NEW DEVELOPMENTS IN
CLINICAL
PSYCHOLOGY

VOLUME II

EDITED BY

FRASER N. WATTS

BPS
BOOKS

WILEY

Published by BPS Books
(The British Psychological Society)
in association with
John Wiley & Sons Limited
Chichester · New York · Brisbane · Toronto · Singapore

© The British Psychological Society, 1988
  First Edition

British Library Cataloguing in Publication Data
New developments in clinical psychology.
  Vol. 2
  1. Clinical psychology
  I. Watts, Fraser N.   II. British
  Psychological Society.
  157'.9
  ISBN 0–471–91998–5

Distributed by
John Wiley & Sons Limited.
Chichester, New York, Brisbane, Toronto, Singapore.

Printed in Great Britain by A. Wheaton & Co. Ltd., Exeter.

CONTENTS

Contents

PREFACE

Clinical psychology continues to develop rapidly, and a variety of factors are contributing to this. The requirements of employers and clients are one prominent influence. Such requirements vary from one country to another. In the UK, the increased priority that clinical psychologists have given to various groups with chronic handicaps is probably a reflection of National Health Service needs. Research developments are another factor affecting professional practice, and are more international. Demonstrations of the promise of new techniques, or closer scrutiny of old ones, influence their use in the clinic.

The 'new developments' represented in this volume reflect changes in the patient groups with whom clinical psychologists are working, a shift towards 'community' work (partly in response to general policies, partly as a response to our limited professional manpower), and the increasingly broad range of interventions that are being used. As in the first volume, each chapter aims to present a topic where new knowledge and practical clinical developments converge. However, the relationship between the two varies. Sometimes research has changed clinical practice; in other cases research has investigated changes in clinical practice which have already occurred. Either relationship seems legitimate and potentially fruitful.

The first few chapters concern the treatment of adult psychological disorders. The techniques of Gestalt therapy are not new, but it is only very recently that research has been carried out to investigate empirically the processes at work. For various reasons, perhaps partly ideological and partly historical, there has been much less research on 'psychotherapeutic' treatments than on cognitive-behavioural ones. (This has perhaps been even more true of the United Kingdom than of North America.) However, there is a growing body of adventurous and clinically-applicable research on psychotherapy, of which Clarke and Greenberg's work on Gestalt techniques is, in my view, an exciting example.

Attributional therapy (Brewin) and problem-solving therapy (Marx) are again not wholly new. However, recent years have seen growing clinical sophistication in their application and an accumulation of research evidence for their effectiveness. They are also both therapeutic developments which are firmly rooted in a body of theory and knowledge about fundamental cognitive processes. In this, they are attractive developments to those of us who wish to see a continuing cross-fertilization between the scientific and practical aspects of clinical psychology, and who believe that clinical psychology benefits from maintaining links with general psychology. Developments in the cognitive-behavioural treatment of agoraphobia (Watts)

1

are a pleasing example of how research and clinical practice have inter-
twined to lead to a broader and more effective approach to one of the
'chestnut' conditions of clinical psychology practice.

One of the important developments in psychological treatment in recent
years has been the move away from exclusive reliance on the dyadic relationship between patient and therapist. These issues are discussed in the
chapters by Bennun and Parry. The patient's social context is potentially of
enormous influence. To ignore it is to allow potentially negative influences
to go unchecked. Equally, it is to fail to harness social resources that may
make a significant contribution to treatment. Social contacts are much more
frequent and sustained than therapeutic contact could ever be, and so can
achieve things that would be impossible for a therapist. In psychological
treatment, we have too often been seduced by the myth of a trained therapist
bringing about permanent changes in a patient's psychological functioning.
In reality, therapists are often bringing about an improvement in a patient's
current level of adjustment by their concurrent social influence, one that will
revert when that influence is withdrawn. This makes it essential for us as a
profession to mobilize the resources of the natural social network.

Chapters 7 and 8 (by Hanley and MacCarthy) are concerned with extending the provision of psychological treatments to groups of clients for whom
they are often not readily available. Treatments which have been developed
largely with young adults are often applicable with only minor modifications
to an elderly population, though they are not used with the elderly as often
as they might be. Ethnic minorities probably provide an even more serious
example of where potentially effective treatments are selectively applied,
with the result that a segment of the population with considerable needs
receives less treatment effort than it deserves. These are issues which arise
with particular force in a public service, where psychologists have a responsibility to see that their resources are deployed where they are needed (or
where they can be most effective). This is not always the place where
demand is most pressing and obvious.

The range of psychological problems with which clinical psychologists
have to concern themselves is never static. New problems arise, and old
problems can gain an increased prominence. The sexual abuse of children
(Dunn Smith) is a good example of a condition which has recently gained
high visibility; it is a problem to which clinical psychologists are now being
pressed to respond, though few have been trained to do so. There is also a
growing demand for psychological work with problems of physical health. In
the UK, the level of service provision in this area is far below what would be
desirable. Aldridge's chapter describes what preventive work with children
can contribute to their physical health. Richer's chapter on nutrition concerns a currently 'hot' topic on the interface of physical and psychological
health, one on which there has been much prejudice (both for and against),
but on which solid evidence is now beginning to accrue. The rehabilitation of

head injury patients is another area within the field of medicine where psychologists are making an increasing contribution. Tyerman and Humphrey's chapter on personal and social rehabilitation in this volume complements that in Volume 1 on cognitive retraining.

Sharrock then contributes the only chapter in this book which is directly concerned with assessment, and this is a reflection of the changing use of assessment in clinical psychology. It is becoming relatively rare for assessment to be carried out except in the context of assessing patients for treatment, monitoring progress in treatment, or assessing the needs of defined clinical populations. However, forensic clinical psychology is a field where assessment remains of central importance. Recent work on eyewitness testimony has important implications for clinical interviewing that have not yet been widely recognized, and these are discussed by Sharrock.

The following two chapters concern evaluation. The movement towards community-based services (for people with either mental illness or mental handicap) is one of the striking changes in the pattern of service provision in recent years. However, it is a change that has often been made for ideological (or financial) reasons with relatively little critical appraisal. Clifford and Damon contribute a valuable review of how such services have been, and can be, evaluated. Financial pressures and a new management style in the National Health Service have made clinical psychologists much more resource-conscious than hitherto. However, there is little expertise within the profession on methods of cost-effectiveness evaluation, and Mangen's chapter will make an important and timely contribution in remedying this. The final chapter (Brown) challenges the predominant concern with work in the NHS which still characterizes most of clinical psychology in the UK, and discusses a style of consultancy work which appears to have significant cost-effectiveness attractions and which can be used in a broader range of institutions.

These chapters do not, of course, represent an exhaustive coverage of what is current or new in British clinical psychology. However, I believe they illustrate the themes which are prominent in current developments: the growing range and effectiveness of methods of psychological treatment; an increasing concern for the social context of their application and the range of clients with psychological problems to whom they are made available; a broadening of the range of problems and client groups with whom clinical psychologists work beyond the traditional fortress of 'adult mental health'; and a growing emphasis on evaluation of patterns of services and the efficient use of resources. Needless to say, there are many other topics which could have been included to illustrate these themes.

Assembling this book has been made easy by the willingness of the contributors to write to guidelines, and their openness to suggestions for revision. As with Volume 1, I have found this book a pleasure to edit. It is a tribute to the healthy state of clinical psychology that a set of chapters such

as these can readily be assembled. I hope readers will enjoy them as much as
I have.

Fraser N. Watts
MRC Applied Psychology Unit, Cambridge
Candlemas, February 1988

CLINICAL RESEARCH ON GESTALT METHODS

Katherine M. Clarke and Leslie S. Greenberg

Gestalt therapy is an integration of a number of theoretical and clinical ideas, drawn from a variety of traditions, into a coherent therapeutic approach. It has been suggested that Gestalt represents a good model for integrating ideas from behavioural, dynamic and humanistic approaches into a technically eclectic approach to therapy. In this type of technical integration, the clinician utilizes a combination of interventions on the basis of what has been demonstrated to be the most effective form of intervention for a particular type of problem.

Some of the methods of intervention developed in the Gestalt approach appear to be particularly effective means of increasing awareness of internal processing, resolving conflict and facilitating complete emotional processing. These Gestalt methods, although originally conceived of as the methods of a particular school or therapeutic philosophy have been shown to contain not only specific interventions appropriate for specific problem states but also to be constituted by a set of identifiable cognitive, behavioural and affective processes (Greenberg and Safran, 1987). This suggests their possible incorporation into a non-dogmatic integrative approach to psychotherapy.

Particular Gestalt methods can thus be extracted from the overall Gestalt therapy. Viewed as complex interventions which utilize particular cognitive, affective and behavioural change processes such as increased awareness of automated thoughts, completion of emotional processing, and exposure to feared stimuli, these can be used to achieve a specific goal at specific times as deemed appropriate by the clinician.

In this regard, a clinician may choose to use particular Gestalt methods to facilitate certain change processes without having to adopt the complete philosophy and theoretical framework of the Gestalt approach.

This chapter presents recent research on Gestalt interventions and, more particularly, the empirical investigations of the 'two-chair' dialogue method.

5

SPECIFICATION OF GESTALT METHODS

Gestalt therapy, like many contemporary schools of therapy, began with a charismatic founder, Fritz Perls, a creative and highly artistic clinician. His intuitive artistry was passed on to various disciples who have continued and developed the art and skill. Perls' writing on Gestalt therapy, like that of his followers, focused primarily on clinical theory and discussed therapeutic incidents as illustrations of the therapy (Perls, 1973; Perls, 1969; Perls *et al.*, 1951; Fagan and Shephard, 1970). Perhaps because of this clinical/therapeutic emphasis, little attention was given to empirical verification of theoretical premises or clinical hunches.

Research on the two-chair technique sprang, then, from a desire to demystify the practice of Gestalt therapy. To do this it was necessary to specify the intervention skills. It was also important to know more about the change process occurring inside clients when this therapy was effective. Essentially, the research was aimed at discovering what worked and when, why, and with whom it worked.

To this end the research began by identifying a technique employed by many Gestalt therapists, describing when it was used, and attempting to define the constellation of interventions which comprised the technique. The two-chair technique was selected because it was often used by Gestalt therapists and because it appeared clinically significant for most clients.

SPLITS

From a formal observation of expert Gestalt therapists at work, it was determined that the two-chair technique was usually implemented when the client expressed a *split* (Greenberg, 1976). A split is a verbal performance pattern in which a client reports a division of the self process into two partial aspects of the self or tendencies (Greenberg, 1979). Three types of split were differentiated according to the relationship between the parts of the self and the person's subjective experience of the split.

Conflict splits are characterized by the two partial aspects of the self being in opposition to one another. The relational feature is a word or words which indicate that the two parts are being set against each other (for example, 'but', 'yet', 'if', 'why'). The person's subjective experience of this type of split is one of struggle, indicated by some process or content cue that the person is involved in an inner struggle, striving or coercion (for example, 'should', 'must', 'want'). An example of a conflict split is, 'I *should* be more tolerant *yet* I *can't* be'.

The *subject/object* split is present when two aspects of the self are in subject–object relationship to each other. One part of the self (the subject) does something to the other part of the self (the object). In this situation, the individual is usually fully invested in one aspect of the self. The relational feature is a pronoun such as 'myself' or 'I' which makes of the self an object. The subjective experience is an indication of discontent or exasperation with the behaviour in which the person is engaged. An example of a subject/object split is, 'I judge myself'.

The third type of split is the split of *attribution*. In an attribution split, a part of the self is attributed to an outside object or person. The relational feature is a third person or object indicator such as 'she', 'they', or 'it'. There are two subclasses of attribution split, distinguished by their subjective features.

An *attribution of opposition* is indicated by the person's hypersensitivity to a minor manifestation of attitudes or feelings expressed by a third person. The subjective feature is that the individual is in disagreement with, struggling with, or strongly bothered by a third person, with whom the self is invested. For example: '*He* thinks what I say is ridiculous. *I get so upset. I can't, I just can't* get him to see my side'.

In an *attribution of agency* split people 'give up their power' to the environment and then feel acted on or alienated by it. The subjective feature is a feeling of passivity or victimization in which the person feels done unto. The locus of control is with a third person, outside the self. A classic example is found in a famous song: '*You made me* love you. *I didn't want to* do it. *I didn't want to* do it.'

THE TWO CHAIRS

Having determined when Gestalt therapists used the two-chair technique, an analysis was made of exactly what they were doing during this often intuitive process of therapeutic interaction. The initial function of the therapist during two-chair work is to set up an experiment to help demarcate the two parts of the self. This usually takes the form of a dialogue between the partial aspects of the self. Perls (1969) popularized the notion of 'top dog' and 'underdog' to describe the process of self-bullying and submission that often characterizes the beginning of these dialogues.

Research and observation has shown that the two chairs can be characterized more profitably as the '*experiencing* chair' and the '*other* chair' (Greenberg, 1976; 1980). The experiencing chair is the experiencing part of the self much like the organism or self in experiential therapies (Rogers, 1961; Perls *et al.*, 1951). An indication of productive dialogue is when this part moves away from whining and excusing ('underdog' talk), and engages in a process of inner exploration and experiencing. This aspect of the self has been shown to engage in dialogue at deeper levels of experiencing on the *Experiencing Scale* (Klein *et al.*, 1969) than does the other chair (Greenberg, 1984). It also uses more 'focused' and 'expressive' voice as measured by the *Vocal Quality Category System* (Rice *et al.*, 1979).

The *other* chair, in contrast to the experiencing chair, is filled with the person's shoulds, negative self statements and attributions and with other people and things. The client in this position usually uses a more externalizing (Rice *et al.*, 1979) or lecturing voice and engages in lower levels of experiencing. Clients speak from the other chair as if they are their automatic thoughts and internal representations of the world. In the face of this other chair, the experiencing chair, vividly reacts, feels and experiences.

This characterization of the two chairs provides a kind of guide for the therapist in intervening to keep the partial aspects of the self separated. Since the client usually presents in an undifferentiated state, where the two sides are not distinguished and therefore are unable to make contact, it is essential for the therapist to recognize what belongs to the experiential self and what belongs to the self talk of the other chair. Only when this separation is made between the two levels of processing can integration and conflict resolution occur.

Research has also determined that resolution of a split is characterized by certain changes in experiencing level and vocal quality in the other chair (Greenberg, 1976; 1980; 1984). The other chair usually moves to deeper levels of experiencing and speaks in a more focused and emotional voice. It is as though the other becomes softer, less critical and more accepting of the self. If on the other hand, an apparent 'resolution' is not accompanied by these measurable changes in the other chair, the therapist or researcher is alerted to a possible pseudo or intellectual resolution.

The therapist's moment by moment interventions, then, are designed to bring to fullness the totality of expression that is occurring in the present. To be effective, the therapist must actively direct the client's attention to more and more aspects of the unfolding phenomenology of the partial aspects of the self and their relationship to one another. To this end the therapist interventions are guided by five principles.

THERAPIST INTERVENTIONS

The five principles which guide the therapist interventions are:

1. maintaining the contact boundary
2. responsibility
3. attending
4. heightening
5. expressing.

Various therapist behaviours may embody one or more of these principles, although most interventions will have one principle as their primary thrust. The principles viewed together define the basic structure of the therapist interventions of the two-chair technique.

1. Maintaining the contact boundary
This principle involves clear *separation* of the partial aspects of the self and clear *contact* between the parts. This is the primary goal of the two-chair work. The therapist intervenes when the dialogue gets bogged down in order to maintain the flow of contact and works continuously to separate out emerging polar opposites of the client's ongoing experience.

2. Responsibility
The premise of this principle is the Gestalt notion of avoidance. Avoidance is conceptualized as the fear of experience, the blocking of awareness and the activity of not taking responsibility. This activity is brought to the person's awareness, usually with a question like: 'What are you avoiding', or, 'Are you aware of avoiding anything?'

A number of approaches may be used to encourage the taking of responsibility. One is *owning* in which the therapist intervenes to get the person to speak in the first person singular, to own what she or he is saying rather than distancing from it. The person might, for example, be asked to say, 'I'm discouraged', rather than 'It's discouraging'. The two-chair technique itself helps clients to take responsibility by requiring them to say what they want and feel from the experiencing chair and to make their demands and criticisms from the other chair. This prevents clients from distancing themselves from their experience by merely talking about and analysing the self.

Another approach is to ask the client to *be congruent* in each aspect of the self and express and embody its true nature. If, for example, the other chair is punishing or bullying, then the person is asked actually to punish or bully themselves. If the person in the experiencing chair is feeling frightened or weak, he or she is asked to say so rather than blaming the other part.

Another way the therapist facilitates congruence is by emphasizing the inner experiencing of the client in the experiencing chair. The suggestion is to change externalized statements to expressions of inner experience.

3. Attending
The purpose of the therapist's intervention here is to direct clients' attention to particular aspects of their experience. This may be done simply by asking clients if they are aware of what they are doing or by encouraging a client to 'stay with' a certain feeling. There are two aspects of attending:
a) Changing perspective. The therapist asks the client to change the focus of his/her attention and to attend to that which is not presently in awareness. Voice quality, posture, facial expression or kinesthetic activity are all examples of experience that might not be in the client's awareness.
b) Focusing. This intervention directs clients' attention to inner processes of which they might not be aware. The therapist might direct the client to 'go inside and pay attention to that feeling'.

4. Heightening
The therapist's interventions are always intended to raise the client's level of

awareness of moment-by-moment experiencing. A variety of methods such as having clients repeat or exaggerate key statements or feeding key statements to the client, serve this goal of heightening ongoing experience.

5. Expressing

The purpose of this intervention is to bring aspects of experiencing into awareness by actually *doing*. It is to counter the tendency to talk 'about'. Expression of both the particular content (what) and the process involved (how) in the two-chair dialogue are pursued. Expressing, in a differentiated fashion, the particular content of an experience can bring detail and concreteness to the process.

Attention is paid to the style of expression in either chair and this is turned into content in the dialogue. The intention is to bring into awareness *how* the client relates to him/herself. A client who speaks loudly and aggressively in the experiencing chair may be asked how this sounds. The reply, 'I sound like a bully', and the subsequent direction to be a bully brings into awareness the client's style of self-relationship.

DIFFERENTIAL EFFECTS

In order to determine the effectiveness of the Gestalt two-chair dialogue in resolving splits it has been compared to a number techniques drawn from other therapeutic orientations. In a number of analogue and therapy studies, the two-chair method was compared to interventions drawn from client-centred therapy ('empathy'), cognitive-behavioural therapy ('problem solving'), and an experiential approach ('focusing'). It should be noted that the purpose of these studies was not to compare the general effectiveness of one therapy over another, but to examine the *specific* effects of a *specific* intervention used for a *specific* client problem state in therapy.

The first studies compared the two-chair technique to high level empathy used for clients experiencing a conflict split. Empathic reflections of feelings were chosen as the comparison intervention because one of their purposes is to increase client awareness and experiencing (Carkhuff, 1970). An initial multiple single case study showed that the two-chair technique led repeatedly to greater depth of experiencing and greater change of awareness than empathic reflection when the interventions followed a client statement of conflict (Greenberg and Rice, 1981).

An analogue study (Greenberg and Clarke, 1979) extended the investigation by examining both process and outcome variables for 16 subjects, used as their own controls, treated by four different therapists. Results indicated that the two-chair technique led to deeper levels of experiencing and more shifts in awareness than did empathic reflections. Particularly important was the finding that subjects reached Level 5 and 6 more often in the two-chair sessions than in the empathic reflection sessions. To reach Level 5, the speaker must pose or define a problem or proposition about him/herself explicitly in terms of feelings. The problem must then be explored in a personal way. To reach Level 6, the content must be 'a synthesis of readily accessible, newly recognized or more fully realized feelings and experiences to produce personally meaningful structures or to resolve issues' (Klein *et al.*, 1969, page 61).

It was evident then, that in this larger subject and therapist pool the two-chair technique led to more resolution of conflict than did empathic reflection. In terms of subsequent behavioural changes following conflict resolution, the majority of subjects in both treatments reported movement in the direction of 'much better than expected' on a post session behavioural measure of goal attainment.

The next study sought to generalize the findings of the analogue study in an investigation of clients in therapy and to look further at post sessional outcome variables (Greenberg and Dompierre, 1981). Ten therapists and 16 clients, used as their own controls, were studied. Two sessions in the course of therapy were designated as experimental sessions. These were programmed to be the fifth and seventh sessions. In order to enhance independence of the treatments the sixth session was designated as a non-experimental treatment session and therapists were instructed not to respond actively to an intrapsychic conflict. Half the clients received the two-chair treatment first and half received empathic reflection first. After the intervening session, each client then received the alternative treatment when they presented a conflict.

Results showed that depth of experiencing and shifts in awareness were higher following the two-chair technique. Reported conflict resolution immediately after the session and in a one-week follow-up was also greater for the two-chair technique. Reported behaviour change after a week and progress over a week were also significantly greater for the Gestalt treatment. Level of discomfort was not significantly different for the two treatments. Investigation of the therapist's level of experience in this study further revealed that expertise did not significantly influence the efficacy of the two-chair technique.

Since these studies all examined the specific differential effects of the two-chair technique compared to empathic reflection, the question arose as to whether or not simply doing something more 'active' was causing the resolution effect. To this end, the two-chair technique was compared to focusing (Gendlin, 1981) followed by empathic reflection. Kantor and Zimring (1976) had suggested that the active technique of focusing operates to supply the client with new possibilities, which leads to a redefinition of the problem. The use of two active techniques, each of which involves directions from the therapist, also added control to therapist expectancy effects.

Results of this analogue study showed that the two-chair technique applied at a split produced significantly greater depth of experiencing than did focusing followed by empathic reflection (Greenberg and Higgins, 1980). Both treatments produced significantly more reported shifts in awareness and progress in target complaints than a no-treatment control group.

Having compared the two-chair technique to a reflective and directive technique drawn from affectively-oriented therapies, the next step was to compare it to an intervention drawn from a cognitive-behavioural orientation (Clarke and Greenberg, 1986). There has been considerable controversy regarding the role of affect and cognition in therapeutic change. The comparison of the two-chair technique to problem-solving (D'Zurilla and Goldfried, 1971) grounded this debate in the specific clinical effects of an affective and cognitive treatment for a specific client problem state, namely decisional conflict.

Decisional conflict is described by Janis and Mann (1977) as 'occurring when there are simultaneous opposing tendencies within the individual to reject or accept a given course of action' (page 42). Because the decision conflict is one of strong affect, that is, feeling torn apart by opposing tendencies, the affectively-oriented therapist may turn to the Gestalt two-chair technique. On the other hand, a therapist working from a cognitive-behavioural stance will recognize this as an appropriate time to implement systematic problem solving. Because no clear preference is felt, a logical weighing of the pros and cons may help to resolve the conflict. The question of differential effects may legitimately be raised because both treatments could be effective in the situation.

For purposes of control and measurement, the decisional conflict was kept uniform. All subjects were experiencing conflict regarding a career decision. The definition of a career decision was kept very broad and decisions ranged from 'I want to tell off my boss but I can't', to, 'I want to work but I feel guilty about leaving my children'. All of the decisions were emotionally significant and current. The dependent variables were degree of undecidedness and stage of decision making.

Forty-eight people were randomly assigned to three groups: a problem-solving group, a two-chair group and a waiting-list control group. Therapists saw clients for two sessions, working on the same decision in each session. Results showed that the two-chair technique was more effective than the problem-solving or no treatment for reducing indecision. Both treatments were more effective than no treatment for facilitating movement through the stages of decision making.

INTENSIVE ANALYSIS

While the differential effects studies addressed the question of what specific treatment helped with resolving conflict, they did not identify how the change takes place. Another important vein of research is the intensive examination of the process of change (Greenberg, 1984). Once we know *what* works, we need to know *how* it works. The identification of the process of change makes it possible to refine treatments for maximal effectiveness.

To this end Greenberg (1980; 1983; 1984) conducted intensive analyses of client performances in successful episodes of conflict resolution and compared these to unsuccessful episodes. The first study developed a typical pattern of depth of experiencing and voice quality for the two chairs (or sides) of the conflict. The two sides of the conflict were found to function as independent systems, proceeding at different levels of experiencing. The other chair proceeds at lower levels of experiencing than the experiencing chair. At a certain point, the systems merge. They become indistinguishable in their experiencing level and, together, show a higher level of experiencing than before merging.

This pattern revealed itself consistently throughout nine events in three clients. This led to characterizing the event as containing two phases, a pre-resolution phase, prior to the increase of experiencing in the other chair, and a resolution phase, in which both chairs tend to increase in depth of experiencing.

Patterns of vocal quality (Rice *et al.*, 1979) corroborated the findings on depth of experiencing which suggested this pattern of pre-resolution phase, merger, and resolution phase. In the pre-resolution phase of each event, the other chair used more limited and external voice than did the experiencing chair. The experiencing chair used more focused (inner-directed) and emotional voice. In the resolution phase, the other chair's use of limited and external voice declines and use of focused and emotional voice increases. This indicates better contact between the partial aspects of the self and of each aspect with itself.

The pattern of performances in these episodes of split resolution led to the construction of a three-stage model of intrapsychic conflict resolution (Greenberg, 1983). The three stages of conflict resolution are *opposition*, *merger*, and *integration*. The first stage is characterized by a relationship of opposition between the two parts in conflict. The aspect of the personality contained in the other chair is critical, hostile, intimidating or threatening towards another part, contained in the experiencing chair. The part in the experiencing chair is initially rebellious, passively compliant, helpless or avoidant.

In successful episodes of conflict resolution, the two chairs or parts of the personality, enter the second phase of the event by changing their manner. They stop relating from positions of opposition and begin to accept one another. During this merging phase, both sides of the conflict are stated clearly, with feeling, each part experiences a greater sense of internal locus of control and the relationship between the parts becomes more affiliative. The experiencing part is sensed from the inside and is accepted as part of the self. It refuses to be seen as 'bad', expresses its wants, and is more assertive of its wants and needs.

The hostile, dominant aspect of the personality takes a less critical stance towards the experiencing chair, expresses its standards, values and felt concerns. It then begins to feel more compassion for the experiencing part of the self. At this stage, the other chair turns inward, experiences its feelings more deeply, and the two chairs become more alike. Finally, in the integration phase of the event, a negotiation or integration takes place between the two sides in which they mutually listen, understand and accept each other. This creates a resolution in which the opposing sides of the split are reconciled.

This three stage model was evaluated by using process instruments which measure the degree of affiliation and independence between the two chairs: 'Structural Analysis of Social Behaviour Scale', Benjamin, 1974; the vocal quality of each chair (Rice *et al.*, 1979); and the experiencing level of each chair (Klein *et al.*, 1969). Greenberg (1984) elaborated this three-phase model into a model containing six components necessary for conflict resolution. In this refined model, through role playing, the critic identifies its harsh, critical evaluations of the experiencing part of the self. The experiencing part, in turn, expresses its affective reactions to the harsh criticism. The harsh critic then moves from general statements to more concrete and specific criticisms of the person or situation. Specific behaviours may be negatively evaluated and specific changes are demanded. In response to these criticisms, the experiencing chair begins to react in a more differentiated fashion until a new aspect of its experience is expressed. A sense of direction then emerges for the experiencer, which is expressed to the critic as a want or a need. The critic, having become more specific, moves to a statement of standards and values. At this point in the dialogue – when there is an assertion of a want or a need in the face of a standard or value – the critic softens. This is followed by a negotiation or an integration, or both, between the two parts. Figure 1 describes this process.

RELATING PROCESS TO OUTCOME

The intensive analyses of successful and unsuccessful conflict resolution events contributes to our understanding of how resolution occurs in a two-chair dialogue. An important clinical question, however, is whether or not these process components are related to outcome. Does a particular performance within therapy predict different post therapy results?

To investigate the relationship between resolution processes and outcome, three essential components of resolution were selected from the model (Greenberg and Webster, 1982). The first essential component was *criticism in the other chair*. This component integrates the standards and values components of the six-part model and ensures that the client has truly

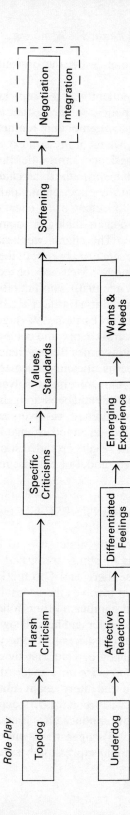

FIGURE 1. Refined Performance Model of Conflict Resolution

engaged in the dialogue by expressing the opposition of one side to the other.

The second essential component was the *expression of felt wants in the experiencing chair*. This component integrates the feelings and wants components of the above model into a component requiring the client to express, from the experiencing chair, wants in the context of feeling. This ensures that the client is deeply experiencing this side of the polarity. The final essential component was a *softening in the other chair*. The previously harsh critic softens in its attitude to the experiencing part.

To relate these processes to outcome, 31 clients completed a six-week program using a Gestalt two-chair dialogue to work on an intrapsychic conflict related to a decision. The clients were classified as resolvers or nonresolvers based on the presence or absence of the three specified components of conflict resolution model. Measures of indecision (Osipow *et al.*, 1976), anxiety (Spielberger *et al.*, 1970), conflict resolution (Greenberg and Dompierre, 1981), target complaints (Battle *et al.*, 1966), symptom intensity (Phillips, 1970), prevailing mood (Epstein, 1979), goal attainment (Kiersuk and Sherman, 1968), behavioural change and conflict resolution were made before treatment and at various times during the six-week process.

Resolvers were found to be significantly less undecided and less anxious after treatment than were nonresolvers. Resolvers also showed greater improvement on target complaints and behaviour change. After the particular session in which the critic softened, resolvers reported greater conflict resolution, less discomfort, greater mood change and greater goal attainment than nonresolvers. These results provided support for the validity and clinical utility of the proposed model of conflict resolution.

CURRENT RESEARCH

A coordinated effort is currently under way to study a second Gestalt therapy event referred to as finishing unfinished business or completing incomplete experience (Greenberg and Safran, 1987; Doldrup *et al.*, in press). This therapeutic event involves the arousal and expression of inhibited emotion to an imagined significant other, followed by recovery, relief and cognitive restructuring. Beutler and his colleagues (Beutler *et al.*, 1986) suggest that conflict over, and constriction of, angry impulses plays a role in back pain and depression. They believe that by defining an appropriate target for the expression of interpersonal anger, directing the client to an imagined dialogue with the feared interpersonal target, and intensifying the expression until a resolution is recognized, the patient gains a sense of completion and control that is conducive to stress reduction.

Greenberg and Safran (1987) suggest that the complete expression of previously interrupted emotional expression brings about an experience of completion and a cognitive reorganization of the experience similar to a process of grieving. Expression of feelings such as loss, anger, and fear in this fashion appears to relieve the person of an internal burden which has constantly clamoured for attention. This change process operates to bring about closure through a cognitive/perceptual reorganization such that the original situation is accepted in some fashion and is no longer perceived as thwarting one's attempts to achieve satisfaction. This event is currently under investigation in both analogue and therapy situations and shows some promise of demonstrating the usefulness of dialogue with a significant other in an empty chair to resolve unfinished business. As Bohart (1977) had initially demonstrated in the study of interpersonal conflict reduction, some combination of emotional expression and cognitive processing appears to be superior to either component alone in helping resolve feelings and change perceptions.

CONCLUSION

The use of the two-chair dialogue between parts of the self for working with intrapsychic conflict and the use of dialogue with a significant other for resolving unfinished interpersonal feelings hold promise as therapeutic methods which can be incorporated into a clinician's general repertoire of skills. These methods are drawn from the practice of Gestalt therapy and have been, to differing degrees, empirically investigated. A number of further events, drawn from Gestalt and other experiential approaches and involving working with emotion, in combination with cognition and action, have been spelled out recently in a discussion of emotion in psychotherapy (Greenberg and Safran, 1987). These await empirical investigation and demonstration of their range of clinical applications so that they can be used to complement the clinician's repertoire of cognitive and behavioural interventions.

REFERENCES

BATTLE, C.C., IMBER, S.D., HOEHN-SARIC, R., STONE, A.R., NASH, E.H. and FRANK, J.D. (1966). Target complaints as criteria of improvement. *American Journal of Psychotherapy*, *20*, 184–192.

BENJAMIN, L.S. (1974). Structural analysis of social behavior. *Psychological Review*. *81*, 392–425.

BEUTLER, L., ENGLE, D., ORO'BEUTLER, M., DOLDRUP, R. and MEREDITH, K. (1986). Inability to express intense affect: A common link between depression and pain. *Journal of Consulting and Clinical Psychology*, *54*, 752–759.

BOHART, A. (1977). Role playing and interpersonal conflict resolution. *Journal of Counseling Psychology*, *24*, 15–24.

CARKHUFF, R. (1970). *Helping and Human Relations: A primer for lay and professional helpers. Vol. 1.* New York: Holt, Rinehart and Winston.

CLARKE, K.M. and GREENBERG, L.S. (1986). Differential effects of the Gestalt two-chair intervention and problem solving in resolving decisional conflict. *Journal of Counseling Psychology, 33*, 11–15.

DOLDRUP, R., BEUTLER, L., GREENBERG, L.S. and ENGLE, D. (in press). *Focused Expressive Psychotherapy*. New York: Guilford.

D'ZURILLA, T. and GOLDFRIED, M. (1971). Problem solving and behavior modification. *Journal of Abnormal Psychology, 78*, 107–126.

EPSTEIN, S. (1979). The stability of behavior: On predicting most of the people much of the time. *Journal of Personality and Social Psychology, 37*, 1097–1126.

FAGAN, J. and SHEPHARD, I. (eds) (1970). *Gestalt therapy now*. Palo Alto, Ca.: Science & Behavior Books.

GENDLIN, E.T. (1981). *Focusing*. New York: Bantam.

GREENBERG, L.S. (1976). A task analytic approach to the study of psychotherapeutic events. Unpublished doctoral dissertation. Downsview, Ontario, Canada: York University.

GREENBERG, L.S. (1979). Resolving splits: Use of the two-chair technique. *Psychotherapy: Theory, Research and Practice, 16*, 316–324.

GREENBERG, L.S. (1980). An intensive analysis of recurring events from the practice of Gestalt therapy. *Psychotherapy: Theory, Research and Practice, 17*, 143–152.

GREENBERG, L.S. (1983). Toward a task-analysis of conflict resolution in Gestalt therapy. *Psychotherapy: Theory, Research and Practice, 20*, 190–201.

GREENBERG, L.S. (1984). A task analysis of intrapersonal conflict resolution. In L.N. Rice and L.S. Greenberg (eds), *Patterns of Change: Intensive Analysis of Psychotherapy Process* (pp. 67–123). New York: Guilford.

GREENBERG, L.S. and CLARKE, K.M. (1979). The differential effects of Gestalt two-chair dialogue and empathic reflection at a conflict marker. *Journal of Counseling Psychology, 26*, 1–9.

GREENBERG, L.S. and DOMPIERRE, L. (1981). Specific effects of Gestalt two-chair dialogue on intrapsychic conflict in counseling. *Journal of Counseling Psychology, 28*, 288–294.

GREENBERG, L.S. and HIGGINS, H.M. (1980). Effects of two-chair dialogue and focusing on conflict resolution. *Journal of Counseling Psychology, 27*, 221–224.

GREENBERG, L.S. and RICE, L.N. (1981). The specific effects of a Gestalt intervention. *Psychotherapy: Theory, Research and Practice, 18*, 31–37.

GREENBERG, L.S. and SAFRAN, J. (1987). *Emotion in psychotherapy: Affect, cognition and the process of change*. New York: Guilford.

GREENBERG, L.S. and WEBSTER, M. (1982). Resolving decisional conflict by two-chair dialogue: Relating process to outcome. *Journal of Counseling Psychology, 29*, 468–477.

JANIS, I.L. and MANN, L. (1977). *Decision-making: A Psychological Analysis of Conflict, Choice and Commitment*. New York: Plenum Press.

KANTOR, S. and ZIMRING, F. (1976). The effects of focusing on a problem. *Psychotherapy: Theory, Research and Practice, 13*, 255–259.

KIERSUK, J.T. and SHERMAN, R.E. (1968). Goal attainment scaling: General method for evaluating community mental health programs. *Community Mental Health Journal, 4*, 443–453.

KLEIN, M.H., MATHIEU, P.L., GENDLIN, E.T. and KIESLER, D.J. (1969). *The experiencing scale: A research and training manual*. Madison: Psychiatric Institute, Bureau of Audio-Visual Instruction.

OSIPOW, S.H., CARNEY, C.G. and BARAK, A. (1976). A scale of educational vocational undecidedness: A typological approach. *Journal of Vocational Behavior*, *9*, 223–243.

PERLS, F.S. (1969). *Gestalt Therapy Verbatim*. Lafayette, Ca.: Real People Press.

PERLS, F.S. (1973). *The Gestalt Approach: Eyewitness to Therapy*. Palo Alto, Ca.: Science & Behavior Books.

PERLS, F.S., HEFFERLINE, R. and GOODMAN, P. (1951). *Gestalt Therapy*. New York: Julian Press.

PHILLIPS, J.P.N. (1970). A new type of personal questionnaire technique. *British Journal of Social and Clinical Psychology*, *9*, 241–256.

RICE, L.N., KOKE, C.J., GREENBERG, L.S. and WAGSTAFF, A. (1979). *Manual for Client Vocal Quality*. Downsview, Ontario, Canada: York University.

ROGERS, C. (1961). *On becoming a person*. Boston: Houghton Mifflin.

SPIELBERGER, C.D., GORSUCH, R.L. and LUSHENE, R.E. (1970). *Manual for the State-Trait Anxiety Inventory*. Palo Alto, Ca.: Consulting Psychologists Press.

ATTRIBUTION THERAPY
Chris R. Brewin

Attribution theory is a branch of social psychology that is concerned with how people account for the events they experience and the actions they observe. According to attribution theory, human beings have a natural desire to explain their world in order to exercise a greater degree of control over it. This search for the causes of their experiences is particularly noticeable when anything unusual, unwanted, or unpleasant occurs (Weiner, 1985a), which is of course precisely the situation of most people who consult clinical psychologists. It is very rare to come across patients who are not concerned in some way or who have not formed some view about the origins of their problems.

The relevance of attribution theory to clinical practice has been discussed at length elsewhere (Antaki and Brewin, 1982), but is basically due to two main factors. First, real-world events are often extremely complex, leaving plenty of scope for misunderstanding or partial appreciation of the causal factors involved. Information about the causes and consequences of different illnesses is often lacking, either because it has not been offered or not remembered. People may have all sorts of misconceptions about the general frequency of the upsetting events they experience, and about important causal elements such as their own abilities and others' motives. Second, the explanations that people make can have a variety of emotional and behavioural consequences, some being likely to exacerbate and some to ameliorate physical and psychological symptoms. These two factors suggest that there may be considerable scope for improving symptoms and distress by altering people's perceptions of the causes of significant experiences. In this Chapter I shall discuss the role played by attributions and explanations, and review attempts to make them the target of therapeutic intervention.

Most attribution theorists have confined themselves to investigating how people identify the factors, internal or external to themselves, that are responsible for some clearly definable event such as an accident or a display of anger. Explanation, particularly in clinical settings, is a more complex process than this, however, and if attribution theory is to be useful it must be set within this wider context. At least four separate functions of explanation can be distinguished (Brewin and Antaki, 1987):

labelling, in which people decide on the nature and meaning of a particular event;
causal attribution, in which the responsible causal factors are identified;
moral judgement, in which people's actions are evaluated against standards of right and wrong; and
self-presentation, in which explanations may be selected in order to put across a particular view of oneself.

Although there is usually some overlap between these different functions, they provide a useful way of thinking about how explanations may go wrong and what kind of intervention is required. I shall give some brief examples of these different functions of explanation in order to illustrate their role in clinical practice.

FUNCTIONS AND CONSEQUENCES OF EXPLANATIONS

Labelling

When an event is experienced, it must first be labelled. This is not always as straightforward as it sounds. For example, husbands and wives may have great difficulty in correctly labelling the early symptoms of schizophrenia as being a product of mental illness. Yarrow *et al.* (1956) describe how wives cannot generally pinpoint the time when their husband's problem emerged. The subjective beginnings are seldom localized in a single strange or disturbing incident, but only after an accumulation of odd behaviour and reactions. At first, these odd behaviours may be denied or normalized and assimilated into existing expectations. Early interpretations of them may shift back and forth a good deal, and are often couched in terms of physical difficulties, character problems, or environmental distress. Although the progressive disruption produced by the symptoms usually leads to an explanation in terms of mental illness, some wives maintain the same explanation throughout, either within or outside a psychiatric framework.

Another example of the difficulty in labelling others' behaviour comes from studies of children referred to psychiatric clinics for 'deviancy' (Lobitz and Johnson, 1975; Rickard *et al.*, 1981). In contrast to what might be expected, these children do not always differ from non-referred controls on behavioural measures. A more reliable distinguishing feature is that their parents label their behaviour as 'deviant', even when it appears to be similar to that of children in general.

Individuals sometimes have difficulty in correctly labelling their own experiences, psychotic patients often developing a complicated delusional system to account for their strange sensations and hallucinations. Johnson *et al.* (1977) reported on the treatment of a 37-year-old male patient, provisionally diagnosed as suffering from paranoid schizophrenia, who complained that he regularly had sexual intercourse with a 'warm form'. Treatment consisted of trying to make the patient more receptive to a new label for his experiences, namely that he had been sexually abstinent for a long period and was inadvertently masturbating by his leg movements.

Explanations for physical illness also vary enormously and demonstrate the effects of medical knowledge and folk beliefs (Watts, 1982). Certain individuals reveal disease phobia (recurrent anxiety about suffering from a variety of illnesses) and disease conviction (a belief in the presence of serious illness that persists despite a lack of medical evidence), both of which are illustrative of a tendency to label physical sensations in a threatening way. There is a lot of scope for errors of this kind in the overlap between the effects of overbreathing and the symptoms of a heart attack, both of which are characterized by an intense feeling of apprehension and distressing physical sensations such as vertigo, blurred vision, palpitations, and numbness. It has recently been argued that panic attacks are the product of mislabelling the symptoms of overbreathing as those of a heart attack or other medical emergency (Clark *et al.*, 1985).

Causal attribution

Once a label has been applied to an event or symptom, the causal factors responsible can be sought. Was the accident due to carelessness, bad luck, or faulty machinery? Was the illness brought about by unhealthy eating or smoking, overwork, too many worries, or some constitutional weakness? It has been suggested that underlying the huge number of potential causal factors are a small number of critical dimensions, having very specific consequences, along which they all vary. According to Weiner (1985b), the perceived causes of an event differ on the three dimensions of internality, stability, and controllability. Attributing successful outcomes to internal factors such as one's own ability leads to positive esteem-related feelings such as pride, whereas attributing unsuccessful outcomes to internal factors leads to shame and lowered self-esteem. Attributing successful outcomes to stable, unchanging factors leads to raised expectations of future success, whereas attributing unsuccessful outcomes to stable factors leads to lowered expectations of success. The controllability dimension is associated with a number of emotional consequences. Weiner suggests that attributing one's own unsuccessful outcomes to factors controllable by oneself, such as lack of effort, leads to feelings of guilt, whereas attributing them to factors controllable by other people produces feelings of anger. On the other hand, attributing other peoples' unsuccessful outcomes to factors not under their control leads to feelings of pity.

It is not possible to do justice to Weiner's theory in the space available, only to point to some of the consequences for patients' motivation and emotional reactions in therapy. The first thing to note is that self-esteem is at least in part dependent on whether or not one blames oneself for one's predicament (for example, Brewin and Furnham, 1986). This relationship with self-esteem is also implied by the 'self-serving bias' in attributions, whereby people generally take more credit for their successes than their failures. The self-serving pattern is, for instance, characteristic of patients with diabetes who are giving explanations for the positive and negative consequences of their illness (Bradley *et al.*, 1984). Recently it has been proposed that certain individuals ('self-handicappers') may go to considerable lengths to avoid having to make damaging internal attributions, even adopting symptoms or destructive personal habits to give themselves an acceptable alibi for failure (for example, Arkin and Baumgardner, 1985). Whether or not patients' symptoms are interpreted in this way, it seems likely that any attempt on the part of the therapist to emphasize the patient's own role in precipitating the problem, for example, by pointing to ineffective coping strategies, runs the risk of threatening the patient's self-esteem and jeopardizing co-operation with therapy.

A second derivation from the theory is that, if the therapist wishes to raise expectations of success and hence the amount of effort expended in treatment, he or she should encourage unstable attributions (bad luck, temporary circumstances) for unsuccessful outcomes and stable attributions (improved competence) for successful outcomes. Sonne and Janoff (1982) reviewed treatments for weight loss that tried to get patients to attribute improvement to their own personal competence rather than to the competence of the therapist. They reported superior maintenance of weight loss in the personal competence group, a better outcome being predicted by perceptions of greater control over and contribution to the weight loss achieved during therapy. Although these studies did not measure the perceived stability of the causes of improvement, it is a reasonable inference that improvement attributed internally would be perceived as more stable than improvement attributed to a time-limited intervention by a therapist.

The theory also suggests that the attributions made by family members for an individual's illness or behaviour may greatly affect their attitudes towards him or her. This has been illustrated recently in a study of mothers' attributions for their child's nocturnal enuresis (Butler *et al.*, 1986). Mothers endorsed a wide range of possible attributions, indicating their uncertainty about the cause. Interestingly, the most commonly favoured attribution, to the child being a heavy sleeper, has received no support from empirical comparisons of the sleep patterns of enuretic and control children (for example, Gillin *et al.*, 1982). As expected, Butler *et al.* found that mothers who attributed the enuresis to factors under the child's control were more likely to be intolerant of the wetting. This is potentially important because parental intolerance is associated with a greater likelihood of prematurely terminating treatment.

Moral judgement

This aspect of explanation is related to the understanding of what *ought* to have happened rather than of what actually happened, and hence is closely tied up with beliefs about appropriateness and standards of conduct. Storms and McCaul (1976) proposed a common mechanism to account for the exacerbation of a variety of anxiety-related behaviours, such as stammering, insomnia, impotence, shyness, and blushing. This mechanism involves (*a*) seeing the cause of unwanted behaviour as one's own negative dispositions or characteristics, (*b*) an increase in an unpleasant emotional state such as anxiety or depression stemming from this negative self-evaluation, and (*c*) a consequent exacerbation of the same unwanted behaviour which gave rise to the initial attribution. They reported evidence that negative self-evaluation is common among stutterers, who often have low self-esteem and experience intense anxiety about speaking. Storms and McCaul's exacerbation model appears to be describing moral as well as causal judgements because it is concerned with people who feel that they ought not to be displaying a particular behaviour and ought not to possess some particular characteristic.

The interdependence of causal and moral judgement is even more apparent in studies of close relationships. Orvis *et al.* (1976) found evidence from their study of attributional conflict in young couples that led them to suggest:

> Attributions are an integral part of the interpersonal evaluative process. The *reasons* for behavior are learned as part and parcel of the *evaluation* of behavior. (Page 379)

Fincham (1985) has also noted that causal ratings for marital difficulties are not value-neutral judgements about an objectively verifiable chain of cause and effect, and has suggested that marital therapists should attend to the partners' expectations regarding appropriate behaviour. Like causal judgements, moral judgements may have a range of emotional and behavioural consequences. Negative evaluation of one's own behaviour is likely to lead to guilt and to attempts to restore positive self-evaluation, whereas negative evaluation of others is likely to lead to feelings of anger and, in some cases, to the taking of retributive action.

Self-presentation

The self-serving bias in attributions for success and failure has already been noted, and it is only necessary to add that even blaming oneself may, under some circumstances, serve a self-presentational function. Appearing to be incompetent and reliant on good luck to achieve success might be a logical tactic for someone who had low expectations of their own ability and was concerned about being found wanting by others. There is some evidence that the depressive tendency to attribute failure to low ability may be sensitive to the presence of an observer and hence reflect a self-presentational concern (House, 1983). From the point of view of the therapist, therefore, care must be taken that the initial explanations offered by patients do in fact reflect their underlying beliefs and are not simply designed to paint themselves in a more favourable light.

Summary. Even from this brief review it is clear that the kind of explanation a person makes for their symptoms and problems may be of great importance. The consequences of mislabelling are very varied, including emotional reactions such as increased anxiety and behavioural reactions such as inappropriate help-seeking. Work by attribution theorists has suggested more specific effects on expectations of success and failure, on emotions related to self-esteem, and on interpersonal emotions. Moral judgements may have similar effects on esteem-related and on interpersonal emotions, as well as sometimes creating an impetus to make recompense for behaviour that falls short of acceptable standards of conduct. Finally, explanations have consequences for the public image of the person offering them.

THE FORMATION OF EXPLANATIONS

Before explanations can be systematically changed, it is necessary to have some appreciation of the factors that influence them. We have already discussed some of the motivational effects of the desire for self-enhancement, whether in one's own eyes or those of other people, and the influence of internalized standards of conduct on moral judgements. Moral judgements are also influenced by considerations of the controllability, foreseeability, and intentionality of a person's actions, so that credit and blame are assigned on the basis of the person's inferred internal state as well as on the basis of their actions. Bad actions that are perceived as intentional, for instance, and for which there appear to be no mitigating factors, attract the most censure. Labelling, on the other hand, is primarily related to the availability of different categories in memory and to the use of decision rules for deciding into what category to place a particular event.

A large amount of research has examined the antecedents of causal attributions (for example, Kelley and Michela, 1980). Apart from the influence of the 'fundamental attribution error' (of which more later), the contributory factors can be roughly divided between those that are based on past experience and those that represent current situational information.

Causal beliefs are suppositions or expectations about cause–effect relations that are based on past experience and that can be called upon to analyze complex or ambiguous situations. These expectations may contain some specific content – for example, that people in authority want to repress those under them or that men are invariably unfaithful – and may result in rapid interpretations being made of behavioural instances that appear to fit the particular pattern. Explanations based on such causal beliefs may come to mind instantly and subjectively may be quite compelling, so that the person might not stop to consider alternative explanations and might angrily reject evidence that is contrary to it. Other beliefs (causal schemata) are concerned with how two or more causes combine to produce a certain effect. For example, it may be believed that either cause A or cause B suffices to produce a given effect (schema for multiple sufficient causes) or that both A and B are necessary (schema for multiple necessary causes).

A particular type of causal belief that has been much discussed in the context of vulnerability to depression is attributional style. It has been proposed (for example, Peterson and Seligman, 1984; Alloy *et al.*, 1988) that people who habitually attribute negative outcomes to internal, stable, and global factors (for example, defects in their ability or character) are more likely to make such an attribution when faced with upsetting or disappointing experiences of unclear origin. These attributions, they suggest, then lead to low self-esteem, hopelessness and depression. The concept of attributional style assumes that certain people show cross-situational consistency in the kinds of attribution they make, regularly putting their successes down to their own efforts, blaming others for failures, and so on. Although some investigators have failed to find evidence for consistent attributional styles in a nondepressed population (Cutrona *et al.*, 1984), it is possible that they might be found within a population at risk for depression. There is some evidence that a person's attributional style in conjunction with subsequent failure does predict the extent of their depressive reaction (Metalsky *et al.*, 1987), although at present it is equally likely that attributional style is a risk factor whether or not a negative experience occurs (Brewin, 1985).

Three types of current situational information relevant to the formation of attributions have been discussed in some detail. Kelley (1967) suggested that for many events the most common causal factors are persons (P), stimuli (S), and occasions or times (T). The attribution of a given P's response to a certain S on a particular occasion (T) depends on the perception of the degree of its consensus with other Ps' responses to S, its consistency with this P's response to S on other occasions, and its distinctiveness from P's response to other Ss. Particular patterns of information are thought to lead to particular attributions. For example, behaviour that is low in consensus, high in consistency, and low in distinctiveness tends to produce person attributions, whereas behaviour that is highly consensual, highly consistent, and highly distinctive tends to be attributed to the stimulus.

This analysis has proven very fruitful, although a number of defects have been pointed out and improvements suggested (Hilton and Slugoski, 1986; Jaspars *et al.*, 1983). It is easy to see how a parent's attribution for a child's misbehaviour with a particular playmate would be influenced by information about how many other children misbehaved with this playmate (consensus), how often the child had misbehaved with this playmate in the past (consistency), and how often the child misbehaved with other playmates (distinctiveness). But many important real-life events, such as accidents, bereavement, or redundancy, do not possess this person–stimulus–occasion structure, with the result that some of this information is unavailable. If the event is only likely to happen once, or if no more then one stimulus is ever likely to be involved, consistency and distinctiveness information may have to be combined to yield a cruder judgement of *how often something similar has happened in the past*. In practice the individual trying to explain an event may not have any ready access to this kind of information other than from his or her own memory. These estimates may be affected by current mood, the recall of past negative outcomes being enhanced and the recall of past positive experiences being inhibited when one is depressed (Blaney, 1986).

Consensus information about how others would have behaved or about the frequency in the general population of a particular experience can also be extremely hard to come by. The assumption is frequently made that others are more similar to oneself than they in fact are, but this 'false consensus effect' is typically absent when a person is depressed (Tabachnik *et al.*, 1983). Consensus beliefs about shameful or embarrassing experiences, which are of more relevance to clinical psychology, have not been specifically investigated, however. It has been suggested (Brewin and Furnham, 1986) that people who are ashamed of experiences they believe to be unusual or deviant will, in the absence of consensus information, tend to make self-attributions and to avoid others they perceive as 'normal'. One of the consequences would be to further restrict their access to normative (consensus) information, thereby prolonging or exacerbating the problem. The existence of biases in individuals' social judgements is also evident in the 'fundamental attribution error', whereby the situational forces that are responsible for others' behaviour tend to be underestimated. This may lead to an excess of inappropriate person attributions by members of a couple trying to account for their partner's negative behaviours.

CHANGING EXPLANATIONS

The multiplicity of factors influencing the formation of explanations means that there are potentially many ways of altering them. The most popular methods have been to offer new and less threatening labels for ambiguous experiences, to suggest explicit alternative attributions for failures of various kinds, and to provide new information that is either unavailable to patients or is inconsistent with their beliefs in the hope that it will lead to attributional change. In a number of cases, the simple provision of a new label or of new information will be greatly reassuring. Doctors and psychologists are constantly making use of these principles by providing non-threatening explanations for worrying symptoms, and by telling people that their problem is much more common than they thought and will not last long. Indeed, there is probably a great deal more scope for the simple providing of information, both to patients and their relatives, when an illness has been newly diagnosed, a new treatment begun, or hospital admission contemplated. Sometimes, though, this new information is in conflict with pre-existing causal beliefs and changing the patient's explanation requires a more structured approach.

Some of the earliest clinically-relevant studies, which are generically-termed 'misattribution therapy' studies, were concerned to relabel physiological arousal. They were influenced by Schachter's theory of the emotions, which claimed that emotional experience consists of an undifferentiated state of physiological arousal that is labelled in various ways according to the way that environmental stimuli are appraised. A number of investigators subsequently tried to mislead subjects into relabelling unwanted feelings of arousal in a less threatening way, for example, by attributing their origin to an emotionally neutral source.

In a well-known example of this approach, Storms and Nisbett (1970) gave people suffering from insomnia a pill to take at bedtime. Although the pills were inert, Storms and Nisbett told half the subjects that the pills would produce symptoms similar to those of high physiological arousal and the other half that they would calm them down. Consistent with the prediction that it would be helpful to relabel the experience of arousal as a side-effect rather than as an internal emotional state, it was found that the former group reported falling asleep more quickly than the latter. Reviewers of the misattribution therapy approach (Brewin and Antaki, 1982; Harvey and Galvin, 1984) have concluded that the findings have been difficult to replicate and that clinically-significant effects have not been established. In part, this must be due to the inherent implausibility of many of the manipulations, as well as to the difficulty of misleading people. This research has demonstrated a useful theoretical point about the importance of labels, but from a clinical point of view there is much more to be gained from providing veridical information to people who have wrongly or unhelpfully labelled their experiences.

Veridical relabelling has been attempted recently as a treatment for panic attacks (Clark *et al.*, 1985; Salkovskis *et al.*, 1986). Hypothesizing that these attacks arise because the symptoms of overbreathing are misinterpreted as signalling a cardiac or other medical emergency, the treatment consists of providing (*a*) a less threatening label for the patient's symptoms (i.e. they are only a sign of overbreathing) and (*b*) information that is compatible with the less threatening label but is incompatible with the more threatening label. This is achieved by having patients practice voluntary overbreathing, then assess their sensations and compare them to those experienced during panic attacks. Patients are encouraged to explore for themselves the similarities between the two sets of sensations, and any discrepancies that might undermine the new label are discussed. In attributional terms, what is being given is consistency and distinctiveness information, that is, that the symptoms covary across time with one event but not with another. The therapist then gives patients an explanation of how overbreathing can induce panic attacks and trains them in a pattern of slow breathing to counteract it. Although this treatment contains a number of elements, so that improvement need not be the result of relabelling, Salkovskis and Clark (1986) argue that the extremely rapid initial reduction in panic attack frequency and self-reported anxiety is suggestive of the importance of the cognitive element.

Watts *et al.* (1973) report a method of modifying the delusional beliefs of chronically-paranoid patients that has elements of both relabelling and reattribution. Their technique was to begin with the least strongly-held beliefs, working up gradually to those that were most strongly held. For each belief they elicited the patient's reasons for holding it, and then discussed alternative explanations. Patients were not directly contradicted, but were encouraged to express alternative explanations for themselves and to discuss the evidence in favour of each until the strength of their belief in the initial explanation began to wane. For example, if a patient based a belief that people thought he looked feminine on the fact that he had a thin waist, other non-masculine features of the body such as facial hair would be discussed and the assumption that women always had thinner waists than men challenged. In essence, the therapeutic focus seems to have been on the available situational information, using data about consensus, distinctiveness, etc., to assess covariation between patients' experiences and the range of possible causal factors. Several other authors have reported successful attempts to modify delusional beliefs, but as yet there are no large-scale outcome studies evaluating this approach.

There have also been attempts to change more general causal beliefs. Layden (1982) obtained information about the habitual attributional styles of low self-esteem and depressed college students from questionnaires and from programmed successes and failures on a number of tests of intellectual and social skills. She then discussed with each individual their tendency to internalize or externalize success and failure, and the importance of accurate attribution. The therapy task was to keep a daily diary of successes and failures, examining each event thoroughly to see if there were internal causes for the successes and external causes for the failures. Subjects were not to make up causes, but to look for real, possible causes they normally missed. In other words, they were to try to acquire a healthier attributional style, by learning to analyze and re-evaluate everyday situations. Layden noted several reactions in her subjects that are consistent with the theoretical link between attributions and self-esteem:

> The responses individuals had to information about their attributional style and to the task they were to do were often dramatic. Some people cried with relief. One said to me that she had never been told that it was acceptable to like herself, to think she brought about successes. Some quoted parents or other authority sources to the effect that one should always feel responsible for all failures encountered to gain humility. Others were glad to be 'ordered' to do the task that they would have liked to do but felt uncomfortable giving themselves permission to do (page 76).

Layden's results indicated that, relative to a control group, subjects receiving attribution retraining over a four- to five-week period changed their attributions in the predicted directions and showed an increase in self-esteem. To the extent that attributional style changed, levels of self-reported depression also improved. Other investigators have subsequently confirmed that this method of supplying causes for everyday events can lead to changes in attributional style (Sober-Ain and Kidd, 1984).

The majority of attempts at systematic reattribution training have concentrated on improving various aspects of academic and intellectual achievement. In a pioneering study, Dweck (1975) undertook the retraining of children who had extreme reactions to failure and easily became helpless in the classroom. These children took less personal responsibility for the outcomes of their behaviour and tended to place relatively little emphasis on the role of effort in determining success and failure. Dweck provided them with a series of problems into which she had pre-programmed a number of failures. Whenever a child failed, he or she was explicitly told that this was because they should have tried harder. As predicted, this reattribution of failure to an unstable and controllable cause led to increased persistence and enhanced performance.

Försterling (1985) has reviewed 15 subsequent studies that aimed to improve reading, arithmetic, general academic performance, and performance on a variety of more specific tasks, mainly by getting subjects to reattribute failure to lack of effort. A variety of techniques have been used, including an operant approach with positive reinforcement of effort attributions, explicit mention or modelling by an experimenter of effort attributions, and the provision of antecedent or 'pre-attributional' information. In spite of the fact that the subjects were mainly selected for their poor levels of performance or low levels of achievement motivation, all bar one of the 15 studies reviewed by Försterling reported very promising results, producing changes in self-report measures and in measures of persistence and performance. In one of the studies to encourage unstable (but not effort) attributions for failure, Wilson and Linville (1982) were able to improve long-term academic performance and improve drop-out rates by simply giving freshman college students two types of information. First, they were told that grades tended to be low at first but improved in later years (information about low consistency), and secondly they were shown videotaped interviews with older students reporting improvement in their grades (information about high consensus). Most studies, however, relied on a number of structured sessions in which subjects worked on a task and were instructed how to explain the occurrence of success and failure.

The information required to change explanations may come from many sources, including the patient's attempts to master difficult situations and gain greater control over symptoms, more accurate self-monitoring, the testimony of others, and modelling by peers or by the therapist. The approaches reviewed above represent a promising beginning, and could be adapted to fit a variety of clinical conditions. Less intensive interventions will be necessary when there are fewer or less strongly held assumptions and causal beliefs to overcome, for example when patients have recently developed a physical or psychiatric condition and are being prepared for hospitalization, surgery, or other treatment. When the condition is a long-standing one, patients are almost certain to have developed a set of attributions and expectations concerning it. If these are based on faulty information or on partial access to relevant information, or if they are being maintained by self-presentational concerns, considerable and imaginative efforts may be needed to alter them in a more adaptive direction.

CONCLUSIONS

Many people seen by clinical psychologists feel that they are exposed to various kinds of threat, that they are relatively powerless to effect particular changes in their own lives, that they are worthless and responsible for the bad things that happen to them, and that they are unable to live up to certain standards they have set themselves. While these views may at times be veridical, they will sometimes be erroneous by virtue of lack of information, distorted information, one-sided information, or powerful causal beliefs that override what accurate information is available. The relation of theories of attribution and explanation to these common problems can be seen in one of two ways. First, it provides an overall framework to account for changes in self-esteem, in expectations of therapeutic success, and in certain emotional states. The *modus operandi* of many different kinds of therapy may lie in the provision of different kinds of information that then influence patients' explanations of and reactions to their problems. For example, a functional analysis of a patient's symptoms attempts to isolate antecedent conditions, typically showing that the symptoms fluctuate in intensity over time (low consistency information) and occur in some situations but not in others (high distinctiveness information). This pattern, particularly if combined with high consensus information, would tend to encourage situational rather than personal attributions as well as fostering attributions to unstable and specific factors.

The second contribution of this theoretical approach is to identify particular maladaptive beliefs that may be directly targeted in therapy and to suggest what types of information may help to modify them. It is neutral, however, about the best way of delivering this information, and a number of possible techniques have been described. Because of this there will never be one instantly identifiable 'attribution therapy'. What is characteristic of all attribution therapies, on the other hand, is an explicit concern with individual explanations of problems and symptoms, and with the consequences of the explanation for the person's emotional and behavioural adaptation.

REFERENCES

ALLOY, L.B., ABRAMSON, L.Y., METALSKY, G.I. and HARTLAGE, S. (1988). The hopelessness theory of depression: Issues of research design, conceptualization and assessment with special reference to attributional styles. *British Journal of Clinical Psychology*, 27, 5–21.

ANTAKI, C. and BREWIN, C.R. (1982). *Attributions and Psychological Change: Applications of attributional theories to clinical and educational practice*. London: Academic Press.

ARKIN, R.M. and BAUMGARDNER, A.H. (1985). Self-handicapping. In J.H. Harvey and G. Weary (eds), *Attribution: Basic issues and applications*. Orlando, Fl.: Academic Press.

BLANEY, P.H. (1986). Affect and memory: A review. *Psychological Bulletin*, 99, 229–246.

BRADLEY, C., BREWIN, C.R., GAMSU, D.S. and MOSES, J.L. (1984). Development of scales to measure perceived control of diabetes mellitus and diabetes-related health beliefs. *Diabetic Medicine*, 1, 213–218.

BREWIN, C.R. (1985). Depression and causal attributions: What is their relation? *Psychological Bulletin*, 98, 297–309.

BREWIN, C.R. and ANTAKI, C. (1982). The role of attributions in psychological treatment. In C. Antaki and C.R. Brewin (eds), *Attributions and Psychological Change*. London: Academic Press.

BREWIN, C.R. and ANTAKI, C. (1987). An analysis of ordinary explanations in clinical attribution research. *Journal of Social and Clinical Psychology*, 5, 79–98.

BREWIN, C.R. and FURNHAM, A. (1986). Attributional versus pre-attributional variables in self-esteem and depression: A comparison and test of learned helplessness theory. *Journal of Personality and Social Psychology*, 50, 1013–1020.

BUTLER, R.J., BREWIN, C.R. and FORSYTHE, W.I. (1986). Maternal attributions and tolerance for nocturnal enuresis. *Behaviour Research and Therapy*, 24, 307–312.

CLARK, D.M., SALKOVSKIS, P.M. and CHALKLEY, A.J. (1985). Respiratory control as a treatment for panic attacks. *Journal of Behavior Therapy and Experimental Psychiatry*, 16, 23–30.

CUTRONA, C.E., RUSSELL, D. and JONES, R.D. (1984). Cross-situational consistency in causal attributions: Does attributional style exist? *Journal of Personality and Social Psychology*, *47*, 1043–1058.

DWECK, C.S. (1975). The role of expectations and attributions in the alleviation of learned helplessness. *Journal of Personality and Social Psychology*, *31*, 674–685.

FINCHAM, F.D. (1985). Attribution processes in distressed and non-distressed couples: 2. Responsibility for marital problems. *Journal of Abnormal Psychology*, *94*, 183–190.

FÖRSTERLING, F. (1985). Attributional retraining: A review. *Psychological Bulletin*, *98*, 495–512.

GILLIN, J.C., RAPPAPORT, J.L., MIKKELSEN, E.J., LANGER, D., VANSKIVER, C. and MENDELSON, W. (1982). EEG sleep patterns in enuresis: A further analysis and comparison with controls. *Biological Psychiatry*, *17*, 947–953.

HARVEY, J.H. and GALVIN, K.S. (1984). Clinical implications of attribution theory and research. *Clinical Psychology Review*, *4*, 15–33.

HILTON, D.J. and SLUGOSKI, B.R. (1986). Knowledge-based causal attribution: The abnormal conditions focus model. *Psychological Review*, *93*, 75–88.

HOUSE, W.C. (1983). Variables affecting the relationship between depression and attribution of outcomes. *Journal of Genetic Psychology*, *142*, 293–300.

JASPARS, J., HEWSTONE, M. and FINCHAM, F.D. (1983). Attribution theory and research: The state of the art. In J. Jaspars, F.D. Fincham and M. Hewstone (eds), *Attribution Theory and Research: Conceptual, Developmental, and Social Dimensions*. London: Academic Press.

JOHNSON, W.G., ROSS, J.M. and MASTRIA, M.A. (1977). Delusional behavior: An attributional analysis of development and modification. *Journal of Abnormal Psychology*, *86*, 421–426.

KELLEY, H.H. (1967). Attribution theory in social psychology. In D. Levine (ed.), *Nebraska Symposium on Motivation, Vol. 15*. Lincoln: University of Nebraska Press.

KELLEY, H.H. and MICHELA, J.L. (1980). Attribution theory and research. *Annual Review of Psychology*, *31*, 457–501.

LAYDEN, M.A. (1982). Attributional style therapy. In C. Antaki and C.R. Brewin (eds), *Attributions and Psychological Change*. London: Academic Press.

LOBITZ, G.K. and JOHNSON, S.M. (1975). Normal versus deviant children: A multimethod comparison. *Journal of Abnormal Child Psychology*, *3*, 353–374.

METALSKY, G.I., HALBERSTADT, L.J. and ABRAMSON, L.Y. (1987). Vulnerability to depressive mood reactions: Toward a more powerful test of the diathesis-stress and causal mediation components of the reformulated theory of depression. *Journal of Personality and Social Psychology*, *52*, 386–393.

ORVIS, B.R., KELLEY, H.H. and BUTLER, D. (1976). Attributional conflict in young couples. In J.H. Harvey, W.J. Ickes and R.F. Kidd (eds), *New Directions in Attribution Research, Vol. 1*. Hillsdale, N.J.: Lawrence Erlbaum.

PETERSON, C. and SELIGMAN, M.E.P. (1984). Causal explanations as a risk factor for depression: Theory and evidence. *Psychological Review*, *91*, 347–374.

RICKARD, K.M., FOREHAND, R., WELLS, K.C., GRIEST, D.L. and McMAHON, R.J. (1981). Factors in the referral of children for behavioral treatment: A comparison of mothers of clinic-referred deviant, clinic-referred non-deviant and non-clinic children. *Behaviour Research and Therapy*, *19*, 201–205.

SALKOVSKIS, P.M. and CLARK, D.M. (1986). Cognitive and physiological processes in the maintenance and treatment of panic attacks. In I. Hand and H.-U. Wittchen, *Panic and Phobias*. Berlin: Springer Verlag.

SALKOVSKIS, P.M., JONES, D.R.O. and CLARK, D.M. (1986). Respiratory control in the treatment of panic attacks: Replication and extension with concurrent measurement of behaviour and pCO_2. *British Journal of Psychiatry*, *148*, 526–532.

SOBER-AIN, L. and KIDD, R.F. (1984). Fostering changes in self-blamers' beliefs about causality. *Cognitive Therapy and Research*, *8*, 121–138.

SONNE, J.L. and JANOFF, D.S. (1982). Attributions and the maintenance of behavior change. In C. Antaki and C.R. Brewin (eds), *Attributions and Psychological Change*. London: Academic Press.

STORMS, M.D. and McCAUL, K.D. (1976). Attribution processes and the emotional exacerbation of dysfunctional behavior. In J.H. Harvey, W.J. Ickes and R.F. Kidd (eds), *New Directions in Attribution Research, Vol. 1*. Hillsdale, N.J.: Lawrence Erlbaum.

STORMS, M.D. and NISBETT, R.E. (1970). Insomnia and the attribution process. *Journal of Personality and Social Psychology*, *16*, 319–328.

TABACHNIK, N., CROCKER, J. and ALLOY, L.B. (1983). Depression, social comparison, and the false-consensus effect. *Journal of Personality and Social Psychology*, *45*, 688–699.

WATTS, F.N. (1982). Attributional aspects of medicine. In C. Antaki and C.R. Brewin (eds), *Attributions and Psychological Change*. London: Academic Press.

WATTS, F.N., POWELL, G.E. and AUSTIN, S.V. (1973). The modification of abnormal beliefs. *British Journal of Medical Psychology*, *46*, 359–363.

WEINER, B. (1985a). 'Spontaneous' causal thinking. *Psychological Bulletin*, *97*, 74–84.

WEINER, B. (1985b). An attributional theory of achievement motivation and emotion. *Psychological Review*, *92*, 548–573.

WILSON, T.D. and LINVILLE, P.W. (1982). Improving the academic performance of college freshmen: Attribution therapy revisited. *Journal of Personality and Social Psychology*, *42*, 367–376.

YARROW, M.R., SCHWARTZ, C.G., MURPHY, H.S. and DEASY, L.C. (1956). The psychological meaning of mental illness in the family. *Journal of Social Issues*, *11*, 12–24.

PROBLEM SOLVING THERAPY

Elisabeth Marx

The relationship between mental health and the ability to solve day-to-day problems which Jahoda proposed in 1958 was neglected in clinical psychology for many years. The way in which people solve problems was the exclusive topic of general psychology, and consequently, the majority of research focused on the analysis of impersonal problem solving, such as anagrams or syllogisms, without any attempt to transfer these findings to the area of real-life or social problem solving. But with the advent of the 'cognitive revolution' (Mahoney, 1974), there was an increasing tendency to overcome the insularity of general and clinical psychological research, in favour of integrating cognitive psychological concepts within the area of clinical psychology. The concept of social problem solving represents an example of this development.

Jahoda's (1958) proposal was taken up again by D'Zurilla and Goldfried (1971) and Spivack *et al.* (1976) with the intention of analysing the basic cognitive operations of social problem-solving processes and utilizing this knowledge for the development of therapeutic interventions. The frequent observation of patients' difficulties in solving everyday problems and adapting to novel situations led to the idea that deficits in social problem solving may be a core feature of psychological disorders. Thus, considering social problem solving as an important component of social competence, the approach is based on the assumptions that

(*1*) some forms of psychological disorders might be causally related to deficits in social problem solving, and
(2) training individuals in the necessary problem-solving skills might be an effective therapeutic approach. (D'Zurilla and Goldfried, 1971; D'Zurilla and Nezu, 1982).

There is ample empirical evidence, albeit of a correlational nature, for the first assumption. Deficits in social problem solving have been found in a variety of psychological disorders, such as maladjusted adolescents (Platt *et al.*, 1974), adult psychiatric patients (Platt and Spivack, 1974), heroin addicts (Platt *et al.*, 1973), alcoholics (Intagliata, 1978), depressed students (Gotlib and Asarnow, 1979) and suicidal psychiatric patients (Schotte and Clum, 1987).

In all of these studies, social problem solving was assessed with the Means–Ends Problem-Solving Test (MEPS; Platt and Spivack, 1975). The MEPS consists of a series of social problem situations in which the beginning and the final outcome of the problem are presented. Subjects have to describe the strategies which will allow the protagonist of the story to reach the stated outcome. Consequently, the inventory assesses step-by-step planning or means–ends thinking. Subjects' answers can be scored for a variety of aspects, of which relevant means and irrelevant means are most commonly utilized. The aforementioned studies demonstrated that, in comparison to non-clinical controls, patients from different clinical populations developed fewer relevant means and more irrelevant means, and that psychiatric patients used more impulsive strategies and less introspection (Platt and Spivack, 1974).

Hence, there has been growing interest in recent years in improving patients' adaptation and social competence by training them in the skills necessary for effective problem solving, as illustrated by the increasing number of publications in this area. Whereas a computer search with the cueword 'problem-solving therapy' only elicited 25 references for the period between 1964 and 1974, it provided 77 references for the subsequent five years, and 131 references for the period between 1981 and 1986.

Social problem solving refers to the process of discovering an effective course of action. It is defined as a

> process, whether overt or cognitive in nature, which (a) makes available a variety of potentially effective response alternatives for dealing with a problematic situation and (b) increases the probability of selecting the most effective response from among these various alternatives. (D'Zurilla and Goldfried, 1971, page 108).

In contrast to behavioural interventions, with their training of discrete behavioural skills for specific situations, the aim of problem-solving therapies is to equip the patient with generalizable strategies which can be applied to a variety of situations. With the development of heuristics for dealing with problematic situations, the therapy does not focus exclusively on solutions to patients' present problems, as in traditional therapies, but intends to enhance their coping skills for future problems, and to help them to become 'their own therapists'.

The aim of this chapter is to provide an overview and analysis of the current status of problem-solving therapy. The underlying theoretical model of problem-solving processes, the major elements of the therapy, and the application in the treatment of various psychological disorders is described.

Finally, an attempt is made to outline advantages and limitations of the problem-solving approach and to offer recommendations for future practice and research.

PROCESS MODEL OF SOCIAL PROBLEM SOLVING

The major theoretical models in the development of problem-solving therapies can be differentiated according to their emphasis on either the analysis of fundamental components of problem solving (Spivack *et al.*, 1976) or on the investigation of the problem-solving process applying a cybernetic concept (D'Zurilla and Goldfried, 1971; Dixon *et al.*, 1979; Heppner, 1978). Characteristic of the first approach is Spivack *et al.*'s (1976) concept of interpersonal cognitive problem-solving skills. Solving real-life problems is not seen as a unitary ability but rather as a set of interrelated fundamental problem-solving skills, such as problem sensitivity, alternative-solution thinking, means–ends thinking, consequential thinking, and causal thinking.

Although this concept has been widely and successfully used within Spivack *et al.*'s therapeutic programmes for teaching problem-solving skills to children, adolescents, and adults, the majority of social problem-solving therapies follow the process model, originally developed by D'Zurilla and Goldfried (1971), and slightly modified by D'Zurilla and Nezu (1982).

In an attempt to define common features of effective social problem solving, D'Zurilla and Goldfried (1971) integrated research findings on impersonal problem solving, creativity training, and decision making in economic contexts. As a result, their model conceptualizes problem solving as a five-stage process, with distinct cognitive operations at each stage. The succeeding implementation of these operations is supposed to enhance the likelihood of finding an effective problem solution. The five phases consist of:

(*1*) Problem orientation
(*2*) Problem definition and formulation
(*3*) Generation of alternatives
(*4*) Decision making
(*5*) Solution implementation and verification.

These sequential phases reflect an ideal-type process. In real-life problem solving the phases overlap, interact, and are linked by feedback loops, and the problem-solving process therefore resembles a cybernetic rather than a linear model. Each phase is stringently analyzed for the fundamental cognitive operations which facilitate effective problem solving, and the recommended heuristics represent the essential components of problem-solving training.

1. Problem orientation

It is a well recognized fact that the way one approaches problems, the general mental set (Heppner, 1978), can have a major effect on the quality of the subsequent problem-solving process. Whether difficult situations are primarily perceived as a challenge or a threat (cf., primary appraisal, Lazarus *et al.*, 1974) will result in the selection of different response alternatives, and will influence the motivation and persistence of the problem solver. The major aim in the problem-orientation phase is to reduce negative emotional reactions and negative self-statements in view of the experienced problems which are likely to inhibit the subsequent problem-solving process, and to replace these with target-oriented behaviour.

A positive problem orientation will be facilitated if the problem solver

(*a*) adopts the general assumption that problems constitute a normal part of life and that most problems can be coped with effectively;

(*b*) recognizes problems once they occur;

(*c*) suppresses the tendency either to act impulsively or to avoid the situation altogether and do nothing.

Thus, the most important aspects of an effective problem orientation are the confidence in one's ability to cope (cf., influence of high self-efficacy on subsequent behaviour, Bandura, 1982), an internal locus of control, a sensitivity for problems (that is, to use the emotional cues which problems evoke for action-oriented behaviour), and a 'stop and think' attitude before acting.

2. Problem definition and formulation

Contrary to well-defined impersonal problems, social problem situations are characteristically vague (one does not know exactly what the problem is) and ambiguous (there are no clear criteria for a situational interpretation). Consequently, social problems require strategies which allow an adequate analysis of the problem and its goal. The problem solver often has to embark on collecting more information about the situation, before he/she is able to define the problem appropriately. The aim is a formulation of the problem that is couched in concrete operational terms, distinguishes relevant from irrelevant aspects, avoids cognitive errors which could lead to the definition of pseudoproblems (Beck, 1967), identifies the major goal, and possibly subdivides the problem into more manageable subproblems. As with situational definitions, the problem-solving goal should be stated in concrete and behavioural terms describing exactly what changes are desired.

Once the problem has been specified and realistic and attainable goals have been set, the problem solver can begin the search for effective strategies.

3. Generation of alternatives

The main purpose of this phase is to produce as many action alternatives as possible in a way that maximizes the likelihood of finding the most effective strategy among the alternatives. One way of achieving this is to apply Osborn's (1963) brainstorming techniques with the main principles of (*a*) quantity breeds quality and (*b*) deferment of judgement. The rationale behind these two rules is that the more alternatives one produces, the more likely it is that high quality solutions will be amongst them. The occurrence of high quality solutions should also be facilitated by deferring the judgement of the produced alternatives to the decision-making phase, and 'let the ideas run'.

Since it is not sufficient for effective problem solving to develop general strategies (like 'pleasing a friend') but these have to be specified in the form of concrete tactics (like 'buying theatre tickets for Monday night'), both general and specific levels have to be included in the brainstorming process. Two different methods can be used in developing specific courses of action.

First, a problem solver may produce as many general strategies as possible, select the best general strategy in the decision-making phase, and subsequently, return to the generation-of-alternatives phase in order to develop as many specific tactics as possible for the selected strategy. The best of these tactics would then be chosen in a second decision-making process.

Second, a problem solver may develop general strategies, roughly screen out the irrelevant ones, and then, in a second brainstorming process produce as many tactics as possible for all the relevant strategies. The range of strategies with their respective potential tactics would then be evaluated in the decision-making phase.

Although the first of these options is more efficient and economical, its application might depend on the kind of problem – with the first option being more appropriate for problems in familiar areas and the second option for problems in unfamiliar areas.

4. Decision making

Selecting the most promising course of action raises the question of what constitutes an effective strategy. Following the utility model of human choice, effectiveness is based upon the value and likelihood of the expected consequences. The problem solver has to select the alternative with the highest probability of changing the situation successfully, that is, the strategy that maximizes positive short- and long-term consequences and minimizes negative consequences, both personally and socially. Consequences which need to be considered in the personal area are: amount of effort, consistency with morals, emotional costs and gains. Social consequences include: effects on friends and family, social reputation, etc. The likelihood that a particular course of action will produce the desired outcome (cf., outcome expectancy, Bandura, 1982) combined with the likelihood that the individual will be able to implement the particular course of action (cf., self-efficacy, Bandura, 1982) determine the final selection of a strategy.

5. Solution implementation and verification

Finally, after a cognitive solution has been found, the selected strategy has to be implemented and evaluated for its effectiveness. In order to implement the strategy effectively, adequate behavioural skills plus facilitative motivation are needed. In order to evaluate the outcome, the problem solver has to observe the consequences, and determine whether they match the desired outcome.

In the case of a match between desired and actual outcome, the problem solver 'exits' the problem-solving process and reinforces him/herself for the successful solution.

In the case of a mismatch between expected and actual consequences, the problem solver should use the negative feedback to find out where the problem-solving process might have failed. On the cognitive level, potential distortions of the process include the setting of unrealistic goals, inadequate consideration of long-term consequences, lack of specificity of tactics, etc. If the cause of ineffective problem solving lies at the cognitive level, the problem solver has to return to the relevant stage and re-run the whole process. On the other hand, if the cause of ineffective problem solving is at the behavioural level, the problem solver has to either acquire the necessary skills or try to reduce emotional inhibitions.

Validity of the model

The elements of D'Zurilla and Goldfried's five-stage-model represent core features of every current process model of social problem solving (Heppner, 1978; Dixon et al., 1979). However, looking at the empirical verification of the various components, little research has been carried out. As the theoretical delineation of the model was based on research on impersonal problem solving, the empirical evidence which D'Zurilla and Goldfried cite is exclusively from that area, such as the correlation between concrete thinking and effective problem solving (Bloom and Broder, 1950) or the importance of the brainstorming technique for creative thinking (Meadow and Parnes, 1959).

This raises the question of how well the findings of general psychological theories of problem solving can be transferred to real-life problem solving. Certainly the definition of a problem in the impersonal area as a 'stimulus organization for which an organism does not have a ready response' (Davis, 1973, page 12) is applicable to the area of social problem solving. And so are the basic operations for the solution of a problem, that is, the analysis of the problem, the definition of the target, and the development of possible strategies. However, real-life problems generally differ from impersonal problems in type and characteristics (Dörner, 1976). In contrast to the well-defined problems in the area of impersonal problem solving which usually only require one of the outlined basic operations, social problems usually require all three of them. That is, the problem solver does not know exactly what the problem is, what the appropriate target is, and what possible strategies can be applied. Apart from differences in problem type, the characteristics of social situations with their high complexity, little transparency, and strongly dynamic features make a simple transfer of findings from impersonal to social problem solving questionable.

To summarize, the special features of social problem solving are:

(a) The problem is 'open' (i.e., ill-defined).
(b) The target is 'open' (i.e., unknown).
(c) The choice of possible strategies is 'open'. In contrast to certain types of problem, for example in mathematics, where the employment of algorithms guarantees the solution of a problem, similarly unfailing strategies do not exist in the social area.

From these considerations, including the fact that real-life problems involve 'hot information' as opposed to the 'cool information' of impersonal problems (Folkman *et al.*, 1979), one might not expect a strong relationship between the two types of problem solving. This is also empirically suggested by a lack of correlation between the two forms of problem solving (Gotlib and Asarnow, 1979) and by the independence of social problem solving from intelligence (Platt *et al.*, 1974).

Nevertheless, the relevance of the recommended heuristics of D'Zurilla and Goldfried's (1971) model for social problem solving has been empirically verified. In studies with college students, Nezu and D'Zurilla (1979) demonstrated that the training in the decision-making criteria resulted in the selection of more effective strategies, and that the implementation of the brainstorming rules increased the number of developed alternatives (Nezu and D'Zurilla, 1981b) and produced more effective solutions (D'Zurilla and Nezu, 1980). Furthermore, the importance of successful management of the early problem-solving phases for later ones has also been demonstrated. Subjects that were trained in specific problem definition and formulation skills made better choices in the decision-making process (Nezu and D'Zurilla, 1981a) and produced more alternatives (Nezu and D'Zurilla, 1981b) than subjects that only received general guidelines for the definition of problems or no guidelines at all.

MAJOR ELEMENTS OF PROBLEM-SOLVING THERAPY

Therapy programmes follow closely the outlined process model of social problem solving. The training involves a graded-tasks approach in which the cognitive operations of each phase have to be successfully managed before proceeding to the next phase. The therapist usually gives a presentation of the underlying principles and necessary strategies of each phase, demonstrates them by verbalizing an exemplary problem-solving process, and subsequently corrects and reinforces the strategies during the problem-solving attempts of the patient. (Therapy protocols are included in Goldfried and Davison, 1976, chap. 9; Falloon *et al.*, 1984, chap. 11; Pekala *et al.*, 1985; therapy manuals are available from Platt and Spivack (no date) and from Duckworth, 1983.)

Various behavioural techniques are used during the therapeutic process, such as modelling, prompting, corrective feedback, reinforcement, role-play, and behavioural rehearsal. In order to facilitate the generalization of the training and to promote patients' capacity for independent problem solving, regular homework assignments are usually included. These may consist of standard work sheets on which the patient has to specify a problem he or she has experienced, list all the possible alternative solutions, evaluate their potential consequences as to their value (e.g., positive, negative, neutral) and likelihood of occurrence (e.g., highly likely, likely, unlikely), and select the best strategy amongst the produced alternatives. The training can be carried out in individual or group settings.

CLINICAL APPLICATION OF PROBLEM-SOLVING TRAINING

Since the developments of the first programmes in the mid-1970s, problem-solving therapy has been extensively used with various clinical groups in different therapeutic contexts. Analogous to the specific intentions of the programmes (D'Zurilla and Nezu, 1982), the different areas of application can be classified as to whether problem-solving training represents.

(*1*) the major therapeutic intervention
(*2*) a treatment maintenance strategy as part of a therapy package (with implications for secondary prevention)
(*3*) competence training with nonclinical groups (with implications for primary prevention).

Representative studies in each of these areas will be briefly reviewed. Only therapy studies with adults are summarized, because problem-solving programmes for children have been primarily used within a psychoeducational context, and because programmes for adults and children differ enormously due to their different state of cognitive development. (For a review of problem-solving training with children, see Urbain and Kendall, 1980.)

1. Problem-solving training as the major therapeutic intervention

Based on the assumption that psychological difficulties may be caused by a deficit in social problem solving, the training of the necessary skills has been a major target for interventions with hospitalized (mostly schizophrenic) patients, depressives, and couples with marital problems.

Although special programmes have been developed for chronic psychiatric patients (Bedell and DeeMichael, 1985) and there have been a number of attempts to use the problem-solving approach with this population, the results of the presently available outcome studies with schizophrenics can only be regarded as preliminary evidence for treatment effectiveness due to imperfections in their design. This is illustrated by the study of Coché and Flick (1975). Apart from some suggestive evidence for the effectiveness of problem-solving therapy for chronic psychiatric patients (Siegel and Spivack, 1976; Pekala *et al.*, 1985), Coché and Flick's (1975) study was the first attempt to test the effectiveness of problem-solving training with hospitalized psychiatric patients in a therapy outcome study. Compared to the control groups (a play-reading attention placebo control group and a no-treatment control group), the group trained in problem solving showed significant improvement in their problem-solving scores.

Although training was successful with regard to the improvement of the problem-solving scores, the study does not allow any conclusions as to whether problem-solving training is a valid intervention for hospitalized psychiatric patients. The lack of a psychopathological outcome measure and of follow-up, and doubt about whether a play-reading group constitutes a credible attention placebo to control nonspecific treatment effects make it impossible to answer the major questions about therapeutic effectiveness. That is, what are the specific treatment effects; does the treatment effect generalize (reduction of psychopathology); and are treatment effects persistent? Consequently, better controlled studies are needed in order to evaluate the potential of problem-solving programmes for hospitalized psychiatric patients.

More stringent research designs including a credible treatment control group and measures of psychological symptomatology were applied in studies that investigated problem-solving therapy with depressives. Thus, Hussian and Lawrence's (1981) study with depressed geriatric patients demonstrated that after a two-week training period, only groups with problem-solving therapy showed a significant reduction of depressive symptoms. The superiority of the problem-solving training was maintained at a two-week follow-up, but showed only a tendency to significance at a three-month follow-up. In order to secure the maintenance of treatment effects, it seems advisable to prolong the treatment period and/or to include booster sessions after treatment termination.

Support for the maintenance of the effects of problem-solving therapy is provided by Nezu's (1986) study with unipolar depressives. After a training period of eight weeks, problem-solving therapy resulted in significantly lower depression scores after treatment and at a six-month follow-up, higher self-evaluation of problem-solving skills and stronger internal locus of control compared to problem-focused therapy and a waiting list control.

Marital therapy is another area in which the importance of problem solving has become increasingly evident. In a series of studies with progressive improvements in design, Jacobson (1977) demonstrated that behavioural therapy, a combined approach of contingency contracting and problem-solving/communication training, was superior to a waiting list control condition, and, with the inclusion of an attention placebo group, suggested that these gains were not due to nonspecific treatment effects (Jacobson, 1978; Baucom, 1982). The differential effects of behavioural versus problem-solving components were subsequently investigated in a dismantling design (Jacobson, 1984), and it was shown that whereas behavioural techniques focus primarily on immediate changes, problem-solving training produced more long-term changes.

Apart from the above areas, there is some indication for the potential usefulness of problem-solving therapy as a method of anxiety reduction in the treatment of agoraphobia (Jannoun *et al.*, 1980). Originally applied as a control condition to test the relevance of exposure in the treatment of agoraphobia, problem solving was found to produce surprisingly good treatment results, especially with regard to the maintenance of the effects. Although a subsequent study (Cullington *et al.*, 1984) could not replicate the positive effects of the problem-solving training, and despite the present controversy whether or not it is a promising treatment strategy for agoraphobia (D'Zurilla, 1985; Butler and Gelder, 1985), further research seems to be indicated. Future studies that include a longer problem-solving training (it was only three-and-a-half hours in the above studies) might produce more consistent results.

In summary, studies which applied problem-solving training as the main therapeutic intervention with various clinical groups have been differentially successful in producing the intended treatment effects. Strongest evidence for the efficacy of the problem-solving approach has been achieved in the treatment of depression and of marital difficulties. By comparison, only preliminary support is available for its effectiveness as a treatment for hospitalized psychiatric patients and for agoraphobia.

The varying evidence for the effectiveness of problem-solving therapies in the different clinical groups might simply be due to differences in the stringency of the research designs of the presented studies (with the strongest treatment effect being demonstrated in depressives using the most stringent design). Alternatively, however, we have to consider the possibility that problem solving might be of differential relevance for different disorders. In fact, a major criticism of the problem-solving approach to psychological disorders concerns its uniformity assumption (Krause and Simons, 1981), that is, the notion that different psychological disorders are caused 'by the same problem-solving deficit'.

Although problem-solving deficits have been found, as outlined earlier, in various diagnostic groups, it is not clear whether the observed deficits are of aetiological importance for the respective disorders or whether they represent concomitant features of psychopathological disorders in general. Furthermore, apart from depression (McLean, 1976), there is a lack of disorder specific theoretical models which incorporate problem-solving deficits as an aetiological factor. Unless empirical evidence is found for the causal relationship between problem-solving deficits and psychological disorders, problem-solving training may, in many cases, be a necessary but not a sufficient main form of treatment.

2. Problem-solving training as a treatment maintenance strategy

Maintenance of treatment gains and prevention of relapse are important aspects of every therapeutic intervention. The application of problem-solving training in this area has focused so far on the treatment of addictive behaviour and on relapse prevention of schizophrenics. The main target is to enhance patients' ability to adapt to novel situations which they are likely to face after treatment termination. These can vary from practical problems (like finding accommodation or a job) to social and intrapersonal problems (like coping with drinking temptations in remitted alcoholics). The aim is to reduce the risk of relapse.

Within the area of addictive behaviours, the promotion of problem-solving skills has been integrated in general therapy programmes with alcoholics and smokers. Studies which examined the effects of problem-solving training given in addition to standard alcoholism programmes (Intagliata, 1978; Chaney et al., 1978) have provided some promising results. Thus, Chaney et al. (1978) showed that additional problem-solving training reduced the duration and severity of relapse in alcoholics.

Similarly successful as a maintenance strategy was problem-solving training in a smoking-reduction program (Supnick and Colletti, 1984). Clients with problem-solving training did not show significant relapse; but this was only the case for clients that were abstinent at the end of the main smoking-reduction treatment, not for clients with a reduced rate of smoking at treatment termination.

One of the most interesting applications of the problem-solving approach has been employed by Falloon and co-workers (Falloon et al., 1984) for the relapse prevention of schizophrenics. As living in a family with high levels of 'expressed emotion' (EE) has been identified as a high risk factor for relapse in schizophrenics (Vaughn and Leff, 1976), the main target of Falloon *et al.*'s intervention was to reduce the level of EE in the family and patients' vulnerability to EE. A therapy package was applied to improve the emotional climate within the family through training in family communication and family problem-solving skills, and to enhance the problem-solving skills of schizophrenics. Studies which compared the intensive family problem-solving training with holistic health therapy plus behaviour or insight-oriented family therapy showed that the problem-solving approach was more effective in reducing relapse rates in patients with schizophrenia, and that EE level in patients' relatives could be significantly lowered (Liberman *et al.*, 1981; Liberman *et al.*, 1984). The differential treatment effect of the problem-solving component cannot be disentangled in these studies as problem solving was combined with communication training; but this multiple therapy approach seems very promising for secondary prevention in schizophrenia.

3. Competence training with nonclinical groups

Although problem-solving training could be particularly useful for primary prevention, for example, to reduce vulnerability in high stress groups (such as individuals who are confronted with drastic life changes), this has hardly been explored. Instead, studies evaluated primarily the effectiveness of problem-solving training in student populations. Dixon *et al.* (1979) demonstrated the effectiveness of their training procedure in comparison to a pre-test–post-test control group, and a post-test only control group. In comparison to the two control groups, students in the problem-solving group developed significantly higher quality solutions, and also indicated that they used less impulsive behaviour during problem solving.

The possibility of improving academic achievement via problem-solving training is suggested by Duckworth's (1983) study. After participation in a problem-solving program students obtained higher standard bachelor's degrees at graduation compared to a no-training control group; they also developed a stronger internal locus of control and had lower neuroticism scores compared to the control subjects. However, because of the post-test only control group design, Duckworth's findings have to be interpreted with caution.

EVALUATION

In summary, problem-solving therapy has been successfully applied in various therapeutic contexts. Empirical studies support its effectiveness in the treatment of depression and marital problems, and there is suggestive evidence for its usefulness in the treatment of agoraphobics and even chronic psychiatric patients. Apart from its function as a main therapy, problem-solving training has been effective as a treatment maintenance strategy. Additional training in problem solving has reduced relapse rates in addictive behaviours (alcoholism and smoking), and it seems to be a promising psychosocial approach to the 'revolving door' problem in schizophrenia.

Thus, the rationale underlying the therapy programmes designed to enhance the patient's general adaptational skills has been empirically confirmed by their wide range of successful application. However, the advantage of a wide range of potential applications is offset by a lack of clarity concerning the differential indication and the 'active ingredient' of the programme.

Problem-solving training seems indicated with patients who are unable to solve difficult situations. This deficiency may cause their psychological maladjustment and/or increase the risk of the persistence of psychological maladjustment. A deficit in social problem solving can be caused by various factors. Patients may

(a) lack the necessary *cognitive* strategies for effective problem solving
(b) possess the necessary cognitive skills but not be able to implement the cognitive solution because of *behavioural deficits* or
(c) possess the necessary cognitive and/or behavioural skills but not be able to use these because of *emotional inhibitions* (D'Zurilla and Goldfried, 1971).

Moreover, effective problem solving does not only require heuristics to develop plans of actions (as represented in the heuristic structure, Dörner, 1976) but also demands sufficient knowledge with which to operate (as represented in the epistemic structure, Dörner, 1976). According to this analysis, a problem-solving deficit may be

(d) caused by a *lack of social knowledge*.

Consequently, depending on the exact nature of the problem-solving difficulties, different forms of therapeutic intervention will be indicated, with *cognitive problem-solving training* in case a, *behavioural skills' training* in b, *anxiety reduction procedures* in c, and *improvement of the epistemic structure* (teaching of relevant social knowledge or restructuring of existing knowledge; König, 1979) in case d.

Therefore, in order to improve decisions as to what form of treatment will be most effective for what patient or diagnostic group, future research will need to focus on the improvement of differential diagnosis. A task analysis of the specific problem-solving deficit is necessary (cf., Schwartz and Gottman, 1976), and for this purpose, a refinement in the assessment methods of problem solving is needed. The current main assessment procedure for social problem solving is the Means–Ends Problem-Solving Test (MEPS;

Platt and Spivack, 1975). Apart from recent criticisms regarding its validity as a problem-solving measure (Krause and Simons, 1981; Butler and Meichenbaum, 1981; D'Zurilla and Nezu, 1982), the MEPS assesses the outcome of the problem-solving process, the cognitive solution, and thus, gives no indication as to where the problem-solving process might have failed. In order to specify cognitive problem-solving deficits, process-oriented measures will have to be developed (Lauth, 1983). These are needed for diagnostic purposes, evaluation of problem-solving interventions and the analysis of the 'active ingredient' of the therapy.

Moreover, there are a number of conceptual issues which will have to be addressed in future. The most pressing questions are:

Is the normative model of social problem solving as proposed by D'Zurilla and Goldfried (1971) a valid description of real life problem solving? When do people use the suggested problem-solving heuristics?

Should the rather 'static' model by D'Zurilla and Goldfried (1971) be extended by taking into account the dynamic character of social problem solving, for example, temporal continuity, feedback from interaction partners, etc. (Kanfer and Busemeyer, 1982)?

What is the translation of cognitive solutions to behavioural performance, and how far can we assume a generalization of treatment effects (Tisdelle and St Lawrence, 1986)?

Finally, the relation between the ability to solve everyday problems and mental health may not be as straightforward as originally proposed. Recent findings by Heppner *et al.* (1987) confirmed the expected relation between self-appraised, ineffective problem solvers and psychological as well as physical symptoms but also indicated potentially negative consequences of self-appraised, highly effective problem solvers. In this study, self-appraised, highly effective problem solvers tended to be more prone to engage in Type A behaviour.

Although research on problem-solving therapy is only in its initial stages, its clinical application has shown promising results. For patients to learn strategies for solving problems is likely to counteract their common feeling of being overwhelmed when confronted with novel or difficult situations, and the associated tendency to either avoid them or to remain passive. The experience that a lot of problems can be solved will enhance motivation for active problem solving, increase feelings of self-efficacy and control, and reduce the general feeling of helplessness which is a concomitant feature of many psychological disorders. The knowledge of potential heuristics is likely to decrease subjective and objective stress levels, both because difficult situations will not have the same threatening character when coping strategies are available (Lazarus *et al.*, 1974), and because more problems will in fact be solved. As a general coping strategy (Prystav, 1981), problem solving can be regarded as an effective agent in counteracting vulnerability to stress.

There is empirical evidence suggesting that social problem solving may serve as a moderator between negative stressful life events and depressive symptoms. In Nezu *et al.*'s (1986) study, self-appraised, effective problem solvers under high levels of stress had significantly lower depression scores compared to self-appraised, ineffective problem solvers under similar levels of stress. In view of the importance of stress factors in the development of many psychological disorders, it is especially in the area of primary prevention that use of the problem-solving approach should be intensified.

Future practice and research should investigate the potential of problem-solving training in high risk groups, for example with individuals prior to drastic environmental, social and personal changes, such as unemployment and divorce. Further important areas of practical evaluation with the aim of secondary prevention could include intervention in attempted suicide, and deinstitutionalization programmes for long-term patients (Edelstein *et al.*, 1980) or for prisoners before release. Since we cannot prevent the occurrence of problems, the promotion of patients to become 'their own therapist' certainly seems a most valuable target.

Acknowledgement

I am very grateful to Atul Vadher, Fraser Watts and Mark Williams for helpful comments on a previous draft of this chapter.

REFERENCES

BANDURA, A. (1982). Self-efficacy mechanisms in human agency. *American Psychologist, 37*, 122–147.

BAUCOM, D.H. (1982). A comparison of behavioral contracting and problem-solving/communications training in behavioral marital therapy. *Behavior Therapy, 13*, 162–174.

BECK, A.T. (1967). *Depression: Clinical, Experimental and Theoretical Aspects.* New York: Hoeber.

BEDELL, J.R. and DEEMICHAEL, D. (1985). Teaching problem-solving skills to chronic psychiatric patients. In: D. Upper and S.M. Ross (eds) *Handbook of Behavioral Group Therapy.* New York: Plenum Press.

BLOOM, B.S. and BRODER, L.J. (1950). *Problem-Solving Processes of College Students.* Chicago, Illinois: University of Chicago Press.

BUTLER, G. and GELDER, M. (1985). Problem solving: Not a treatment for agoraphobia. A reply to D'Zurilla (1985). *Behavior Therapy, 16*, 548–550.

BUTLER, L. and MEICHENBAUM, D. (1981). The assessment of interpersonal problem-solving skills. In: P.C. Kendall and S.D. Hollon (eds) *Assessment Strategies for Cognitive-Behavioral Interventions.* New York: Academic Press.

CHANEY, E.F., O'LEARY, M.R. and MARLATT, G.A. (1978). Skill training with alcoholics. *Journal of Consulting and Clinical Psychology, 46*, 1092–1104.

COCHÉ, E. and FLICK, A. (1975). Problem-solving training groups for hospitalized psychiatric patients. *Journal of Psychology, 91*, 19–29.

CULLINGTON, A., BUTLER, G., HIBBERT, G. and GELDER, M. (1984). Problem solving: Not a treatment for agoraphobia. *Behavior Therapy, 15*, 280–286.

DAVIS, G.A. (1973). *Psychology of Human Problem-solving: Theory and Practice.* New York: Basic Books.

DIXON, D.N., HEPPNER, P.P., PETERSEN, C.H. and RONNINNG, R.R. (1979). Problem-solving workshop training. *Journal of Counselling Psychology, 26*, 133–139.

DÖRNER, D. (1976). *Problemlösen als Informationsverarbeitung.* Stuttgart: Kohlhammer.

DUCKWORTH, D.H. (1983). Evaluation of a programme for increasing the effectiveness of personal problem solving. *British Journal of Psychology, 74*, 119–127.

D'ZURILLA, T.J. (1985). Problem solving: Still a promising treatment strategy for agoraphobia. *Behavior Therapy, 16*, 545–548.

D'ZURILLA, T.J. and GOLDFRIED, M.R. (1971). Problem-solving and behavior modification. *Journal of Abnormal Psychology, 78*, 107–126.

D'ZURILLA, T.J. and NEZU, A. (1980). A study of the generation-of-alternatives process in social problem solving. *Cognitive Therapy and Research, 4*, 67–72.

D'ZURILLA, T.J. and NEZU, A. (1982). Social problem solving in adults. In: P.C. Kendall (ed.) *Advances in Cognitive-Behavioral Research and Therapy.* New York: Academic Press.

EDELSTEIN, B.A., COUTURE, E., CRAY, M., DICKENS, P. and LUSEBRINK, N. (1980). Group training of problem solving with psychiatric patients. In: D. Upper and S.M. Ross (eds) *Behavioral Group Therapy. An Annual Review Vol. II.* Champaign, Illinois: Research Press.

FALLOON, I.R.H., BOYD, J.L. and McGILL, C.W. (1984). *Family Care of Schizophrenia.* New York: Guilford Press.

FOLKMAN, S., SCHAEFER, C. and LAZARUS, R.S. (1979). Cognitive processes as mediators of stress and coping. In: V. HAMILTON and D.M. WARBURTON (eds) *Human Stress and Cognition: An Information-Processing Approach.* Chichester: Wiley.

GOLDFRIED, M.R. and DAVISON, G.C. (1976). *Clinical Behavior Therapy.* New York: Holt, Rinehart & Winston.

GOTLIB, I.H. and ASARNOW, R.F. (1979). Interpersonal and impersonal problem-solving skills in mildly and clinically depressed university students. *Journal of Consulting and Clinical Psychology, 47*, 86–95.

HEPPNER, P.P. (1978). A review of the problem-solving literature and its relationship to the counseling process. *Journal of Counseling Psychology, 25*, 366–375.

HEPPNER, P.P., KAMPA, M. and BRUNNING, L. (1987). The relationship between problem-solving self-appraisal and indices of physical and psychological health. *Cognitive Therapy and Research, 11*, 155–168.

HUSSIAN, R.A. and LAWRENCE, P.S. (1981). Social reinforcement of activity and problem-solving training in the treatment of depressed institutionalized elderly patients. *Cognitive Therapy and Research, 5*, 57–69.

INTAGLIATA, J.C. (1978). Increasing the interpersonal problem-skills of an alcoholic population. *Journal of Consulting and Clinical Psychology, 46*, 489–498.

JACOBSON, N.S. (1977). Problem solving and contingency contracting in the treatment of marital discord. *Journal of Consulting and Clinical Psychology, 45*, 92–100.

JACOBSON, N.S. (1978). Specific and nonspecific factors in the effectiveness of a behavioral approach to the treatment of marital discord. *Journal of Consulting and Clinical Psychology, 46*, 442–452.

JACOBSON, N.S. (1984). A component analysis of behavioral marital therapy: The relative effectiveness of behavior exchange and communication/problem-solving training. *Journal of Consulting and Clinical Psychology, 52*, 295–305.

JAHODA, M. (1958). *Current Concepts of Positive Mental Health.* New York: Basic Books.

JANNOUN, L., MUNBY, M., CATALAN, J. and GELDER, M. (1980). A home-based treatment program for agoraphobia: Replication and controlled evaluation. *Behavior Therapy, 11*, 294–305.

KANFER, F.H. and BUSEMEYER, J.R. (1982). The use of problem solving and decision making in behavior therapy. *Clinical Psychology Review, 2*, 239–266.

KÖNIG, F. (1979). Problemlösen und kognitive Therapie. In: N. Hoffmann (ed.) *Grundlagen Kognitiver Therapie.* Bern: Huber.

KRAUSE, R. and SIMONS, D. (1981). Problemlösen – eine Analyse des Konzepts und seiner Anwendung in der Psychotherapieforschung. *Zeitschrift für Klinische Psychologie, 10*, 265–280.

LAUTH, G. (1983). Erfassung von Kognitionsverläufen in Problemlösungstherapien. *Zeitschrift für Klinische Psychologie, 13*, 18–38.

LAZARUS, R.S., AVERILL, J.R. and OPTON, E.M. (1974). The psychology of coping: Issues of research and assessment. In: G.V. Coelho, D. Hamburg and J.E. Adams (eds) *Coping and Adaptation.* New York: Basic Books.

LIBERMAN, R.P., FALLOON, J.R. and AITCHISON, R.A. (1984). Multiple family therapy for schizophrenia: A behavioral problem-solving approach. *Psychosocial Rehabilitation Journal, 7*, 60–77.

LIBERMAN, R.P., WALLACE, C.J., FALLOON, J.R. and VAUGHN, C.E. (1981). Interpersonal problem-solving therapy for schizophrenics and their families. *Comprehensive Psychiatry, 22*, 627–630.

MAHONEY, M.J. (1974). *Cognition and Behavior Modification.* Cambridge, Mass.: Ballinger.

McLEAN, P. (1976). Therapeutic decision making in the behavioral treatment of depression. In: P.O. Davidson (ed.) *The Behavioral Management of Anxiety, Depression, and Pain.* New York: Brunner/Mazel.

MEADOW, A. and PARNES, S.J. (1959). Evaluation of training in creative problem-solving. *Journal of Applied Psychology, 43*, 189–194.

NEZU, A.M. (1986). Efficacy of a social problem-solving therapy approach for unipolar depression. *Journal of Consulting and Clinical Psychology, 54*, 196–202.

NEZU, A. and D'ZURILLA, T.J. (1979). An experimental evaluation of the decision-making process in social problem solving. *Cognitive Therapy and Research, 3*, 269–277.

NEZU, A. and D'ZURILLA, T.J. (1981a). Effects of problem definition and formulation on decision making in the social problem-solving process. *Behavior Therapy, 12*, 100–106.

NEZU, A. and D'ZURILLA, T.J. (1981b). Effects of problem definition and formulation on the generation of alternatives in the social problem-solving process. *Cognitive Therapy and Research, 5*, 265–271.

NEZU, A.M., NEZU, C.M., SARAYDARIAN, L., KALMAR, K. and RONAN, G.F. (1986). Social problem solving as a moderating variable between negative life stress and depressive symptoms. *Cognitive Therapy and Research, 10*, 489–498.

OSBORN, A.F. (1963). *Applied Imagination: Principles and Procedures of Creative Problem-Solving* (3rd ed.). New York: Scribner.

PEKALA, R.J., SIEGEL, J.M. and FARRAR, D.M. (1985). The problem-solving support group: Structured group therapy with psychiatric inpatients. *International Journal of Group Psychotherapy, 35*, 391–409.

PLATT, J.J., SCURA, W.C. and HANNON, J.R. (1973). Problem-solving thinking of youthful incarcerated heroin addicts. *Journal of Community Psychology, 1*, 278–281.

PLATT, J.J. and SPIVACK, G. *Workbook for Training in Interpersonal Problem-solving for Adults and Adolescents*. Philadelphia, Pa.: Department of Mental Health Sciences, Hahnemann University.

PLATT, J.J. and SPIVACK, G. (1974). Means of solving real-life problems: I. Psychiatric patients versus controls, and cross-cultural comparisons of normal females. *Journal of Community Psychology, 2*, 45–48.

PLATT, J.J. and SPIVACK, G. (1975). *Manual for the Means–Ends Problem-Solving Procedure (MEPS): A measure of interpersonal problem-solving skills*. Philadelphia, Pa.: Hahnemann Medical College and Hospital.

PLATT, J.J., SPIVACK, G., ALTMAN, N., ALTMAN, D. and PEIZER, S.B. (1974). Adolescent problem-solving thinking. *Journal of Consulting and Clinical Psychology, 42*, 787–793.

PRYSTAV, G. (1984). Psychologische Copingforschung: Konzeptbildungen, Operationalisierungen und Messinstrumente. *Diagnostica, 27*, 189–214.

SCHOTTE, D.E. and CLUM, G.A. (1987). Problem-solving skills in suicidal psychiatric patients. *Journal of Consulting and Clinical Psychology, 55*, 49–54.

SCHWARTZ, R. and GOTTMAN, J. (1976). Toward a task analysis of assertive behavior. *Journal of Consulting and Clinical Psychology, 44*, 910–920.

SIEGEL, J.M. and SPIVACK, G. (1976). Problem-solving therapy: The description of a new program for chronic psychiatric patients. *Psychotherapy: Theory, Research and Practice, 13*, 368–373.

SPIVACK, G., PLATT, J.J. and SHURE, M. (1976). *The Problem-Solving Approach to Adjustment*. San Francisco: Jossey-Bass.

SUPNICK, J.A. and COLLETTI, G. (1984). Relapse coping and problem-solving training following treatment for smoking. *Addictive Behaviours, 9*, 401–404.

TISDELLE, D.A. and ST LAWRENCE, J.S. (1986). Interpersonal problem-solving competency: Review and critique of the literature. *Clinical Psychology Review, 6*, 337–356.

URBAIN, E.S. and KENDALL, P.C. (1980). Review of social-cognitive problem-solving interventions with children. *Psychological Bulletin, 88*, 109–143.

VAUGHN, C.E. and LEFF, J.P. (1976). The influence of family and social factors on the course of psychiatric illness: A comparison of schizophrenic and depressed neurotic patients. *British Journal of Psychiatry, 129*, 125–137.

AGORAPHOBIA: THE CHANGING FACE OF TREATMENT

Fraser N. Watts

Clinical psychologists have been treating agoraphobia longer than most conditions. In the UK, it was behaviour therapy which established psychologists' role in treatment, and within behaviour therapy phobias were the first condition where clear evidence of effectiveness was demonstrated. Of course, the simple phobias which respond best to desensitization have always been relatively rare in the National Health Service, so it was largely to agoraphobia that we applied desensitization.

Despite psychologists' long involvement with agoraphobia, treatment tactics have not gone unchanged. Research and theory on agoraphobia has continued unabated (80 entries in a recent *Psychological Abstracts*). Research on agoraphobia has been unusually productive and practically-orientated; we now understand a great deal more about agoraphobia than we did 20 years ago, and more effective treatment approaches have become available.

Early treatment approaches emphasized the similarity of agoraphobia to simple phobias, and applied the same treatment methods to both. Recent thinking about agoraphobia has emphasized its dissimilarity (for example, Hallam, 1978). It is much rarer in the general population (6 per 1000), has an older age of onset in the late 20s (Thorpe and Burns, 1983), and a much greater association with other psychological problems (Chambless, 1985). To anticipate points that will be discussed in more detail later, physiological arousal has a more central place in agoraphobia. It is more likely to occur independently of specific external precipitation, and to be itself a focus of fear. Also, fear in agoraphobia seems to be cognitively mediated to a much greater extent than in simple phobias. Finally the degree of anxiety is more dependent on the interpersonal context.

GROUP AND HOME BASED APPROACHES

The most important practical developments in the treatment of agoraphobia in the 70s related to the involvement of other people (beside the individual patient with a therapist) in the treatment process. Involving other patients in a group-based approach and involving the spouse in a home-based approach were both found to be at least as effective as the individual therapist treating a patient alone, perhaps more so. Both are also clearly more economical of therapist time. They thus represented major practical advances in the treatment of agoraphobia. One or other of these treatment methods would now normally be the preferred way of treating agoraphobia in standard clinical practice.

Group-based methods

The consistent finding from studies of *in vivo* exposure in groups is that it is at least as effective as the treatment of patients individually (Hand *et al.*, 1974; Emmelkamp and Emmelkamp-Benner, 1975; Hafner and Marks, 1976; Teasdale *et al.*, 1977).

The initial study of Hand *et al.* provided group exposure on a relatively intensive basis, that is, three sessions of four hours each within a single week. The treatment method had a strong emphasis on coping with anxiety rather than minimizing it. Patients were required to enter phobic situations and not to withdraw from them before the anxiety had declined. Some patients were treated in 'structured' groups, others in 'unstructured' groups. In the structured condition, patients met for half an hour before the *in vivo* exercises to discuss strategies for coping with anxiety, and were encouraged to help each other during *in vivo* exercises. Explicit attempts were made by the therapist to promote cohesiveness within the group. In the 'unstructured' groups, there was no opportunity for group discussion of the exposure exercises. The two kinds of group did not differ in their initial response to treatment; the structured groups continued to improve in the follow-up period, apparently making it one of the most efficacious treatment procedures for agoraphobia to have been reported. However, this conclusion has to be treated with some caution (see Mathews *et al.*, 1981, p. 105) as it was not possible to obtain data on all patients at follow-up and some of the more severe patients may have been omitted. However, group exposure was clearly at least as effective as individual treatment.

There is independent evidence to indicate that it is helpful to supplement group exposure with other group procedures. Jones *et al.* (1980) found that combining group exposure with group discussion and counselling of significant others increased its effectiveness. Also, Sinnotti *et al.* (1981) found that there were particular benefits in arranging that patients in each group were living in geographical proximity to each other. Patients were able to use each others' homes as targets for *in vivo* exercises and seemed to benefit from the additional social contact. The particular benefits of group treatment are not confined to overcoming phobic avoidance behaviour. Hafner and Marks

(1976) found that group treatment produced greater improvements in social and leisure behaviour than individual treatment.

Initially there was concern that in group treatments the more handicapped patients would act as negative 'models' for the other patients in the group and have a deleterious effect. However, experience has not borne this out. In a cohesive group, the least handicapped patients seem to feel a responsibility to the rest of the group to 'blaze the trail' while the most handicapped patients feel a responsibility not to hold the others back. At both ends of the spectrum the social pressures produced by the group are helpful. It is also, of course, possible to subdivide the group in some of the *in vivo* exercises they undertake.

Home-based treatment

Home-based treatment, like group treatment, is relatively economical of therapist time. In the most thoroughly investigated version of this treatment developed at Oxford (see Mathews *et al.*, 1981) the therapist pays about five visits to the patient's home over a month, taking a total of seven hours, compared to the 20 hours which might be spent in ordinary individual treatment. It is made clear at the start that the patients will be running their own treatment programme, and a suitable person, usually the spouse, is recruited to help with it. Details of the therapeutic programme are provided in manuals, one for the patient and one for the partner; the role of the psychologist is that of an adviser. He/she explains the treatment programme and discusses progress but does not take part in *in vivo* exposure.

Results with this approach have been very encouraging. The advantage comes, not in the initial treatment period, where gains are comparable to those with other methods, but with continuing improvement in the follow-up period. In the five years following spouse-aided treatment, patients were less likely to report exacerbations of their symptoms or to seek further psychiatric help than those treated individually (see Mathews *et al.*, 1981, page 138).

It has been found that the manuals produced for the spouse-aided treatment can, even without any therapist involvement at all, produce improvements (Mathews *et al.*, 1981, p. 131). Nevertheless, the incremental advantage of involving a therapist in home-based practice probably justifies the relatively small amount of time involved.

The home-based treatment programme has two important features which reflect current thinking about the treatment of agoraphobia. Firstly, as in most group-based approaches there is an emphasis on training patients in the management of anxiety encountered during exposure. Secondly, because a significant person in the patient's life, usually the spouse, is involved in a therapeutic role, it has an opportunity of addressing directly the inter-

personal context of agoraphobia. These two themes in the growing refinement of the treatment of agoraphobia will be considered in more detail.

COGNITIVE, PHYSIOLOGICAL AND BEHAVIOURAL ASPECTS OF TREATMENT

Recent thinking on agoraphobia has emphasized its multi-faceted nature
(Foa *et al.*, 1984), usually adopting Lang's 'three systems' approach (fear,
avoidance behaviour, physiological responsiveness) (Lang, 1968; Himadi *et
al.*, 1985). Though there is undoubted value in a multi-component view of
phobic anxiety, the idea that there are exactly three components has been
adopted over-rigidly in the behaviour therapy literature. Scherer has a
somewhat similar *five*-component approach to emotion (Scherer, 1984)
which distinguishes subjective feeling states from cognitive stimulus processing (which are confused in some versions of the 'three systems' approach),
and also distinguishes motivation/behavioural tendencies from motor expression.

Various 'three-system' measures of agoraphobia are now available such as
those of Michelson and Mavissakalian (1983) and Chambless (Chambless *et
al.*, 1984; Chambless *et al.*, 1985). The point has also been made that
agoraphobics differ in the severity of their pathology in the various response
systems, and there is evidence that it is helpful to provide treatment targeted
specifically at the chief problem area (Michelson, 1986).

Cognitive, physiological and behavioural aspects of the treatment of
agoraphobia are now discussed in turn.

Cognitive anxiety-management

The behavioural treatment of agoraphobia initially concentrated on the
desensitization of fear responses to physical/geographical cues. More recent
thinking (for example, Hallam, 1978; Chambless and Goldstein, 1978) has
emphasized instead the importance of 'fear of fear'. The anxiety of agoraphobics, unlike other groups of phobics, is often secondary to the physiological responses which occur when they become frightened. There seems to
be a feedback loop in which initial physiological responses are amplified by
the anxious cognitions that they produce. This has led to increasing use of
cognitive anxiety-management skills as an adjunct to exposure treatment.

A considerable variety of cognitive approaches to agoraphobia is now
available based on the modification of self-statements (Last, 1984), cognitive restructuring (Emmelkamp and Mersch, 1982), the adaptation to phobias of Beck's cognitive treatment of depression (Beck and Emery, 1985),
problem-solving (Jannoun *et al.*, 1980), guided mastery (Williams *et al.*,
1984) and paradoxical intention (Michelson, 1986). There is such substantial

overlap between these that an empirical comparison of them would probably not be appropriate.

Though early evidence cast doubt on whether the addition of explicit cognitive components enhanced the effectiveness of exposure treatment (Emmelkamp and Mersch, 1982), more recent evidence has been encouraging (for example, Marchione *et al.*, 1987). One reason why it has sometimes been difficult to demonstrate the incremental effectiveness of cognitive additions to treatment is that good exposure treatment already entails a degree of cognitive modification.

The importance of cognitive training is particularly clear in patients with panic attacks. It is beyond the scope of this chapter to review the recent controversy in the psychiatric literature regarding the notion of panic disorder as a distinct nosological entity (see Gelder, 1986). However, because many agoraphobic patients also experience panic attacks, recent work on the treatment of panic has a place in the treatment of agoraphobia too. Clark (1986) has shown the cognitive treatment of panic to be very promising. 'Exposure' is still important, but it is to the physiological reactions which cue anxious cognitions rather than to geographical situations. Hyperventilation is crucial in providing such exposure as it is often important in the development of panic. However, even if this were not so, deliberate over-breathing in the context of therapy would remain a pragmatically useful way of eliciting some of the physiological reactions which cue anxiety.

Physiological vulnerability

The prominence of somatic complaints in agoraphobia, and the recently demonstrated effectiveness of cognitive treatments for them, raises fundamental issues about the relative primacy of physiological and cognitive features. No consensus on this has yet emerged. Hallam (1985) has recently provided a strong and closely argued statement of a cognitive position which rejects the adequacy of 'mechanistic' (physiological or behaviouristic) accounts of agoraphobia and focuses instead on the processes of attribution and construal which lead to the particular patterns of complaint found in agoraphobia. An important part of such an argument is that the physiological responses associated with anxiety can be found under conditions in which they do *not* lead to the experience of anxiety (for example, Taylor *et al.*, 1986).

While rejecting a physiological theory of agoraphobia which has no place for cognitive appraisal, it might be a mistake to downgrade physiological factors too far. A radically cognitivist view might say that agoraphobics do not differ at all from normal control subjects in the frequency and severity of initial physiological reactions *until* they cue abnormal cognitive processes. Though this strong view has not been definitely excluded by research, it lacks clinical plausibility. It is more likely that agoraphobics also have abnormal vulnerability to the physiological reactions that cue anxiety, in which case comprehensive treatment should work on these as well as on their cognitive appraisal.

For example, recent, as yet unpublished, work by Arnold Wilkins and myself suggests that agoraphobics are unusually vulnerable to the kind of stressful visual stimuli which can also trigger migraine headaches and epileptic seizures in light-sensitive epileptics (Wilkins *et al.*, 1984). This might be just one example of a family of sensory and physiological vulnerabilities in agoraphobics. As with migraine headaches, understanding the nature of physiological vulnerability could lead to an education programme that could substantially reduce the frequency with which stressful physiological reactions occur.

Mechanisms of exposure treatment

Enthusiasm for cognitive approaches should also not be allowed to deflect attention from the therapeutic mechanisms of *in vivo* exposure. Though cognitive interventions can be effective on their own, the balance of evidence indicates that cognitive therapy should be used as an adjunct to exposure, not a substitute for it. For example, Emmelkamp *et al.* (1978) showed that cognitive restructuring alone was significantly *less* effective than *in vivo* exposure alone.

Recent thinking indicates that securing *effective* (that is, functional) exposure is not always straightforward. Phobics have a repertoire of avoidance strategies which permit them to be in the presence of a phobic stimulus without attending to it in the way which would produce the therapeutic benefits of exposure (Borkovec, 1982; Foa and Kozak, 1986). Some of these strategies are externally observable, such as avoidance of eye gaze. Others involve attentional and cognitive strategies which are not directly observable, such as phobics imagining that they are somewhere else during exposure treatment.

It is not unusual to find therapists who encourage phobics in the use of strategies such as distraction which permit them to remain in the presence of the phobic stimulus while reducing the amount of anxiety they experience. However, it is doubtful whether this facilitates overall clinical improvement. Though distraction may well reduce short-term anxiety, the long-term benefits of exposure treatment depend on attention to the anxiety-producing stimulus, so that a clear cognitive representation of it can be formed (Watts, 1979). The implications of this for the conduct of exposure treatment have not yet been fully assimilated.

Before beginning exposure treatment, it may be advisable to investigate phobics' attentional strategies, and their propensity to engage in cognitive avoidance. Watts (in press) has developed a questionnaire that can be used for this purpose. It is, of course, not easy for phobics to maintain focused attention under high levels of anxiety. The therapist should, however, train the phobic patient to do this as much as possible, but also to try to keep anxiety levels within the range where focused attention *can* be maintained. It may also be relevant to examine patients' perception of their physiological responses, as Borkovec (1973) found that patients who were inaccurate in this were less likely to benefit from exposure. The concept of cognitive avoidance is not confined to external anxiety-arousing situations; avoidance of physiological cues is also possible. It is possible that prior training in accurate physiological monitoring would reduce cognitive avoidance of physiological reactions and so increase the effectiveness of exposure to treatment.

A key issue in exposure treatment is how gradually anxiety cues should be presented. The current consensus is for graded exposure in which anxiety is neither minimized as in classical desensitization, nor maximized as in flooding. However, the rationale for this preference for an intermediate level of exposure has not always been made clear. In fact, it is at intermediate levels of anxiety that functional exposure is likely to be maximized. If anxiety is excessive, cognitive avoidance will make good functional exposure impossible. However, if anxiety is minimized, anxiety may not be accessed sufficiently for it to be effectively modified.

One formulation of this latter point is in terms of Lang's concept of the 'emotion prototype', a cognitive representation involving stimulus, response and meaning components (see Watts and Blackstock, 1987). Lang has argued that the emotion prototype needs to be fully accessed before it can be modified, which is unlikely to happen if the therapist tries to minimize anxiety during exposure. There is an important conceptual distinction here between stimulus and response aspects of anxiety. Lang sees response features of anxiety as particularly fundamental, and has predicted, for example, that the effects of imaginal desensitization would be enhanced by prior training in *response* imagery. However, the empirical evidence for this is not good. Watts, in contrast, has argued that it is focused attention to anxiety producing *stimuli* that is particularly critical if anxiety decrement is to occur (see Watts and Blackstock, 1987; Lang, 1987).

PERSONALITY AND RELATIONSHIPS

Another important theme of recent work on agoraphobia has been attention to the interpersonal context. Twenty years ago, this was usually ignored in behavioural treatment. Now, it is generally regarded as central to the treatment of agoraphobia. This represents yet another way in which agoraphobia may differ from other groups of phobias; the interpersonal context does not seem to be of similar importance in simple phobias such as spider phobia.

Several propositions have been advanced about the importance of personality and interpersonal features in agoraphobia:

1. *Agoraphobics have dependent personalities and low levels of self-sufficiency which are related to their patterns of upbringing* (for example, Bowlby, 1980; Goldstein and Chambless, 1978; Thorpe and Burns, 1983; Guidano, 1987). However, hypotheses about premorbid personality features are notoriously difficult to test and evidence for this claim is not compelling.

2. *Agoraphobic symptoms arise in the context of interpersonal conflict* (Goldstein and Chambless, 1978). This claim, though plausible, is based largely on clinical series and there is a lack of comparison with the levels of interpersonal conflict in a control non-agoraphobic sample of comparable age.

3. *The husbands of female agoraphobics show personality abnormalities, and are unusually resistant to independence in their wives.* One of the most thorough studies of this hypothesis, Buglass *et al.* (1977), found little evidence for it, though as Hafner (1982), has pointed out, their findings, on detailed examination, are not as negative as they suggest in their report.

4. *The outcome of phobic treatment can be predicted from measures of pre-therapy marital interaction.* The evidence for this proposition is relatively strong (for example, Milton and Haffner, 1979; Bland and Hallam, 1981; Hafner and Ross, 1983). However, negative results have also been reported (Himadi *et al.*, 1986). There is also the point that an association between marital dissatisfaction and treatment outcome might not represent a causal effect; both might be the product of some third variable such as patient depression.

5. *The amount of anxiety that agoraphobics experience in a phobic situation depends heavily on whether they are accompanied by someone they can trust to help them.* This is a universal clinical observation. The interpersonal context is less relevant to simple phobias, and seems to operate in a different way; a spider phobic may find it helpful to have someone else around to remove the spider, but would not look to that person to help and support *them* in coping with their anxiety in a way that an agoraphobic would.

6. *Reductions in agoraphobic avoidance behaviour often lead to a deterioration in the marital relationship.* Evidence that this *can* occur is reasonably strong (for example, Hafner, 1982; Barlow *et al.*, 1981). However, it is equally clear that this is by no means a universal reaction. Attention is now focusing on identifying which cases are likely to show marital deterioration (Hafner, 1982; Hafner, 1984).

7. *Cognitive-behavioural treatment of agoraphobia can be improved by including the spouse as an agent of treatment.* Again, there is good evidence that this is at least sometimes the case (Hafner *et al.*, 1983; Barlow *et al.*, 1984). This evidence is considered by Bennun in the following chapter of this book in the context of a general review of the advantages of involving spouses and families in treatment.

It will be seen that research evidence for these propositions is somewhat variable, though there are sufficient positive findings to justify the currently prevailing clinical view that attention to the interpersonal context of agoraphobia is helpful. As yet, there are many unresolved issues about the exact nature of the relationship between marital problems and phobic symptoms. For example, some might argue that personal and interpersonal problems lead directly to panic attacks, and that resolution of these underlying problems is necessary if the frequency of panic attacks is to be reduced. Others might emphasize that reductions in avoidance behaviour increase the independence of the phobic in a way that disrupts a pathological marital adjustment. This, it might be argued, leads to avoidance behaviour being resumed in order to safeguard the marriage. Of course, there is no incompatibility between these two views. However, there is not yet sufficient research to compare critically the validity of alternative formulations about the way in which the marital context impinges on the treatment of agoraphobia.

One point on which there is general agreement is that attention to the marital context is more important in determining long-term than short-term treatment gains. Even enthusiasts for the interpersonal context would generally concede that substantial short-term improvements *can* result from an intensive programme of *in vivo* exposure. The concern is rather that these may reach a plateau that falls short of adequate clinical improvement, or may even be reversed, unless broader contextual issues are also attended to.

One helpful impact of recent work on the interpersonal context is the emphasis that has resulted on the diversity of agoraphobics (for example, Chambless and Goldstein, 1981). Most authorities recognize that there is at least a minority of agoraphobics, sometimes called 'simple' agoraphobics, who can be treated by *in vivo* methods alone whereas other 'complex' ones require attention to the interpersonal context. However, there is no uniformity as yet about where to draw the boundary between simple and more complex cases. Some (for example, Chambless and Goldstein, 1978) have suggested that the distinction depends on whether agoraphobia arises in the context of interpersonal or of medical problems; others (Hafner, 1982) would emphasize clinical and psychometric measures of marital adjustment and extra-punitive hostility.

There are various ways in which spouses can be involved in treatment. One of the simplest is to use them as therapeutic agents in an exposure-based treatment programme, such as the home-based programme described earlier. In principle, this might be risky, in that it gives spouses a position of

NDCP E

influence that they could use to undermine the treatment programme. However, it may also make them ego-involved in its success, and therefore much less likely to undermine progress than if they have no role in the treatment. A variety of other ways of involving spouses are also available. For example, in the two-week intensive programme of Chambless and Goldstein (1981), group *in vivo* exposure is supplemented by psychotherapy groups for agoraphobics, a separate group for spouses or significant others, and conjoint sessions.

SAFETY SIGNALS

It is a welcome reflection of the changing climate in psychological treatment that a growing awareness of the importance of interpersonal factors in agoraphobia has led to the incorporation of 'psychotherapeutic' elements into a behavioural treatment programme, without any sense of opposition between them. However, diversification of treatment methods has often been at the cost of a clear and unifying theoretical formulation. Rachman's recent theoretical work on agoraphobia (Rachman, 1983, 1984a, 1984b) provides a revised learning-theory based formulation which can readily incorporate interpersonal features.

Rachman sees the behaviour of agoraphobics as being determined by a balance of danger and safety signals. The effects of signals of danger (for example, panic, illness, death) are offset by signals of safety (being in a safe place, with a trusted companion, having reliable coping strategies). The concept of 'safety signals' has a clearly articulated place in certain theories of avoidance behaviour in animals (Gray, 1971), in which avoidance behaviour is seen as being maintained by the safety signals that reinforce it.

It is clear how, within this 'safety' perspective, the interpersonal features discussed above can readily be incorporated (see Bennun, 1986). For example, the development of agoraphobia after bereavement or loss is explicable in terms of the effects of the withdrawal of a crucial 'safety' signal. Recent emphasis on the importance of strategies for coping with anxiety as part of the treatment of agoraphobia can also be seen as the provision of additional safety-promotion strategies.

The 'safety signal' perspective also has implications for how exposure treatment is organized. Rachman formulates the principle like this: 'Place safety signals in the avoided situations and encourage the agoraphobic person to travel towards the safety signals in these new settings . . . Instead of training people to travel away from safety, as we do in current practice, we would begin training people to move towards safety signals'. This is a helpful proposal, though empirical evidence that it increases the effectiveness of exposure treatment to organize it on this basis remains to be reported. At present, the 'safety signal' approach is probably more important as an integrating theoretical perspective than as a source of new treatment strategies.

CONCLUSION

Changes in the treatment of agoraphobia during the last 15 years reflect many ideals of good clinical practice. Developments in treatment methods have arisen from a fruitful interplay of careful clinical observation and more formal empirical research. Theories and treatment methods have been broadened where necessary with little evidence of fruitless controversy between hard-line positions. Treatment has been rendered more effective than it used to be, and ways have also been found of reducing the amount of therapist time needed. These are the kind of developments that one hopes will increasingly characterize clinical psychology in its maturity.

REFERENCES

BARLOW, D., MAVISSAKALIAN, M. and KAY, L. (1981). Couples treatment of agoraphobia: changes in marital satisfaction. *Behaviour Research and Therapy*, *19*, 245–255.

BARLOW, D., O'BRIEN, G. and LAST, C. (1984). Couples treatment of agoraphobia. *Behaviour Therapy*, *15*, 41–58.

BECK, A.T. and EMERY, G. (1985). *Anxiety Disorders and Phobias: A Cognitive Perspective*. New York: Basic Books.

BENNUN, I. (1986). A composite formulation of agoraphobia. *American Journal of Psychotherapy*, *40*, 177–187.

BLAND, K. and HALLAM, R.S. (1981). Investigation of agoraphobic patients' responses to exposure in *in vivo* treatment in relation to marital satisfaction. *Behaviour Research and Therapy*, *19*, 335–338.

BORKOVEC, T.D. (1973). The role of expectancy and physiological feedback in fear research: a review with special reference to subject characteristics. *Behaviour Therapy*, *4*, 491–505.

BORKOVEC, T. (1982). Facilitation and inhibition of functional CS exposure in the treatment of phobias. In J.C. Boulougoris (ed.) *Learning Theory Approaches to Psychiatry*. Chichester: John Wiley.

BOWLBY, J. (1980). *Attachment and Loss. Vol. 2*. London: Hogarth Press.

BUGLASS, D., CLARK, J., HENDERSON, A., KREITMAN, N. and PRESLEY, A. (1977). A study of agoraphobic housewives. *Psychological Medicine*, *7*, 73–86.

CHAMBLESS, D.L. (1985). The relationship of severity of agoraphobia to associated psychopathology. *Behaviour Research and Therapy*, *23*, 305–310.

CHAMBLESS, D.L. and GOLDSTEIN, A.J. (1978). A reanalysis of agoraphobia. *Behaviour Therapy*, *9*, 47–59.

CHAMBLESS, D.L. and GOLDSTEIN, A.J. (1981). Clinical treatment of agoraphobia. In M. Mavissakalian and D.H. Barlow (eds). *Phobias: Psychological and Pharmacological Treatment*. New York: Guilford Press.

CHAMBLESS, D.L., CAPUTO, G.C., BRIGHT, P. and GALLAGHER, R.

(1984). The assessment of fear in agoraphobics: the Body Sensations Questionnaire and the Agoraphobic Cognitions Questionnaire. *Journal of Consulting and Clinical Psychology*, *52*, 1090–1097.

CHAMBLESS, D.L., CAPUTO, G.C., JASIN, S., GRACELY, E. and WILLIAMS, C. (1985). The Mobility Inventory for Agoraphobia. *Behaviour Research and Therapy*, *23*, 35–44.

CLARK, D.M. (1986). A cognitive approach to panic. *Behaviour Research and Therapy*, *24*, 261–270.

EMMELKAMP, P.M.G. and EMMELKAMP-BENNER, A. (1975). Effects of historically portrayed modelling and group treatment on self-observation: A comparison with agoraphobics. *Behaviour Research and Therapy*, *13*, 135–139.

EMMELKAMP, P.M.G. and MERSCH, P. (1982). Cognition and exposure *in vivo* in the treatment of agoraphobia: Short-term and delayed effects. *Cognitive Therapy and Research*, *6*, 77–90.

EMMELKAMP, P.M.G., KUIPERS, A.C. and EGGERAAT, J.B. (1978). Cognitive modification versus prolonged exposure *in vivo*: A comparison with agoraphobics as subjects. *Behaviour Research and Therapy*, *16*, 33–41.

FOA, E.G. and KOZAK, M.J. (1986). Emotional processing and fear: exposure to corrective information. *Psychological Bulletin*, *99*, 20–35.

FOA, E.B., SKEKETEE, G. and YOUNG, M.C. (1984). Agoraphobia: phenomenological aspects, associated characteristics, and theoretical considerations. *Clinical Psychology Review*, *4*, 431–457.

GELDER, M.G. (1986). Panic attacks: New approaches to an old problem. *British Journal of Psychiatry*, *149*, 346–352.

GOLDSTEIN, A. and CHAMBLESS, D. (1978). A reanalysis of agoraphobia. *Behaviour Therapy*, *9*, 47–59.

GRAY, J.A. (1971). *The Psychology of Fear and Stress*. London: Weidenfeld.

GUIDANO, V.F. (1987). *Complexity of the Self: A Developmental Approach to Psychopathology and Therapy*. New York: Guilford Press.

HAFNER, R.J. (1982). The marital context of the agoraphobic syndrome. In D.L. Chambless and A.J. Goldstein (eds). *Agoraphobia: Multiple Perspectives on Theory and Treatment*. New York: John Wiley.

HAFNER, R.J. (1984). Predicting the effects on husbands of behaviour therapy for wives' agoraphobia. *Behaviour Research and Therapy*, *22*, 217–226.

HAFNER, R.J. and MARKS, I. (1976). Exposure *in vivo* of agoraphobics: Contributions of diazepam, group exposure, and anxiety evocation. *Psychological Medicine*, *6*, 71–88.

HAFNER, R.J. and ROSS, M.W. (1983). Predicting the outcome of behaviour therapy for agoraphobia. *Behaviour Research and Therapy*, *21*, 375–382.

HAFNER, R.J., BADENOCH, A., FISHER, J. and SWIFT, H. (1983). Spouse-aided versus individual therapy in persisting psychiatric disorders: a systematic comparison. *Family Process*, *22*, 385–399.

HALLAM, R.S. (1978). Agoraphobia: A critical review of the concept. *British Journal of Psychiatry*, *133*, 314–319.

HALLAM, R.S. (1985). *Anxiety: Psychological Perspectives on Panic and Agoraphobia*. London: Academic Press.

HAND, I., LAMONTAQUE, Y. and MARKS, I.M. (1974). Group exposure (flooding) *in vivo* for agoraphobics. *British Journal of Psychiatry*, *124*, 588–602.

HIMADI, W.G., BOICE, R. and BARLOW, D.H. (1985). Assessment of agoraphobia: triple response measurement. *Behaviour Research and Therapy*, *23*, 311–323.

HIMADI, W.G., CERNY, J.A., BARLOW, D.H., COHEN, S. and O'BRIEN,

G.T. (1986). The relationship of marital adjustment to agoraphobia treatment outcome. *Behaviour Research and Therapy, 24,* 107–115.

JANNOUN, L., MUNBY, M., CATALAN, J. and GELDER, M. (1980). A home-based treatment programme for agoraphobia: replication and controlled evaluation. *Behaviour Therapy, 11,* 294–305.

JONES, R.B., SINNOTTI, A. and FORDHAM, A.S. (1980). Group *in vivo* exposure augmented by the counselling of significant others in the treatment of agoraphobia. *Behavioural Psychotherapy, 8,* 31–35.

LANG, P.J. (1968). Fear reduction and fear behaviour. In J. Schlein (ed.) *Research in Psychotherapy.* Washington: American Psychological Association.

LANG, P.J. (1987). Image as action: a reply to Watts and Blackstock. *Cognition and Emotion, 1,* 407–426.

LAST, C.G. (1984). Cognitive treatment of phobia. In M. Hersen, R.M. Eisler and P.M. Miller (eds). *Progress in Behaviour Modification. Vol. 16.* London: Academic Press.

MARCHIONE, K.E., MICHELSON, L., GREENWALD, M. and DANCU, C. (1987). Cognitive behavioural treatment of agoraphobia. *Behaviour Research and Therapy, 25,* 319–328.

MATHEWS, A.M., GELDER, M.G. and JOHNSTON, D.W. (1981). *Agoraphobia: Nature and Treatment.* London: Tavistock; New York: Guilford Press.

MICHELSON, L. (1986). Treatment consonance and response profiles in agoraphobia: the role of individual differences in cognitive, behavioural and physiological treatments. *Behaviour Research and Therapy, 24,* 263–275.

MICHELSON, L. and MAVISSAKALIAN, M. (1983). Temporal stability of self-report measures in agoraphobia research. *Behaviour Research and Therapy, 21,* 695–698.

MILTON, F. and HAFNER, R.J. (1979). The outcome of behaviour therapy for agoraphobia in relation to marital adjustment. *Archives of General Psychiatry, 36,* 807–811.

RACHMAN, S. (1983). The modification of agoraphobic avoidance behaviour: some fresh possibilities. *Behaviour Research and Therapy, 21,* 567–574.

RACHMAN, S. (1984a). Agoraphobia – a safety-signal perspective. *Behaviour Research and Therapy, 22,* 59–70.

RACHMAN, S. (1984b). The experimental analysis of agoraphobia. *Behaviour Research and Therapy, 22,* 631–640.

SCHERER, K.R. (1984). On the nature and function of emotion: a component approach. In K.R. Scherer and P. Ekman (eds). *Approaches to Emotion.* Hillsdale, N.J.: Lawrence Erlbaum.

SINNOTTI, A., JONES, R.B., SCOTT-FORDHAM, A. and WOODWARD, R. (1981). Augmentation of *in vivo* exposure treatment for agoraphobia by the formation of neighbourhood self-help groups. *Behaviour Research and Therapy, 19,* 339–347.

TAYLOR, C.B., SHEIKH, J., AGRAS, W.S., ROTH, W.T., MARGRAF, J., EHLERS, A., MADDOCK, R.J. and GOSSARD, D. (1986). Ambulatory heart rate changes in patients with panic attacks. *American Journal of Psychiatry, 143,* 478–482.

TEASDALE, J.D., WALSH, P.A., LANCASHIRE, M. and MATHEWS, A.M. (1977). Group exposure for agoraphobics: A replication study. *British Journal of Psychiatry, 130,* 186–193.

THORPE, G.L. and BURNS, L.E. (1983). *The Agoraphobic Syndrome: Behavioural Approaches to Evaluation and Treatment.* Chichester: John Wiley.

WATTS, F.N. (1979). Habituation model of systematic desensitization. *Psychological Bulletin, 86,* 627–637.

WATTS, F.N. (in press). Attentional strategies and agoraphobic anxiety. *Behavioural Psychotherapy*.

WATTS, F.N. and BLACKSTOCK, A.J. (1987). Lang's therapy of emotional imagery. *Cognition and Emotion*, *1*, 391–405.

WILLIAMS, S.L., DOSSEMAN, G. and KLEIFIELD, E. (1984). Comparative effectiveness of guided mastery and exposure treatment for intractable phobias. *Journal of Consulting and Clinical Psychology*, *52*, 505–518.

WILKINS, A.J., NIMMO-SMITH, I., TAIT, A., McMANUS, I.C., DELLA SALA, S., TILLEY, A., ARNOLD, K., BARRIE, M.A. and SCOTT, S.G.C. (1984). A neurological basis for visual discomfort. *Brain*, *107*, 989–1017.

INVOLVING SPOUSES AND FAMILIES IN THE TREATMENT OF ADULT PSYCHOLOGICAL PROBLEMS

Ian Bennun

The personal influence that most people exert upon those with whom they live is both substantial and reciprocal. The family unit essentially carries the initial burden of a developing psychological problem in one of its members. The reciprocal effects between the individual with the identified problem and their family/spouse can lead to either an exacerbation or a containing of their problem. Kuipers and Bebbington (1985) note that, while these issues have received extensive theoretical coverage, little has permeated clinical practice. This is particularly surprising given the detrimental effects that certain problems can have on families.

Jacob (1980) has described the adverse impact that excessive drinking has on the family. The alcoholic's spouse carries the additional burden of being responsible for the financial, domestic and childcare arrangements as well as maintaining his/her own and the children's safety. Similarly, the burden of caring for old people at home falls on the family, usually on an elderly spouse, daughter or daughter-in-law (Gilhooly, 1984). The effects of relatives' behaviour on schizophrenia is now well established through the research on expressed emotion (EE) (Leff and Vaughn, 1985), and taken together, these clinical examples suggest the need to explore the clinical utility of involving the spouse and family in treating different psychological problems.

This chapter addresses various ways that staff and/or the family can be used in the treatment of adult psychological problems. The distinction between systemic and spouse- or family-aided treatment will be elaborated as will the use of family-systemic principles within inpatient settings.

There are various ways in which a family can be involved in treatment, not all of which involve systemic family therapy. Patients admitted to hospital are often treated in isolation and the family system, of which they are a part, is largely ignored. A family member may be used as an informant on admission but will not necessarily become part of the treatment regime. An alternative approach, sometimes used, is to include the family in the inpatient treatment and partly formulate the problem in systemic terms thus not seeing the patient's problem in isolation. In some instances, whole families have been admitted as a method of treatment (Dydyk *et al.*, 1982). Similarly, a combination of the individual and systemic approach is evident in outpatient treatment.

FORMS OF CARE

The decision to include the family in treatment is well illustrated by examining the study conducted by Fenton *et al.* (1982) where a controlled comparison was carried out between home and psychiatric hospital treatment. The study evaluated the clinical effectiveness and cost effectiveness of community treatment as opposed to admitting patients into hospital. The home treatment comprised a prompt initial family clinical assessment including all those in the family who would be assisting with the treatment. Hospital staff remained available to the family, were in constant contact with the family via home visits, and observed the family together on repeated occasions. Families were randomly assigned to either home or hospital care and were followed up after one year. The results showed that community-based treatments relieved symptoms of psychiatric disorder at least as effectively as the hospital-based treatment. In terms of cost effectiveness, home-based community treatments were less expensive, were less disruptive and were as safe as the hospital-based treatment. This study suggests that family-facilitated home treatments are a viable treatment option.

A second form of care involving the family is exemplified in the family-oriented psychiatric inpatient unit (Harbin, 1979). This does not involve the admission of whole families but is the application of family therapeutic approaches and interpersonal systems concepts to the treatment of hospitalized individuals. In creating this type of inpatient unit, families are routinely included as an integral part of treatment. This does however meet with certain difficulties given that admission not only removes the family's immediate source of anxiety, but also decreases their potential for change. Hence, their inclusion in the treatment enables the changes that occur on the ward to generalize to the external environment. This can occur either through a shift in family functioning or the family carrying out instructions to maintain change.

These two modes of family involvement represent two contrasting methods of formulation and intervention. In commenting on relatives as a treatment resource, Kuipers and Bebbington (1985) state 'the family should be seen as a positive and irreplaceable resource: no one else will provide such continued interest in the care for patients in the community' (page 469).

The use of the spouse and family can enhance compliance with treatment. It has been suggested that poor treatment outcomes resulting from non-compliance could account for a proportion of treatment failures (Becker and Green, 1975). There are a number of reasons why patients fail to comply with treatment directives. Shelton and Levy (1981) suggest three sources of non-compliance: patients may lack the necessary skills and knowledge to complete the task, there may be interfering cognitions that impede completing assignments and, thirdly, the patient's particular environment may elicit non-compliance. Among the many recommendations suggested to improve compliance is the use of the family and thus engaging others to ensure that the patient has an improved chance of a favourable clinical outcome.

In many respects it is good clinical practice to focus on patient–family interactions to improve compliance. Some aged or disabled people depend on their families to assume responsibility for their adherence to treatment programmes, so the health beliefs and attitudes of other family members are important. Sometimes, the family is used as an intermediary in order to ensure that patients comply with treatment regimes. However, the family can also exert a normative influence on the patient. Thus, they might reinforce treatment compliance or model attitudes and behaviours that will improve compliance and goal attainment. Becker and Green (1975) suggest that through communication, role modelling, pressure and other avenues of influence the family's beliefs and behaviours will influence health actions. If other members of the family become involved in supporting the professionally-prescribed standards, then compliance is more likely. Conversely, the family may interfere with compliance especially when there is a lack of knowledge or support with respect to particular regimes or where existing family patterns do not function effectively with treatment requirements.

Given the family's potential influence in supporting treatment regimes and the deleterious effects that persistent problems have on family functioning, there are good theoretical reasons to include the family as (co-) agents of change. By including them in the treatment, relatives can improve their attitudes towards the patient, can increase their knowledge about the presenting disorder and can increase their usefulness in patients.

TREATING THE SYMPTOM OR THE SYSTEM

The preceding discussion introduces the theoretical and empirical debate concerning the essential treatment focus. Both systemic and individual problem-oriented therapists and theorists have dealt with this topic extensively (see Bennun 1985, 1986b) so a brief description will suffice. The individual or problem-oriented approach differs quite fundamentally from systemic notions of presenting problems and change. Within a problem-oriented perspective, presenting difficulties are seen as residing within individuals and are assumed to represent personal and internal sources of discomfort. Treatment is directed towards removing the symptom with less emphasis on how others in the patient's immediate environment contribute to the distress. On the other hand, a systemic or interactional approach posits that symptoms are signs or manifestations of relationship problems occurring within the individual's psychosocial environment. Treatment within this perspective is directed at the social context within which that individual lives and functions.

The problem-solving approach can take a variety of different forms. It can be examined in terms of antecedents and consequences which may be elaborated by a comprehensive functional analysis. The environmental contingencies operating which maintain the symptom become the focus of treatment with symptomatic change being the desired goal. Alternatively, following a problem-solving format, family members may be included in the treatment as co-agents of change. Spouses, children or significant others in the patient's environment will collaborate with both the therapist and patient and so carry out specific tasks that will alter inappropriate distressing behaviour.

In contrast, the systemic approach pays particular attention to the family and the wider psychosocial environment in explanations of presenting problems. Within systems theory, the family represents a functioning, operational system or unit comprising a set of collected inter-related parts of subsystems with each participant's functioning being determined in part by the relationships between members/generations/subsystems. The couple/family therefore organize themselves in self-regulating, homeostatic ways that determine how they deal with their environmental contingencies. The goal of therapy is to help the family change the rules maintaining the homeostasis and, in so doing, alter the intrafamilial conditions that maintain problematic behaviours/interactions.

There is little empirical evidence to guide the clinician in the decision whether to work systemically or not. In most instances, choices are made on unvalidated assumptions about the kinds of people or problems that would respond most favourably to one approach or the other. The research that has examined this question (Bennun, 1985, 1986b; Emmelkamp et al., 1984; Szapocznik et al., 1983) suggest that both approaches are equally effective; however these reports do not address the question how to decide which treatment is most appropriate. Given that the approaches are often viewed as two contrasting orientations cf., behaviour therapy versus psychoanalytic therapy) it would, to some, appear to be an irrelevant question. It is possible that results of such an enquiry would reveal the same information (and difficulties) as the meta-analyses contrasting individual therapy studies.

While the distinction between these two approaches is clear it is of course possible to use the family system in the treatment of an individual's psychological problem. The two approaches are not mutually exclusive and both theoretical and empirical reports have shown a combination of approaches to be clinically effective. Hafner and his colleagues (1981, 1983) have shown that using a spouse in treatment has positive effects in relieving distress with many presenting problems.

In the remainder of this chapter, more detail is given to specific methods of using spouses or the family in treatment. The context of the systemic approach is placed in the light of the theoretical argument, that in order to alter the behaviour of an individual, the system needs to be a focus. This is followed by a survey of some conjoint approaches to dealing with psychological problems and, finally, an account of spouse-aided therapy.

A SYSTEMIC PERSPECTIVE

It has already been stated that the systemic perspective formulates presenting problems in terms of networks or interactions between components of the individual's interpersonal, social system. For example, a father's depression may be the manifestation of his dilemma about a changing role in relation to a change in the family, for example, the last child leaving home; or a woman's obsessive-compulsive problem may signal some dissatisfaction within her marriage. Few studies have compared systemic with alternative treatments but some have shown the efficacy of systemic (family) interventions *per se*.

Gurman *et al.* (1986) have reviewed the family therapy research with adult presenting problems. They note that the formative investigations were in the treatment of schizophrenia, but they also note that there is little research evaluating systemic treatment. Affective and anxiety disorders which are commonplace within the growing community mental health movement have been represented in broader systemic therapy evaluation studies (Bennun, 1986b), but in themselves, have not been rigorously assessed.

Those investigating and evaluating systemic therapy need to resolve the issue of 'who is the patient?' If it is only those in the consulting room, then only those present will be represented as indices of change. However, adopting Pinsof's (1983) view, the unit of evaluation should be the *patient's system*. This includes all those who are significantly involved in the maintenance and/or resolution of the presenting problems. The concept of 'patient system' does not dictate who is involved in the treatment, rather who must be considered in planning and evaluating any particular intervention. In adopting the systemic perspective, the investigations need to include the feedback process that links the therapist and the patient system. This system critically affects the process and outcome of all forms of treatment and should, therefore, become part of the process research equation. Thorough investigations cannot ignore this wider system, and until the methodology allows for it, evaluations of systemic therapy will remain sparse.

CLINICAL APPLICATIONS OF CONJOINT TREATMENT

The principle of using and training family members in psychological and psychiatric treatments is not new and has been extensively used with child-focused problems (Graziano, 1977; Herbert, 1985). Behaviour modification techniques in particular frequently rely on persons in the patient's social and interpersonal environment as effective agents of change since learning theory emphasizes the importance of the relationship between behaviours and controlling events. The clinical implications of using family members are many: they are able to provide a degree of behavioural constancy towards the patient and are likely to record behavioural targets accurately. Furthermore, they are likely to be positive in maintaining changes and are able to facilitate the generalization of these behavioural changes. Compliance with treatment, as already noted, is another reason to include others in the treatment. Cobb *et al.* (1984) described the spouse as a potential ally who may make the treatment more powerful and enhance the gains achieved over time. In addition to the programmes detailed below, reports of spouse involvement in the treatments of hypertension (Hoelscher *et al.*, 1986), chronic pain (Moore and Chaney, 1985), and smoking (Lichstein and Stalgaitis, 1980) have been described.

Agoraphobia

The partners of agoraphobics may play an important role in the maintenance and treatment of agoraphobia. The results of studies investigating dyadic factors (Barlow *et al.*, 1981; Barlow and O'Brien, 1984; Hafner, 1977, 1984; Hafner and Ross, 1983) and family factors (Hudson, 1974) suggest that individuals in the patient's immediate interpersonal environment can be useful therapeutic agents in the treatment of agoraphobia. Mathews (1976) outlined the need for support and encouragement for those patients undertaking the home treatment programme. The reasoning behind this was that spouses know more about their partner's special problems. Practice is best undertaken from the home and most often agoraphobics feel safer with other people, who in addition can monitor their progress and become involved in joint practice. Evaluations of home-based treatments (Jannoun *et al.*, 1980; Mathews *et al.*, 1977) have shown this approach to be effective in relieving symptoms, although in the study by Jannoun, the comparison problem-solving approach was as effective as the exposure treatment.

In a study where the spouse was used as a co-therapist, Cobb *et al.* (1984) conducted a home-based treatment which included graded exposure, the use of the Mathews (1976) treatment manual and self help. The agoraphobic's partner was instructed to help the patient carry out any homework tasks, and further encourage their efforts at self help rather than encourage dependence. The results on the main measures of outcome indicated that the spouse treatment was as effective as the already established exposure treatment. Those patients in the spouse-assisted treatment rated their partner's involvement as extremely valuable, being as important as their own efforts. This suggested that the patients in this treatment had a different perception of help received from those in individual treatment. Some of the dyadic measures, specifically sexual satisfaction, reflected the value of conjoint treatment. While there were no overall group differences, the authors concluded that there was nothing against including the spouse in treatment; however, equally, there seems little to be gained from insisting that spouses participate in treatment.

If the conjoint treatment is placed in a systemic context, then both symptomatic and marital factors interact in maintaining behavioural avoidance. The studies by Cobb *et al.* (1984) and Barlow *et al.* (1981) where spouses were used as co-therapists, suggest that the marital system may have to be reorganized both for treatment purposes and for the maintenance of therapeutic change. If poor marital adjustment is predictive of both poor spouse cooperation and poor treatment responsiveness then a dual focus of the treatment as described by Hafner (1981) and Hafner *et al.* (1983) seems to be indicated.

Obesity

Stunkard and Mahoney (1976) have suggested that where patients have completed an obesity programme to reduce weight, and then returned to an interpersonal environment which is so structured and rigid that little support is forthcoming, it is likely that the weight lost will be regained. Many reports have suggested that the spouse and family can be used effectively both to reduce weight and to maintain treatment gains (Brownell *et al.*, 1978; Dubbert and Wilson, 1984; Israel and Saccone, 1979; Pearce *et al.*, 1981; Weisz and Bucher, 1980). However, an overall review of studies shows that including the partner of an obese patient in treatment does not significantly enhance efficacy in the long term (Brownell and Stunkard, 1981).

As in the treatment of many other problems, training the spouse in behaviour modification procedures has also been undertaken with obesity (Brownell *et al.*, 1978). In this study, the treatment condition that included the cooperative spouse involved instruction in stimulus control, modelling, monitoring, and differential reinforcement of other behaviours that were incompatible with eating and subsequent weight gain. In addition, spouses were requested to be supportive and encouraging in any attempts that their obese partners made in weight control. A similar study by Weisz and Bucher (1980) also used behavioural principles in individual versus conjoint treatment. The attending spouse was trained to reinforce their partner's improvements, to cue appropriate eating behaviour and to consult with the therapist when difficulties arose. Although the conjoint treatment was not significantly more effective, the involvement of husbands showed positive effects in the client's self reports of marital satisfaction and depression.

Drinking Problems

In a recent review, Orford (in press) pointed out that treatment of problem drinking is more effective if family members are involved. The major features of the treatment involved family members encouraging and reinforcing abstinence and learning how to deal with drinking episodes. With drinking problems, it is not just the patient alone experiencing the distress, so there are direct benefits for all family members should treatment be successful.

One way that families and spouses have been included in treatment is through support for the non-drinking family members (Cadogan, 1973; Sisson and Azrin, 1986) or specific training in behavioural methods to reduce alcohol consumption (Azrin *et al.*, 1982; Cheek *et al.*, 1971). While most of these programmes have been directed towards the female spouse, Williams and Klerman (1984) have described the need for husbands to be involved in the treatment of their alcoholic wives.

By way of illustration, Sisson and Azrin's (1986) controlled study is one example of family member involvement. Two treatment groups were compared, one offering a traditional programme (education, supportive counselling, self help groups) and the other offering a reinforcement treatment programme. This latter treatment condition made extensive use of the family to initiate and promote treatment of the drinker. The programme included the following procedures:

(*1*) awareness of the problem, focusing on elucidating the problems caused by the drinker;
(*2*) motivation training for the non-drinker to do something about the distress produced by the drinker;
(*3*) training in the use of positive reinforcement for non-drinking;
(*4*) instruction in scheduling competing activities in drinking;
(*5*) activities to decrease dependence on the drinker;
(*6*) awareness of drinking and training in negative consequences for excessive drinking;
(*7*) responsibility for self correction so that the drinker is held responsible for his/her activities;
(*8*) training in dealing with dangerous situations and
(*9*) joint counselling.

The results showed that the family involvement condition was significantly superior to the alternative treatment suggesting that the training of spouses and other family members in reinforcement procedures is a feasible method of persuading an alcoholic to obtain treatment and decrease drinking.

Obsessive compulsive disorders

There are several reasons why spouse involvement may be particularly advantageous in the treatment of obsessive compulsive disorders. In addition to those already mentioned, spouses are often actively involved in the rituals and inadvertently reinforce the disorder and impede treatment progress. Both Stern and Marks (1973) and Emmelkamp and DeLange (1983) note that marital disharmony can accompany and exacerbate this behavioural disturbance.

Vogel *et al.* (1982) used a variant of thought stopping and habituation as treatment directives. They introduced overt satiation as a technique where treatment could occur outside of the session with the aid of a spouse or significant other. This person was identified as the surrogate therapist (ST), who then reinforced the non-occurrence of the obsessive ideation and provided some social reinforcement about what the patient was thinking.

Emmelkamp and DeLange (1983) investigated whether spouse involvement enhanced self-controlled exposure treatment. Patients were randomly assigned to self-controlled or partner-assisted exposure. In the partner-assisted condition, the couple attended conjointly. They both received the treatment rationale and the partner was requested to participate in the homework exposure assignments. The results of the study showed the partner-assisted treatment to be more effective on all measures of outcome.

Depression

Using family members in the treatment of depression has not been widely used although there are reports describing how significant others can be included in the treatment. Hooley (1986) examined the dyadic interactions between depressed patients and their spouses in an attempt to identify factors that may mitigate against symptomatic improvement. Using EE as one independent variable, spouses rated as high on EE were both more negative and less positive towards their partners. Compared to low EE spouses, they made more critical remarks, were more frequently in disagreement with their spouse and were less likely to accept what a depressed spouse said to them. The results of the study offer indications regarding how spouses of depressed patients can benefit from conjoint treatment.

In an earlier report, Rush *et al.* (1980) suggested that cognitive therapy for depression may be enhanced if the spouse actively supported treatment. They conceptualized depression in part as a failure to resolve developmental changes or a failure to correct a maladaptive relationship. Thus, depression was placed in an interpersonal context and logically included that context in treatment. The non-depressed spouse was trained both in schedule keeping and in eliciting and correcting maladaptive cognitions.

The elderly

The effective management of older adults depends greatly on the provision of assistance to them by their relatives (Clark and Rakowski, 1983; Glosser and Wexler, 1985). Education and support groups enable carers to carry out their responsibilities more effectively and gain support in this often arduous task. Ratna and Davis (1984) note that failure to work with the caring network can increase the incidence of crises. Family support and training regarding the provision of structure and skills in management techniques can help alleviate the adverse effects of the varied 'intolerable problems' that carers experience (Gilhooly, 1984). Some of these include incontinence, night wandering, sleep disturbances, neglect of cleanliness, bizarre and dangerous behaviours, mood disturbance, demands for attention and interpersonal conflicts.

Specific programmes for families of the elderly have been developed (Pinkston and Linsk, 1984; Safford, 1980). In introducing her programme, Safford (1980) states that relatives represent the most responsible and caring element to act on behalf of the elderly person. The features of the programme include:

(*1*) educating relatives about the causes of elderly disabilities;
(*2*) descriptions of the behavioural consequences of brain damage in the elderly;
(*3*) teaching relatives how to assume an active role in relationships with professionals and
(*4*) steps to provide practical protective care. Pinkston and Linsk (1984) describe a family approach to care of the elderly in which relatives were trained in behavioural procedures to promote better quality care.

Two interesting reports describe some innovative work with this group of patients. La Wall (1981) described a conjoint approach using the 'well' spouse as co-therapist specifically to gather information and to help with reality testing. They were also used to enhance cognitive performance in reality orientation and to monitor treatment and responsiveness. Another aspect of the conjoint treatment was to focus on the spouse who is not the identified patient. This gave the therapist the opportunity to assess the well spouse given the increased likelihood of morbidity with age. In a second report, a case is described where the physician used a grand-daughter to monitor and administer a contingent reinforcement programme to increase adherence to a complex medical regime for an elderly cardiac patient (Dapcich-Miura and Hovell, 1979). This involved recording behavioural objectives, monitoring diet and ensuring compliance with medication. This case report illustrates, like so many others, that when using the family as a treatment agent, teaching behavioural techniques to the individual to be recruited as the co-therapist seems to be particularly important.

The rationale for involving the spouse or family in a problem-focused way seems to vary from one problem to another. In the case of drinking problems, the evidence tends to suggest that including significant others improves the efficacy of treatment. Often, drinking problems reflect family problems and inclusion of those obviously affected (and on occasions those at risk) seems to be of primary importance. While it has been suggested that agoraphobia may also represent a marital problem, the evidence is less conclusive. If exposure is the treatment of choice, then transferring the treatment to the home environment may at least prove to be more cost effective. If the EE evidence concerning depression indicates the reactivity of this problem to the interpersonal environment, then there are good theoretical arguments for including the patient's close interpersonal network in treatment, and in a different way, a good reason to include the family where care is also a burden. In caring for an elderly relative, the dictum 'a problem shared is a problem halved' may help with this task.

SPOUSE-AIDED THERAPY

Hafner and his colleagues (Hafner, 1981; Hafner *et al.*, 1983) developed a spouse-aided therapy and construed it as a novel treatment that was neither individual nor marital, but combined elements within both approaches. Essentially the patient's spouse (or co-habitee) plays a direct and active role in the treatment process as a co-therapeutic agent. These authors state that treatment can also be viewed as 'marriage resource therapy' (Hafner, 1981).

Other writers have noted that spouses are often involved in the genesis and maintenance of persisting psychological disorders (for example, Bennun, 1986a; Hand and Lamontagne, 1976). However these problems are often treated with individual therapy because they are not perceived in marital-systemic terms whether by clinicians, spouses or the patients themselves. Hafner has drawn together both systemic and individual therapy principles particularly for married patients who are resistant to engaging in marital therapy but where one partner presents with a persisting problem. It is most applicable where symptoms are seen as an alternative to overt marital conflict and where the couple prefer that the symptom rather than the system be the appropriate treatment focus.

There are five elements to the approach: first, a direct and personal invitation to the spouse or significant other is made to involve him/her in treatment. It is stated at the outset that the therapy is not marital but provides the spouse with the opportunity to be involved in the treatment as an agent of change or co-therapist. The second element, the spouse interview, enables the therapist to obtain the spouse's account of the patient's disorder and develop a trusting therapeutic alliance. This may also provide the therapist with the opportunity to approach other personal problems initially in relation to the presenting symptoms, and to assess whether there are obstacles to the treatment approach. These may include low motivation, a lack of commitment to the marriage, the spouse's ignorance or disinterest about the nature of the presenting problem.

Having completed these initial phases of the treatment process, the third aspect is the establishment of treatment goals and the therapy framework. This is usually conducted conjointly (with both partners together) where the treatment goals pertaining to the spouse, the patient or the marriage are elucidated. Most important here, is to achieve a consensus about the major treatment goals. If these cannot be established, then spouse-aided therapy may be undermined. This element in the treatment is crucial as it enables the therapist to explore the degree of flexibility within the marital system and alter the treatment focus should this need arise. In order to overcome resistance and a negative therapeutic relationship with the spouse, the therapist should remind the spouse of his/her active involvement in both goal setting and the treatment in general.

The fourth phase concerns achieving the treatment goals and overcoming the possible problems and obstacles that arise within these regimes. It is recommended that in addition to implementing the particular treatment of choice, the therapist examines the couple's problem-solving capacity and so anticipates later difficulties. Finally, to expand the therapy, it is preferable to help the couple perceive the presenting problem in terms of marital or family interaction and so increase the treatment foci. In this way, the systemic shift is initiated to continue the work with the couple in a constructive manner in an improved marital relationship.

This approach is clearly similar to problem solving but does include some systemic principles. The gradual shift from spouse as co-therapist to spouse as co-patient demonstrates the subtlety of what can be a very successful treatment approach. In a controlled trial of spouse-aided versus individual therapy, spouse-aided therapy was found to be superior to individual therapy with the latter decreasing marital satisfaction and increasing depression at follow-up (Hafner *et al.*, 1983).

In reviewing their results, Hafner discussed the mechanisms operative within successful spouse-aided treatments. Two central themes emerged: communication and the spouse's personal change. Early in treatment, the spouse's perception of their partner's symptoms became more accurate largely through therapist clarification and correcting distortions. Educating the spouse about the nature and extent of the patient's symptoms seemed to be a powerful therapeutic contribution. The accuracy with which the partners perceived each other was further improved through shared problem-solving. Where difficulties arose, the therapist addressed these with both partners and guided them away from self-defeating activities. The second theme, that of personal change, became increasingly apparent when the patient raised the alternative of leaving the marriage. In a way this addressed the complacency within the non-symptomatic spouse and forced him/her to reappraise their position within the marriage.

In concluding this discussion it is worth noting the comments of Cobb *et al.* (1980) concerning their distinction between conjoint and marital therapy. Conjoint therapy refers to those involved in the treatment whereas marital therapy construes the relationship as a major presenting problem.

CONCLUSIONS

The use of the spouse and family in the treatment of adult psychological problems is promising even if the empirical literature does not necessarily support their inclusion. Systemically, the alterations for the family following both the emergence and treatment of problems are profound. Similarly the family can be facilitative in enhancing treatment even if the mechanisms through which this is attained remain unclear. However, Emmelkamp and DeLange (1983) question the routine use of the partner in behavioural treatments as their inclusion may unwittingly reinforce the dependence of the symptomatic spouse on the 'well' partner. Madanes (1980) has described the power dynamics that may be evident when one partner presents with a psychological psychiatric problem. Hierarchical incongruities can occur with the symptomatic partner being weak because of having difficulties but also being powerful because their spouse cannot change the symptom. Yet, the non-symptomatic partner is strong in being symptom free, and weak in being unable to free their partner of the difficulty. Therapists who ignore this delicate balance may run the risk of threatening the relationship if this dynamic is not considered during treatment. Where elderly disabled patients are involved, the inclusion of the family can almost always be helpful. However, whether the aid of another as a co-therapist is useful, needs to be carefully considered for each individual case.

REFERENCES

AZRIN, N., SISSON, R., MEYERS, R. and GODLEY, M. (1982). Alcoholism treatment by disulfiram and community reinforcement therapy. *Journal of Behavior Therapy and Experimental Psychiatry*, *13*, 105–112.

BARLOW, D. and O'BRIEN, G. (1984). Couples treatment of agoraphobia. *Behavior Therapy*, *15*, 41–58.

BARLOW, D., MAVISSAKALIAN, M. and HAY, L. (1981). Couples treatment of agoraphobia: changes in marital satisfaction. *Behavior Research and Therapy*, *19*, 245–255.

BECKER, M. and GREEN, L. (1975). A family approach to compliance with medical treatment. *International Journal of Health Education*, *18*, 173–182.

BENNUN, I. (1985). Two approaches to family therapy with alcoholics: problem solving and systemic therapy. *Journal of Substance Abuse Treatment*, *2*, 19–26.

BENNUN, I. (1986a). A composite formulation of agoraphobia. *American Journal of Psychotherapy*, *40*, 177–188.

BENNUN, I. (1986b). Evaluating family therapy: a comparison of the Milan and problem solving approaches. *Journal of Family Therapy*, *8*, 225–242.

BROWNELL, K. and STUNKARD, A. (1981). Couples training, pharmacotherapy, and behaviour therapy in the treatment of obesity. *Archives of General Psychiatry*, *38*, 1224–1229.

BROWNELL, K., HECKERMAN, C., WESTLAKE, R., HAYS, S. and MONTI, P. (1978). The effect of couples training and partner cooperativeness in the behavioural treatment of obesity. *Behavior Research and Therapy*, *16*, 323–333.

CADOGAN, D. (1973). Marital group therapy in the treatment of alcoholism. *Quarterly Journal of Studies on Alcohol*, *34*, 1187–1194.

CHEEK, F., FRANKS, C., LAUCIUS, J. and BURTLE, V. (1971). Behaviour modification training for wives of alcoholics. *Quarterly Journal of Studies on Alcohol*, *32*, 456–461.

CLARK, N. and RAKOWSKI, W. (1983). Family care givers of older adults: improving helping skills. *The Gerontologist*, *23*, 637–642.

COBB, J., McDONALD, R., MARKS, I. and STERN, R. (1980). Marital versus exposure therapy: psychological treatments of co-existing marital and phobic obsessive problems. *European Journal of Behavior Analysis and Modification*, *4*, 3–17.

COBB, J., MATHEWS, A., CHILDS-CLARKE, A. and BLOWERS, C. (1984). The spouse as co-therapist in the treatment of agoraphobia. *British Journal of Psychiatry*, *144*, 282–287.

DAPCICH-MIURA, E. and HOVELL, M. (1979). Contingency management of adherence to a complex medical regimen in an elderly heart patient. *Behavior Therapy*, *10*, 193–201.

DUBBERT, P. and WILSON, G. (1984). Goal setting and spouse involvement in the treatment of obesity. *Behavior Research and Therapy*, *22*, 227–242.

DYDYK, B., FRENCH, S., GERTMAN, C. and MORRISON, N. (1982). Admission of whole families. *Canadian Journal of Psychiatry*, *27*, 640–643.

EMMELKAMP, P. and DELANGE, I. (1983). Spouse involvement in the treatment of obsessive compulsive patients. *Behavior Research and Therapy*, *21*, 341–346.

EMMELKAMP, P., VAN DER HELM, M., MacGILLAVRY, D. and VAN ZANTEN, B. (1984). Marital therapy with clinically distressed couples: a comparative evaluation of system-theoretic, contingency contracting and communication skills approaches. In K. Hahlweg and N. Jacobson (eds) *Marital Interaction: Analysis and Modification*. New York: Guilford.

FENTON, F., TESSIER, L., STRUENING, E., SMITH, F. and BENOIT, C. (1982) *Home and Hospital Psychiatric Treatment*. London: Croom Helm.

GILHOOLY, M. (1984). The social dimensions of senile dementia. In I. Hanley and J. Hodge (eds). *Psychological Approaches to the Care of the Elderly*. London: Croom Helm.

GLOSSER, G. and WEXLER, D. (1985). Participants' evaluation of educational/support groups for families of patients with Alzheimer's Disease and other dementias. *The Gerontologist*, *25*, 232–236.

GRAZIANO, A. (1977). Parents as behavior therapists: In M. Hersen, R. Eisler and P. Miller (eds). *Progress in Behavior Modification*, *vol. 4*. London: Academic Press.

GURMAN, A., KNISKERN, D. and PINSOF, W. (1986). Research on the process and outcome of marital and family therapy. In S. Garfield and A. Bergin (eds) *Handbook of Psychotherapy and Behaviour Change*. New York: Wiley.

HAFNER, R. (1977). The husbands of agoraphobic women and their influence on treatment outcome. *British Journal of Psychiatry*, *131*, 289–294.
HAFNER, R. (1981). Spouse aided therapy in psychiatry: an introduction. *Australian and New Zealand Journal of Psychiatry*, *15*, 329–337.
HAFNER, R. (1984). Predicting the effects on husbands of behaviour therapy for wives' agoraphobia. *Behavior Research and Therapy*, *22*, 217–226.
HAFNER, R. and ROSS, M. (1983). Predicting the outcome of behaviour therapy for agoraphobia. *Behavior Research and Therapy*, *21*, 375–382.
HAFNER, R., BADENOCH, A., FISHER, J. and SWIFT, H. (1983). Spouse aided versus individual therapy in persisting psychiatric disorders: a systematic comparison. *Family Process*, *22*, 385–399.
HAND, I. and LAMONTAGNE, Y. (1976). The exacerbation of interpersonal problems after rapid phobia removal. *Psychotherapy*, *13*, 405–411.
HARBIN, H. (1979). A family-oriented psychiatric inpatient unit. *Family Process*, *18*, 281–291.
HERBERT, M. (1985). Triadic work with children. In F. Watts (ed.) *New Developments in Clinical Psychology, vol. 1*. Leicester: The British Psychological Society/ John Wiley & Sons Ltd.
HOELSCHER, T., LICHSTEIN, K. and ROSENTHAL, T. (1986). Home relaxation practice in hypertension treatment: objective assessment and compliance induction. *Journal of Consulting and Clinical Psychology*, *54*, 217–221.
HOOLEY, J. (1986). Expressed emotion and depression: interactions between patients and high versus low expressed emotion spouses. *Journal of Abnormal Psychology*, *95*, 237–246.
HUDSON, B. (1974). The families of agoraphobics treated by behaviour therapy. *British Journal of Social Work*, *4*, 51–59.
ISRAEL, A. and SACCONE, A. (1979). A follow-up of effects of choice of mediator and target of reinforcement on weight loss. *Behavior Therapy*, *10*, 260–265.
JACOB, T. (1980). An introduction to the alcoholic's family. In: M. Galanter (ed.) *Currents in Alcoholism, vol. 7*. New York: Grune & Stratton.
JANNOUN, L., MUNBY, M., CATALAN, J. and GELDER, M. (1980). A home-based treatment programme for agoraphobia: replication and controlled evaluation. *Behavior Therapy*, *11*, 294–305.
KUIPERS, L. and BEBBINGTON, P. (1985). Relatives as a resource in the management of functional illness. *British Journal of Psychiatry*, *147*, 465–470.
LA WALL, J. (1981). Conjoint therapy of psychiatric problems in the elderly. *Journal of the American Geriatrics Society*, *29*, 89–91.
LEFF, J. and VAUGHN, C. (1985). *Expressed Emotion in Families: Its Significance for Mental Illness*. New York: Guilford Press.
LICHSTEIN, K. and STALGAITIS, S. (1980). Treatment of cigarette smoking in couples by reciprocal aversion. *Behavior Therapy*, *11*, 104–108.
MADANES, C. (1980). Marital therapy when a symptom is presented by one spouse. *International Journal of Family Therapy*, *2*, 120–136.
MATHEWS, A. (1976). *A Home Treatment Programme for Agoraphobia. Parts 1 & 2*. Oxford: University Department of Psychiatry.
MATHEWS, A., TEASDALE, J., MUNBY, M., JOHNSTON, D. and SHAW, P. (1977). A home based treatment programme for agoraphobia. *Behavior Therapy*, *8*, 915–924.
MOORE, J. and CHANEY, E. (1985). Out-patient group treatment of chronic pain: effects of spouse involvement. *Journal of Consulting and Clinical Psychology*, *53*, 326–334.
ORFORD, J. (in press). Alcohol Problems in the Family. To appear in *Research*

Advances in Alcohol and Drug Problems. New York: Plenum Publishing Corporation. (Published for Addiction Research Foundation of Toronto, Canada).

PEARCE, J., LE BOW, M. and ORCHARD, J. (1981). Role of spouse involvement in the behavioural treatment of overweight women. *Journal of Consulting and Clinical Psychology, 49*, 236–244.

PINKSTON, E. and LINSK, N. (1984). *Care of the Elderly: A Family Approach*. New York: Pergamon.

PINSOF, W. (1983). Integrative problem-centred therapy: toward the synthesis of family and individual psychotherapies. *Journal of Marital and Family Therapy, 9*, 19–36.

RATNA, L. and DAVIS, J. (1984). Family therapy with the elderly mentally ill. *British Journal of Psychiatry, 145*, 311–315.

RUSH, A., SHAW, B. and KHATAMI, M. (1980). Cognitive therapy of depression: utilising the couples' system. *Cognitive Therapy and Research, 4*, 103–113.

SAFFORD, F. (1980). A programme for families of mentally impaired elderly. *The Gerontologist, 20*, 656–660.

SHELTON, J. and LEVY, R. (1981). *Behavioral Assignments and Treatment Compliance*. Champaign, Illinois: Research Press.

SISSON, R. and AZRIN, N. (1986). Family member involvement to initiate and promote treatment of problem drinkers. *Journal of Behavior Therapy and Experimental Psychiatry, 17*, 15–21.

STERN, R. and MARKS, I. (1973). Contract therapy in obsessive compulsive neurosis with marital discord. *British Journal of Psychiatry, 123*, 681–684.

STUNKARD, A. and MAHONEY, M. (1976). Behavioral treatment of eating disorders. In H. Leitenberg (ed.) *Handbook of Behavior Modification and Behavior Therapy*. Englewood Cliffs, N.J.: Prentice-Hall.

SZAPOCZNIK, J., KURTINES, W., FOOTE, F., PEREZ-VIDAL, A. and HERVIS, O. (1983). Conjoint versus one-person family therapy: some evidence for the effectiveness of conducting family therapy through one person. *Journal of Consulting and Clinical Psychology, 51*, 889–899.

VOGEL, W., PETERSON, L. and BROVERMAN, I. (1982). A modification of Rachmans habituation technique for treatment of the obsessive compulsive disorder. *Behavior Research and Therapy, 20*, 101–104.

WEISZ, G. and BUCHER, E. (1980). Involving husbands in the treatment of obesity – effects of weight loss, depression and marital satisfaction. *Behavior Therapy, 11*, 643–650.

WILLIAMS, C. and KLERMAN, L. (1984). Female alcohol abuse: its effects on the family, In S. Wilsnac and L. Beckman (eds) *Alcohol Problems in Women*. New York: Guilford Press.

MOBILIZING SOCIAL SUPPORT

Glenys Parry

In much of their work, clinical psychologists aim to promote independence, autonomy and self-reliance in their patients or clients. This emphasis is consistent with a wider cultural value placed upon these qualities in modern life. Whilst pursuing these laudable aims, it is easy to forget that every one of us lives in a social network of mutual interdependence. Pilisuk and Parks (1986) have argued that until relatively recently, humans have lived out their lives within a stable group of about 50 people. In a socially and geographically mobile post-industrial society, we are no longer guaranteed a lifetime's social network. Affiliations are made and broken more frequently than when our grandparents were young, and the concept of 'duty' to help social network members is not so widespread. Despite these changes, the human need for mutual aid and social embeddedness remains. A related feature of recent times has been the rise of professions providing aid. Although the majority of health care continues to be provided by relatives, friends and neighbours, helping professionals supplement this care. Clinical psychologists have a specialist contribution to make to the psychological well-being of many client groups, but particularly people whose needs are least likely to be met by a natural support system: people who have a mental handicap, who are elderly, who suffer mental illness. We are among those versed in the delicate art of helping strangers.

There has been an explosion of research on social support and social networks in the last decade. Broadly this has found that mental health is related to adequate social support and that, conversely, those who lack love, companionship and aid are at greater risk of psychological problems. It is possible to argue from this that humans defy their needs for attachment and social relatedness at their peril. It has certainly suggested to a number of helping professionals that they should become more aware of the social ecology to which their clients belong, rather than treat people out of social context. The current policy of caring for mentally ill and handicapped people in the community rather than in hospitals has made it even more untenable to provide psychological services on the same model as surgical interventions. Any successful community service depends on an understanding of what a 'community' is, and an important part of this concerns the types and functions of support provided by social relationships in natural settings.

This chapter introduces research on social support and social networks in order to provide a background for its clinical application. The review is necessarily very brief, limited and selective. Those wishing to explore the theoretical background further are referred to other sources (Cobb, 1976; Wortman, 1984; Leavy, 1983; Cohen and Wills, 1985; Pilisuk and Parks, 1986). I shall describe ways in which clinical psychologists, among others, can intervene to enhance and promote social support in community settings. These interventions aim to work with networks directly. However, most clinical psychologists continue to provide psychological therapies to individuals, and it is here that a largely unmet challenge is faced. Can we apply what we know about social support to our work with individual clients? It is possible that if individual therapy could be made more ecologically valid, its effectiveness would be increased, as would the range of clients who could benefit. The final section of the chapter, therefore, outlines ways in which cognitive behaviour therapy can help clients to mobilize support and use it appropriately – even to the point where they become agents of change within their own social networks.

ISSUES IN SOCIAL SUPPORT RESEARCH

What is social support?

Sidney Cobb has formulated a widely adopted definition of social support:

> Information leading individuals to believe (they) are (*1*) cared for and loved; (*2*) esteemed and valued; and that they (*3*) belong to a network of communication and mutual obligation (Cobb, 1976).

This is essentially a cognitive definition and as such is particularly useful to psychologists. It is worth examining other authors' definitions too:

> Interpersonal transactions that involve the expression of positive affect, the affirmation or endorsement of the person's beliefs or values and/or the provision of aid or assistance (Kahn and Antonucci, 1980).

> The degree to which a person's basic social needs are gratified through interaction with others (Kaplan *et al.*, 1977).

> Behavior which assures people that their feelings are understood by others and considered normal in the situation (Walker *et al.*, 1977).

We see from these that the term 'social support' refers to a range of different psychosocial processes and is not a unitary entity. Various authors have developed taxonomies of different types of support (House, 1981; Caplan, 1974; Cobb, 1976). These can be summarized as follows (adapted from Wortman, 1984):

the expression of positive affect (including information that one is loved, cared for and esteemed)

the expression of agreement with (or acknowledging the appropriateness of) a person's belief, interpretations or feelings; encouraging their open expression

offering advice or information, or access to new, diverse information

provision of material aid

provision of information that the person is part of a network of mutual obligation or reciprocal help.

It will be clear that these cannot easily be distinguished empirically, since many forms of helping behaviour combine more than one category. Barrera and Ainley (1983) include 'positive social interaction' (as in mutual interests or activities) in their factorial breakdown of supportive behaviours. This may include elements of more than one type of support.

Social support becomes available in the context of a social network, but is not synonymous with it – hence the term 'social support network' is rather confusing and is best avoided. Not all network relationships are supportive, but the type of network one inhabits may affect the way support is mobilized. One crucial concept here is that the people in an individual's personal network may or may not know each other. Two different types of network are illustrated in Figure 1. One is a small network, and most people within it know each other – this is characteristic of networks dominated by kinship. The second is not only larger but much less closely knit – there are several sub-clusters of friends, kin, colleagues linked only by weak ties. A field of research which studies social network characteristics (such as size, density, boundary density, strength, dispersal, etc.) has only recently been linked to the study of social support (Wellman, 1981). So far, there have been few consistent relationships discovered between network parameters and mental health outcomes. On the other hand, network structure appears to be related to other important variables, for example, satisfaction with social support (Stokes, 1983) and the uptake of professional services (McKinlay, 1973; Birkel and Reppucci, 1983). There is also some evidence that although crisis support may be more speedy in small dense networks (Walker *et al.*, 1977), when it comes to longer term adaptational tasks, these lack the range

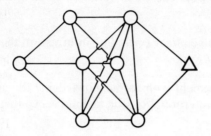

Small, dense kinship network (N = 8, D = 64.3%)

Low density with sub-clusters (N = 15, D = 20%)

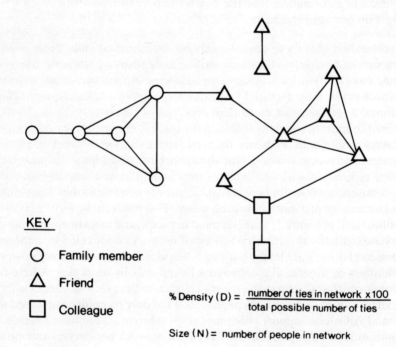

KEY

○ Family member

△ Friend

□ Colleague

% Density (D) = $\dfrac{\text{number of ties in network} \times 100}{\text{total possible number of ties}}$

Size (N) = number of people in network

Figure 1. Two forms of social network

of resources of low density networks with sub-clusters and weak ties (Hirsch, 1981; Wellman, 1979).

Epidemiological research has yielded information about the relationship of social support to mental health using survey methods in general population samples to examine the prevalence of psychiatric disorder in supported and unsupported groups (see for example, Andrews *et al.*, 1978; Henderson *et al.*, 1981). Other researchers have studied social networks, either in the general population (Wellman and Leighton, 1979), high risk groups (Hirsch, 1981; McLanahan *et al.*, 1981) or in patient groups (Hammer, 1981; Cuter and Tatum, 1983).

It is not possible to review this research in detail here and the reader is referred to other recent reviews (Broadhead *et al.*, 1983; Heller and Swindle, 1983; Leavy, 1983; Cohen and Wills, 1985; Kessler and McLeod, 1985). The field has its share of conceptual and methodological problems. Researchers have used a wide variety of social support indices – for example, marital status, the quality of the marital relationship, membership of community groups, available support in a crisis and size of social network have all been used – and the field has only recently begun to emerge from a confusion of definitions and the widespread use of measures with poor psychometric qualities. Many studies report an association between indices of social support and better mental health in general population samples. Some have found that support has a stress-buffering role, so that the relationship between support and health is only observed among those who have suffered a stressful life event (Henderson *et al.*, 1981; Brown and Harris, 1978). Others have reported that support can also be beneficial to mental health for those who have low levels of life event stress – that is, in routine circumstances as well as in a crisis (Aneshensel and Stone, 1982; Parry and Shapiro, 1986). One important conceptual distinction is that between global, diffuse or structural indices of support (such as membership of community groups) and specific, stress-related support (such as the availability of a confiding person). The first is tapping social integration, contributes to the 'psychological sense of community' (to use S.B. Sarason's (1974) term), and tends to yield direct, independent effects; the second is differentially important following a stressful life event, and is more likely to act as a stress buffer (Cohen and Wills, 1985).

The way that crisis-related support can act to protect individuals from the mental health consequences of severe stress is not yet fully understood. Some authors have discussed the role of support in maintaining self-esteem and providing a sense of mastery over the environment (Pearlin *et al.*, 1981; Brown and Harris, 1978). Thoits (1986) argues that social support processes are a form of coping assistance, and like coping, can be conceptualized as problem and emotion focused. Finally, it is possible that those who perceive themselves to be supported (which is what most studies have measured) have personalities which are more resilient to stress, whereas poor perceived support is associated with neuroticism and stress vulnerability (Henderson, 1984). This possibility must be examined carefully, since it has important implications for the clinical psychologist.

The role of the individual

The epidemiological approach to the study of social support has tended to see it as an environmental factor acting upon individuals in a given population. This is unsatisfactory, although it may be a justifiable simplification in research using statistical techniques such as general linear modelling where reciprocal causes and feedback loops are difficult to test. The clinician requires a more realistic conceptualization of the support process (see Hobfoll, 1985, for a useful discussion of this issue). There is a good deal of evidence that whilst social isolation and the lack of confiding intimacy do affect mental health, so do mental health and personality affect the amount and quality of social support received. The degree to which this has been neglected in psychosocial stress research can be judged by the fact that Henderson (1984) found it necessary to remind his readers that 'social support is obtainable only through social relationships which are themselves achieved only by having competence in establishing and maintaining them'. Indeed, some authors have gone so far as to suggest that most of the social support findings could be accounted for by social competence (Heller, 1979; Hansson *et al.*, 1984).

The majority of studies which have found associations between support and mental health outcomes have measured *perceived* social support rather than behavioural tallies of support received. This presents us with a problem, because it suggests either that social support outcomes are cognitively mediated or that correlations between perceived support and depression are spuriously high because the two measures are confounded. Of course, both possibilities could be true, and the clinician can have little doubt that all things being equal, depressed mood is likely to alter an individual's perception of how supported he or she is. However, evidence from a prospective study (Henderson *et al.*, 1981) where non-depressed individuals who perceive themselves to be poorly supported are subsequently more likely to become depressed, makes the first possibility worth considering.

Perceived support is, like 'loneliness', only partly accounted for by the actual support available to or received by an individual (Cutrona, 1982; Stokes, 1985). 'Feeling supported' is of course a *psychological* rather than a sociological phenomenon, based on an internal representation of self in relation to others. Where this self is perceived as unloved and unvalued, there may be a tendency to discount or devalue support. Here we can remember Cobb's (1976) definition of support as 'information leading individuals to believe they are cared for and loved'. When someone is clinically depressed, although their social environment may indeed be deficient in

support, any supportive behaviours which do occur are likely to be interpreted negatively rather than to lead the person to believe they are loved and
cared for. All support processes are linked to dependency relationships
which have the potential for negative as well as positive messages about the
self. I believe this is a fundamental issue too for the mobilization phase of the
social support process.

A number of studies have investigated individual characteristics which are
associated with perceived social support (Duckitt, 1984; Ganellen and
Blaney, 1984; Sarason and Sarason, 1982; Stokes, 1985; Sarason *et al.*
(1985). Unfortunately these are correlational studies using student samples,
and so lose generalizability compared to well-designed epidemiological
surveys. In these studies, those who perceive themselves as lacking social
support have been found to be less socially competent than 'high support'
individuals, to be more introverted, to have higher trait anxiety, to be
intolerant of psychological problems in others, to report unhappier experiences of their childhood relationships with parents, to have more pessimistic
views about the benefits of social relationships, to have a passive, unin-
volved stance towards life events and to see these as a burden to be endured
and to have external locus of control.

When facing a stressful life event of any severity, the belief that one is
supported will, at some point, be tested. There is a great difference between
believing you would be helped in a crisis and actually being helped in a crisis.
The translation of potential support into mobilized support is likely to be
influenced both by the individual and by characteristics of his or her network. We know that some socio-demographic variables affect the mobilization process; for example, women may make more use of support following
stress than men (Butler *et al.*, 1985), and those with a higher level of
education report more mobilized support following a stressful event (Eckenrode, 1983). We also need to understand why some individuals are less
effective at mobilizing help than others. There may be two elements in this,
help-*seeking* and help-*using*.

There is a body of social psychology research on recipients' reactions to
aid which, although isolated from the social support field, is relevant to
understanding how help can be rejected. Fisher *et al.* (1983) discuss two
clusters of reactions to aid: a negative, defensive reaction and a positive,
accepting one. Evidence from a range of sources illuminates the circumstances which elicit cluster 1 rather than cluster 2 reactions, showing that aid
is more likely to be rejected when the recipient is unable to reciprocate
(Gross and Latane, 1974), when the donor's motivation is negative (Gergen
and Gergen, 1974), when it poses a threat to the autonomy of the recipient
(Gergen & Gergen, 1971), when aid is requested rather than offered (Fisher
and Nadler, 1974), and when aid is greatly needed rather than less needed
(Morse and Gergen, 1971).

Various theoretical frameworks have been used to make sense of these findings. Equity theory is based on the principle that there is a desire in social exchange relationships to maintain equity and that lack of equity causes distress. However, Fisher and Nadler argue that none of these account for the full range of findings as parsimoniously as the hypothesis that people reject aid when it poses a threat to their self-esteem. If we link this to the social support and personality findings, we can hypothesize that individuals with vulnerable self-esteem are less likely to mobilize help effectively. If support is perceived as carrying negative messages about the self, this might lead to humiliation, embarrassment and shame. Rather than allow this, the self is protected, but at the cost of rejecting (or even sabotaging) offers of support. It should be clear that this approach has direct relevance for depression, because the depressed person is more likely to perceive (perhaps accurately, but certainly selectively) the negative implications of accepting help.

ENHANCING SOCIAL SUPPORT – COMMUNITY INTERVENTIONS

There are a number of ways in which clinical psychologists can intervene in social networks with the aim of enhancing the ability of the system to provide support for its members. This model of therapy takes the eco system as the focus of intervention, not the individual.

Of course, much conventional clinical work promotes social support. For example, I have already noted how most people depend on kinship for reliable support, both routinely and in a crisis. However, some kin systems do not function well in this regard, and are a source of stress rather than support for the people who live together. Family therapists use a variety of structural and systemic techniques which, if successful, make the family more able to provide for its members' needs (see the previous chapter). Other examples of clinical psychology practice which can be seen as social support interventions would include systems consultation, staff support in homes for mentally-handicapped people, promoting patient self-support groups – such as for people suffering panic disorders or having been the childhood victims of incest – and transmitting skills to volunteers and 'para-professionals'.

In addition to these methods, there are some which are not yet widely practised in the UK but which interest a number of clinical psychologists who work in community settings. These include family networking, neighbourhood organization and consultation with natural helpers.

Family networking

Family networking (Speck and Attneave, 1972; Speck and Attneave, 1973) evolved out of the work of family therapists as a way of mobilizing the resources of a family's social network in response to a crisis with a family member, usually an identified patient. The approach has been slow to gain ground, perhaps because, as originally described, it involves stage-managing an assembly of between 40 and 50 network members – a daunting prospect for mental health professionals trained to work with small groups. More recent reports show that the approach is being implemented in the US, particularly with patients suffering from schizophrenia (Beels, 1981) and with antisocial adolescents (Trimble, 1981). The method is often adapted to work with smaller groups of between 10 and 30 network members (Rueveni, 1979). Published reports of work in the UK are not yet available.

The goal of social networking is to promote change in the patient's network so that it is able to provide effective social support of all kinds. This is done by assembling the network members, often at the patient's home. One criterion for this approach is, therefore, that the family is willing to invite the relatives, friends and neighbours to a meeting. The network assembly lasts from three to four hours and is undertaken by a team of professional workers, one of whom takes responsibility for leading the session, whilst the other two or three mingle with the network and facilitate the process by supporting the leader. The goal is to identify resources in the network and facilitate a sense of cohesiveness which will allow people to solve each others' problems. This 're-tribalization' can be encouraged by the use of non-verbal 'encounter' techniques. Indeed, the original work was very much a product of the human potential movement associated with the *zeitgeist* of the late 60s and early 70s. The intervention team takes care to reflect back responsibility for solving problems to the network itself. They communicate a belief in the capacity of ordinary people to find the necessary resources. Self help and mutual aid are encouraged by the team through a variety of techniques.

The network may have between one and six meetings, and a typical first session might proceed as follows. The assembly begins with a brief 'sales pitch' from the leader followed by a non-verbal warm-up exercise. Often a set of concentric circles are formed to allow an inner group to be surrounded by a less involved outer group. Diverse opinions about the problem are elicited and the team model constructive discussion and listening to all views. They also emphasize openness and the importance of not having 'polite secrets' between network members. Information is shared and misinformation is corrected. The leader ends with a brief restatement of a specific problem, sets the next time to meet and may give the network a specific task to address in the interim. The team members then exit unobtrusively leaving the network members taking refreshments and talking amongst themselves.

The approach has a number of advantages. First, it is an intervention which addresses social support deficits in the most direct manner. It accepts that the contribution made by specialist psychological input is a very small part of the total set of social influences on a patient, and that individual problems are linked to damaged social networks. For these reasons the approach is attractive to those who wish to apply findings in social support research to psychiatric problems in community settings. On the other hand, a number of criticisms can be made. Social network theorists are sceptical about the naive concept of 'network' underlying this intervention, which assumes that the 'tribe' is a solidary network. It is known empirically that most social networks consist of highly complex systems of sub-clusters with different strengths of tie performing different functions. 'Re-tribalization' seems to be based, to network theorists, on a romantic notion of an ideal social form, bearing little resemblance to reality (see Wellman, 1981). More practically, there is the danger when intervening in any ecological system, of setting up chains of events which lead to unpredicted and negative consequences (Willems, 1973). This is demonstrably the case with biological systems, and the occurrence of 'iatrogenic' problems within the network should be monitored carefully. Finally, the intervention can be seen as very expensive and time-consuming for many people. Having said that, there is evidence that it may be both effective and cost-effective in certain cases, particularly where there has been a heavy demand on professional services over a long period with, perhaps, the accompanying threat of hospitalization.

Schoenfeld *et al.* (1985) report an outcome study of this intervention in 12 social networks. The study is, as the authors note, methodologically flawed, in that families were not randomly assigned to the treatment and comparison groups; the latter consisted of families who were ineligible for networking: either because they were unwilling to call a meeting, or the social network was not large enough. In addition, the assessment of clinical improvement is anecdotal. Despite this, the results are of interest. The main outcome measured was the number of contacts the families had with professional agencies in the three months prior to networking and during two consecutive three-month periods following the intervention. These authors found a 76 per cent reduction in professional contact in the three months following the intervention compared to a 19 per cent reduction in the comparison group. Most of the effect can be accounted for by three families. A further four decreased their contact, and the level of professional input was unchanged in five. The clinical outcomes were (anecdotally) good, but no formal measures were taken. Since the types of family described in this study make heavy demands on professional time, and would normally be very difficult to help, the results reported are promising and may commend the approach to those working in psychiatric settings where the emphasis is on preventing initial or recurrent hospitalization. In addition to the sources already mentioned, details of technique can be found in Trimble (1980), Halevy-Martini *et al.* (1984) and Hemley-Van der Velden *et al.* (1984).

Other community interventions

A related method of work is the community worker's role in neighbourhood organization, a role which can be undertaken by a community psychologist. The 'clients' are residents in a defined geographical area who are organizing themselves to improve the quality of life in a particular way. A classic example of this type of intervention was the Tenderloin project discussed by Minkler (1981). Isolated elderly residents of a single-room occupancy hotel in a high crime area were involved in a health preventative programme. Health workers set up a health screening and blood pressure stall in the lobby of the hotel which served an additional purpose – to promote mutual aid and to break down isolation. As residents met, they began to socialize, to assist each other with tasks such as shopping, and eventually, to organize meetings to discuss rent and living conditions. The project eventually included eight houses linked by a self-help organization which liaised with the police and city officials in providing protection from local crime.

A final approach to a community network intervention is to identify 'natural helpers' in the community (Cowen *et al.*, 1979; Pancoast, 1980, Leutz, 1976). It has been argued that: 'bartenders and hairdressers, funeral home directors and, of course, clergy, represent a literal army of confidants and counselors providing social support to those in need' (Pilisuk and Parks, 1986; p. 157). For example, Wiesenfeld and Weis (1979) devised a programme to enhance the listening skills of hairdressers. This approach has been evaluated in the UK by Milne and Mullin (1987) who demonstrated that such a programme was effective in transmitting counselling skills and, furthermore, that the trained hairdressers were rated as significantly more helpful. Milne has extended this principle to training ex-clients in behavioural management of anxiety (Milne *et al.*, 1987). Having benefitted from such an intervention themselves, clients are potentially a valuable resource to transmit these skills within their communities.

SOCIAL SUPPORT IN COGNITIVE BEHAVIOUR THERAPY

Although there has been a growing interest in social network interventions, most clinical psychologists in the UK, particularly in the field of mental health, work with individuals. It is not always appreciated that social support is relevant to therapy with the individual. Psychological therapists have become aware that factors in the patient's social network and support system can either enhance or undermine the effects of treatment. I shall take cognitive behaviour therapy (CBT) as a paradigm example of a widely used approach which has been developed independently of the patient's social context. It is possible (although as yet untested) that patients who still have significant deficits in their social support system at the end of therapy will be less able to maintain their clinical improvement. If problems in social support can be addressed the value of CBT may be enhanced, as any therapy which aims to be effective in the long term should have a preventative as well as a curative function. Although problems in social relationships are certainly a common focus for CBT, this is sometimes done in a way which is unfocused and unsystematic, and attention to the theoretical issues identified above leads to some enhancements of technique.

The process can be summarized as follows:

Assess social network and social support

Identify characteristic patterns of behaviour which lead to support being devalued, unused or abused

Elicit the self-related cognitions accompanying such behavioural sequences

Challenge these cognitions, and

Teach new skills in eliciting support.

Assessment methods

The psychologist begins by developing an accurate understanding of the patient's social relationships. This includes mapping the network and its features (such as size, density, proportion of kin), assessing the frequency and type of helping behaviours already accepted by the patient, identifying areas of strength and deficit and discrepancies between the support available and the patient's perceived social support. To upgrade one's technique in this field requires a knowledge of appropriate measures. These are essential in formulating the problem during assessment and in monitoring change. More than this, though, they are a central part of the intervention, since patients also learn to use these instruments as a way of discovering their own social reality. There are many published scales which measure different aspects of support. In practice the clinical psychologist need use only three: a social network analysis, a measure of perceived support, and a measure of helping behaviours. These allow the therapist to 'triangulate' the social support process for a given individual.

Some of the principles and practicalities of social network analysis are described by Walker *et al.* (1977), Hirsch (1981), Wellman (1981) and Maguire (1983). Typically, a list of primary group members is elicited by recording the names of all the people the patient meets to talk to regularly. Relatives, friends, neighbours, colleagues and professionals are included, but not those with whom there is only superficial contact (for example, nodding acquaintances, shopkeepers, etc.). People who are significant but are rarely seen can be included, for example, relatives and friends who are geographically distant and those with whom the patient has lost touch as a result of the psychiatric episode. The 'map' of the social network is then drawn by establishing for each possible pair of people in the list, whether or not they have a personal relationship *independently* of the patient (see Figure 1). It is then asked how often the patient sees each member, and the nature of the social transaction, particularly which types of support (information, emotional, companionship or material aid) are given. This aspect of the analysis is made more precise by using an inventory of socially supportive behaviours (for example, as described by Barrera and Ainley (1983)). In clinical practice it is best to modify the method from a retrospective one to a diary keeping format. Examples of supportive behaviour which are recorded by this type of instrument are given in Table 1.

Table 1. Sample items from the *Inventory of Socially Supportive Behaviors* (Barrera and Ainley, 1983)

Directive guidance
Gave you some information on how to do something.
Suggested action you should take.
Gave you some information to help you understand a situation you were in.
Taught you how to do something.

Non-directive support
Told you that she/he feels very close to you.
Let you know that he/she will always be around if you need assistance.
Told you that you are OK just the way you are.
Comforted you by showing you some physical affection.

Positive social interaction
Did some activity to help you get your mind off things.
Talked with you about some interests of yours.

Tangible assistance
Gave you over £25.
Provided you with a place to stay.
Provided you with some transport.

The map of the social network can be used in conjunction with the helping behaviour inventory to analyse how much of the network has been mobilized and in which areas, in order to pinpoint specific support deficits. The network measure is then used to identify potential sources of help with the patient's current problems and is the basis for planning behavioural assignments in support elicitation (described by Maguire, 1983). The method of using unexploited resources within the network to help the patient solve problems can best be conceptualized as coping assistance (Thoits, 1986), and is the individual therapy equivalent to the networking interventions described above.

A measure of perceived support is also of great value, and there are many available. The Perceived Social Network Inventory (Orritt *et al.*, 1985) is a useful example, partly because it focuses on coping assistance and also because efforts have been made to establish its psychometric properties (although not in British samples). This measure requires the individual to identify those people to whom he or she could turn when under stress or in need of help, then goes on to establish the type of support available from each, how often given, whether reciprocal and whether the relationship is characterized by negative feelings. Part of the questionnaire is reproduced in the Appendix.

This type of questionnaire is primarily useful as a baseline measure of support perception. The intervention is aimed not just at altering the amount of support elicited from the network, but to alter the patient's perception of that support. Hence an outcome measure is needed which taps this variable, ideally at the time of referral, as therapy starts, at the end of therapy, and at follow-up. In addition, a comparison of the perceptual measure with the behavioural inventory can be the starting point for identifying dysfunctional cognitive processes about support.

Changing cognitions and behaviours

Therapy continues with a systematic examination of the individual's perception of being unsupported and identifies repetitive social interactions in which support is being devalued, rejected, abused or unmobilized. Fundamental to both aspects of the work is precision in identifying the specific ways for this particular individual, that supportive acts are being interpreted as threatening self-esteem. Dysfunctional beliefs about the social support process readily emerge and such statements as these (taken from clinical material) will probably be familiar to most psychological therapists.

'If he loved me, I wouldn't have to ask him to help me.'

'I can't tell my (adult) children about my operation because it would worry them.'

'Well, she did offer to babysit but I know she didn't really mean it.'

'It's embarrassing to admit I can't cope.'

'He only said he would take me out because he feels sorry for me.'

'I feel bad going round to her house yet again because I can't give anything to her.'

'You are only helping me because it's your job.'

Here we see processes of attribution and equity beliefs which can be challenged successfully and the consequences of an alternative belief tested out. Each remark arises from a personal belief held by the patient about interpersonal relationships (see Ryle, 1982, for an account of these). All these beliefs lead to support being devalued or rejected, not out of wilful self-defeating wrongheadedness, but as a *self-protective strategy*. In my experience, the therapeutic alliance is strengthened if this is understood and acknowledged by the therapist. The messages about the self implied by admitting one cannot cope, accepting that some one feels sorry for one, or having to ask for help are identified, challenged, and alternatives tested. These alternatives may involve, for example, discovering the intrinsic value of the support regardless of the motives of the donor, accepting that less than perfect care is a normal aspect of reality, learning to tolerate self-consciousness and embarrassment, or the legitimate use of gratitude as 'payment' in social transactions.

As work on the individual's personal beliefs and automatic thoughts proceeds, new behaviours can be tested in the social network. In an excellent discussion of this issue, Winefield (1984) recommends that new skills in how to elicit support can be taught using behavioural assignments. She notes that traditional social skills teaching is unlikely to be helpful, and that behavioural interventions should focus on teaching patients (*a*) the social norms for intimacy and its reciprocation, (*b*) how much and when to complain, (*c*) how to attend to and display interest in the other person and (*d*) how to reward the other for helping by responding positively.

Two principles behind a social support intervention are: first, that the individual, not the therapist, is to take responsibility for mobilizing the network; and second, that behavioural assignments should take account of the social norms of the network. Although there is nothing intrinsically difficult about this form of work, it is an area where it is easy to make poorly focused interventions due to ignorance about the ecological setting. Support cannot always be artificially 'grafted on' to an existing network; if it is inappropriate it may be rejected – just as a transplanted organ poorly matched for tissue type will be rejected by the living organism. This is what a social ecology is. Any such intervention must be planned carefully, on the basis of the social network analysis, to be a logical extension of natural support or a mobilization of existing support. For example, a therapist may be aware that the patient's network is small and restricted in friendship and sources of information. A recommendation about 'joining a club' or 'going to an evening class' is often entirely alien to the values of the network. In this case it is often better to examine the network for potential 'bridging ties' to other networks. These are weak ties which offer potential access to new friends and activities (Granovetter, 1973; Walker *et al.*, 1977).

Summary

This chapter has reviewed some of the theoretical background to social support interventions. The network can be the direct target of the intervention, through networking, neighbourhood organization or consultation with natural helpers. Alternatively, clinical psychologists can intervene at the individual level, enhancing the effectiveness with which support is mobilized. Both approaches have theoretical justification.

Acknowledgements

I should like to thank Derek Milne for useful discussions of the ideas in this chapter and comments on an earlier draft.

Appendix 1

Perceived Support Network Inventory (from Oritt *et al.*, 1985)

The support we receive from family, friends, professional helpgivers and others during times of stress seems to play an important role in determining our reaction to that stress. The interaction that we have with supportive individuals appears to help us feel better faster after failing an exam, losing a job, or experiencing conflict with someone. This questionnaire attempts to gather information about your perceptions and experiences with your support network in response to stressful events that have occurred in your life.

SUPPORT NETWORK

Write the first name and initial of the surname of all the people you would go to if you needed support or help during a stressful time in your life. Tick the appropriate column that describes your relationship with each person. You do not have to fill out this list in any order. You do not have to use all the spaces available.

First name and initial of surname	Spouse or partner	Family member	Friend	Co-worker	Professional helpgiver	Religious leader	Self-help group member

HELPING BEHAVIOURS

Support from people during stressful events can be broken down into five categories of helping behaviours:

(a) *Emotional support* – someone listening to your private thoughts and feelings regarding a stressful event and/or giving you physical affection.
(b) *Material aid support* – someone lending you money or the use of some valuable object like a car or an appliance during a stressful event.
(c) *Advice and information* – someone suggesting what to do or where to get needed information during a stressful event.
(d) *Physical assistance* – someone helping with jobs around the house, errands, or favours you might need during a stressful event.
(e) *Social participation* – someone offering you the opportunity to engage in pleasant social activities during a stressful event.

SUPPORT NETWORK INFORMATION

On the following pages are questions about the people whose names you wrote down on the Support Network list. Please write the first name and initial of the last name of the *first person* you listed and answer the questions about him/her. Then write the first name and initial of the last name of the *second person* you listed and answer the questions about him/her. Go through your entire Support Network list. Each set of questions for each person takes less than a minute to answer, so the following pages will not take you long.

First name _____

Rate the extent to which you agree with the following statement by circling the appropriate numbers.

	Almost never		Sometimes		Usually		Almost always

During times of stress:

I seek this person out for support or help	1	2	3	4	5	6	7
This person provides me with support or help when I ask	1	2	3	4	5	6	7
I am satisfied with this person's support or help	1	2	3	4	5	6	7

Place a tick next to the categories you might expect to receive from this person during times of stress:

_____*a*) Emotional Support
_____*b*) Material Aid Support
_____*c*) Advice and Information
_____*d*) Physical Assistance
_____*e*) Social Participation

This person receives support from me during times of stress for him/her

1	2	3	4	5	6	7
Almost Never		Sometimes		Usually		Almost Always

Generally speaking, I have serious conflicts with this person

7	6	5	4	3	2	1
Almost Never		Sometimes		Usually		Almost Always

REFERENCES

ANDREWS, G., TENNANT, C., NEWSON, D.M. and VAILLANT, G.E. (1978). Life event stress, social support, coping style and risk of psychological impairment. *Journal of Nervous and Mental Disease, 166*, 307–316.

ANESHENSEL, C.S. and STONE, J.D. (1982). Stress and depression: a test of the stress buffering model of social support. *Archives of General Psychiatry, 39*, 1392–1396.

BARRERA, M. and AINLEY, S.L. (1983). The structure of social support: a conceptual and empirical analysis. *Journal of Community Psychology, 11*, 133–143.

BEELS, C. (1981). Social networks and the treatment of schizophrenics. *International Journal of Family Therapy, 3*, 310–316.

BIRKEL, R.C. and REPPUCCI, N.D. (1983). Social networks, information seeking and the utilization of services. *American Journal of Community Psychology, 11*, 185–205.

BROADHEAD, W., KAPLAN, B., JAMES, S., WAGNER, E., SCHOEN-BACH, V., GRIMSON, R., HEYDEN, S., TIBBLIN, G. and GEHLBACH, S. (1983). The epidemiologic evidence for a relationship between social support and health. *American Journal of Epidemiology, 117*, 521–537.

BROWN, G.W. and HARRIS, T. (1978). *Social Origins of Depression: A Study of Psychiatric Disorder in Women*. London: Tavistock.

BUTLER, T., GIORDIANO, S. and NEREN, S. (1985). Gender and sex-role attributes as predictors of utilization of natural support systems during personal stress events. *Sex Roles, 13*, 515–524.

CAPLAN, G. (1974) (ed.) *Support Systems and Community Mental Health*. New York: Basic Books.

COBB, S. (1976). Social support as a moderator of life stress. *Psychosomatic Medicine, 38*, 300–314.

COHEN, S. and WILLS, T.A. (1985). Stress, social support and the buffering hypothesis. *Psychological Bulletin, 98*, 310–357.

COWEN, E., GESTEN, E., BOIKE, M., NORTON, P., WILSON, A. and DESTEFANO, M. (1979). Hairdressers as caregivers: 1. A descriptive profile of interpersonal helpgiving involvements. *American Journal of Community Psychology, 7*, 633–648.

CUTER, D.L. and TATUM E. (1983). Networks and the chronic patient. *New Directions for Mental Health Services, 19*, 13–22.

CUTRONA, C.E. (1982). Transition to college: Loneliness and the process of social adjustment. In L.A. Peplau and D. Perlman (eds). *Loneliness: A Sourcebook of Current Theory, Research and Therapy*. New York: Wiley.

DUCKITT, J. (1984). Social support, personality and the prediction of psychological distress: An interactionist approach. *Journal of Clinical Psychology, 40*, 1199–1205.

ECKENRODE, J. (1983). The mobilization of social supports: some individual constraints. *American Journal of Community Psychology, 11*, 509–528.

FISHER, J.D. and NADLER, A. (1974). The effect of similarity between donor and recipient on reactions to aid. *Journal of Applied Social Psychology, 4*, 230–243.

FISHER, J.D., NADLER, A. and DE PAULO, B.M. (eds) (1983). *New Directions in Helping. Volume 1. Recipient Reactions to Aid*. New York: Academic Press.

GANELLEN, R.J. and BLANEY, P.H. (1984). Hardiness and social support as moderators of the effects of life stress. *Journal of Personality and Social Psychology, 47*, 156–163.

GERGEN, K.J. and GERGEN, M. (1971). International assistance from a psychological perspective. *1971 Yearbook of World Affairs, volume 25.* London: Institute of World Affairs.

GERGEN, K.J. and GERGEN, M. (1974). Understanding foreign assistance through public opinion. *1974 Yearbook of World Affairs, volume 27.* London: Institute of World Affairs.

GRANOVETTER, M.S. (1973). The strength of weak ties. *American Journal of Sociology, 78,* 1360–1372.

GROSS, A.E. and LATANÉ, J.G. (1974). Receiving help, giving help, and interpersonal attraction. *Journal of Applied Social Psychology, 4,* 210–223.

HALEVY-MARTINI, J., HEMLEY-VAN DER VELDEN, E., RUHF, L. and SCHOENFELD, P. (1984). Process and strategy in network therapy. *Family Process, 23,* 521–533.

HAMMER, M. (1981). Social supports, social networks and schizophrenia. *Schizophrenia Bulletin, 7,* 45–57.

HANSSON, R.O., JONES, W.H. and CARPENTER, B.N. (1984). Relationship competence and social support. In P. Shaver (ed.). *Review of Personality and Social Psychology, Volume 5.* Beverly Hills: Sage.

HELLER, K. (1979). The effects of social support. Prevention and treatment implications. In A.P. Goldstein and F.H. Kanfer (eds). *Maximizing Treatment Gains: Transfer Enhancement in Psychotherapy.* New York: Academic Press.

HELLER, K. and SWINDLE, R.W. (1983). Social networks, perceived social support and coping with stress. In R.D. Feiner, L.A. Jason, J. Moritsugu and S.S. Farber (eds). *Preventive Psychology. Theory Research and Practice in Community Intervention.* Oxford: Pergamon Press.

HEMLEY-VAN DER VELDEN, E., HALEVY-MARTINI, J., RUHF, L. and SCHOENFELD, P. (1984). New developments in network therapy. *International Journal of Family Therapy, 6,* 68–81.

HENDERSON, S. (1984). Interpreting the evidence on social support. *Social Psychiatry, 19,* 49–52.

HENDERSON, S., BYRNE, D.G. and DUNCAN-JONES, P. (1981). *Neurosis and the Social Environment.* Sydney: Academic Press.

HIRSCH, B. (1981). Natural support systems and coping with major life changes. *American Journal of Community Psychology, 7,* 263–277.

HOBFOLL, S.E. (1985). Limitations of social support in the stress process. In I.G. Sarason and B.R. Sarason (eds). *Social Support: Theory, Research and Applications.* Dordrecht: Martinus Nijhoff Publishers.

HOUSE, J.S. (1981). *Work, Stress and Social Support.* Wokingham: Addison Wesley.

KAHN, R. and ANTONUCCI, T. (1980). Convoys over the life course: Attachments, roles and social supports. In P.B. Baltes and D. Brim (eds) *Life-span Development and Behaviour.* Boston: Lexington Press.

KAPLAN, B.H., CASSEL, J.C. and GORE, S. (1977). Social support and health. *Medical Care, 15,* 47–58.

KESSLER, R.C. and McLEOD, J. (1985). Social support and mental health in community samples. In S. Cohen and L. Syme (eds). *Social Support and Health.* New York: Academic Press.

LEAVY, R.L. (1983). Social support and psychological disorder. A review. *Journal of Community Psychology, 11,* 3–21.

LEUTZ, W. (1976). The informal community caregiver: A link between the health care system and local residents. *American Journal of Orthopsychiatry, 46,* 678–688.

MAGUIRE, L. (1983). *Networking with individuals. In Understanding Social Networks.* Beverly Hills: Sage Publications.

McKINLAY, J.B. (1973). Social networks, lay consultation and help-seeking behaviour. *Social Forces, 51*, 275–292.

McLANAHAN, S.S., WEDEMEYER, N.V. and ADELBERG, T. (1981). Network structure, social support and psychological well-being in the single parent family. *Journal of Marriage and the Family, 43*, 601–612.

MILNE, D.L., JONES, R. and WALTERS, P. Ex-clients as therapists: an empirical analysis. Unpublished paper presented to the British Association for Behavioural Psychotherapy, Exeter.

MILNE, D.L. and MULLIN, M. (1987). Is a problem shared a problem shaved? An evaluation of hairdressers and social support. *British Journal of Clinical Psychology, 26*, 69–70.

MINKLER, M. (1981). Application of social support theory to education: Implications for work with the elderly. *Health Education Quarterly, 8*, 147–165.

MORSE, S. and GERGEN, K. (1971). Material aid and social attraction. *Journal of Applied Social Psychology, 1*, 150–162.

ORRITT, E.J., PAUL, S.C. and BEHRMAN, J.A. (1985). The Perceived Support Network Inventory. *American Journal of Community Psychology, 13*, 565–582.

PANCOAST, D. (1980). Finding and enlisting neighbors to support families. In J. Garbarino and H. Stocking (eds). *Protecting Children from Abuse and Neglect*. San Francisco: Jossey-Bass.

PARRY, G. and SHAPIRO, D.A. (1986). Social support and life events in working class women. Stress buffering or independent effects? *Archives of General Psychiatry, 43*, 315–323.

PEARLIN, L.I., LIEBERMAN, M.A., MENAGHAN, E.G. and MULLAN, J.T. (1981). The stress process. *Journal of Health and Social Behavior, 19*, 2–21.

PILISUK, M. and PARKS, S.H. (1986). *The Healing Web. Social Networks and Human Survival*. Hanover: University Press of New England.

RUEVENI, U. (1979). *Networking Families in Crisis*. New York: Human Services Press.

RYLE, A. (1982). *Psychotherapy: A Cognitive Integration of Theory and Practice*. London: Academic Press.

SARASON, S.B. (1974). *The psychological sense of community*. San Francisco: Jossey Bass.

SARASON, I.G. and SARASON, B.R. (1982). Concomitants of social support: Attitudes, personality characteristics and life experiences. *Journal of Personality, 50*, 331–344.

SARASON, I.G., SARASON, B.R. and SHEARIN, E.N. (1986) Social support as an individual difference variable: its stability, origins and relational aspects. *Journal of Personality and Social Psychology, 50*, 845–855.

SARASON, B.R., SARASON, I.G., HACKER, T.A. and BASHAM, R.B. (1985). Concomitants of social support: social skills, physical attractiveness and gender. *Journal of Personality and Social Psychology, 49*, 469–480.

SCHOENFELD, P. HALEVY-MARTINI, J., HEMLEY-VAN DER VELDEN, E. and RUHF, L. (1985). Network therapy: an outcome study of twelve social networks. *Journal of Community Psychology, 13*, 281–287.

SPECK, R. and ATTNEAVE, C. (1972). Network therapy. Ch. 22 in A. Ferber, M. Mendelson and A. Napier (eds). *The Book of Family Therapy*. Boston: Houghton Mifflin.

SPECK, R. and ATTNEAVE, C. (1973). *Family networks*. New York: Pantheon.

STOKES, J.P. (1983). Predicting satisfaction with social support from social network structure. *American Journal of Community Psychology, 11*, 141–152.

STOKES, J.P. (1985). The relation of social network and individual difference variables to loneliness. *Journal of Personality and Social Psychology, 48*, 981–990.

THOITS, P.A. (1986). Social support as coping assistance. *Journal of Consulting and Clinical Psychology, 54*, 416–423.

TRIMBLE, D. (1980). A guide to the network therapies. *Connections, 3*, 9–21.

TRIMBLE, D. (1981). Social network intervention with antisocial adolescents. *International Journal of Family Therapy, 3*, 208–275.

WALKER, K., MacBRIDE, A. and VACHON, M. (1977). Social support networks and the crisis of bereavement. *Social Science and Medicine, 11*, 35–41.

WELLMAN, B. (1979). The community question. *American Journal of Sociology, 84*, 1201–1231.

WELLMAN, B. (1981). Applying network analysis to the study of social support. In B.H. Gottlieb (ed.) *Social Networks and Social Support.* Beverly Hills: Sage Publications.

WELLMAN, B. and LEIGHTON, B. (1979). Networks, neighbourhoods and communities. *Urban Affairs Quarterly, 15*, 363–390.

WIESENFELD, A. and WEIS, H. (1979). Hairdressers and helping: Influencing the behaviour of informal caregivers. *Professional Psychology, 10*, 786–792.

WILLEMS, E.P. (1973). Go ye into all the world and modify behavior: an ecologist's view. *Representative Research in Social Psychology, 4*, 93–105.

WINEFIELD, H.R. (1984). The nature and elicitation of social support: Some implications for the helping professions. *Behavioural Psychotherapy, 12*, 318–330.

WORTMAN, C.B. (1984). Social support and the cancer patient. Conceptual and methodological issues. *Cancer, 53*, 2339–2360.

PSYCHOLOGICAL TREATMENT OF EMOTIONAL DISORDERS IN THE ELDERLY

Ian Hanley

In recent years there has been an increasing interest in the application of psychological theory and principles to the assessment and treatment of mental health problems in elderly adults. However, very few clinical psychologists in this country work with old people (Tatham, 1984; Toner, 1985) and so a small segment (approximately 6 per cent) of a small profession confronts a massive challenge from a population in which the 18.5 per cent over retirement age have high morbidity rates. Psychologists working with the elderly have not been 'slow in coming forward' to promote the potential of the profession to advance health care for the elderly. Indeed, to one observer (Garland, 1986), the claims of psychologists are often unrealistic, overly vociferous and many publications 'resound with confidence verging on euphoria'. Other commentators point to the slender evidence on which many interventions rest (Davies and Crisp, 1985) and the need for a sounder empirical base.

Much of the interest to date has been focused not on functional disorders but rather on the psychological treatment of the organic conditions that can be catalogued under the broad descriptors of dementia or mental impairment in old age. This reflects the major demands placed on health and social service provisions by the expanding army of such sufferers commonly referred to as 'the rising tide'. Functional disorders have been relatively neglected as a consequence of this emphasis on dementia. Moreover it is becoming clear that although the separate categorization of organic and functional disorders makes eminent sense from the aetiological and treatment planning perspectives they can and often do occur together, and functional disorders in the context of dementia deserve recognition and treatment in their own right.

The contribution of life span developmental psychology to our understanding of the problems faced by the elderly has provided a fresh perspective (Jeffery and Saxby, 1984) and a new understanding of clearly age-related factors that need to be recognized and built in to the practice of any psychological therapy with the elderly. As with younger people depression and anxiety are the most common affective disorders experienced by the old. In general the techniques of therapy appropriate to the adult population are being recognized as relevant to the elderly provided they are realistically adapted to meet their special needs in relation to psychological therapy (Church, 1986; Woods and Britton, 1985). Considerable attention is now being paid to the basic process of forming an effective psychotherapeutic relationship with elderly clients. This demands a major reappraisal of interactional style for many psychologists used to working only with younger adults. Specific therapeutic techniques can only be influential when carefully woven into a 'whole person' approach that has been effective in committing the elderly person to stay in therapy – 'techniques' rarely stand on their own with this client group. This often makes therapy, especially with the very old (over 75 years), a slow and more cautious business and one that often aims for more modest gains than with younger adults. Perhaps our gradually increasing knowledge about old age is finally being integrated into the ways we practice. Gone, hopefully, are the days, when in the hasty search for a sound empirical base for psychological therapy, numerous simplistic overgeneralizations were made as to what was therapeutic for 'the elderly' as a population.

There now seems to be a real commitment to the principles of individual assessment and a recognition of the heterogeneity of elderly people. No longer do we assume for example that all elderly people benefit from reminiscence (Coleman, 1986; Coleman, 1987) or indeed that engagement is always a reliable measure of psychological well-being, demanding that we prescribe 'activity programmes' (Simpson *et al.*, 1981). Greater attention is being paid to individual differences in the way elderly clients perceive their past and present lives. Thus the importance of covert cognitive variables is increasingly recognized and total reliance is no longer placed on overt behavioural measurement.

What follows is a necessarily brief and selective review of some of the basic issues underlying psychological approaches to functional disorders in the elderly, as well as a description of a few examples of the techniques being applied. When appropriate, reference will be made to the results of controlled trials. As a consequence, however, of the relative scarcity of well-designed and genuinely informative controlled trials of therapeutic approaches to functional disorders in the elderly (Hodge, 1984) somewhat greater attention is given to the findings from single case study research.

GENERAL FACTORS IN THERAPY WITH THE ELDERLY

In assessing each elderly individual with a functional disorder the therapist needs to start by bearing in mind the tendency of ageing to increase dependency on the environment in its broadest sense. A number of potential obstacles to the therapist–patient relationship need careful consideration.

Intellectual impairments

Church (1983) has reviewed some of the evidence relating to changes in language, memory and abstract ability that occur in normal ageing. This suggests that as therapy becomes more verbal and interpretive in its nature so the elderly client will have increasing difficulty. This suggests specific modifications to the way in which a therapist might carry out therapy regardless of therapeutic persuasion.

Take for example those working today from the perspective of dynamic psychotherapy. Freud made the sweeping statement that 'psychotherapy is not possible near or above the age of 50, the elasticity of the mental processes on which the treatment depends is as a rule lacking – old people are not educable' (Freud, 1905). Although intellectual changes in the very old may make interpretive therapies more difficult to pursue, modern psychotherapy rejects Freud's extreme opinion (Hilderbrand, 1986; Sparacino, 1979; Verwoerdt, 1981). As Hilderbrand points out, what started as a general rule of thumb became somehow enshrined in a rigid operating rule and convention. When tested in practice, albeit in modified form, psychotherapy has been shown to work, at least with selected cases (Hilderbrand, 1986). Perhaps this is because the over 60 or over 65 population is not homogeneous. Walker (1982) found, for example, that the failure rate on a test of ability to shift set (possibly linked in some way to the ability to make shifts in 'interpretive' therapy) rose dramatically from 10 per cent in those aged 60 to 64 years, to 92 per cent in those aged over 80. Woods (in a recent letter to the author) rightly stresses caution in using such unvalidated measures to reach decisions on which elderly individuals might benefit from therapy.

To enhance therapeutic communication with elderly people it follows however that the therapist should seek to:

(*1*) adopt a less abstract, interpretive approach

(*2*) compensate for reduction in memory for meaning

(*3*) adopt a flexible and often reduced session length

(*4*) focus on explicit, concrete and realistic goals

(*5*) focus on patients' emotional wavelength through both verbal and nonverbal means.

It has been demonstrated that responsivity to nonverbal affective stimuli is maintained, even in conditions of severe mental impairment, as reported by Hoffman *et al.* at a conference in 1985.

Social, physical and sensory impairments

Elderly clients, in addition to presenting psychological distress, often experience real physical and social limitations. Depression and physical ill health are closely related in older people (Bergmann, 1982). On the one hand physical illnesses may precipitate or present as depression. On the other hand the person may present as physically ill, with a number of somatic symptoms, which in fact are manifestations of depression. Patients' judgements of their physical health are often accurate and may even be more accurate than those of their physicians in predicting survival (Kay et al., 1966). With many elderly patients it is important for the psychologist to work closely with a medical colleague who can advise on the presence and the likely effects of the various physical disorders and of medications. For a fuller review of the relationships between physical and psychological factors in the presentation of functional disorder in the elderly the reader is referred to Woods and Britton (1985) and Wattis and Church (1986).

A further important difference from the younger client is likely to be in the experience of loss. The older patient is more likely to have undergone a greater number of losses than his younger counterpart and there is a close association between the experience of severe life events in general and depression. Severe life events include bereavement, life-threatening illness of someone close, disruption of other significant relationships and major personal illness as already discussed. Sensory loss of one form or another is so commonplace in the elderly population that it tends to be ignored. In extreme form, for example, registered blindness or deafness, such losses fall into the category of severe life events and can have a major impact on psychological well-being.

Murphy (1982) found for a large sample of elderly living in the community that the risk of developing depression was 25 per cent following one severe event, 44 per cent when a severe event occurred in the context of a marked personal health difficulty, and 50 per cent when a severe event was combined with a major social difficulty. Of those subjects with all three risk factors, 80 per cent developed depression. Coleman (1986) echoes these findings in his excellent longitudinal study of the role of reminiscence in the lives of elderly people. Feelings of depression and low morale as measured by the Life Satisfaction Index and the MMPI Depression Scale corresponded to both physical and social loss, in particular the loss of a spouse or on becoming housebound.

Levin (1967) has argued that the term 'loss' does not adequately describe the types of psychological stress involved in severe life events. He invokes the additional concepts of 'attack', 'restraint' and 'threat' to understand the impact of events. An elderly patient restricted to bed after a coronary, for example, may become depressed as a result of either this restricted activity ('restraint') or because of the coronary itself ('attack') or both. When it comes to therapy it is important to identify precisely what factor is triggering the reaction and this requires a differential diagnosis of 'stress' in terms of its meaning to the individual. For our bedfast patient the concept of 'threat' may be the more important, warning him or her of future loss, attack or restraint. Social adversity however, although related to depression in the elderly, should not be regarded as sufficient explanation for the symptoms or an indication that therapy will not be effective. Attention should be focused instead on the individual's attributional framework and on the influence of cognitive factors. This is discussed in more detail later.

The existence of real social and physical limitations, once assessed, does require a number of factors to be taken into account to enhance therapeutic contact. These include:

(*1*) Clear recognition of the patient's limitations.

(*2*) Flexibility of session location.

(*3*) Increased activity by the therapist – the assuming of greater initiative, even extending into direct intervention in the patient's life.

(*4*) Limited goals.

(*5*) Provision of formal social resources and support – to search for a rational balance between dependence and independence.

(*6*) Symbolic giving – the therapeutic relationship is offered as a partial substitute for some of the cumulative losses the person has experienced. The therapist is more prepared to talk about his or her own life, family etc.

(*7*) The correction of sensory deficits through prostheses and modified styles of staff to patient communication.

Sparacino (1979) expands on many of these points.

Attitudes and the concept of transference

Emery (1981) recommends an educational model to socialize the patient into treatment. The elderly patient is often not used to a 'talking' therapy and may be expecting medication or physical treatment. Often there is a perception of symptoms as due to ageing or physical illness rather than depression or anxiety. When entering into the therapist–patient relationship the patient takes with him or her characteristic attitudes and ways of relating to others derived from earlier life experiences. Transference phenomena also vary, depending on the type of clinical setting and the personality and age of the therapist (Verwoerdt, 1981). The latter may be seen as a parental figure, regardless of age differences or, more commonly, as belonging to the generation of the patient's children or grandchildren. The age difference may affect empathy and make it more difficult for the therapist to maintain an appropriate level of control in the relationship. It often takes considerable tact to shift from one dimension, say a deferential respect for the patient's age, experience and opinions to another where the therapist needs to prescribe specific advice and have this taken seriously. Some degree of dependence and attachment may need to be encouraged, giving the elderly patient confidence to face external difficulties and his or her own deficits in an adaptive fashion. The sense of control thus experienced by the patient in the therapeutic relationship may help combat fears of helplessness and enable a feeling of safety.

Goldfarb (1967) goes so far as to propose that the patient be permitted to regard the therapist as a parent surrogate. With the physically frail or mentally impaired patient positive transfer can be facilitated by the therapist doing simple day to day things with the patient – perhaps sharing a meal or assisting in a task such as tidying personal belongings. For the depressed patient with low self-esteem as much choice as possible should be given to the patient. Attention should be given to simple things like where the patient would like to sit, whether the curtains should be drawn, etc. Where depression or mental impairment prevents recall of personal experiences the therapist should avoid 'what and why' questions and instead cite the patient's experiences so that his/her (often unimpaired) recognition memory can be used to full advantage.

Many have commented that therapeutic work with elderly people is often compromised by the 'gerophobia' of the therapist. This view contends that a therapist's own unresolved fears of ageing and death make it difficult to relate to and work effectively, especially with the very old. The obvious constraints in having to set limited therapeutic goals and the contemporary cultural emphasis on youth and attractiveness are added burdens. The age gap can make empathy more difficult and how many of us are comfortable with physical touch as an aid to communicating with the very old and frail?

'Gerophobia' may overstate the case but all therapists need to review their own attitudes, expectations and behaviour from time to time. Hilderbrand (1986) is one of the few to recognize that elderly people often bring the skills and experiences of a lifetime into therapy and often make satisfying patients to work with.

Before turning to a more specific review of the psychological techniques that have been applied to functional disorders in the elderly it should be noted that psychologists have documented only a very limited involvement in the management of the *more severe* psychological and psychiatric disturbances that make up the bulk of repeated admissions to elderly units and which place the greatest burden upon health service resources. Church (1986) suggests that psychologists have failed to face the challenge of both applying psychological interventions in inpatient settings and adapting to a multi-level model of intervention. This model views biochemical, psychological and social interventions as different and co-existing rather than as competitive alternatives. The avoidance by psychologists of involvement with severe forms of disorder may help explain the views of many psychiatrists, of whom Post (1981) is typical, when he comments in relation to the treatment of depression: 'I have been unimpressed by the value of any therapies which do not attack the mood disorder at central nervous system level'.

THE PSYCHOLOGICAL TREATMENT OF ANXIETY

To allay anxiety all the therapeutic principles underlying the optimal therapist–patient relationship must be observed. Although there is relatively little reported work some studies have successfully applied behaviour therapy to cases of simple phobias and agoraphobia. The incidence of the latter is unreported but appears to be high in the elderly from this writer's experience. Woods (1982) reports success with a patient who was too anxious to go out of the house or do housework, using graded exposure with anxiety management. A group approach was used in which anxiety management skills were taught including relaxation techniques flexibly altered to take into account physical problems. The group went on a graded series of excursions away from the day-hospital and practised homework exercises between sessions.

In line with the principles of adjusting the environment to suit the patient and adopting more limited goals with older patients the treatment goal for elderly agoraphobics is often suitably modest, for example, being able to walk to the corner shop or being able to take the dog to the local park. Often the problem may be traced to a specific incident, perhaps a fall or a 'dizzy turn' when shopping. One particularly unfortunate woman treated by the present writer had experienced three traumatic episodes in quick succession when away from home. In the first, she fainted when shopping; in the second, she was knocked down by a car; and on the third occasion, she suffered a severe panic attack. In retrospect, increasing anxiety was apparent between these episodes and, by the time of referral, some six months after the panic attack, she was completely housebound. Treatment was only successful in getting her to walk in the garden and a short distance with her dog down the street. This particular case also illustrates the need to adopt a family or systems approach on some occasions. This patient's increased dependency was welcomed by her husband who had recently retired and taken enthusiastically to the business of shopping, cooking and cleaning! Attempts to alter the reinforcement he was providing for the *status quo* were singularly unsuccessful.

Thyer (1981) reports the successful treatment of a 70-year-old woman with a debilitating fear of dogs subsequent to being attacked by a large St Bernard. Prolonged *in vivo* exposure to dogs was used and anxiety reduced quickly during the first two sessions. After five sessions she was once again able to leave the house and no longer experienced nightmares or insomnia. Three years of verbal psychotherapy before this behavioural programme had not led to symptom alleviation. Hussian (1981) used 'stress inoculation training' to successfully treat four residents of an institution who experienced anxiety travelling in lifts. This involved the construction and practice of positive coping statements. Residents were encouraged to imagine themselves going into the lift whilst practising these positive self-statements. This was needed before *in vivo* graded exposure could be used and illustrates that imaginal procedures can be helpful with the elderly.

Verwoerdt (1981), among others, has stressed that *within* a comprehensive psychological treatment plan work is conducted on three main levels, none of which should be omitted. Individual psychotherapy, or 'throughput therapy', is the first necessary element in the total spectrum. The next is protective intervention: the breaking up of any vicious circles of interacting social, psychological and somatic factors, and adjusting the environment to the patient rather than vice versa ('input therapy'). The third level is involved with improving activity and action patterns ('output therapy'). Related to this is the premise of Church (1986) that levels *other* than the psychological, in particular the social and the biochemical, need to coexist in therapy to optimize the chance of success – the traditional multidisciplinary perspective. The following case illustrates the application of both these multilevel models to the treatment of an elderly woman with multiple problems revolving round severe anxiety.

Case 1

Mrs B was a 68-year-old widow from the Scottish Borders living alone in a small flat in the same block as her married daughter. She had a five-year history of suspected angina dating back to the death of her husband from cardiovascular disease. She experienced frequent attacks of 'chest pain' which occasioned her to ring her daughter and GP in a panic, especially late at night or early in the morning.

Extensive investigations, including stress testing and numerous ECG examinations, failed to show any abnormality. Interesting background information obtained at the first interview revealed that:

1. Mrs B had never gone through the normal grief process following the death of her husband. She had not attended his funeral, had never visited his grave, and frequently talked as if he were still alive. She talked about him at length during the first interview in a highly distressed fashion.

2. She had had numerous close experiences of death through cardiovascular disease. Several members of the family had died from cardiac arrests and she referred to herself as having a 'heart problem'. She was also frightened to bath alone for fear of an 'attack'.

3. She had never lived alone prior to the death of her husband. Living in a terraced street she had always had someone close by when he was at work. More recently she had, apparently, never experienced chest pain when on prolonged visits to a sister-in-law in Edinburgh. At other times, when living on her own, she became noticeably anxious in the evening, felt compelled to draw the curtains early, and retired to bed because she was unable to settle in the living room.

The problems identified for treatment were as follows:

1. unresolved grief
2. excessive dependency characterized by negative demands on daughter's family and GP leading to alienation of both and a tendency for daughter to avoid Mrs B
3. mis-labelling of chest pain as 'heart failure'
4. excessive anxiety when alone with suspected causal link to chest pain
5. inability to bath alone
6. lack of social activity.

Table 1 illustrates the multi-level approach to treatment negotiated between the relevant parties – the present writer, Mrs B, the GP and Mrs B's family. As noted earlier, 'input' refers to the adjustment of the environment to reduce demands on the patient, 'throughput' to the business addressed in psychotherapy and 'output' to activities demanded of the patient.

As is so frequently the case in treatment it took several sessions to build up this therapeutic strategy as a more detailed assessment of the problems gradually emerged. No data were collected to measure outcome but the concensus of opinion of all concerned was that an obvious improvement had resulted in all six identified problems.

A note should be made here on the particular appropriateness of bereavement counselling with elderly clients. A review by Parkes (1980) makes the point that supportive counselling can reduce the risk for a high-risk bereaved person to that of a low-risk person. Many elderly would fall into the high-risk category as defined by the presence of the following factors: a particularly traumatic bereavement, a highly ambivalent relationship with the deceased and the presence of another major concurrent life crisis. Worden (1983) reviews the techniques involved in grief counselling.

PSYCHOLOGICAL TREATMENT OF DEPRESSION

Depression remains the most common psychiatric disorder in the elderly (Kay *et al.*, 1966; Gurland, 1976; Gurland *et al.*, 1983) and up to two-thirds of admissions to acute psychiatric units for the elderly have a primary

Table 1. Multi-level treatment of an anxious elderly woman

	Input	*Throughput*	*Output*
Social	Increased visits to sister-in-law during winter months. GP provides regular monthly consultations. Daughter makes regular daily visit.	Social activities counselling.	Bake for daughter's family. Attend pensioners club. Invite grandchildren to help in baking, etc.
Psychological	Ongoing support from psychologist.	Grief therapy. Rational restructuring re. chest pain. Positive coping statements re. chest pain, relaxation training.	Graduated exposure to bathing and staying up longer in the evening.
Physical	Analgesics, tranquillizers.	Counselling on use of medication.	Patient to reduce extra demands on family and GP, i.e., not phone when having pain. Patient to assume greater control over when she takes medication.

diagnosis of depression. The exact prevalence is difficult to establish as this is dependent on the precise criteria used in diagnosis. Reliance cannot be placed purely on the numbers receiving formal psychiatric treatment as depression in the elderly is frequently missed by GPs (Williamson *et al.*, 1964; Kline, 1976). Of those cases diagnosed by GPs many are treated successfully without a psychiatric referral (Post, 1981). Hospitalized, depressed, elderly patients clearly constitute a more difficult group to treat with perhaps only 25–35 per cent making a sustained recovery (Post, 1972; Murphy, 1983). Re-admission rates are high while complete remission and good adjustment between episodes is rare. For a more complete review of the incidence, phenomenology and prognosis of depression in the elderly the reader is referred to Post (1981) and Hanley (1984). As a rough guide it can be taken that the prevalence of psychiatrically-diagnosed depression in the elderly is around 10 per cent while community samples employing less strict criteria report much higher figures (Murphy, 1983).

Psychiatric practice still rests heavily on physical treatments, notably tricyclic antidepressants, monoamine oxidase inhibitors and ECT. To make a contribution in this area, psychologists will have to fully understand and employ the multi-level model of depression (Akiskal and McKinney, 1975), typified by a case study reported by Church and Wattis at a conference in 1984. This is one of very few reports in which an obviously severe depression was tackled from a combined biochemical, psychological and social perspective.

Case 2

A 69-year-old married woman was admitted at a greater than yearly frequency with depressive illness (including four suicide attempts) in a 13-year period up to her admission in 1981. She suffered from severe depressive delusions, e.g., 'There is no blood in my body', 'I'm dead', tended to be negative and uncooperative and had very low self-esteem.

Table 2 shows the main interventions employed and their timing. Psychological aspects were tackled in different ways throughout the stages of her recovery. The behavioural component involved structuring an increase in staff-initiated contact with her, but a reduction in the time spent with her when she was being negative and uncooperative. The cognitive part of the programme involved nursing staff terminating their efforts to argue with the patient when she expressed delusional ideas and, instead, rationally restructuring in a positive fashion the patient's self statements and then walking away for a short period.

For example, *Nurse:* 'Let's get your hair done this afternoon and make it look nice'.

Patient: 'I'm no good, I'm ugly'.

Nurse: 'I know you believe that, but you are not ugly and I am not going to stay here and listen to you being hurtful to yourself like that'.

While no single intervention produced a dramatic change, neglecting any one might have led to a treatment failure or a partial response. Church and Wattis identified the social change as responsible for her continued well-being. After discharge it was possible to rehouse the woman closer to her daughter and grandchildren. This allowed her to regain the constructive life she had led prior to her children leaving home and her first episode of depression. Follow-up revealed she had been well for two years and without antidepressants for one year.

Table 2. Multi-level treatment of a depressed elderly woman

Intervention	Time span
1. Section for admission and treatment	1st wk–4th wk
2. Antidepressant therapy (amytryptyline)	1st wk–54th wk
3. Behavioural/cognitive strategy for delusions	3rd wk–9th wk
4. Counselling and advice for daughters	3rd wk onwards
5. Marital cotherapy (problem solving/cognitive)	9th wk onwards
6. Discharge and follow-up	19th wk onwards
(*a*) compliance	
(*b*) problem solving	
(*c*) gradual reduction in reliance on hospital staff	
7. Identification and treatment of new medical state (arthritis)	25th week
8. Social change (house move to live near daughter and grandchildren)	32nd week

Source: Church (1986). In Hanley and Gilhooly (1986), page 12. With permission.

Therapeutic realism combined with data from controlled trials with younger depressives (Blackburn *et al.*, 1981) would suggest that combined treatments hold the best prospect for successful interventions like the one just described, although evidence has been presented, again from trials with younger adults, that cognitive therapy alone is as effective as cognitive therapy combined with tricyclic antidepressants (Murphy *et al.*, 1984; Beck *et al.*, 1985; Rush *et al.*, 1977). The most useful summary of cognitive therapy with the elderly is presented by Thompson *et al.* (1986), who explore a range of special issues that require consideration in applying the techniques with other patients.

Evidence for the value of individual cognitive therapy (see Beck *et al.*, 1979) and individual behaviour therapy (modelled after Lewinsohn, 1974) when applied with elderly depressives has emerged from a controlled trial by Gallagher and Thompson (1982). Using the Hamilton Rating Scale for Depression and the Beck Depression Inventory they obtained substantial improvements with 16 sessions of therapy conducted over a 12-week period. Follow-up revealed that approximately two-thirds of those treated were still using specific skills learned in therapy to help them cope with potentially depressogenic situations that had occurred over time. Not surprisingly those patients who met the study's criteria for an endogenous type of depression responded less well than those not categorized as endogenous. A study comparing the efficacy of cognitive/behavioural therapy and treatment with antidepressants for a well defined sample of depressed elderly patients is urgently required. Gallagher and Thompson acknowledge that for cases of severe depression pharmacotherapy may act to reduce distress sufficiently for patients to effectively participate in cognitive therapy. Much more research is required before firm statements can be made concerning the factors that may be associated with differential treatment outcome, for example, initial intensity of depressed mood, endogeneity, background personality disorder.

Reference was made earlier to the link between stressful life events and a higher incidence of depression in the elderly (Murphy, 1983). A recent study by Lam *et al.* (1987) investigated the relationship between cognitive phenomenology and experienced adversity in depressed hospital patients and community controls. Dysfunctional attitudes, negative automatic thoughts and hopelessness were measured in four groups of subjects, namely depressed patients and controls who either had or had not experienced adversity, as established by the methods developed by Brown and Harris (1978). The depressed elderly reported more negative cognitions than the nondepressed elderly, supporting the view that the patterns found in younger depressed adults are equally characteristic of elderly samples. The other major finding was that social adversity was *not* related to depressive cognitions in either the clinical or community samples. This implies that physical illness or other adversity should not be regarded as a sufficient explanation for cognitive symptoms of depression. These results also indirectly support the use of cognitive therapy approaches, for which some success has been reported above, and confirm that cognitive measures can be sensibly employed for the purpose of patient selection.

The personal helplessness model of depression is a useful framework for explaining how individuals perceive and respond to life events. There is a direct link between cognitive distortions and the attribution of helplessness as per the reformulated model of Abramson *et al.* (1978).

FUNCTIONAL DISORDERS IN DEMENTIA

Emotional problems, in particular anxiety and depression, are frequently either overlooked in dementia or dismissed as untreatable consequences of central nervous system impairment. However, when efforts are made, either directly or indirectly, to tackle emotional disorder the results are often encouraging. Both Church (1984) and Hanley (1986) report successful single case treatments of confused and problematic behaviour in elderly female dementia patients whose admission to care had been triggered in both cases by the death of a spouse. Care was taken to ensure the formation of a good therapeutic relationship in these cases and also to attend in a sensitive fashion to the expressed wishes of the elderly patients themselves. Both were cognitively impaired and frequently became agitated, insisting that their husbands were alive and that they should be allowed home to look after them. Through the creative application of bereavement therapy methods in the context of reality orientation both became orientated to the reality of their loss, agitation reduced and behaviour problems were eliminated.

It has been argued that the reduction of emotional disturbance in dementia is a primary goal of reality orientation (RO) techniques (Hanley, 1984; Hanley, 1986). Further support for this view is also obtained from the work of Greene *et al.* (1983). They investigated the effects of providing psychogeriatric day patients with brief personal orientation sessions and adopted a well-controlled ABA single case study method. Independent behaviour ratings, conducted by casegivers at home, revealed significant improvement in the mood of patients during the RO phase. This, in.turn, seemed to have a causal effect in enhancing the mood of the caregivers themselves. This is an area worthy of further investigation.

CONCLUSION

Relatively little systematic work has been done on the psychological treatment of functional problems in the elderly. A number of single case studies demonstrate however that the treatment methods used for younger patients are equally applicable for the elderly providing they are modified to the individuals' needs viewed from the perspective of life-span developmental psychology. In general, a multi-level approach is advocated following the establishment of a sound psychotherapeutic relationship. In view of the higher rate of relapse in old-age depression and of the dangers of long-term antidepressant medication and other physical treatments in some older patients there is a great need to ensure a psychological component to treatment. Finally there is great scope for treating functional problems in elderly patients with dementia.

REFERENCES

ABRAMSON, L.Y., SELIGMAN, M.E.P. and TEASDALE, J.D. (1978). Learned helplessness in humans: critique and reformulation. *Journal of Abnormal Psychology, 87*, 49–74.

AKISKAL, H.S. and McKINNEY, W.T. (1975). Overview of recent research in depression. *Archives of General Psychiatry, 32*, 285–304.

BECK, A.T., RUSH, J.A., SHAW, B.F. and EMERY, G. (1979). *Cognitive Therapy of Depression*. New York: Guilford Press.

BECK, A.T., HOLLON, S., YOUNG, J., BEDROSIAN, R., and BUDEMY, D. (1985). Treatment of depression with cognitive therapy and amitriptyline. *Archives of General Psychiatry, 42*, 142–148.

BERGMANN, K. (1982). Depression in the elderly. In B. Isaacs (ed.) *Recent Advances in Geriatric Medicine, 2*. Edinburgh: Churchill Livingstone. 159–182.

BLACKBURN, I.M., BISHOP, S., GLEN, A., WHALLEY, L.S. and CHRISTIE, J. (1981). The efficacy of cognitive therapy in depression: a treatment trial using cognitive therapy and pharmacotherapy, each alone and in combination. *British Journal of Psychiatry, 139*, 181–189.

BROWN, G.W. and HARRIS, T.O. (1978). *Sound Origins of Depression*. London: Tavistock.

CHURCH, M. (1983). Psychological therapy with elderly people. *Bulletin of The British Psychological Society, 36*, 110–112.

CHURCH, M. (1984). Some aspects of bereavement counselling with elderly people. *Psychologists Special Interest Group in the Elderly Newsletter (The British Psychological Society), No. 12*, 6–9.

CHURCH, M. (1986). Issues in psychological therapy with elderly people. In I. Hanley and M. Gilhooly (eds) *Psychological Therapies for the Elderly*. London: Croom Helm.

COLEMAN, P.G. (1986). Issues in the therapeutic use of reminiscence with elderly people. In I. Hanley and M. Gilhooly (eds) *Psychological Therapies for the Elderly*. London: Croom Helm.

COLEMAN, P.G. (1987). *Ageing and Reminiscence Processes*. Chichester: John Wiley.

DAVIES, E.D.M. and CRISP, S.G. (1985). The Clinical Psychology of the Elderly. In M.S.J. Pathy (ed.) *Principles and Practice of Geriatric Medicine*. Chichester: John Wiley.

EMERY, G. (1981). Cognitive therapy with the elderly. In G. Emery, S.D. Hollon and R.C. Bedrosian (eds), *New Directions in Cognitive Therapy*. New York: Guilford, 84–98.

FREUD, S. (1905). *On Psychotherapy*. Standard Edition 7, London: Hogarth.

GALLAGHER, D. and THOMPSON, L.W. (1982). Treatment of major depressive disorder in older adult outpatients with brief psychotherapies. *Psychotherapy: Theory, Research and Practice, 19*, 482–490.

GARLAND, J. (1986). Promise or performance? Clinical psychology's contribution to the well being of older people in Britain. *Psychologists Special Interest Group in the Elderly Newsletter (The British Psychological Society), No. 21*, 12–18.

GARLAND, B.J., COPELAND, J., KURIANSKY, J., KELLEHER, M., SHARPE, L., and DEAN, L.L. (1983). *The Mind and Mood of Ageing: Mental Health Problems of the Community Elderly in New York and London*. London: Croom Helm.

GOLDFARB, A.I. (1967). Geriatric psychiatry. In A.M. Freedman and H.I. Kapean (eds) *Comprehensive Textbook of Psychiatry*. Baltimore: Williams and Wilkins. 1464–1487.

GREENE, J.G., TIMBURY, G.C., SMITH, R. and GARDINER, M. (1983). Reality orientation with elderly patients in the community: an empirical evaluation. *Age and Ageing, 12*, 38–43.

HANLEY, I.G. (1984). Understanding and treating depression in the elderly. In I. Hanley and J. Hodge (eds) *Psychological Approaches to the Care of the Elderly*. London: Croom Helm.

HANLEY, I.G. (1986). Reality orientation – three case studies. In I.G. Hanley and M. Gilhooly (eds) *Psychological Therapies for the Elderly*. London: Croom Helm.

HILDERBRAND, P. (1986). Dynamic psychotherapy with the elderly. In I. Hanley and M. Gilhooly, *Psychological Therapies for the Elderly*. London: Croom Helm.

HODGE, J. (1984). Towards a behavioural analysis of dementia. In I. Hanley and J. Hodge (eds) *Psychological Approaches to the Care of the Elderly*. London: Croom Helm.

HUSSIAN, R.A. (1981). *Geriatric Psychology: A Behavioural Perspective*. New York: Van Nostrand Reinhold.

JEFFERY, D. and SAXBY, P. (1984). Effective psychological care for the elderly. In I. Hanley and J. Hodge (eds) *Psychological Approaches to the Care of the Elderly*. London: Croom Helm.

KAY, D.W.K., BERGMANN, K., FOSTER, E. and GARSIDE, R.F. (1966). A four-year follow-up of a random sample of old people originally seen in their own homes: a physical, social and psychiatric enquiry. In *Proceedings of the 4th World Congress of Psychiatry*. Excerpta Medica. Excerpta Medica Intern. Congress Series No. 150. Amsterdam: 1668–1670.

KLINE, N. (1976). Incidence and prevalence and recognition of depressive illness. *Dissertations on the Nervous System*, *37*, 10.

LAM, D.H., BREWIN, C.R., WOODS, R.T. and BETTINGTON. P.E. (1987). Cognition and social adversity in the depressed elderly. *Journal of Abnormal Psychology*, *96*, 1.

LEVIN, S. (1967). Depression in the aged: the importance of external factors. In S. Levin and R.J. Kahanna, *Psychodynamic Studies in Ageing, Creativity, Reminiscing and Dying*. New York: International University Press.

LEWINSOHN, P.M. (1974). A behavioural approach to depression. In R. Freedman and M. Katy (eds) *The Psychology of Depression*. New York: Winston and Co.

MURPHY, E. (1982). Social origins of depression in old age. *British Journal of Psychiatry*, *141*, 135–142.

MURPHY, E. (1983). The prognosis of depression in old age. *British Journal of Psychiatry*, *142*, 111–119.

MURPHY, G.E., SIMMS, A.D., WETZEL, R. and LUSTMAN, P. (1984). Cognitive therapy and pharmacotherapy, singly and together in the treatment of depression. *Archives of General Psychiatry*, *41*, 33–41.

PARKES, C.M. (1980). Bereavement counselling. *British Medical Journal*, *281*, 3–6.

POST, F. (1972). The management and nature of depressive illness in late life: A follow-through study. *British Journal of Psychiatry*, *121*, 393–404.

POST, F. (1981). Affective Illnesses. In T. Arie (ed.) *Health Care of the Elderly*. London: Croom Helm.

RUSH, A.J., BECK, A., KOVAIS, M. and HOLLON, S. (1987). Comparative efficacy of cognitive therapy and pharmacotherapy in the treatment of depressed outpatients. *Cognitive Therapy and Research*, *1*, 17–37.

SIMPSON, S., WOODS, R.T. and BRITTON, P.G. (1981). Depression and engagement in a residential home for the elderly. *Behavioural Research and Therapy*, *19*, 435–438.

SPARACINO, J. (1979). Individual psychotherapy with the aged: A selective review. *International Journal of Ageing and Human Development*, *9*, 197–220.

TATHAM, A. (1984). Survey of psychologists working with elderly people. *Psychologists Special Interest Group in the Elderly Newsletter (The British Psychological Society)*, No. 12, p. 15.

THOMPSON, L.W., DAVIES, R., GALLAGHER, D. and KRANTY, S.E. (1986). Cognitive therapy with older adults. In T. Brink (ed.) *Clinical Gerontology: a Guide to Assessment and Intervention*. New York: The Haworth Press.

THYER, B.A. (1981). Prolonged in vivo exposive therapy with a 70-year-old woman. *Journal of Behaviour Therapy and Experimental Psychiatry, 12*, 69–71.

TONER, H.L. (1985). Manpower figures for psychologists working with the elderly in Scotland. *Division of Clinical Psychology Newsletter, The British Psychological Society, 49*, 23–27.

VERWOERDT, A. (1981). Psychotherapy for the elderly. In T. Arie (ed.), *Health Care of the Elderly*. London: Croom Helm.

WALKER, S. (1982). An Investigation of the Communication of Elderly Subjects. M. Phil. thesis, University of Sheffield.

WATTIS, J.P. and CHURCH, M. (1986). *Practical Psychiatry of Old Age*. London: Croom Helm.

WILLIAMSON, J., STOKOE, I.H., GRAY, S., FISHER, M., SMITH, A., McGHEE, A. and STEPHENSON, E. (1964). Old people at home: their unreported needs. *Lancet, 1*, 1117–1120.

WOODS, R.T. (1982). The psychology of ageing: assessment of defects and their management. In R. Levy and F. Post (eds) *The Psychiatry of Late Life*. Oxford: Blackwell. 68–113.

WOODS, R.T. and BRITTON, P.G. (1985). *Clinical Psychology with the Elderly*. London: Croom Helm.

WORDEN, J.W. (1983). *Grief Counselling and Grief Therapy*. London: Tavistock.

CLINICAL WORK WITH ETHNIC MINORITIES

Brigid MacCarthy

Britain is now a multi-cultural society. At the 1981 census, 6.3 per cent of the population was born outside Britain, but in many inner city areas about one third of the population belong to immigrant households. Within this significant minority individuals hold diverse relationships with indigenous British society. Each ethnic group has a unique history, shaped by the circumstances surrounding their migration, the attitudes prevalent in Britain when they first arrived, and the degree to which they themselves welcome assimilation. Recent migrants include refugees, transitory workers, students, and permanent voluntary settlers. Second and third generation, British-born children of migrants represent an increasingly important subgroup, whose attitudes towards the assimilation of British culture are still more diverse than those of their parents. Ethnic minorities, therefore, are far from homogeneous. However, it is the problems they have in common, rather than issues specific to particular cultures which are discussed here.

Ethnic identity is assumed to be a natural rather than a social fact, which is determined by skin colour and cultural background. In practice, however, ideological, political and economic interests combine to define groups which might not otherwise be discriminated by genetics or culture (Cohen, 1974). The drive to sort the social world into in-groups and out-groups appears to be universal, but inter-group differences based on perceived ethnic identity can be played down or emphasized as ideology dictates. Faith in a melting-pot ideology and colour-blindness has given way to active recognition of ethnic differences. However, individuals do not belong exclusively to discrete ethnic groups, but rather to a *set* of cultural groups (Bochner, 1982) and the extent to which each person feels part of an ethnic minority varies with time and context.

Very few trained clinical psychologists working in the UK belong to an ethnic minority. Clinical psychologists are likely, therefore, to find themselves sometimes working with patients whose culture is substantially different to their own. This issue is rarely confronted in research or professional discussion (Bird, 1986). To date there has been no survey of the effectiveness of services offered by psychologists to ethnic minorities in Britain, although there is a burgeoning American literature on the subject (for example Atkinson, 1985; Pedersen, 1985; Wilkinson, 1986).

As clinical psychologists are rarely the primary contact in mental health services, they have less contact with ethnic minorities than do other professionals. However, psychologists involved with service planning and assessment have to confront issues arising from differences between host and sending populations in rates of disorders, cultural differences in the expression of and response to disturbance, and use of services. Psychologists treating individuals, families or groups from ethnic minorities have to work with unfamiliar symbolic systems, and different world views, expectations and values. Also, in all settings both therapists and their patients have to deal with the consequences of implicit or explicit racist beliefs – categorical assumptions which interfere with the perception of others as individuals.

EPIDEMIOLOGICAL FACTORS

Overall, migrants and their British born descendants are no freer of psychological disturbance than the indigenous population, yet, except in certain specialized services, they are relatively rarely referred to psychologists for assessment or treatment. In the US, by the early 1970s, a similar pattern of under-referral and under-use was changed by the growth of an urban, self-confident and more assertive middle-class black population and by the development of community mental health programmes. Black and Hispanic Americans began to ask for their fair share of mental health services. As the process of acculturation develops in Britain, and British-born descendants of migrants make up the majority of ethnic minority groups, the American experience is likely to be repeated here.

Some mental health professionals have more contact with minority groups than would be predicted by the proportion of the population represented by minorities, and some have less contact, depending on the clinical setting in which they work (Harrison *et al.*, 1984). Adequately controlled studies which correct for age and sex (Malzburg, 1969) indicate that overall, immigrants and their descendants have similar rates of disturbance as the indigenous population. Asian groups show a prevalence roughly equivalent to, or slightly below the indigenous population for major psychiatric illnesses while Afro-Caribbeans and Africans have an increased likelihood of being given such a diagnosis, but tend to recover rapidly. All immigrant groups show an increased admission rate for schizophrenia. Apart from the Irish and the Greeks, most immigrant groups present a lower rate of minor disorders than the indigenous population. Minority group members are referred proportionally less often to out-patient settings, and tend to be poor attenders when they are referred (Harrison *et al.*, 1984).

Three kinds of arguments have been advanced to explain putative differences.

1. Base rates in the sending society may differ from that of the host society, because of genetic or cultural differences. Although rates for schizophrenia round the world have proved to be remarkably similar (Sartorius *et al.*, 1986) there is more variation in rates of depression between first and third world centres, and between urban and rural environments. However, the phenomenology, course and prognosis of both disorders show the effect of cultural variation even when Western diagnostic procedures are used, which mask differences in identification and response to disturbance (Cooper and Sartorius, 1977).

2. Selection may influence the likelihood that a psychiatrically-disturbed individual will migrate. Pre-existing abnormalities were originally thought to lie behind the impulse to emigrate, but, in some circumstances only the most competent were able to migrate. Only a detailed knowledge of the factors which prompted specific minorities to migrate can predict the direction of this effect (Rack, 1982).

3. The stress of migration such as the loss of familiar culture, language or social networks may increase vulnerability to disturbance. However, the stress of migration depends on the circumstances of departure, and the fit between aspirations and opportunity in the host country. For instance, a lowly-paid industrial job may still satisfy the aspirations of immigrants from a peasant culture, but West Indian women with white collar qualifications, who are forced to take on full-time menial work are likely to feel that it violates strong conventions about the importance of family life (Rack, 1982). Disturbance and breakdown occur more frequently in migrants only after several years in the host country, which suggests that if migrants are subject to special stresses, these are related more to the long-term process of acculturation, rather than the immediate impact of changing countries. The more obvious stress of living with pervasive social and economic disadvantage and the consequences of racism are likely to increase rates of disturbance and may even affect British-born minority group members more profoundly than the generations who migrated. Ambiguous attitudes to assimilation of white culture and aspirations constantly frustrated by racism may increase vulnerability to severe disturbance, particularly if individuals do not have a strong allegiance to a separate, positive ethnic identity (McGovern and Cope, 1987).

Research findings have been inconsistent (see London, 1986, for a thorough review). Local patterns of service provision and the ethnic composition of the population served, cohort effects due to acculturation, shifts in attitudes and policies affecting minorities, and difficulty in devising satisfactory experimental methods have all contributed to this. In Britain, surveys have concentrated on migrants, and on those already in contact with services, usually with in-patient facilities. As a result, the particular problems of non-migrant minority groups have been ignored and information about the 'true' prevalence of the full range of disorders in the community is limited.

Questions about differential uptake of services have rarely been addressed. Culturally-determined variations in the expression of distress, attitudes to seeking professional help, the use made of indigenous healers and the effects of racism all play a part in this.

The expression of distress is governed by language and cultural norms, which allow certain demonstrations of discomfort and repress others. For example, it was long believed that Africans had a different psychology to Westerners, which prevented their experiencing depression (Littlewood and Lipsedge, 1982). Subsequently, sensitivity to the ethnocentrism of this assumption has led to the realization that depression may be differently expressed in other cultures. Non Westerners express much psychic distress either by literal somatization, or through somatic metaphors. In contrast, Westerners use more mentalistic metaphors and psychological symptoms to express distress (Marsella, 1979). Western doctors often respond only to the physical symptoms, so that the psychological aspects of the complaint are neglected. This may partly explain the apparently low rate of minor psychiatric disorders in African and Asian groups. Although Asians visit their GPs at least as frequently as their white neighbours, they are less often given a psychiatric diagnosis or treatment (Murray and Williams, 1986).

At the other extreme, both African and Afro-Caribbean groups have apparently higher rates of schizophrenia than the native, white population. British-born Afro-Caribbeans are very much more likely to be given a psychotic diagnosis than both immigrants and white Britons (for example, McGovern and Cope, 1987). However the phenomenology and prognosis for many of these patients has shown that 'atypical psychotic reaction' might be a more appropriate label. The onset is often acute; violently-disturbed behaviour and delusions with a subcultural content are more common. This may go some way towards explaining why Afro-Caribbeans are over-represented in emergency services, compulsory admissions and inpatient facilities. However, the resolution of the acute disturbance is both faster and different to that of nuclear schizophrenia since depressive features emerge as the person recovers (Littlewood and Lipsedge, 1981).

A greater suspicion of psychiatry and fear of stigma, plus culturally-valued coping preferences for cheery denial, repression or self-reliance may partly account for low rates of referral or attendance in informal services (Maultsby, 1982). Cultural factors also set the threshold for labelling behaviour as disturbed: signs of internal, psychological distress which do not impinge on social behaviour are seen as deserving professional attention only in Western middle-class society (Heller *et al.*, 1980). Admission may be delayed until disturbance becomes so severe that it is unavoidable. Thus an unfortunate cycle of fear and stigma is created for some minority groups, as psychiatric services become exclusively associated with violence and extremes of insanity.

Informal support systems, or indigenous 'folk' healers may be used, particularly for the treatment of minor, or more nebulous distress. Over 200 hakim serve the Indian community in Britain, and obeah seems to be used occasionally by Afro-Caribbeans (Rack, 1982) The scale and effectiveness of these alternative services, usually used in conjunction with mainstream services, has not been established. Some communities, such as the Chinese, and Hasidic Jews insulate themselves from most aspects of British life, including psychiatric services, so that very little is known about either the prevalence of disturbance or mental health practices in these groups (Watson, 1977).

Finally, racist attitudes have an impact on the use of services by minority groups. Unusual behaviour, particularly if the subject has a distinctive skin colour, is more apparent and readily pathologized in a prejudiced society. For instance, the effects of this process have been noted in school-teachers' responses to West Indian children's behaviour (Cochrane, 1979). Mental health professionals are subject to many of the same biases: diagnostic and treatment decisions are influenced by assumptions based on racial stereotypes, even when the personnel are themselves from an ethnic minority (Littlewood and Lipsedge, 1982).

COGNITIVE AND ATTITUDINAL DIFFERENCES

Some features of cognition and, specifically, of the process of psychotherapy appear to be universals. However, concepts, values and goals which profoundly affect expectations and experience of assessment and treatment do show considerable variation.

Unconcsious ethnocentric bias may cause professionals to mistake Western, dominant ways of thinking for universals. Unless psychologists are aware of the impact of culture on such factors, mutual incomprehension and failure may be mistakenly attributed to individual dynamics.

Ideas about illness and mental disorder, about causality and control in the natural world and about the nature of personhood differ significantly between cultures. Norms and values governing behaviour and roles also vary widely. Differences in vocabulary and grammar both reflect and constitute fundamental differences in how the world is construed.

The relative salience of cause, symptom and course in providing an adequate diagnosis differs considerably. In Western medicine, eliciting and categorizing symptoms, particularly physical symptoms, are key aspects of the diagnostic process, and are expected to precede the formulation of treatment plans, whereas non-Western cultures are more interested in why the illness occurred (Comoroff, 1978). Western thinking is particularly oriented to providing physical explanations for illness, including psychiatric disorder, whereas traditional societies have looked to social relationships to account for disturbance. How health and illness are explained not only indicates an appropriate mode of intervention, but also apportions moral responsibility and exemption from blame in order to manage the relationship between the sick person and the social environment (Parsons, 1964). Morgan (1975) argues that in the West, the physical world seems controllable and predictable, and therefore explanations couched in physical terms carry conviction and reassurance, while in traditional societies, since the physical world is a mystery, the social world seems safer, more controllable and better able to explain frightening phenomena.

Moral attitudes towards illness vary considerably between cultures. In the West, people are encouraged to attribute problems to intra-psychic factors, and to seek a cure through self-examination, although this varies with class and disease (Pill and Stott, 1982; Helman, 1984). Psychiatric illness, particularly if it is chronic, is often attributed to internal factors, to which blame is attached (Mechanic, 1975). Non-Western cultures, however, appraise the symptoms of (for instance) schizophrenia, less judgementally and see its effect on the person as more circumscribed. Perhaps as a consequence of this, families are more willing to accommodate to the needs of discharged patients, and seem able to find appropriate unstressful roles which minimize the rate of relapse (Cooper and Sartorius, 1977; Jenkins *et al.*, 1986).

Concepts of personhood show much cross-cultural variation. The distinction between mind and body, the definition of a self-conscious subject of experience and the relationship between the human self and the behavioural environment, are fixed by culture. Generally, Western culture has a highly mentalistic model of the person: individuals are autonomous and exist prior to social relationships. By contrast, more holistic societies mute recognition of the individual and the inner self, stressing social roles in defining identity (White, 1982). Emotions, which are private experiences, located within the inner self in individualistic cultures, are often externalized in traditional cultures and located in the relationship between the subject and object of the feeling (Pina-Cabral, 1986).

Beliefs about control and its value also vary. Agency is located in the outside world, in a variety of real and imaginary phenomena: blame for failure may be attributed to witches, ancestors or the spirit world. Passive acceptance of fate is often prescribed, and the struggle to gain autonomy or control is regarded as spiritual failure (Bharati, 1985). Disadvantaged minorities within Western cultures may also believe in external control (Porter and Washington, 1979; Pill and Stott, 1982). Such beliefs help to form expectations about the therapeutic process.

Differences in symbolic systems prevent clear communication and the establishment of accurate empathy and depth of self-disclosure. Paradoxically, problems are less acute when differences are most obvious. Subtle misinterpretations of words or gestures which appear familiar disrupt therapeutic relationships more than blank incomprehension (Draguns, 1981). Non-verbal behaviour can also be confusing. Gestures can have radically different implications and a protective coping strategy may be misinterpreted as rudeness or stupidity (Caldwell-Colbert and Jenkins, 1982).

Comparison of curing practices in traditional and Western cultures show that some features of psychotherapeutic encounters are universal (Lévi-Strauss, 1968; Torrey, 1978). Naming and explaining disorder, gratifying a need for acceptance and warmth, exercising status and prestige, communicating understanding to the client in order to generate perceptions of therapists' competence and concern, and the intention to produce change through mobilizing endogenous resources seem to be universal (Draguns, 1981). However, conflicting expectations about the process or outcome of a consultation or treatment influence its content, duration and outcome (Goldstein, 1981). Western beliefs and values predispose the therapist to take personal growth as an ultimate aim of treatment, and expect patients to achieve it through self-exploration. Yet patients may expect or prefer explicit directives and rapidly achieved improvement in functioning.

Therapist credibility, derived from perceptions of expertise, trustworthiness and attractiveness is an important process variable which is threatened in cross-cultural work (Sue, 1981). Credibility is most readily ascribed and easily achieved when the level of perceived similarity between psychologist and client is high. Perceptions of ethnic dissimilarity encourage a process of de-individuation in which behaviour is attributed to cultural determinants. Individual differences are ignored, yet attributions for events and behaviour are biased towards personal, i.e., racial, rather than situational factors (Bochner, 1982). Psychologists may place too much emphasis on issues related to clients' genetic origins which are irrelevant to their individual adjustment (Sue and Zane, 1987).

Since psychologists usually belong to the dominant culture, the hierarchy implicit in consultative or therapeutic relationships may reproduce that in society at large. This can create problems for minority group clients who may be struggling with issues of low self-esteem, fear or resentment generated by racism (Maultsby, 1982). Perceived differences in race lead to lower levels of self-disclosure, exploration and satisfaction with treatment and discourage clients from returning for further help (for example, Banks, 1971). The drop out rate after one session runs at 50 per cent for Blacks, Hispanics, and native Americans, compared to 30 per cent for the 'white' population in the US (Sue, 1977). Similar findings are reported in Britain (Harrison *et al.*, 1984).

PROBLEMS IN ASSESSMENT AND TREATMENT APPROACHES

a. Assessment

Cultural bias has been identified in the form and content of tests, their administration procedures, and the usage to which they are put. Although controversy has mainly focused on intelligence and attainment testing with children, cultural biases in personality and behavioural assessments have also been identified.

On most commonly used IQ tests, non-Caucasians' mean scores are about one standard deviation below those of middle-class Caucasians. This finding has formed the basis of a long-running battle about the relationship between race and intelligence (see, for example, Jensen, 1980). On the one hand it is argued that due to cultural bias, the tests underestimate the abilities of ethnic minorities, and on the other, that test results show up the unfairness of the effects of economic and social deprivation which prevent non-dominant ethnic groups from realizing their full potential. There have been many attempts to design culture-fair tests which give children an equal chance to demonstrate their true abilities. Stimulus materials are used which avoid or balance culture-specific references. Procedures which minimize the use of unfamiliar linguistic forms, and do not penalize test-taking attitudes which may reflect cultural values, such as a reluctance to work at speed, have been devised. Equal weight is given to skills at which minority groups are known to excel (Kaufman, 1984). Finally, the use to which such test results are put have been questioned. Although the tests appear to have predictive validity, since their results correlate with subsequent attainment, the effects of the cycle of deprivation and of self-fulfilling prophesies on individual and group achievements are likely to account for much of the apparent strength of the correlations.

Given this, do standardized attainment tests have any useful role in clinical work with ethnic minorities? Preference should be given to those tests which are designed to be culture fair, and only norms appropriate to the ethnicity of the assessee should be employed. Psychologists working frequently with particular minority groups might develop their own set of norms, formally or informally. A very comprehensive range of abilities should be assessed, using verbal and non-verbal and structured and unstructured interview strategies. Extrapolation from results to actual or potential abilities must be made very cautiously, and extrinsic comparisons avoided, particularly in discussions with those involved with the child in the long term.

Cultural norms and child-rearing practices are thought to influence acquisition of certain stable personality traits. Anthropologists have had limited success in demonstrating systematic variations which can be confidently linked to cultural factors (Leighton and Hughes, 1961). However, standardized self-report personality tests are subject to the same caveats about item content, test-taking attitudes and construct validity as attainment tests and can only be interpreted if relevant norms are available. Some symptom rating scales have been carefully validated for use with culturally distinct groups (for example, Orley *et al.*, 1979; Sen *et al.*, 1987). However, they may not accurately reflect the subjective impact of the rated level of disturbance since cultural factors, which cannot be measured by such scales, play a significant part in managing illness behaviour (Kleinman, 1987). Thus, the use of standardized instruments generally raises complex difficulties in cross-cultural assessment and cannot substitute for face-to-face, culturally-sensitive interviewing.

b. Behaviour modification

Because it avoids mentalistic constructs by focusing on objectively-observable phenomena, and since culture has been defined as a matrix of socially-determined reinforcers (Bochner, 1982), behaviour modification seems peculiarly well-adapted to cross-cultural work. Programmes which have successfully treated individuals and groups from ethnic minorities have been reported (Turner, 1982).

However, behaviour modification has been viewed with suspicion, particularly by those groups with a history of oppression or exploitation by the dominant culture (Maultsby, 1982). Issues of control and manipulation, with overtones of a master/slave relationship which, to the general public seem to be key features of behavioural procedures, are highly salient for such populations. Psychologists working in community settings are recommended to use behavioural principles to shape both staff and recipient attitudes to this treatment approach before introducing specific programmes. There is also a fear that applications of behavioural procedures will teach minority members to adapt to a maladaptive environment. Behavioural theory has been criticized for ignoring the social and political level of analysis, and therefore having little to say about how to modify institutions and environmental conditions which contribute to psychopathology. (Saafir, 1982).

Attempts to use social skills assessment and treatment with non-Caucasian populations has highlighted the lack of cultural specificity in the stimulus content and norms of both self-report questionnaires and observer-rated behavioural assessments. Assertiveness and dating behaviour are highly charged areas, and appropriate cues are easily missed or misinterpreted by observers unfamiliar with the informal social norms and values and non-verbal behaviour of another culture. White observers rated the assertiveness of black subjects considerably lower than black observers in video-taped assessments (Turner *et al.*, 1984). Black Americans have developed patterns of assertive behaviour which are designed to confuse or mislead the white majority in a society which has punished assertiveness in minorities assigned a low status. Social skills checklists in common use have been shown to sample some irrelevant situations and score some responses wrongly (Caldwell-Colbert & Jenkins, 1982). Culture-specific measurement instruments and norms are needed. Fellow group-members and therapists who share the patient's culture are essential if behavioural feedback is to reflect cultural norms accurately.

Sexuality is also governed by a number of culturally-specific beliefs and practices. Expectations about both male and female sexuality are highly diverse, and each culture carries myths about the appetite and potency of each sex. Preferences for particular styles of intercourse, and the boundary defining perversity also vary (Tucker, 1982). Attempts to modify sexual behaviour in the direction of the therapist's norms may be deeply offensive or threatening, while therapists themselves may risk being offended by culturally-determined sexual stereotypes which contrast with their own beliefs. Careful preliminary negotiation of treatment targets with individual clients, and a willingness to work within a set of expectations which are not the therapist's own, are prerequisites.

c. Family therapy

Some theorists appear to believe that structures which signal health in Western, nuclear families are universally healthy. In nuclear families, clear differentiation between generations, close bonding within the immediate family, together with developing independence among the children are all signs of good functioning, while enmeshment is pathological. However, the form and content of roles in families differ substantially between cultures. Obligation, mutual dependence, and continuing loyalty to the parental family may be prescribed and greater or lesser flexibility in roles and definition of between-generational boundaries may be tolerated than is acceptable within Western middle-class families (Lau, 1984). In the 1960s and 70s in the States and in Britain, black family structures were regarded as deficient and blamed for providing a disadvantaging environment for children. More recently, the strengths of their strong kinship networks and adaptability have been recognized: ties of blood rather than marriage define the stable family unit. Single parent and extended family types are more common and acceptable in some cultures than they are in the majority of British culture. Roles within the family may be distributed differently – the 'parental child', apparently common in black American and Afro-Caribbean families, is one example of this. However, there is also potential for diverse structures within cultures, as families evolve through their life-cycle (Hodes, 1985).

Therapists working with families from unfamiliar cultures are faced, therefore, with a problem of distinguishing functional from dysfunctional systems. Since they are often prescriptive in their approach, family therapists may inadvertently challenge systems which are culturally valued and functional because they seem pathological from a different cultural perspective. The communicative power of symptoms in the identified patient is a useful tool in family work but in an unfamiliar culture, the symbolic value of a symptom or the end it seeks to achieve, can be easily misunderstood (Lau, 1984).

Conflict between generations within immigrant families often concerns the issue of acculturation and how closely the family should keep to the old tradition. Objects or ways of behaving may become symbols of the parental and of the new culture. Parents often feel powerless to assert their authority or provide a model for their children who may be more confident in the host culture than they are themselves. Where acculturation is at the centre of conflict, therapists who are not of the same culture are unlikely to win the trust of all family members sufficiently to establish a working alliance.

Family life is often thought to be a private area, which should not be exposed to the public gaze, so that attempts to interview or treat whole families may be experienced as prying or threatening. Antagonism between the Afro-Caribbean community and the state over child-care and adoption issues in recent years has contributed to suspicion of family interventions. In the United States, black families seem to be resistant to family therapy, but often only attend because they have been forced to by other agencies. Difficulties arising during the process of initial engagement should not be interpreted as resistance. Preliminary exploration of family structures with genograms (diagrams of the family tree), and delaying intimate questioning until considerable trust has been established has been recommended (Boyd-Franklin, 1984). Short-term problem-focused contracts, which aim to make existing structures more functional without expecting fundamental changes in personality or family systems, are reported to be more acceptable and a flexible attitude to lateness and absenteeism has encouraged black families to remain in treatment.

d. *Cognitive-behaviour therapy*

Cognitive therapists assume that mental illness is fundamentally a disorder of thinking. The exploration of a patient's cognitive 'set' identifies underlying premises, assumptions and attitudes which influence behaviour. Many beliefs and values which compose this 'set' are culturally determined. Patients may assume that social mores are logical necessities rather than arbitrary conventions, in a way which prevents them thinking clearly about their present experience and future options. The focus of intervention is the presence of maladaptive ideas or the absence of problem-solving and coping skills. Techniques such as verifying assumptions and generating alternative solutions are particularly useful in cross-cultural work, since the acceptability of a range of behavioural options within specific social contexts can be explored as an integral part of therapy. These are useful techniques for addressing problems of adaptation which arise through migration and acculturation. Therapist and patient can pool their knowledge of their separate cultures in order to clarify the arbitrary but culturally-given basis for assumptions, and generate solutions to the problems posed by living between two cultures.

However, despite the relativism implicit in cognitive psychology, cognitive therapy, paradoxically, often relies on prescribing 'healthy' ways of thinking. Moral authority is vested in the beliefs and values of the therapist, and passed on to the patient through a system of rhetoric (Totman, 1982). Major figures in the field speak of teaching people to think straight, or to think more logically and rationally (Goldfried and Goldfried, 1980), which makes the approach particularly susceptible to ethnocentric bias. The affective impact of many cognitions partly depends on the set of beliefs and values shared by a salient social group. Some of the healthy thoughts prescribed by cognitive therapists may be congruent with the values and experiences of middle-class whites in America or Britain, but clash damagingly with the world views and practical and economic experience of many ethnic minorities.

The struggle for personal control in the external world is of great importance in an individualistic society, and is also at present a realistic possibility for middle-class whites. The sense of self-blame in the face of failure or misfortune is thus likely to be peculiarly depressing, and success attributed to personal factors peculiarly gratifying. However, in several Asian cultures, with a background in Buddhist or Hindu beliefs, merging the autonomous self with a general fate, mastering personal ambition, as well as honouring the rights and duties owed to others are core prescriptions (Bharati, 1985). Even among highly Westernized Japanese, theories and coping strategies contained in the cognitive approach are unrecognizable or unwelcome (Weisz *et al.*, 1984). If patients are encouraged to acquire a set of cognitions which contradict those prevailing in their social network, the new skills are unlikely to generalize outside treatment sessions.

For disadvantaged minorities living in a relatively choiceless world, the experience of hopelessness and helplessness is common and appears to arise from a realistic appraisal of their situation. However, this helplessness is usually attributed to universal rather than personal factors, so that self-esteem, which is severely threatened in such circumstances can be preserved (Porter and Washington, 1979). Universal helplessness encourages low outcome expectations, however, since no response seems likely to produce a desirable outcome (Green, 1982). While cognitive methods may help individuals who blame themselves for circumstances beyond their control to identify the potential for change both at a personal and social level, there is a danger that an approach which encourages the search for personal auton-omy may increase distress by cutting across adaptive cognitions held by socially-disadvantaged patients. For instance, one such patient remarked: 'You want me to stop feeling anything' (Beck and Emery, 1979).

With minority group patients, the emphasis in this approach should avoid prescribing specific positive cognitions or proscribing negative ones, but concentrate instead on challenging the style of negative thinking, making it less ruminative, intrusive and inhibiting. With this emphasis, cognitive therapy can be as compatible with Buddhist values as with those of Amer-ican 'enterprise' culture.

e. Psychoanalysis

Cultures which place less value on the existence of the autonomous indi-vidual also have less faith in the power of insight to produce change. Psychoanalysis is the indigenous psychology of the West, since it emphasizes the split between the external and internal world, and between the mind and body (Cunningham and Tickner, 1981). The isolated, self-conscious ego, which is the subject of many transactions in psychoanalysis may be unavail-able to introspection, or unrecognizable when its boundaries extend to include spirits, ancestors, or aspects of the physical environment. Analysts' attempts to apply Freudian ideas in Africa has led to controversy, and some profound criticism of the cultural specificity of the theory. Some workers have felt that useful work can be done, providing analysts are aware of how radically different notions of the self can be (Ortigues, 1973). Others argue that basic tenets of the theory, such as the structure of the Oedipal situation and the intensity of the feelings it generates depend on features of economic and political power relations which exist only in capitalist systems (for example, Deleuze and Guattari, 1977).

Feelings which arise in the transference may reflect hierarchical rela-tionships which are partly a product of racism and which are a potent source of stress for the patient. Since analytic work relies on elucidating and con-taining such feelings within the therapist–patient relationship, its techniques may be well equipped to handle these painful issues. There is a danger that the process of containment and working through may teach a patient to accept unsatisfactory circumstances passively, but it can release constructively focused energy necessary to create a more facilitative environment.

Unresolved countertransference based on explicit or unrecognized racial attitudes may distort the therapeutic relationship. Attempts to assuage guilt by over-identification with the patient's culture, or avoidance of confronta-tion, as well as insistence on the universality of a patient's problems, thereby ignoring their culturally-specific features have been cited as manifestations of racially-based countertransference (Griffith, 1977). Repeatedly, workers experienced in the field emphasize the importance of therapists developing insight into the extent of their own racial prejudices.

TRAINING AND SERVICE DEVELOPMENT

How mental health services might adapt to the needs of minority groups has rarely been discussed in the British literature. (See Rack, 1982, and Littlewood and Lipsedge, 1982, as notable exceptions.) By contrast, American psychologists passed a formal resolution in 1974 which stated that counselling culturally diverse individuals without specialist training was unethical. Since then, the pitfalls and efficacy of the process have been energetically researched, without having much influence on clinical practice (Casas *et al.*, 1986; Sue and Zane, 1987). Despite this, the American literature can offer guidelines about how we might modify training, service planning and treatment techniques, to develop a more culturally-responsive network of services (see chapters in Marsella and Pedersen, 1981, Turner and Jones, 1982, and Jackson, 1983, for accounts of innovative projects).

There can be no substitute for ensuring that patients who seek assessment or treatment see a psychologist from their own culture. The percentage of psychologists from ethnic minorities, working in the health and social services in Britain is unknown, but in the States, a recent survey showed that less than 5 per cent of mental health workers and a still smaller proportion of researchers in the field were non-Caucasian (Maultsby, 1982). The proportions in Britain seem likely to be even less fairly representative. Clearly a drive to recruit ethnic minority trainees is needed. However, many of the research and therapeutic paradigms used in professional psychology are highly culture-specific. Unless more radical changes in undergraduate and graduate curricula are made, the chances are that trainees will only be offerred a white, middle-class psychology on which to base their practice. Cultural awareness training packages have been devised in the States, but have not so far effectively increased therapists' acceptability across cultures (Christensen, 1984). Multi-cultural issues in education are given considerable attention in teacher-training courses in Britain. These might serve as profitable models for innovation in the training of psychologists.

Alternative services have been devised in the States to meet the needs of culturally-diverse communities. Some community mental health centres specialize in providing service and training resources for particular minority groups. These have been welcomed because they can offer a less stigmatizing and more flexible service than traditional facilities. Similarly, outreach schemes which try to avoid institutionalizing abnormality entirely and which involve the patient's wider social network in the process of treatment have proved successful. In some cases they mirror informal or indigenous healing practices which increases their acceptability and efficacy. Diagnostic and therapeutic practices need to follow models which are familiar and meaning-ful within the patient's own culture as closely as possible. Rack (1982) suggests procedures for collaborating with indigenous healers, or for em-ploying idioms which represent a compromise between models familiar to both patients and Western-trained professionals. Awareness of selection factors which influence local rates of attendance and decisions about treat-ment disposal will also sensitize psychologists to the potential for misdiagno-sis, discrimination in referral procedures or local under-provision of services.

In summary, a number of recommendations are relevant to all the approaches outlined above. Therapists need to tolerate preferences for treatment contracts which may be more short-term, flexible, and focused on limited, functional change. Differences in preferences and aims should not necessarily be interpreted as resistance to change. An active, directive approach which is highly nurturant, but practical rather than introspective has achieved positive results with black and Hispanic Americans (for exam-ple, Boyd-Franklin, 1984). However, the uncritical use of such recipes may gloss over important differences between cultures and encourage psycholog-ists to ignore patients' individual preferences, their degree of integration and the nature of their relationship with the host culture. Psychologists can become paralysed by striving for too much cultural relativity. Individual differences and phenomena which are also maladaptive in the patient's own culture can be misattributed to cultural differences (Rack, 1982). Ultimate-ly, a therapeutic relationship aims to facilitate change in the patient. Therap-ists working cross-culturally have to strike a balance between avoiding a wholesale prescription of the dominant culture's values and norms and providing sufficient structure for new learning experiences to take place.

REFERENCES

ATKINSON, D.R. (1985). A meta-review of research on cross-cultural counseling and psychotherapy. *Journal of Multicultural Counseling and Development, 13*, 138–153.

BANKS, W.M. (1971). The differential effects of race and social class in helping. *Journal of Clinical Psychology 28*, 90–92.

BECK, A.T. and EMERY, G. (1979). *Cognitive Therapy of Anxiety and Phobic Disorders*. Philadelphia: Center of Cognitive Therapy.

BHARATI, A. (1985). The self in Hindu thought and action. In A.J. Marsella, G. Devos and F.L.K. Hsu (eds) *Culture and Self. Asian and Western Perspectives*. New York: Tavistock.

BIRD, D. (1986). Ethnic minorities in clinical psychology. *Clinical Psychology Forum*, April issue.

BOCHNER, S. (1982). The social psychology of cross-cultural relations. In S. Bochner (ed.) *Cultures in Contact: Studies in Cross-Cultural Interaction*. Oxford: Pergamon Press.

BOYD-FRANKLIN, H. (1984). Issues in family therapy with black families. *The Clinical Psychologist, 37*, 54–57.

CALDWELL-COLBERT, A.T. and JENKINS, J.O. (1982). Modification of interpersonal behaviour. In S.M. Turner and R.T. Jones (eds), *Behaviour Modification in Black Populations: Psychosocial Issues and Empirical Findings*. New York: Plenum Press.

CASAS, J.M., PONTEROTTO, J.G. and GUTIERREZ, J.M. (1986). An ethical indictment of counseling research and training: The cross-cultural perspective. *Journal of Counseling and Development, 64*, 347–349.

CHRISTENSEN, C.P. (1984). Effects of cross-cultural training on helper response. *Counselor Education & Supervision, 23*, 311–320.

COCHRANE, R. (1979). Psychological and behavioural disturbance in West Indians, Indians and Pakistanis in Britain: A comparison of rates among children and adults. *British Journal of Psychiatry, 134*, 201–210.

COHEN, A. (1974). *Two Dimensional Man: An Essay on the Anthropology of Power and Symbolism in Complex Society*. London: Routledge & Kegan Paul.

COMOROFF, J. (1978). Medicine and culture: some anthropological perspectives. *Social Science & Medicine, 12B*, 247–254.

COOPER, J. and SARTORIUS, N. (1977). Cultural and temporal variations in schizophrenia: A speculation on the importance of industrialization. *British Journal of Psychiatry, 130*, 50–54.

CUNNINGHAM, A. and TICKNER, D. (1981). Psychoanalysis and indigenous psychology. In P. Heelas & A. Lock (eds) *Indigenous Psychologies*. London: Academic Press.

DELEUZE, G. and GUATTARI, F. (1977). *Capitalism and Schizophrenia: Anti-Oedipus*. New York: Viking Press.

DRAGUNS, J.G. (1981). Cross-cultural counseling and psychotherapy: History, issues, current status. In A. Marsella and P. Pedersen (eds) *Cross-Cultural Counseling and Psychotherapy*. New York: Plenum Press.

GOLDFRIED, M.R. and GOLDFRIED, A.P. (1980). Cognitive change methods. In F.H. Kanfer and A.P. Goldstein (eds) *Helping People Change, 2nd edn*. New York: Pergamon.

GOLDSTEIN, A.P. (1981). Evaluating expectancy effects in cross-cultural counseling and psychotherapy. In A. Marsella and P. Pedersen, (eds) *Cross-Cultural Counseling and Psychotherapy*. New York: Plenum Press.

GREEN, L. (1982). A learned helplessness analysis of problems confronting the black community. In S.M. Turner and R.T. Jones (eds), *Behavior Modification in Black Populations: Psychosocial Issues and Empirical Findings*. New York: Plenum Press.

GRIFFITH, M. (1977). The influence of race on the psychotherapeutic relationship. *Psychiatry, 40*, 27–40.

HARRISON, G., INEICHEN, B., SMITH, J. and MORGAN, H.G. (1984). Psychiatric hospital admissions in Bristol, II. Social and clinical aspects of compulsory admission. *British Journal of Psychiatry, 145*, 605–611.

HELLER, P.L., CHALFANT, H.P., WORLEY, M., QUESADA, G. and BRADFIELD, C.D. (1980). Socio-economic class, classification of abnormal behaviour and perceptions of mental health care: A cross-cultural comparison. *British Journal of Medical Psychology, 53*, 343–348.

HELMAN, C. (1984). *Culture, Health and Illness. An Introduction for Health Professionals*. Bristol: John Wright.

HODES, M. (1985). Family therapy and the problem of cultural relativism: a reply to Dr Lau. *Journal of Family Therapy 7*, 261–272.

JACKSON, A.M. (1983). Treatment issues for black patients. *Psychotherapy: Theory, Research & Practice, 20*, 143–151.

JENKINS, J.H., KARNO, M., DE LA SELVA, A. and SANTANA, F. (1986).

Expressed emotion in cross-cultural context: Familial responses to schizophrenic illness among Mexican-Americans. In M.J. Goldstein, I. Hand, and K. Hahlweg (eds) *Treatment of Schizophrenia: Family Assessment and Intervention*. New York: Springer Verlag.

JENSEN, A.R. (1980). *Bias in Mental Testing*. New York: Free Press.

KAUFMAN, A.S. (1984). The K-ABC and controversy. *Journal of Special Education 18*, 409–444.

KLEINMAN, A. (1987). Anthropology and psychiatry. The role of culture in cross-cultural research on illness. *British Journal of Psychiatry, 151*, 447–454.

LAU, A. (1984). Transcultural issues in family therapy. *Journal of Family Therapy, 6*, 91–112.

LEIGHTON, A.H. and HUGHES, J.M. (1961). Cultures as causative of mental disorder. *Millbank Memorial Fund Quarterly, 39*, 446–470.

LÉVI-STRAUSS, C. (1968). The effectiveness of symbols. In *Structural Anthropology*. London: Allen Lane.

LITTLEWOOD, R. and LIPSEDGE, M. (1981). Acute psychotic reactions in Caribbean-born patients. *Psychological Medicine, 11*, 303–318.

LITTLEWOOD, R. and LIPSEDGE, M. (1982). *Aliens and Alienists: Ethnic Minorities and Psychiatry*. Harmondsworth: Penguin.

LONDON, M. (1986). Mental illness among immigrant minorities in the United Kingdom. *British Journal of Psychiatry, 149*, 265–273.

MALZBERG, B. (1969). Are immigrants psychologically disturbed? In S.C. Plog & R.B. Edgerton, (eds) *Changing Perspectives in Mental Illness*. New York: Rinehart and Winston.

MARSELLA, A.J. (1979). Depressive affect and disorder across cultures. In H. Triandis and J. Draguns (eds) *Handbook of Cross-Cultural Psychology, Vol. 5*. New Jersey: Allyn & Bacon.

MARSELLA, A. and P. PEDERSEN (1981). *Cross-Cultural Counseling and Psychotherapy*. New York: Plenum Press.

MAULTSBY, M. (1982). A historical view of black distrust of psychiatry. In S.M. Turner & R.T. Jones (eds), *Behaviour Modification in Black Populations: Psychosocial Issues and Empirical Findings*. New York: Plenum Press.

McGOVERN, D. and COPE, R.V. (1987). First psychiatric admission rates of first and second generation Afro-Caribbeans. *Social Psychiatry, 22*, 139–149.

MECHANIC, D. (1975). Sociocultural and social-psychological factors affecting personal response to psychological disorder. *Journal of Health & Social Behaviour, 16*, 393–404.

MORGAN, D. (1975). Explaining mental illness. *Archives of European Sociology, 16*, 262–280.

MURRAY, J. and WILLIAMS, P. (1986). Self-reported illness and general practice consultations in Asian-born and British-born residents of West London. *Social Psychiatry, 21*, 139–145.

ORLEY, J., BLITT, D.M. and WING, J.K. (1979). Psychiatric disorder in two African villages. *Archives of General Psychiatry, 36*, 513–520.

ORTIGUES, E. (1973). La théorie de la personnalité en psychanalyse et en ethnologie. In *La Notion de Personne en Afrique Noire*. Paris: No. 544 of Colloques Internationaux du Centre National de la Recherche Scientifique.

PARSONS, T. (1964) Definitions of health and illness in the light of American values and social structure. In T. Parsons *Social Structure and Personality*. London: Free Press of Glencoe.

PEDERSON, P.B. (ed.) (1985). *Handbook of Cross-Cultural Counseling and Therapy*. Westport, CT: Greenwood Press.

PILL, R. and STOTT, N.C.H. (1982). Concepts of illness causation and responsibility. Some preliminary data from a sample of working class mothers. *Social Science & Medicine, 16*, 43–52.

PINA-CABRAL, J. (1986). *Sons of Adam, Daughters of Eve: The Peasant World View in Alto Minho.* Oxford: Clarendon Press.

PORTER, J.R. and WASHINGTON, R.E. (1979). Black identity and self-esteem: A review of studies of black self-concept, 1968–1978. *Annual Review of Sociology, 5*, 53–74.

RACK, P. (1982). *Race, Culture and Mental Disorder.* London: Tavistock.

SAAFIR, R.K. (1982). Implementing community programs. The black perspective in behavioral community psychology. In S.M. Turner and R.T. Jones (eds), *Behaviour Modification in Black Populations: Psychosocial Issues and Empirical Findings.* New York: Plenum Press.

SARTORIUS, N., JABLENSKY, A., KORTEN, G., ANKER, M., COOPER, J.E. and DAY, R. (1986). Early manifestations and first-contact incidence of schizophrenia in different cultures. *Psychological Medicine, 16*, 909–928.

SEN, B., WILKINSON, G. and MARI, J.J. (1987). Psychiatric morbidity in primary health care. A two-stage screening procedure in developing countries: Choice of instruments and cost-effectiveness. *British Journal of Psychiatry, 151*, 33–38.

SUE, D.W. (1981). Evaluating process variables in cross-cultural counseling and psychotherapy. In A. Marsella and P. Pedersen (eds) *Cross-Cultural Counseling and Psychotherapy.* New York: Plenum Press.

SUE, S. (1977). Community mental health services to minority groups: Some optimism, some pessimism. *American Psychologist, 32*, 616–624.

SUE, S. and ZANE, N. (1987). The role of culture and cultural techniques in psychotherapy. *American Psychologist, 42*, 37–45.

TORREY, E.F. (1978). What Western psychotherapists can learn from witchdoctors. *American Journal of Orthopsychiatry, 42*, 69–76.

TOTMAN, R. (1982). Philosophical foundations of attribution therapies. In C. Antaki and C. Brewin (eds) *Attributions and Psychological Change. Applications of Attributional Theory to Clinical and Educational Practice.* London: Academic Press.

TUCKER, C.M. (1982). Sexual disorders. In S.M. Turner and R.T. Jones (eds), *Behavior Modification in Black Populations: Psychosocial Issues and Empirical Findings.* New York: Plenum Press.

TURNER, S.M. (1982). Introduction. In S.M. Turner and R.T. Jones (eds), *Behavior Modification in Black Populations: Psychosocial Issues and Empirical Findings.* New York: Plenum Press.

TURNER, S.M., BEIDEL, D.C., HERSEN, M. and BELLACK, A.S. (1984). Effects of race on rating of social skill. *Journal of Consulting and Clinical Psychology, 52*, 474–475.

TURNER, S.M. and JONES, R.T. (eds) (1982). *Behavior Modification in Black Populations: Psychosocial Issues and Empirical Findings.* New York: Plenum Press.

WATSON, J.L. (1977). *Between Two Cultures: Migrants and Minorities in Britain.* Oxford: Blackwell.

WEISZ, J.R., ROTHBAUM, F.M. and BLACKBURN, T.C. (1984). Standing out and standing in. The psychology of control in America and Japan. *American Psychologist, 39*, 955–969.

WHITE, G.M. (1982). The ethnographic study of cultural knowledge of 'mental disorder'. In A.J. Marsella and G.M. White (eds) *Cultural Conceptions of Mental Health and Therapy.* The Hague: D. Reidel.

WILKINSON, C.B. (ed.) (1986). *Ethnic Psychiatry.* New York: Plenum.

SEXUAL ABUSE OF CHILDREN

Jane E. Dunn Smith

Sexual contact between adults and children is not new. In some eras and in some cultures it has been accepted; in others it has been variously condemned as a sin by the Christian church or religious authority, or defined as a crime by the legal-judicial systems or as deviant by mental health professionals (Mrazek, 1983). In the Western world child care professionals in the USA and the UK are now conceptualizing adult–child sexual contact as child abuse, and the problem is being managed within the legal and statutory systems set up originally to deal with physical child abuse (Smith, 1984).

The climate of public opinion in the Western world has only comparatively recently moved to a point where it has become acceptable to discuss various sorts of sexual anomalies. Adults who experienced unwelcome sexual contacts during childhood are now encouraged to reveal their experiences: in therapy, in autobiographical accounts, in TV documentaries and in response to research questionnaires. Two powerful groups have taken up the cause: the child protection movement, following the sequential stages of the 'discovery' of child abuse suggested by Kempe (1979); and the feminist movement, lobbying against the exploitation of women. The resulting publicity has contributed to the 'dramatic rise in visibility' (Finkelhor, 1982) of the phenomenon. Public opinion and the media are reacting to child sexual abuse in the '80s with the same outrage (and disbelief) accorded to the 'battered baby syndrome' in the '60s. The emotional climate of the reaction is heightened by two consistently recurring findings. Among reported perpetrators to date almost 90 per cent are men, and this holds whether the abused children are boys or girls. More than 70 per cent of the 'victims' are female. In the majority of cases the perpetrator is already known to the child, rather than being a stranger. (In at least 50 per cent of reported cases to date the perpetrator is the father or father surrogate of the child.) Sexual abuse is, therefore, popularly conceived as being committed primarily by men upon children (usually girls) within the family.

As with physical child abuse (Smith, 1984) there has been a time-lag of nearly a decade between the American and UK discovery of the phenomenon of sexual abuse, and this is reflected in the literature. Our current data base is largely American, and is primarily retrospective, obtained from self-report of adult clinical samples, surveys of non-clinical volunteers (usually college students), or studies of deviant populations such as prisoners or prostitutes. More recently, population surveys of adult victims based on random sampling techniques (for example, Russell, 1983) are beginning to appear in the American literature, together with reports on cohorts of recently-abused children collected by large-scale combined service and research programmes in the USA. Much of the available data suffers from serious methodological limitations (Mrazek, 1983; Finkelhor, 1986b) and the conclusions drawn from it are of questionable validity.

Foremost amongst the methodological problems is that of definition. Conceptualizing adult–child sexual contact as child abuse does not make it simply a sub-category of physical abuse (Finkelhor, 1982); there are more subtle complexities involved. Any definition will be not only culture-bound and time-bound, but will also be a direct reflection of the specific professional discipline making the definition (Mrazek, 1983). Most Western countries now have legal sanctions against child sexual abuse, but such sanctions vary from country to country, and from state to state in the USA. Thus for legal purposes a global working definition such as 'the exploitation of a child for the sexual gratification of an adult' will have to be expanded (Fraser, 1981) so that it clearly specifies what sexual activity is and is not permissible *within any legislation*, and exactly what each form of abuse consists of. In contrast, from a mental health perspective, the emphasis will be on the presumed harmfulness to the child rather than the punishment of the abuser.

The idea of 'exploitation' of the child is central to any definition from a child protection perspective, and the most widely referenced definition is that of Schechter and Roberge (1976). These authors refer to the sexual exploitation of children as

> the involvement of dependent, developmentally immature children and adolescents in sexual activities that they do not fully comprehend, are unable to give informed consent to, and that violate the social taboos of family roles (Schechter and Roberge, 1976, page 129).

However, such global definitions raise a number of questions. 'Sexual activities' may involve physical contact (ranging from fondling to intercourse) or may be non-contact (for example, exposure to pornographic material or exhibitionism). Should they all be regarded as equally exploitative or damaging? What about the relative ages of the victim and the perpetrator? At what age should an adolescent be considered able to comprehend and give consent? What about consensual experimentation between peers? Does violence or bribery affect the degree of abusiveness?

Does frequency of abuse (a single act, or a continuum of acts over time) make a difference? What about the social taboos? Is victimization by a stranger different from that by a known, unrelated adult, and is that different from abuse by a blood relation, that is, incest? (There is a general belief that the effects of intra-familial sexual abuse will be more devastating to the child than extra-familial abuse; a belief that seems to stem from culturally transmitted feelings about incest. Bixler, 1981.)

In the present climate of public and professional anxiety about sexual abuse the tendency is towards over-inclusiveness in definition. In practice, as with physical child abuse, referral to the child protection services for suspected abuse often becomes the sole criterion for inclusion in a research project.

The professionals concerned with the identification, management and treatment of child sexual abuse include hospital and community medical practitioners, psychiatrists, psychologists, social workers, the police and the legal professions. Each discipline is producing its own literature, and tends to read mainly its own journals, so that there is a lack of cross-fertilization (Finkelhor, 1986a). Psychologists on both sides of the Atlantic have become involved, as they did with physical child abuse (Smith, 1984) at a comparatively late stage in the discovery of the phenomenon. Their contribution to the tightening up of research methodology will be vital, but as yet is barely perceptible (Finkelhor, 1986b). Clinical psychologists in the UK at the present time are likely to stumble upon child sexual abuse in a variety of contexts: to suspect its masked presence in other presenting problems, such as depression or anxiety; to be consulted as 'experts' about it by other professionals; to find themselves the recipients of unsolicited disclosures from patients (both adults and children) that 'it' has happened to them. Not only is it a subject surrounded by taboo, particularly the incest taboo, but because the majority of victims in every study to date are female and the majority of perpetrators are male, the subject raises issues of subjective and emotional reactions in professionals of both sexes which are far more highly charged than with many other problems. There is debate about the value judgements inherent in the terminology used in the literature, with feminists preferring to refer to 'survivors' rather than 'victims'. As it is impossible within the scope of one chapter to cover the whole field I shall focus on the abused rather than the abusers, and for the sake of simplicity and congruence with the bulk of the child protection literature, I shall refer to 'perpetrators' and 'victims'.

What then is actually known about the phenomenon of child sexual abuse, based on empirical findings rather than speculation, prejudice or anecdote; and what, if any, guidelines for good clinical practice exist in the present state of our knowledge?

INCIDENCE AND PREVALENCE

It is impossible to establish true prevalence rates for any type of child abuse (Smith, 1984). A 'rash of conflicting numbers' supposedly establishing the prevalence of child sexual abuse suddenly began to appear in the 1980s, and has led to confusion and scepticism about the extent of the problem (Peters *et al.*, 1986). Suggested prevalence rates in the USA range from Finkelhor's (1979) estimate of a one per cent prevalence of father–daughter incest (based on his questionnaire survey of college students) to Russell's (1983) estimate of 28 per cent of adult women experiencing at least one incident of either intrafamilial or extrafamilial sexual abuse before the age of 14, and 38 per cent experiencing at least one incident before the age of 18 (based on a methodologically-stringent random sample of adult women in San Francisco). Estimates based not on retrospective recall by adults but on the number of cases *reported* to agencies are much lower. In the UK Baker and Duncan's (1985) ten per cent prevalence rate is based on a MORI public opinion survey, with its attendant quota sampling problems, and uses a very broad definition of abuse. (Approximately half the experiences reported by their sample involved no physical contact, but were *perceived* as abusive by the victims.)

These 'conflicting numbers' may thus arise from various factors, which are not mutually exclusive (Peters *et al.*, 1986): variations in the definitions of child sexual abuse used in a study; methodological problems over sample recruitment; variations in methods of interviewing and training of interviewers in different studies; and the possibility of true differences in prevalence among certain ethnic groups or in certain geographical locations. There is the additional complication that as public and professional awareness of the problem rises in any country, so do the incidence figures rise. Recent reviews by psychologists suggest that the most important factors in accounting for discrepancies in prevalence rates may be differences in the methods of data collection (Wyatt and Peters, 1986a and b).

VICTIMS AND PERPETRATORS

Virtually all the studies which have included men as well as women have found higher abuse rates for women (Peters *et al.*, 1986). By combining all the methodologically-sound surveys to date that have interviewed both men and women, Finkelhor and his colleagues arrive at a mean rate of 2.5 women abused for every man. In agency-based surveys of *reported* abuse the difference is wider: five girls to every boy (Reinhart, 1987). It has been suggested that incestuous abuse of males may be consistently under-reported because of the dual taboos of incest and homosexuality (Finkelhor, 1980; Forseth and Brown, 1981). It has also been suggested that it may be particularly difficult for adolescent boys to report any abuse because of a fear that participation in a homosexual experience will result in their becoming homosexual (Pierce and Pierce, 1985). In fact such views are merely speculation, and we do not have enough data on male victims from which to generalize.

Among reported perpetrators of abuse 90 per cent or more are male, and are more likely to be known to the victim than to be strangers. Natural fathers or father-surrogates have been found to be the most likely perpetrators in both clinical and non-clinical samples. In her community sample, Russell (1984) found that one in every six women who had a stepfather as a principal figure in her childhood years was sexually abused by him, compared to one in every 40 women living with biological fathers. It has been suggested that young male perpetrators (adolescents) are more likely to abuse males than females. The few reports of female perpetrators are of single cases (for example, Chasnoff *et al.*, 1986) and the victims include neonates.

LONG AND SHORT TERM EFFECTS

What are the effects of child sexual abuse on the victims: how serious a problem is it in mental health terms? Browne and Finkelhor's (1986) review paper (which is limited to female victims) goes very carefully through the current state of knowledge of the effects of child sexual abuse and concludes that immediate or short-term effects which rate as pathological disturbance are manifest in between 20 per cent and 40 per cent of abused children seen by clinicians. These are especially reactions of fear, anxiety, depression, anger and hostility, and inappropriate sexual behaviour. But Browne and Finkelhor warn that lack of standardized outcome measures and adequate comparison groups make these conclusions 'sketchy'. The long-term impact of child sexual abuse is described as slightly more clear-cut: eight non-clinical studies of adults, including three random sample community surveys, found that child sexual abuse victims in the 'normal' population had identifiable degrees of impairment when compared with non-victims. This impairment is not necessarily severe, but Browne and Finkelhor point out that all the studies which have looked for it so far have found it, with the exception of one (Tsai *et al.*, 1979). The authors conclude that the implication of their review is that a history of child sexual abuse *is* associated with a greater risk for mental health and adjustment problems in adulthood, but that the *degree* of impairment is much less clear, and most non-clinical victims show up as only slightly impaired or normal. Less than 20 per cent show serious psychopathology.

> These findings give reassurance to victims that extreme long-term effects are not inevitable. Nonetheless, they also suggest that the risk of initial and

long-term mental health impairment for victims of child sexual abuse should be taken very seriously. (Browne and Finkelhor, 1986 page 72).

The study by Tsai *et al*. (1979), although it has been criticized for its use of a self-selected non-clinical sample, nevertheless raises some interesting ideas about why some victims escape relatively unscathed. The authors suggest that the reported support of friends and family and the lack of perceived blame at the time of the abuse, and sympathetic and understanding sexual partners later, may have served as protective factors for their 'well adjusted' adult victims (Tsai *et al*., 1979, p.416). In a more recent study Herman *et al*. (1986) also discuss factors which may mediate the long-term effects of abuse. They compared adult victims referred for therapy with women identified as incest victims in Russell's (1983) community random sample. The victims who had become patients were more likely to have suffered severe forms of abuse: of longer duration, associated with violence, and perpetrated by fathers or stepfathers. All of the community sample said that they had been upset at the time, but roughly half considered that they had recovered well – and likelihood of a good recovery was related to abuse experiences which did not involve force or intrusive physical violation, and which occurred only once or infrequently. Both these studies point to the need for future research to identify the environmental factors, both at the time of the abuse and in adult life, which may promote long-term recovery for the victims.

Until further research has identified such protective factors we are left in clinical practice with little knowledge about *which* children are likely to come through the experience relatively unscathed. There is little evidence on which to base decisions about whether or not to intervene in cases of unclear suspicions. The ambiguity about long-term effects does suggest that clinical psychologists working with clinical populations of adults and adolescents referred for other problems (depression, anxiety, self-destructive behaviour, sexual maladjustment, substance abuse, eating disorders, low self-esteem, victimization as adults, feelings of isolation and stigma) should be aware of child sexual abuse as a possible aetiological factor. Routine questioning of adolescent psychiatric patients to elicit such possibilities is now reported from the USA, and a very high proportion of American adult psychiatric patients are reporting histories of abuse. If a previous history of abuse is revealed by a patient already seeking help for other problems, clinical experience suggests that the abuse will need to be dealt with in therapy.

IDENTIFICATION OF SEXUAL ABUSE

The first important step in the identification of recent or ongoing sexual abuse of children is for professionals to be able to entertain the idea of sexual abuse as a possible differential diagnosis. This may be difficult for the investigating professional, especially where the child's family (that is, those adults who potentially might be the perpetrators of abuse) are respectable, middle-class and/or professionals themselves. The second step is to be aware that even very young children may be being abused. Some North American studies of cohorts of children referred to hospitals specifically designated to respond to child sexual abuse report that approximately one third of the child victims reported were six years of age or younger. Abuse in young children is often revealed accidentally – by observation by a third party, as a result of medical injury or sexually transmitted diseases, or because of sexualized behaviour, play or comments by the victim – rather than through purposeful disclosure by the victim. Any observations, symptoms, or indication of sexual behaviour or information in a young child is potentially meaningful, and should be pursued (Mian *et al.*, 1986).

What observable symptoms or behaviour should arouse suspicions? Clinical psychologists may be consulted by other professionals or lay-persons about indices of suspicion, and need to be aware of the gross physical symptoms which suggest a possible diagnosis of sexual abuse. Unexplained vaginal bleeding, recurrent vaginitis, anogenital trauma or irritation, and unexplained genital pain or dysuria should always elicit a thorough physical examination of the child and a full social and medical history (Felman and Nikitas, 1983). Descriptions of the medical assessment of sexually abused children can be found in Paul (1977) and Kerns (1981). In the present climate of heightened awareness of the problem, coupled with lack of professional expertise in diagnosis and management, there is an urgent need for education of professionals. Cantwell (1983), and Hobbs and Wynne (1986) argue that routine inspection of the anus and genital areas should be carried out on all children in any physical examination. Only then will doctors become sensitized to distinguishing between the normal and abnormal appearance of an area which is often omitted in routine physical examinations.

It is also important to realize that abuse which stops short of digital or penile penetration, such as fondling, fellatio or cunnilingus, may be more difficult to detect unless the doctor or paediatrician is aware of the need for further investigation of any trauma, however slight, in the anogenital region. Any suspicion of a sexually transmitted disease in a child should also be investigated. Felman and Nikitas's (1983) review is one of several papers recently appearing in the paediatric literature which emphasize that the discovery of any sexually transmitted disease (ranging from gonorrhoea and syphillis to genital herpes) in children should point to a possible diagnosis of sexual abuse. A literature search during March, 1987, revealed only one paper which describes HIV infection (in a ten-year-old child) contracted through sexual abuse (Leiderman and Grimm, 1986); but this will undoubtedly become an additional area of concern over the next decade whenever sexual abuse is suspected.

The observation of behavioural signs which may be indicative of sexual abuse is more problematic. Checklists of behavioural indicators are currently fashionable but, as I have discussed elsewhere, it is important to keep in mind that such lists are based on symptoms which have all been observed in *some* abused children, but which are not necessarily diagnostic of abuse (Smith, 1987). Likewise, drawings with either explicit or symbolic sexual content have been produced by some victims, and are often described as 'evidence' of abuse, but we have little normative data against which to measure them. Yates *et al.* (1985) compared drawings by child victims of incest with drawings by children referred for other problems and found few differences between the two groups.

The interviewing of children and adolescents to establish whether or not sexual abuse has occurred raises various complex issues. There is a growing body of American data indicating that children and adolescents presenting with a variety of other problems in medical and psychiatric settings may in fact be 'masked presentations' of sexual abuse (Hunter *et al.*, 1985). There is a clear need for any professionals involved in assessment interviews with children and adolescents (and their parents) to feel both competent at and comfortable with making routine enquiries about sexual abuse in an appropriate matter. David Mrazek describes such psychiatric interviews in general terms (Mrazek, 1980; Mrazek and Mrazek, 1985) and discusses the necessity of taking the child's developmental level into account in conducting an interview – but does not elaborate on how this might be done.

Apart from the routine enquiry in a psychological or psychiatric history-taking there is also the so-called 'disclosure interview' with a child, particularly a young child, when a case arousing a high index of suspicion is investigated. Investigative interviewing may be undertaken by a variety of different professionals – paediatricians, social workers, psychiatrists, clinical psychologists, police – and while each discipline may be concerned to establish exactly what has happened to the child they may want to do so for different purposes (protection or treatment of the child; prosecution of the offender). Videotaped recordings of disclosure interviews may be submitted as evidence in court proceedings (Davies and Drinkwater, 1987). How to conduct such 'disclosure interviews' is a matter of considerable concern to UK professionals at the present time – who should interview, whether the police should be present, how to protect the child from too many interviews. There is a clear need for skills training for professionals engaged in such work, but this is rarely available. Child sexual abuse teams, following the American model, are often hastily set up in the UK, with little or no training provided for team members.

In the USA, educational films are available on how to conduct interviews, as well as a variety of props: play materials, books of anatomical drawings, anatomically correct dolls (advertised as 'available in Caucasian, Hispanic or Black ...' Jones and McQuiston, 1986). Yet the detailed advice on interviewing is still based solely on clinical experience. Case studies such as that described by Jones and Krugman (1986) describe how skilful interviewing of even very young children can elicit information from the child which may later be fully corroborated by the perpetrator – but such success stories may place a covert onus on all professionals working with children to do likewise. Excellent advice, based on clinical experience, on how to elicit information from a child can be found in Jones and McQuiston (1986) – use the language the child uses, don't mimic the perpetrator's intrusiveness, beware of the significance of touching – but the *interpretation* of such information still relies on clinical judgement. Empirical investigation of how normal (non-abused) children would play with anatomically correct dolls is only just beginning (Jampole and Weber, 1987) so that interpretation of a suspected victim's play is as dubious as is interpretation of the suspected victim's drawings (Yates *et al.*, 1985).

There is the additional problem of whether a young child is telling the 'truth' or being led by the interviewer's questions, and whether a child who retracts a previous allegation of abuse should be believed or not. The most useful framework for deciding whether or not a young child is telling the truth is that described by De Young (1986). She describes a sequence of careful investigative steps, based on a knowledge of children's cognitive development, and concludes that young children are unlikely to lie about sexual abuse – and that if they *do* lie, they are probably being coerced into lying.

MANAGEMENT AND TREATMENT OF CHILD SEXUAL ABUSE IN THE USA

The word 'management' is used intentionally here: remarkably little has been published on treatment process and outcome. American professionals were overwhelmed by problems of identification and crisis management thrown up by the rapidity with which reports of sexual abuse escalated in the late '70s. Philosophical differences between police, child protective agencies and medical and mental health personnel over how such cases should be managed made the coordination of services more difficult (Finkelhor, 1983). In the '80s the emphasis has moved to prevention, and the more difficult issues of treatment are side-stepped.

In the USA, the management of all forms of child abuse is dictated by the legal framework of mandatory reporting laws and the role of the child protection services (Smith, 1984). Within this framework, treatment is most likely to be either court-ordered or to be required by the child protection agency as the means by which a family may avoid court proceedings. In most States sexual abuse reporting is also mandatory and child protection services focus on ensuring the safety of the child from further abuse as their first priority. Early treatment approaches were usually geared towards working with the victim, while the perpetrator was removed (for example, Sgroi, 1982).

In 1971, in California, Hank Giaretto, a psychologist, set up his Child Sexual Abuse Treatment Program (CSATP), the first treatment programme based on a family systems approach (Giaretto, 1979). Whole families were treated in close conjunction with the local judicial system, and the backing of a court order to ensure compliance with treatment was strongly advocated. This family systems framework has subsequently been adopted by several other treatment programmes in the USA, and is seen as the treatment of choice by the majority of programmes. The goals of treatment have gradually changed from the initial punitive attitude towards the perpetrator to the goal of family rehabilitation, so that the perpetrator and the victim could be returned to the home whenever this was judged to be clinically justified.

Giaretto's Child Sexual Abuse Treatment Program in California was externally evaluated in 1978 (Kroth, 1979). The overall evaluation was positive, but the researchers had some caveats. Kroth was emphatic that, in the absence of other outside empirical data with which to compare his study, 'one must necessarily draw conclusions with hesitation'. However, no such hesitation is to be found in Giaretto's own eulogy of CSATPs in Giaretto (1982a), nor in his treatment and training manual (Giaretto, 1982b). There have been no further objective evaluations of any treatment approaches appearing in the literature to date. We still have no satisfactory longitudinal data on any of the variables (for example, recidivism rates, family reunification rates, victim delinquency rates, parental or victim sexual dysfunction rates) which might allow us to make informed judgements about which treatments work with sexually abusive families, or for whom they work. The same situation pertains as with child physical abuse (Smith and Rachman, 1984). Without methodologically-sound controlled treatment trials we cannot make any empirically-based claims about the value of any particular treatment approach.

In the absence of any objective evaluation in the USA it would appear that a multi-modal treatment approach is being used: a combination of individual, group and family therapy, depending on the assessment of each individual case. For the abused child, group therapy is cited as the preferred treatment; for the perpetrators, group and family therapy are preferred (Forseth and Brown, 1981). It is important to keep in mind the difficulties of working with these families. Bander *et al.* (1982) point out that in most families referred for treatment, sexual abuse is not an isolated problem in an otherwise well functioning family. The family is far more likely to have multiple problems, and to require a high level of clinical input from a multidisciplinary team. Interagency cooperation (between health departments, police, hospitals, courts and welfare departments, as well as with child protection agencies) is often fraught with difficulty, and exacerbated by professionals' attitudes towards the problem and the perpetrators.

Group therapy with abused children of all ages is advocated by Berliner and Ernst (1984), and groups are usually kept within particular age limits. Groups for adolescent girls are described by Blick and Porter (1982), who also provide useful practical advice on the setting up and running of such a group. In addition, particularly in the adult psychotherapy literature, there are accounts of groups for adult women who have disclosed a history of childhood sexual abuse during individual therapy (for example, Herman and Schatzow, 1984; Tsai and Wagner, 1978).

A recent suggestion by two American psychologists (Lindberg and Distad, 1985a and b) conceptualizes the symptoms experienced by adult and adolescent incest victims referred for therapy (anxiety, intrusive imagery or recurring nightmares, insomnia, depression, anger, guilt and mistrust) as a post-traumatic stress syndrome. Self-destructive behaviours, such as suicide attempts, self-mutilation, alcohol and drug abuse, running away, explosive anger and seductiveness and/or promiscuity can be viewed as 'survival responses'. Treatment stemming from this conceptualization, whether in individual or group settings, would evolve from a planned advocacy role by the therapist. It would focus on the goals of establishing trust; helping the victim to realize that his or her participation in the incest experience was in no way the victim's fault or responsibility; recognizing the self-defeating behaviours as survival responses; and learning how to manage self-destructive behaviours and build up new adaptive behaviours.

MANAGEMENT AND TREATMENT IN THE UK

In contrast to the mandatory reporting system in the USA, the identification and management of child abuse in the UK is based on voluntary cooperation at a local level. Each Health Authority is responsible for making its own arrangements based on guidelines issued by the Department of Health and Social Security. A recommendation was made in 1980 that criteria for inclusion on the Child Abuse Registers should be widened to include other forms of abuse, such as neglect and emotional abuse, as well as physical injury, and most areas have now revised their procedures to include child sexual abuse. Because of the local rather than centralized arrangements, data are not available nationally from these Registers. However, in the areas where the National Society for the Prevention of Cruelty to Children Special Units have taken over the maintenance of the Registers the reports of child sexual abuse placed on these Registers since 1981 have risen from 3 per cent of all abused children reported to 18 per cent, according to Creighton in a paper presented at a conference in 1987. This rapid rise in the number of reported cases in the five years 1981–1986 parallels that described by Fink-

elhor (1983) as occurring in the USA between 1977–1982. The same philosophical differences over management, strong emotional reactions, and
professional clamour for workshops and training sessions in the USA described in the '70s by Finkelhor (1983) can be observed in the UK in the late
'80s, resulting in a similar chaotic management of sexual abuse cases. In the
absence of mandatory reporting and the legalistic framework obtaining in
the USA there is much less consistency over police involvement and the
prosecution of offenders. A very honest description of the initial chaotic
management of an ultimately successful intervention can be found in Dale
et al. (1986). In the UK, child protection agencies (Social Services
Departments and the National Society for the Prevention of Cruelty to
Children) are being swamped with sexual abuse referrals at a time when
they are suffering from inadequate financial resources after several years of
severe constraints on public expenditure. These agencies are also doubtful
about their professional competence to offer effective treatment for such
cases.

Thus, where treatment *is* offered in the UK, it is still very much on an *ad
hoc* basis. Family therapy is usually advocated as the treatment of choice
(CIBA, 1984; Furniss, 1984) although to date there are no published data
critically evaluating its effectiveness in the UK. Clinical descriptions of
family therapy are available (for example Will, 1983). The back-up of
statutory agencies and of both civil and legal mandates to ensure cooperation in treatment are considered essential. Treatment is undertaken with all
family members on the multimodal treatment model advocated by Giaretto
(1979). However, such a multimodal approach requires considerable professional resources, rarely available outside specialized hospital or treatment
unit settings. Dale *et al.* (1986) describe family therapy, with its goal of
rehabilitating the family, as being in direct contrast to the feminist viewpoint
which sees male dominance over women and children and masculine abuse
of power as the problems to be addressed in therapy. Feminists advocate
group work with victims (and their mothers) as the preferred treatment,
since it provides a sense of mutual support and a common identity. (Feminists have also been critical of psychoanalytic approaches with incest victims,
arguing that the female victim is then isolated and required to focus on her
own emotional problems, guilt and feelings of inadequacy, instead of having
her consciousness raised by group participation. Vander Mey and Neff,
1982).

An alternative and more useful conceptualization to the family therapy–
feminist group work polarization may be to consider treatment as being
based either on an adult-oriented (family rehabilitation or offender treatment) perspective or on a child-oriented perspective. The child-oriented
perspective sees the ultimate goal of therapy in any child abuse case as an
acceptable global quality of life for the child. This may, in some cases,
involve separating the child from a family unwilling or unable to change

(Smith and Rachman, 1984). This perspective requires careful assessment of the *child's* needs in each individual case. The assessment may then lead to individual counselling and/or group or family treatment, if appropriate to that particular case.

Individual counselling with adolescent and adult victims of sexual abuse may be particularly reliant on the therapist's ability to provide support and to be empathic and non-judgemental, in view of victims' frequent reports of their difficulties in trusting other people. It has been suggested that cognitive therapy techniques may be useful in identifying and modifying victims' self-blaming and self-defeating thoughts (Gold, 1986) and that exploration of a victim's relationship with parents, particularly the mother, may be important. Certainly in group work with adolescent girls in the UK (Dunn Smith *et al.*, in preparation) issues of guilt and relationships with parents had to be dealt with by the group before the girls were able to move on to tackle the more usual concerns of adolescence (peer and heterosexual relations, leaving home, becoming independent).

Clinical psychologists in the UK may also find themselves involved in the rehabilitation of perpetrators of child sexual abuse in forensic settings. A useful starting point for anyone new to working with sex offenders can be found in Cook and Howells (1981), and in Chapters 3 and 4 in Finkelhor *et al.* (1986). Lanyon (1986) discusses the theoretical rationale for offender treatment, and an annotated bibliography on adolescent sex offenders can be found in Ryan (1986).

PROFESSIONAL ATTITUDES AND THERAPIST VARIABLES

In the present state of our knowledge therapeutic intervention largely relies on what Kroth (1979) has described as 'various therapeutic myths'.

> The professional community, itself influenced by the pervasive incest taboo, must try to discriminate between the potpourri of mythologies heretofore given to it as explanation of the problem and advice on how to treat it. (Kroth, 1979, page 301)

The pervasiveness of the incest taboo results in value-judgements of which the professionals themselves may be completely unaware. In the UK Eisenber *et al.* (1987) have recently reported an empirical investigation of the attitudes of health care professionals involved in child sexual abuse cases. They found, for example, that the type of sexual activity involved affected respondents' attitudes (with sexual intercourse perceived as more harmful to the child than fondling), and that incestuous abuse was generally considered (especially by female respondents) to be harmful to the victim. More such studies are urgently needed.

Despite the difficulties over establishing prevalence rates there is general agreement in the literature that the rising incidence rates, as public and professional awareness rises, indicate that the size of the problem is still underestimated (Peters *et al.*, 1986). If the increase is in *identified* cases, rather than an increase in real incidence, then there is likely to be a substantial proportion of the adult population (and particularly the adult female population) who have been themselves undisclosed victims of child sexual abuse. And that group of undisclosed victims is likely to include a relative proportion of mental health professionals. Their sensitivity to the question of how victims are affected may be heightened, and their professional judgement affected, by subjective issues. It may well be that it is *not* appropriate for all professionals to be involved in child sexual abuse cases. Therapist variables may be particularly important with this population (Mrazek, 1981). Gender differences may also prove important: Attias and Goodwin (1985) found male professionals more sceptical about abuse allegations, and the particular difficulties experienced by male therapists working with female victims have been commented on by Finkelhor (1982) and Dale *et al.* (1986).

PREVENTION

Finkelhor (1986b) has suggested that sexual abuse prevention 'promises to be one of the great social experiments of the decade'. In America a variety of prevention programmes have been developed for use in schools: the problem is how to evaluate their effectiveness. Children may demonstrate greater knowledge about sexual abuse after they have participated in training packages (for example Wurtele *et al.*, 1986), but how do we know whether they are able to translate that knowledge into action? The use of a stooge to make advances to children in a simulation study immediately raises a number of ethical issues (Leventhal, 1987; Conte, 1987) as well as demonstrating that, in fact, current prevention programmes may *not* change children's behaviour.

In the UK similar educational initiatives are getting under way, and various books are available to use with children (for example, Elliott, 1986). Perhaps the present emphasis on prevention is to be expected. It is easier for professionals to handle than the discovery, management or treatment of child sexual abuse.

REFERENCES

ATTIAS, R. and GOODWIN, J. (1985). Knowledge and management strategies in incest cases: a survey of physicians, psychologists and family counselors. *Child Abuse and Neglect, 9*, 527–533.

BAKER, A.W. and DUNCAN, S.P. (1985). Child sexual abuse: a study of prevalence in Great Britain. *Child Abuse and Neglect, 9*, 457–467.

BANDER, K., FEIN, E. and BISHOP, G. (1982). Child sex abuse treatment: some barriers to program operation. *Child Abuse and Neglect, 6*, 185–191.

BERLINER, L. and ERNST, E. (1984). Group work with pre-adolescent sexual assault victims. In I.R. Stuart, and J.G. Greer, (eds). *Victims of Sexual Aggression: Treatment of Children, Women and Men*. New York: Van Nostrand Reinhold.

BIXLER, R.H. (1981). The incest controversy. *Psychological Reports, 49*, 267–283.

BLICK, L. and PORTER, F. (1982). Group therapy with adolescent female incest victims. In S. Sgroi, *Handbook of Clinical Intervention in Child Sexual Abuse*. Lexington, Mass.: Lexington Books.

BROWNE, A. and FINKELHOR, D. (1986). Impact of child sexual abuse: a review of the research. *Psychological Bulletin, 99*, 66–77.

CANTWELL, H.B. (1983). Vaginal inspection as it relates to child sexual abuse in girls under 13. *Child Abuse and Neglect, 7*, 171–176.

CHASNOFF, I.J., BURNS, W.J., SCHNOLL, S.H., BURNS, K., CHISUM, G., and KYLE-SPORE, L. (1986). Maternal neonatal incest. *American Journal of Orthopsychiatry, 56*, 577–580.

CIBA Foundation (1984). *Child Sexual Abuse Within the Family*. London: Tavistock Publications.

CONTE, J.R. (1987). Ethical issues in evaluation of prevention programs. *Child Abuse and Neglect, 11*, 171–172.

COOK, M. and HOWELLS, K. (eds) (1981). *Adult Sexual Interest in Children*. New York: Academic Press.

DALE, P., WATERS, J., DAVIES, M., ROBERTS, W. and MORRISON, T. (1986). The tower of silence: creative and destructive issues for therapeutic teams dealing with sexual abuse. *Journal of Family Therapy, 8*, 1–25.

DAVIES, G. and DRINKWATER, J.M. (1987). The child witness: do the courts abuse children? *Issues in Criminological and Legal Psychology, No. 13*. Leicester: The British Psychological Society.

DE YOUNG, M. (1986). A conceptual model for judging the truthfulness of a young child's allegation of sexual abuse. *American Journal of Orthopsychiatry, 56*, 550–559.

DUNN SMITH, J.E., EVERED, C. and RICHARDS, D. (in preparation), Group treatment for sexually abused adolescent girls.

EISENBERG, N., OWENS, R.G. and DEWEY, M.E. (1987). Attitudes of health professionals to child sexual abuse. *Child Abuse and Neglect, 11*, 109–116.

ELLIOTT, M. (1986). *The Willow Street Kids: it's your right to be safe*. London: Marilyn Malin Books.

FELMAN, Y.M. and NIKITAS, J.A. (1983). Sexually transmitted diseases and child sexual abuse. Parts I and II *New York State Journal of Medicine, 83*, 341–343 and 714–716.

FINKELHOR, D. (1979). *Sexually Victimized Children*. New York: Free Press.

FINKELHOR, D. (1980). Risk factors in the sexual victimization of children. *Child Abuse and Neglect, 4*, 265–273.

FINKELHOR, D. (1982). Sexual abuse: a sociological perspective. *Child Abuse and Neglect, 6*, 95–102.

FINKELHOR, D. (1983). Removing the child – prosecuting the offender in cases of sexual abuse: evidence from the national reporting system for child abuse and neglect. *Child Abuse and Neglect, 7*, 195–205.

FINKELHOR, D. (1986a) Introduction. In D. Finkelhor, S. Araji, L. Baron, A.

Browne, S.D. Peters and G.E. Wyatt. *A Sourcebook on Child Sexual Abuse.* Beverly Hills: Sage.

FINKELHOR, D. (1986b). Prevention: a review of programs and research. In D. Finkelhor, S. Araji, L. Baron, A. Browne, S.D. Peters and G.E. Wyatt. *A Sourcebook on Child Sexual Abuse.* Beverly Hills: Sage.

FINKELHOR, D., ARAJI, S., BARON, L., BROWNE, A., PETERS, S.D. and WYATT, G.E. (1986). *A Sourcebook on Child Sexual Abuse.* Beverly Hills: Sage.

FORSETH, L.B. and BROWN, A. (1981). A survey of intrafamilial sexual abuse treatment centers: implications for intervention. *Child Abuse and Neglect, 5,* 177–186.

FRASER, B.G. (1981). Sexual child abuse: the legislation and the law in the United States. Ch. 5 in P. Beezley Mrazek and C.H. Kempe (eds) *Sexually Abused Children and their Families.* Oxford: Pergamon.

FURNISS, T. (1984). Organizing a therapeutic approach to intrafamilial child sexual abuse. *Journal of Adolescence, 7,* 309–317.

GIARETTO, H. (1979). Humanistic treatment of father–daughter incest. In R. Helfer and C.H. Kempe (eds). *Child Abuse and Neglect: the Family in the Community.* Cambridge, Mass: Ballinger Publishing Co.

GIARETTO, H. (1982a). A comprehensive child sexual abuse treatment program. *Child Abuse and Neglect, 6,* 263–278.

GIARETTO, H. (1982b) *Integrated Treatment of Child Sexual Abuse: a Treatment and Training Manual.* New York: Science and Behaviour Books.

GOLD, E.R. (1986). Long-term effects of sexual abuse in childhood: an attributional approach. *Journal of Consulting and Clinical Psychology, 54,* 471–475.

HERMAN, J. and SCHATZOW, E. (1984). Time-limited group therapy for women with a history of incest. *International Journal of Group Psychotherapy, 34,* 605–616.

HERMAN, J., RUSSELL, D. and TROCKI, K. (1986). Long-term effects of sexual abuse in childhood. *American Journal of Psychiatry, 143,* 1293–1296.

HOBBS, C.J. and WYNNE, J.M. (1986). Buggery in childhood: a common syndrome of child abuse. *Lancet, 8510,* 792–796.

HUNTER, R.S., KILSTROM, N. and LODA, F. (1985). Sexually abused children: identifying masked presentations in a medical setting. *Child Abuse and Neglect, 9,* 17–25.

JAMPOLE, L. and WEBER, M.K. (1987). An assessment of the behaviour of sexually abused and non-sexually abused children with anatomically correct dolls. *Child Abuse and Neglect, 11,* 187–192.

JONES, D.P.H. and KRUGMAN, R.D. (1986). Case report: Can a three-year-old child bear witness to her sexual assault and attempted murder? *Child Abuse and Neglect, 10,* 253–258.

JONES, D.P.H. and McQUISTON, M. (1986). *Interviewing the Sexually Abused Child, Volume 6,* Kempe Center Series. Denver: National Center for the Prevention and Treatment of Child Abuse and Neglect.

KEMPE, C.H. (1979). Recent developments in the field of child abuse: Opening address to 2nd International Congress on child abuse and neglect. *Child Abuse and Neglect, 3,* ix–xv.

KERNS, D.L. (1981). Medical assessment of child sexual abuse. Ch. 10 in P.B. Mrazek and C.H. Kempe (eds). *Sexually Abused Children and their Families.* Oxford: Pergamon.

KROTH, J.A. (1979). Family therapy impact on intrafamilial child sexual abuse. *Child Abuse and Neglect, 3,* 297–302.

LANYON, R.I. (1986). Theory and treatment in child molestation. *Journal of Consulting and Clinical Psychology, 54*, 176–182.

LEIDERMAN, I.Z. and GRIMM, K.T. (1986). A child with HIV infection (letter). *Journal of the American Medical Association, 256*, 3094.

LEVENTHAL, J.M. (1987). Programs to prevent sexual abuse: what outcomes should be measured? *Child Abuse and Neglect, 11*, 169–171.

LINDBERG, F.H. and DISTAD, L.J. (1985a) Post-traumatic stress disorders in women who experienced childhood incest. *Child Abuse and Neglect, 9*, 329–334.

LINDBERG, F.H. and DISTAD, L.J. (1985b) Survival responses to incest: adolescents in crisis. *Child Abuse and Neglect, 9*, 521–526.

MIAN, M., WEHRSPANN, W., KLAJNER-DIAMOND, H. and LEBARON, D. (1986). Review of 125 children 6 years of age and under who were sexually abused. *Child Abuse and Neglect, 10*, 223–229.

MRAZEK, D. (1980). The child psychiatric examination of the sexually abused child. *Child Abuse and Neglect, 4*, 275–284.

MRAZEK, P.B. (1981). Special problems in the treatment of child sexual abuse. Ch. 12 in P.B. Mrazek and C.H. Kempe (eds) *Sexually abused children and their families*. Oxford: Pergamon.

MRAZEK, P.J. (1983). Sexual abuse of children. Ch. 6 in B.B. Lahey and A.E. Kazdin (eds) *Advances in Clinical Child Psychology, Vol. 6*. New York: Plenum.

MRAZEK, D. and MRAZEK, P. (1985). Child maltreatment. Ch. 43 in M. Rutter and L. Hersov (eds) *Modern Approaches to Child Psychiatry* (2nd ed). Oxford: Blackwell.

PAUL, D.M. (1977). The medical exam in sexual offences against children. *Medicine, Science and the Law, 17*, 251–258.

PETERS, S.D., WYATT, G.E. and FINKELHOR, D. (1986). Prevalence. Ch. 1 in D. Finkelhor, S. Araji, L. Baron, A. Browne, S.D. Peters and G.E. Wyatt: *A Sourcebook on Child Sexual Abuse*. Beverly Hills: Sage Publications.

PIERCE, R. and PIERCE, L.H. (1985). The sexually abused child: a comparison of male and female victims. *Child Abuse and Neglect, 9*, 191–199.

REINHART, M.A. (1987). Sexually abused boys. *Child Abuse and Neglect, 11*, 229–235.

RUSSELL, D.E.H. (1983). The incidence and prevalence of intrafamilial and extrafamilial sexual abuse of female children. *Child Abuse and Neglect, 7*, 133–146.

RUSSELL, D.E.H. (1984). The prevalence and seriousness of incestuous abuse: stepfathers vs biological fathers. *Child Abuse and Neglect, 8*, 15–22.

RYAN, G. (1986). Annotated bibliography: adolescent perpetrators of sexual molestation of children. *Child Abuse and Neglect, 10*, 125–131.

SCHECHTER, M.D. and ROBERGE, L. (1976). Sexual exploitation. In R.E. Helfer and C.H. Kempe (eds). *Child Abuse and Neglect: the Family and the Community*. Cambridge, Mass.: Ballinger Publishing Co.

SGROI, S.M. (1982) (ed.). *Handbook of Clinical Intervention in Child Sexual Abuse*. Lexington, Mass: Lexington Books.

SMITH, J.E. (1984). Non-accidental injury to children, Part I: A review of behavioural interventions. *Behaviour Research and Therapy, 22*, 331–347.

SMITH, J.E. (1987). Working with child-abusing parents: problems and practice. *Educational and Child Psychology, 3*, 169–176.

SMITH, J.E. and RACHMAN, S.J. (1984). Non-accidental injury to children, Part II: a controlled evaluation of a behavioural management programme. *Behaviour Research and Therapy, 22*, 349–366.

TSAI, M. and WAGNER, N.N. (1978). Therapy groups for women sexually molested as children. *Archives of Sexual Behaviour, 7*, 417–427.

TSAI, M., FELDMAN-SUMMERS, S. and EDGAR, M. (1979). Childhood molestation: variables relating to differential impacts on psychosexual functioning in adult women. *Journal of Abnormal Psychology, 88*, 407–417.

VANDER MEY, B.J. and NEFF, R.L. (1982). Adult–child incest: a review of research and treatment. *Adolescence, 17*, 717–735.

WILL, D. (1983). Approaching the incestuous and sexually abusive family. *Journal of Adolescence, 6*, 229–246.

WURTELE, S.K., SASLAWSKY, D.A., MILLER, C.L., MARRS, S.R. and BRITCHER, J.C. (1986). Teaching personal safety skills for potential prevention of sexual abuse: a comparison of treatments. *Journal of Consulting and Clinical Psychology, 54*, 688–692.

WYATT, G.E. and PETERS, S.D. (1986a) Issues in the definition of child sexual abuse in prevalence research. *Child Abuse and Neglect, 10*, 231–240.

WYATT, G.E. and PETERS, S.D. (1986b) Methodological considerations in research on the prevalence of child sexual abuse. *Child Abuse and Neglect, 10*, 241–251.

YATES, A., BEUTLER, L.E. and CRAGO, M. (1985). Drawings by child victims of incest. *Child Abuse and Neglect, 9*, 183–189.

PRIMARY PREVENTION IN BEHAVIOURAL MEDICINE WITH CHILDREN

Jan Aldridge

There has been an enormous growth in enthusiasm in recent years for a more psychological approach towards the problems of illness and health with children. Such an approach has been well documented in the area of child behavioural and developmental problems (for example, McAuley and McAuley, 1977; Kazdin, 1979; Herbert, 1981). A considerable literature is also developing on the use of behavioural principles in the alleviation of medical problems, such as asthma and seizure control (Khan, 1977; Cabral and Scott, 1976; Russo and Varni, 1981). A further area of increasingly accepted application is work with children and young people with chronic physical illnesses (Fielding, 1985). In the context of chronic illness care may be seen as having an equal commitment to 'management' as to 'treatment'. Clinical psychologists are being called upon increasingly to help with this total care of children with long-term physical illnesses. The range of problems and groups of patients studied is large and growing rapidly; these include studies in such diverse areas as problems of adjustment (Pless, 1984), of self-esteem (Schowalter, 1977), and levels of family stress (Walker *et al.*, 1987).

This chapter, however, is not a review of these increasingly accepted areas of application. As well as responding to these problems of illness, clinical psychologists working with children are beginning to be involved with work in the area of prevention, health maintenance and life style change. There is growing realization that we cannot stem the tide of child problems by simply engaging in more treatment (Peterson *et al.*, 1980) and the beginnings are detectable of an adjustment of priorities, emphasizing the prevention of new disorders in addition to treating existing ones. The focus of this chapter is on this area of prevention in behavioural medicine with children. As yet this is a new and developing area, not clearly delineated, but one which shows healthy signs of becoming increasingly important in the future.

PREVENTION

The general area of prevention has traditionally been divided into either two or three subsections (Caplan, 1964; Casey *et al.*, 1986; Fielding, 1987). Most workers are agreed in defining primary prevention as work designed to prevent the occurrence of new cases or disorders in a population. Some workers further subdivide work in this area into secondary prevention, with its goal of reducing the prevalence of disorders, and tertiary prevention or rehabilitation, with its goal of preventing or reducing further sequelae from established chronic disorders (Caplan, 1964; Offord, 1987). Other workers have regarded the term secondary prevention, first used in this narrow sense by Caplan (1964), of dubious value and essentially equivalent to the more traditional word, treatment. They have defined secondary prevention as interventions with children 'at risk' for further problems because of existing disorders, such as chronic illness or developmental disability (Casey *et al.*, 1986). This definition of secondary prevention, as referring to those prog- rammes that are applied to individuals who are already identified as targets in order to prevent or minimize further difficulties, is gaining increasing acceptance (Forgays, 1984). Clinical psychology has made, and is continuing to make, a significant contribution to this area of secondary prevention in behavioural medicine with children. Examples are work on maximizing compliance in young people (Stark *et al.*, 1987); studies of the impact of chronic illness on child-rearing practices (Markova *et al.*, 1980); preparation for stressful medical procedures (Schultheis *et al.*, 1987); improving social group functioning in young handicapped people (Wallander and Hubert, 1987). However, this chapter concerns itself with primary prevention and defines it as work aimed at preventing problems developing in the first place.

PRIMARY PREVENTION AND BEHAVIOURAL MEDICINE

A range of primary prevention programmes have been and continue to be developed in some of the more traditional areas of child clinical psychology. For example, in the prevention of sleep problems, Schmitt (1986) discussed the use of anticipatory guidance to help parents avoid three common types of sleep disorder: trained night feeding, trained night crying and fearful night crying. In the area of parent training Christopherson (1986) provided anticipatory guidance on discipline with basic guidelines stressing the value of much brief, non-verbal, physical contact with restraint from spanking, yelling and verbal reprimands. The prevention of common feeding problems in infants and young children has also received some attention. Finney (1986), for example, outlined behavioural management strategies for use by health visitors to help develop positive food experiences and parent–child interactions during meal times. While primary prevention programmes in these areas of child clinical psychology continue to develop apace, another exciting range of potential targets for prevention exists within the behavioural medicine field.

Prevention in behavioural medicine with children is particularly important as many of the problems that lead to serious adult illnesses are the result of life styles that develop in childhood. As John Knowles remarked, 'over ninety-nine per cent of us are born healthy and made sick as a result of personal misbehaviour and environmental conditions' (Knowles, 1977). Patterns of eating, of under-activity and of use of drugs constitute some of the major causes of avoidable illnesses in Western societies (Haggerty, 1977).

A significant impetus for primary prevention in behavioural medicine has come from America and Canada. Prevention in similar areas to those noted by Haggerty (1977) has been emphasized by the US Preventative Services Task Force in 1986: the modification of behavioural risk factors such as smoking, substance abuse, lack of exercise, inadequate nutrition and stress. In the United Kingdom, the Royal College of General Practitioners in 1982 published *Healthier Children – Thinking Prevention*, emphasizing the case for preventive child care in general practice. Increasingly, psychologists are collaborating with health professionals from other disciplines to develop ways of keeping people healthy. In the present chapter, examples of collaborative primary prevention work in two areas are considered, alcohol abuse and smoking. They are discussed as illustrative examples of work in this emerging field. Other areas where psychologists are active include drug abuse (Kandel and Logan, 1984), exercise (Keir and Lauzon, 1980) and weight control (Puska, 1982; Dietz, 1986).

Alcohol abuse

Illicit use of alcohol is one of the foremost drug problems among young people. Alcohol-related traffic accidents constitute the most frequent cause of death and disablement in American youth (Douglass, 1982). There is evidence (Parker *et al.*, 1980) that even social drinking in young adults may produce a marked loss of cognitive functioning. Additionally it is being suggested that social drinking in early pregnancy is as damaging to the embryo as constant heavy drinking (Sulik *et al.*, 1981), and more damaging than the effect of tobacco on the foetus (Abel, 1981).

Such research, together with the modest successes of treatment programmes, has led to an increasing emphasis on the prevention of alcohol abuse among adolescents. Alcohol education programmes are by far the most common form of primary preventive service offered. The goal of such programmes has been generally to increase knowledge about the effects of alcohol and thereby produce changes in attitudes to consumption and in consumption itself. However, in the past, most of those who have studied the effects of these health education programmes have rated them somewhere between being merely unsuccessful (Haggerty, 1977) to being 'abysmal at best' (Knowles, 1977). Stuart (1974), for example, evaluated a school alcohol and drug abuse prevention programme which was aimed at increasing knowledge. He suggested that this programme was actually iatrogenic rather than just missing the mark. It actually increased the use, favourable attitudes towards, and selling of, certain drugs and alcohol relative to a control group not receiving the programme. Overall, it seems there is general agreement that such programmes can demonstrate significant gains in adolescent knowledge of alcohol but have mixed success in producing attitude and behaviour change (Randall and Wong, 1976).

However, despite the problems of some of the earlier research in this area, some well-executed and theoretically well-founded studies have begun to emerge more recently. One such study (Schlegel *et al.*, 1984), illustrates how much can be learned from a carefully executed evaluation of a prevention programme. The researchers recognized that one of the main problems in the literature on alcohol education was that many of the programmes repeatedly failed to incorporate the theoretical relationship between knowledge, attitudes, intentions and behaviour. It has been known for a long time that the giving of facts might improve knowledge but not necessarily change attitudes (Lewin, 1947). In a similar way changes in intentions and behaviour do not automatically follow from changes in attitude (McGuire, 1972; Flay *et al.*, 1980). Explicitly accepting that changes in attitude might, or might not, lead to changes in intentions and behaviour, Schlegel *et al.* (1984) attempted a more deliberate and theoretically-based attempt to translate knowledge and attitudes into actual behaviour.

Their study asked if 13-year-old schoolchildren could be assisted in some systematic way to make decisions about their intentions and behaviour so that these decisions might serve as guidelines for future behaviour. They drew broadly on the work of Hoyt and Janis (1975) who developed a motivational balance sheet procedure whereby a person analyses the consequences of a decision. The anticipated gains or benefits, and costs or losses, are categorized into four major types of consequence:

utilitarian gains or losses to self
utilitarian gains or losses to significant others
self-approval or disapproval
approval or disapproval from significant others.

This decision-making procedure maps out a structure for action, with the intention of helping to translate facts and values into an actual decision concerning behaviour. It has potential uses in a number of areas and has been found particularly helpful for reaching and keeping to decisions in areas such as career choice, weight reduction and physical activity (Hoyt and Janis, 1975; Wankel and Thompson, 1976). It is possible that self-persuasion is one of the mediating processes accounting for the positive effects of the balance sheet procedure, with the subjects becoming more aware of the facts and values supporting a given course of action (Schlegel *et al.*, 1984). This receives some support from work by Wright (1983), who found that self-persuasion was a powerful tool in modifying both attitudes and subsequent behaviour.

Schlegel *et al.* (1984) examined the use of a decisional balance sheet as a guided decision-making procedure for the prevention of adolescent alcohol abuse and compared its effectiveness with two other educational approaches, (*a*) a facts only based approach, using discovery learning methods; and (*b*) a facts + values clarification approach, using values exposition, values clarification and the achievement of values consonance (Harmon *et al.*, 1973). They predicted that the facts only exposure would affect the knowledge about alcohol use, that the facts + values clarification would affect attitudes as well as knowledge, and that the addition of a guided decision-making process (facts + values clarification + decision making) would affect intentions and behaviour as well.

The results are interesting. They found that contrary to their expectations, the facts only group showed the lowest levels of drinking both initially and at six month follow-up. The guided decision-making group showed the greatest increase in starting to drink, albeit at moderate levels. It is apparent that the decision-making procedure had a counterproductive effect in this group in that more young people actually started drinking. To explain these results they suggested that the guided decision-making procedure precipitated a volitional choice not to abstain. This decision was then translated into actual behaviour, as reflected by the increased incidence of new drinking.

Education is one commonly-used form of primary prevention with children and adolescents. Another is to focus on training young people to develop specific skills for resisting peer pressures. Such an approach is particularly relevant with adolescents, with the increasing role of peer influences as a primary determinant of intentions and behaviour. The variable of 'similarity' is one of the most powerful factors in whether people like each other or not; and in adolescence peer acceptance, support and approval is very important indeed. Many adolescents are afraid of opting out of an activity and risking peer disapproval or rejection. In such a social climate the immediate rewards of acceptance by a peer group outweigh the values of both the immediate and potential long-term rewards for performance of health behaviours. It is against this background that it is useful to look at smoking prevention amongst adolescents.

Smoking

There has been a considerable amount of pioneering work on social influence and smoking in adolescence. There are two reasons why work in the area of smoking is particularly important; childhood experience with cigarettes frequently leads to chronic adult tobacco use, and smoking behaviour is linked to a high rate of other problem behaviours. Smoking is regarded by many as the greatest single preventable health hazard of our time. In spite of a decrease in adult smoking there is discouraging evidence that smoking among teenage boys is virtually constant and among girls is actually increasing.

The importance of prevention is highlighted by the limited success of cessation programmes. Most school children believe smoking is dangerous to health. Children of between four and eleven years even attempt to persuade their parents to stop, yet in spite of this many school children begin smoking in their early adolescent years. It seems that peer pressure, parental modelling and the mass media may override the belief of the adolescent that smoking is dangerous. The pressure to conform to group norms is difficult to resist, particularly for those whose group membership is new or uncertain. Taking into account the important influence of the peer group in adolescence, a number of prevention programmes have focused on training adolescents to develop skills for resisting peer pressures.

In an elegant series of studies, Evans *et al.* (1981) examined various types of intervention strategies within a framework of social-psychological communication models (McGuire, 1974) and social learning theory (Bandura, 1971), and evaluated their effectiveness in deterring the onset of frequent smoking in young adolescents. Evans *et al.* (1978) developed a smoking deterrence strategy that used persuasive communication and cognitive inoculation in a series of videos and posters that identified the social pressures and counter-arguments from peers, parents and the media on adolescents to smoke. Detailed techniques for recognizing and coping with such social influences on smoking were modelled via videoed role-plays by children of the same age as the subjects. Additional messages dramatized the immediate physiological consequences of smoking instead of focusing on the less effective but more frequently used fear-arousing communications about cancer and heart disease in the future (Evans *et al.*, 1975). Between 1352 and 3296 secondary age school children were involved. Evans *et al.* (1981) found that the treatment group smoked less frequently and were significantly less likely to begin smoking than the controls, and that this group maintained its advantage at follow-up.

Other workers (for example Perry *et al.*, 1980; Hurd *et al.*, 1980) have investigated smoking prevention programmes incorporating variants of these techniques developed by Evans, for example, modelling of desired behaviour using people of a similar age, role-playing ways of resisting social pressures to smoke, covert rehearsal of counter-arguing, guided practice and positive social approval oriented reinforcement. Overall, their work suggests much promise for programmes approaching primary prevention by providing skills for coping with peer pressure drawing on social learning theory and social influence 'inoculation' techniques.

There are, however, two recurrent problems in a number of studies in this area: one is generalization, the other is long-term maintenance. It is important that the health behaviours generalize across situations in the adolescents' lives, and that they are maintained. Bandura (1978) has argued that psychological functioning involves a continuous reciprocal interaction between behaviour, cognitive and environmental influences and, therefore, that the likelihood that a given behaviour will be performed or not can vary markedly in different environmental settings, with different people, and at different times. Programmes aimed at preventing the use of tobacco, alcohol and drugs with adolescents should therefore investigate the value of deliberately exposing the individual to a range of settings; for example, in role-play, getting the adolescent to refuse drugs in a variety of situations rather than just one. Similarly, prevention programmes might investigate the value of incorporating multiple role models with whom the subject can identify, rather than single role models; for example, the use of assertive, non-assertive, sophisticated and naive models with the individuals portrayed being sufficiently similar to the target individuals that they are able to identify with the manner in which the situation is handled. Long-term follow-up is obviously of considerable importance in the area of prevention. However, when such follow-ups have been carried out, a number of studies have shown disappointing results, often finding that when the programme is discontinued the effects do not outlast the programme by more than a few months.

When attempting to increase positive long-term effects it is clinically-relevant to bear in mind the distinctions that social learning theory makes among the three basic sub-processes of change – induction, generalization and maintenance of behaviour. The analysis of prevention programmes in terms of these sub-processes provides a more informative basis for evaluation and improvement than do undifferentiated assessments of outcome. From this perspective the general issue of programme efficacy is divided into the more specific questions of whether a method initiates psychological changes, whether the changes generalize across situations and response systems (behavioural, affective and attitudinal) and whether the changes are maintained over time. In the area of prevention it seems that some methods are effective for creating changes, but require specific incorporation of supplemental generalization and maintenance or 'booster' programmes, rather than just leaving generalization and maintenance to fortuitous circumstances.

THE APPLICATION OF PRIMARY PREVENTION PROGRAMMES TO LARGER POPULATIONS

Psychology is in the process of rapidly developing its theoretical and practical contribution to a range of areas within the broad field of health maintenance and enhancement. An exciting challenge in this area is the sheer scale of the number of people who can be reached. This is a significant attraction for clinical psychologists who share David Hawks' (1987) impatience with 'the benefits conferred by one-to-one patient consultations'. As he provocatively put it: 'while not underestimating the benefit to the patient, the sum total of the good one could do always seemed to me too paltry to justify a professional life'.

The traditional way in which psychological services are provided to the public is based on a disease model. However, in the area of personal well-being the disease model no longer seems appropriate. As psychology significantly increases its contribution to this area, the inappropriateness of the disease model increases. It is worth considering Bandura's (1984) views on this topic.

> Because most of our psychological practices have embodied the disease ideology we offer remedies for the few rather than benefits to the many. The relevance of research, the adequacy of behavioural analyses, and the utility of psychological procedures all tend to be measured against the pathology metaphor. We have the knowledge and the means to bring benefit to many. We have the experimental methodology with which to advance psychological knowledge and practice. But to accomplish this calls for a broader vision of how psychology can serve people, and a fundamental change in the uses to which our knowledge is put.

Ways of applying medical and psychological knowledge to the benefit of large numbers of people are beginning to be explored, in particular the use of the mass media in large scale prevention programmes is being investigated (Maccoby and Alexander, 1980; Ferstl *et al.*, 1977). Maccoby and Alexander were concerned with the reduction of risk of cardiovascular disease on a community-wide basis. They found that the media, including television and posters, were successful in producing significant reductions in risk factors. Less promising results for the use of television were found by Ferstl *et al.* (1977) when they investigated the Max Planck Institute of Psychiatry's use of German television in a programme for weight control. There are a number of possible reasons for these conflicting results. In the German study the programme was mounted over a much shorter time period (seven months) than the two-year American study. Given that market research suggests that frequent multiple impacts are necessary to change buying patterns even marginally, it is possible that the length and density of imputs was not great enough to achieve significant impact. Another possibility is that certain kinds of behaviours are more amenable to influence via the mass media than others. For example, it might be hypothesized that in reducing the risk of cardiovascular disease an important part of the task is to inform people. If the information is given in a positive way people might take this information and effectively persuade themselves. With weight control it is arguable that it is not so much getting the information across that is most important – most people know it is less healthy to be overweight – the task is more to persuade people to change certain habits and behaviour. In this case we know that simply offering information and advice has rarely been associated with changes in behaviour. In this area it is more effective to enlist the active participation of the individual.

The studies of Ferstl *et al.* (1977) and Maccoby and Alexander (1984) involved problems which are mainly associated with adulthood and both were targeted at adult populations. Nonetheless, it can be argued that concomitant with familial predispositions, these conditions often have their aetiology in habits laid down in the more formative years. Perhaps then the challenge for child clinical psychology and the media is to organize joint ventures aimed at early prevention.

Ferstl *et al.* (1977) had a most striking finding. Bibliotherapy on its own was effective, and certainly more effective than television on its own. Preventive literature, taking developmental stages into account, and not attempting to appeal to five and fourteen-year-olds simultaneously, is one way forward. It has been suggested that while the mass media is limited in its ability to persuade, it can be effective in bringing specified matters to the public's attention for discussion (McCombs and Shaw, 1972). 'The press may not be successful in telling people what to think, but it is stunningly successful in telling its readers what to think about' (Cohen, 1963). In terms of prevention, telling children what to think about and gaining their interest, may be a modest and sensible goal in this emergent area. The effectiveness of the mass media in influencing different types of health-related behaviours with children is an area very much in need of further study. In particular the comparative efficacy of television and books merits further consideration.

CONCLUSIONS

Advances have wiped out many of the earlier killer diseases of the twentieth century but others remain in which life-style behaviour plays a very prominent role. It has been said that people experience physical debilities and die prematurely, mostly of preventable bad habits (Bandura, 1984). A new orientation towards health is becoming apparent. It is concerned with the importance of 'taking care' of our helath and our selves rather than just treating dysfunction when it occurs. This area is sometimes referred to as 'behavioural health' (Matarazzo, 1980), of which primary prevention is very much a part. It is this behaviour or life style of the individual that is today's frontier in the study and understanding of health and illness. Many of the problems that lead to serious adult illnesses, such as diet, exercise, smoking, are the result of life styles that develop in childhood. This, together with the growing problems of addictive behaviour among young people and the attendant treatment problems, suggests that preventive aspects of health care might assume much greater importance with child clinical psychology services in the future.

Clinical psychology has the potential to make significant contributions to this relatively unexplored frontier of promoting health behaviour with currently healthy individuals who wish to decrease their risk of losing this healthy state. In making a contribution psychologists can draw on the broader body of psychological knowledge. The value of seeing prevention in behavioural medicine with children in the context of this broader body of knowledge cannot be overestimated. Prevention is a complex problem and contributions have been made from areas as diverse as social psychology, learning theory, communications and developmental psychology.

Social learning theory in particular has offered a particularly fruitful conceptual framework, helping to integrate contributions from different models or areas of psychology. A specific example is Bandura's (1978) reciprocal interaction model which proposed that human behaviour is regulated by immediate situational influences, by the person's performance skills and by the anticipations of the consequences for different courses of action. In any one programme different techniques might therefore usefully be applied to different aspects of the problem. For example, modelling, role-playing, peer group influences, might be used to help with situational aspects; social skills training might be used to help develop a person's personal performance and coping skills, problem-solving training might help the handling of conflicts; rehearsal, role-play, counter-arguing or guided decision making might all be useful in helping a person anticipate the consequences of different courses of action. It is clear that preventive action must take many forms, and draw on many models, often using a combination of techniques.

When working with children it is also clear that prevention must be considered within a developmental context. Indeed it is perhaps true for any age that a developmental perspective is helpful in promoting and defining productive areas of research and practice. Budman and Wertlieb (1979) argued explicitly that preventive health interventions might be most effective when based on a model of human development through the life span. Certainly, with children and young people, if a prevention strategy is to be effective it must be geared appropriately to the developmental level of the individual. For example, Schlegel *et al.*'s (1984) guided decision-making procedure appeared to actually induce early onset of alcohol use with 13-year-olds; the facts information type of intervention (using active, discovery learning methods) was more appropriate to this age group. With older adolescents, who were already drinking, the guided decision-making procedure had advantages in achieving responsible drinking. The potential interaction of the goals of prevention with the developmental level and tasks of an age group has a number of potential implications for how a prevention programme is approached. How particular aspects of an illness interact with age-related developmental tasks is an area that is beginning to be discussed (Cerreto and Travis, 1984; Perrin and Gerrity, 1984), but it has been investigated relatively little in preventive work.

There are many challenges for psychologists. The challenge of collaboration across professional divisions; the challenge of defining optimal strategies for conducting preventive work in different areas with different age groups; the challenge of mass-mediated communications as well as face-to-face situations; the challenge of both short and long-term evaluation; the challenge of ethical and moral issues; the challenge of highlighting a prevention model in a profession which often finds itself constrained within a variety of treatment models. Finally, there is the challenge of identifying and surveying those young people who have been successful at maintaining health behaviours and not adopting deviant habits, and exploring the methods they have used and how the commonality of their experiences might be used profitably.

Exciting possibilities exist in the application of psychological knowledge to the maintenance of health. Enough work has been started in prevention for us to realize that opportunities in behavioural health will present themselves with increasing frequency in the future.

REFERENCES

ABEL, E.L. (1981). Behavioural teratology of alcohol. *Behavioural Bulletin, 90*, 564–581.

BANDURA, A. (1971). *Social Learning Theory*. Morristown, N.J.: General Learning Press.

BANDURA, A. (1977). *Social Learning Theory*. Englewood Cliffs, N.J.: Prentice Hall.

BANDURA, A. (1978). The self system in reciprocal determinism. *American Psychologist, 33*, 344–358.

BANDURA, A. (1984). On paradigms and recycled ideologies. In S. Rachman *Contributions to Medical Psychology: Volume 3*. Oxford: Pergamon Press.

BUDMAN, S.H. and WERTLIEB, D. (1979). Psychologists in health care settings: an introduction to the special issue. *Professional Psychology, 10*, 397–401.

CABRAL, R.J. and SCOTT, D.F. (1976). Effects of two desensitization techniques, biofeedback and relaxation on intractable epilepsy: a follow-up study. *Journal of Neurology, Neurosurgery and Psychiatry, 39*, 504–507.

CAPLAN, G. (1964). *Principles of Preventive Psychiatry*. New York: Basic Books.

CASEY, P.H., BRADLEY, R.H., COLDWELL, B.M. and EDWARDS, D.R. (1986). Developmental intervention: a pediatric clinical review. In *Prevention in Primary Care Clinics of North America, 33*, 4, 899–924.

CERRETO, M.C. and TRAVIS, L.B. (1984). Implications of psychological and family factors in the treatment of diabetes. *Pediatric Clinics of North America, 31*, 3, 689–710.

CHRISTOPHERSON, E.R. (1986). Anticipatory guidance on discipline. *Pediatric Clinics of North America, 33*, 4, 789–798.

COHEN, B.C. (1963). *The Press, the Public and Foreign Policy*. Princeton: Princeton University Press.

DIETZ, W.H. (1986). Prevention of childhood obesity. *Pediatric Clinics of North America, 33*, 4, 823–833.

DOUGLASS, R. (1982). *Youth, Alcohol and Traffic Accidents*. Alcohol and Health Monograph, 4, Washington, D.C. U.S. Department of Health and Human Services. National Institute on Alcohol Abuse and Alcoholism.

EVANS, R.I., ROZELLE, R.M., MAXWELL, S.E., RAINES, B.E., DILL, C.A., GUTHRIE, T.J., HENDERSON, A.H. and HILL, P.C. (1981). Social modelling films to deter smoking in adolescents: results of a 3-year field investigation. *Journal of Applied Psychology, 66*, 399–414.

EVANS, R.I., ROZELLE, R.M., MITTELMARK, M.B., HANSEN, W.B., BANE, A.L., and HAVIS, J. (1978). Deterring the onset of smoking in children: knowledge of immediate physiological effects and coping with peer pressure, media pressure and parent modelling. *Journal of Applied Social Psychology, 8*, 2, 126–135.

EVANS, R., ROZELLE, R.M., NOBLITT, R. and WILLIAMS, D.L. (1975). Explicit and implicit persuasive communications over time to initiate and maintain behaviour change: new perspective utilizing a real-life dental hygiene situation. *Journal of Applied Social Psychology, 5*, 2, 150–156.

FERSTL, R., HENRICH, G., RICHTER, M., BUHRINGER, G. and BRENGELMANN, J.C. (1977). Die Beeinflussing des Ubergewichts. Munich: The Max Planck Institute for Psychiatry.

FIELDING, D. (1985). Chronic illness in children. In F. Watts (ed.) *New Developments in Clinical Psychology*, The British Psychological Society, Leicester, 1985.

FIELDING, D. (1987). Working with children and young people. In J.S. Marzillier and J. Hall (eds) *What is Clinical Psychology?* Oxford: Oxford Medical Publications.

FINNEY, J.W. (1986). Preventing common feeding problems in infants and young adolescents. *Pediatric Clinics of North America, 33*, 4, 775–788.

FLAY, B.R., DITECCO, D.A. and SCHLEGEL, R.P. (1980). Mass media in health promotion: an analysis using an extended information-processing model. *Health Education Quarterly, 7*, 127–147.

FORGAYS, D.G. (1984). Primary prevention of psychopathology. In M. Hersen, A.E. Kazdin and A.S. Bellack *Clinical Psychology Handbook*, pp.701–733.

HAGGERTY, R.J. (1977). Changing lifestyles to improve health. *Preventive Medicine, 6*, 276–289.

HARMAN, M., KIRSCHENBAUM, H. and SIMON, S.B. (1973). *Clarifying values through subject matter*. Winston: Minneapolis.

HAWKS, D. (1987). Touching the hot stove. *Clinical Psychology Forum, 11*, 4–5.

HERBERT, M. (1981). *Behavioural Treatment of Problem Children: A Practice Manual*. New York: Grune and Stratton.

HOYT, M.F. and JANIS, I.L. (1975). Increasing adherence to a stressful decision via a motivational balance-sheet procedure: a field experiment. *Journal of Personality and Social Psychology, 31*, 5, 833–839.

HURD, P.D., JOHNSON, C.A., PECHACEK, T., BAST, L.P., JACOBS, D.R. and LUKPKER, R.V. (1980). Prevention of cigarette smoking in seventh grade students. *Journal of Behavioural Medicine, 3*, 15–28.

KANDEL, D.B. and LOGAN, J.A. (1984). Patterns of drug use from adolescence to young adulthood: 1. Periods of risk for initiation, continued use and discontinuation. *American Journal of Public Health, 74*, 660.

KAZDIN, A.E. (1979). Advances in child behaviour therapy: applications and implications. *American Psychologist, 34*, 10, 981–987.

KEIR, S. and LAUZON, R. (1980). Physical activity in a healthy life style. In P.I. Davidson and S.M. Davidson (eds) *Behavioural Medicine: Changing Health Lifestyles*. New York: Brunner/Mazel.

KHAN, A.U. (1977). Effectiveness of biofeedback and counter conditioning in the treatment of bronchial asthma. *Journal of Psychosomatic Research, 21*, 97–104.

KNOWLES, J.H. (1977). The responsibility of the individual. In J.H. Knowles (ed.) *Doing Better and Feeling Worse: Health in the United States*. New York: W.W. Norton.

LEWIN, K. (1947). Group decision and social change. In *Committee on the teaching of social psychology. Readings in social psychology*. New York: Henry Holt and Co.

McAULEY, R. and McAULEY, P. (1977). *Child Behaviour Problems: An Empirical Approach to Management*. New York: Macmillan.

McCOMBS, M. and SHAW, D. (1972). The agenda-setting function of mass media. *Public Opinion Quarterly, 36*, 176–187.

MACCOBY, N. and ALEXANDER, J. (1980). Use of media in lifestyle programmes. In P.O. Davidson and S.M. Davidson (eds). *Behavioural Medicine: Changing Health Lifestyles*. New York: Brunner/Mazel.

McGUIRE, W.J. (1974). Communication-persuasion models for drug education: experimental findings. In M. Goodstadt (ed.) *Research on methods and programmes of drug education*. Toronto: Addiction Research Foundation.

MARKOVA, I., MacDONALD, K. and FORBES, C. (1980). Impact of haemophilia on child-rearing practices and parental cooperation. *Journal of Child Psychology and Psychiatry, 21*, 153–162.

MATARAZZO, J.D. (1980). Behavioural health and behavioural medicine: frontiers for a new health psychology. *American Psychologist, 35*, 807–817.

MICKALIDE, A.D. (1986). U.S. preventive services task force. In *Prevention in Primary Care, Pediatric Clinics of North America, 33*, 4, 1007–1009.

OFFORD, D.R. (1987). Prevention of behavioural and emotional disorders in children. *Journal of Child Psychology and Psychiatry, 28*, 1, 9–19.

PARKER, E.S., BIRNBAUM, I.M., BOYD, R.A. and NOBLE, E.P. (1980). Neuropsychologic decrements as a function of alcohol intake in male students. *Alcoholism: Clinical and Experimental Research, 48*, 129–142.

PERRIN, E.C. and GERRITY, P.S. (1984). Development of children with a chronic illness. *Paediatric Clinics of North America, 31*, 19–31.

PERRY, C., KILLEN, B.A., TELCH, M., SLINKARD, M.A. and DONAHER, B.K. (1980). Modifying smoking behaviour of teenagers: a school-based intervention. *American Journal of Public Health, 70*, 722–725.

PETERSON, L., HARTMANN, D.P. and GELFAND, D.M. (1980). Prevention of child behaviour disorders: a life style change for child psychologists. In P.O. Davidson and S.M. Davidson (eds) *Behavioural Medicine: Changing Health Life Styles*. New York: Brunner/Mazel.

PLESS, I.B. (1984). Clinical assessment: physical and psychological functioning. *Pediatric Clinics of North America, 31*, 33–45.

PUSKA, P. (1982). The North Karelia youth project: evaluation of two years of intervention in health behaviour and CVD risk factors among 13–15 year old children. *Preventive Medicine, 11*, 550–570.

RANDALL, D. and WONG, M.R. (1976). Drug education to date: A review. *Journal of Drug Education, 6*, 1–21.

ROYAL COLLEGE OF GENERAL PRACTITIONERS (1982). *Healthier Children – Thinking Prevention. Report from General Practice, 22*. London: Royal College of General Practitioners.

RUSSO, D.C. and VARNI, J.W. (eds) (1987). *Behavioural Pediatrics: Research and Practice*. New York: Plenum Press.

SCHLEGEL, R.P., MANSKE, S.R. and PAGE, A. (1984). A guided decision-making program for elementary school students: a field experiment in alcohol (pp.407–440). In P.M. Miller and T.D. Nirenberg (eds). *Prevention of Alcohol Abuse*. New York: Plenum Press.

SCHMITT, B.D. (1986). The prevention of sleep problems and colic. *Pediatric Clinics of North America, 33*, 4, 763–774.

SCHOWALTER, J.E. (1977). Psychological reactions to physical illness and hospitalization in adolescence: a survey. *Journal of the American Academy of Child Psychiatry, 16*, 500–516.

SCHULTHEIS, K., PETERSON, L. and SELBY, V. (1987). Preparation for stressful medical procedures and person × treatment interactions. *Clinical Psychology Review, 7*, 329–352.

STARK, L.J., DAHLQUIST, L.M. and COLLINS, F. (1987). Improving children's compliance with diabetes management. *Clinical Psychology Review, 7*, 223–242.

STUART, R. (1974). Teaching facts about drugs: pushing or preventing. *Journal of Educational Psychology, 66*, 189–201.

SULIK, K.K., JOHNSTON, M.C. and WEBB, M.A. (1981). Fetal alcohol syndrome: embryogenics in a mouse model. *Science, 214*, 936–938.

WALKER, L.S., FORD, M.B. and DONALD, W.D. (1987). Cystic fibrosis and family stress: effects of age and severity of illness. *Pediatrics, 79*, 2.

WALLANDER, J.L. and HUBERT, N.C. (1987). Peer social dysfunction in children with developmental disabilities: empirical basis and a conceptual model. *Clinical Psychology Review, 7*, 205–221.

WANKEL, L.M. and THOMPSON, C. (1976). Motivating people to be physically active: self-persuasion versus balanced decision-making. *Journal of Applied Social Psychology, 7*, 332–340.

WRIGHT, S. (1983). *Cognitive change and the motivation to perform an unpleasant task*. Unpublished Ph.D. Thesis, St George's Hospital Medical School: University of London.

NUTRITION AND DISTURBED BEHAVIOUR

John Richer

CONCEPTS AND CONFLICTS

Polarization of views

Mix together:
– one research field of great complexity fraught with confusions of logic and poverty of good scientific description (human behaviour studies),
– another research field of enormous interactive complexity (human physiology and nutrition),
– detailed, sophisticated and useful lay knowledge dating back thousands of years (of behaviour and food),
– numerous individual cases of lay success after long histories of professional failure (individuals altering their diets and finding remedies for problems where traditional medicine could not help),
– some individual cases of 'remedies' going seriously wrong (for example, children being put on dangerously deficient diets),
– a climate of public (and some medical) opinion more sympathetic to complementary approaches to medicine,
– some parts of the medical profession feeling the need to defend traditional scientific values and objectivity against bias and anecdote,
– sections of the lay public feeling that the profession is dismissive of what they see as plain fact,
– pepper to spice the argument and salt to taste.
Stir well and leave to simmer, but take care the sauce does not separate!

Unfortunately there has been a separation; views on the effects of nutrition on behaviour have tended to polarize. On the one side are those, let us caricature them as the 'cranks', who see the world through food coloured spectacles, who look for a nutritional cure for most ailments (and in fact make some interesting single case findings on the way), but who sometimes are reported to engage in dangerous experiments with their own or their

172

children's diets. On the other side are the 'conservatives' who believe that the effects of food on behaviour are insignificant and that reported cases can be better explained in other ways (placebo effects, etc.). However, they are accused of dismissing the interesting, and now large, accumulation of evidence often from single cases, and of relying on often rather poor large group studies, which fail to show significant associations between diet and behaviour, but which are unsympathetic to the existence of subgroups where this connection might exist.

The cranks see the conservatives as rigid, status conscious, and afraid for their professional reputations, the conservatives see the cranks as over-zealous, fad followers and unscientific.

Rippere (1983) writes in strong terms about the plight of many who have not been helped by traditional medicine, who have often been given a psychiatric label, but who, through self diagnosis and sometimes the help of one of the rare clinical ecologists, have discovered that they have adverse reactions to particular substances eaten, touched or breathed in, and that avoidance of these improves their problems. She writes that even then, as well as before their self diagnosis, many have experienced the disbelief, criticism and dismissal of their medical practitioners.

There is clearly a need for an approach which is sympathetic to the possibility of dietary effects on behaviour. There is also clearly a need for good empirical studies; some are now emerging.

INVESTIGATING FOOD-BEHAVIOUR LINKS: CONCEPTS AND APPROACHES

In this paper I make no attempt to discuss the physiological aspects of nutritional effects on behaviour. Of methodological and behavioural aspects a few points need first to be made briefly before empirical studies are discussed, since simple errors in the understanding of behaviour and logic are frequently made which fuel the polarization between conservatives and cranks.

Ingested chemicals. It is universally accepted (conservatives included) that some drugs profoundly affect behaviour, but there is no *a priori* reason in this context for separating foods from drugs; both are ingested chemicals. The fact that drugs may not be nutritious does *not* imply some foods do *not* affect behaviour. Again, the fact that food affects one type of organism activity, our metabolism, is not an *a priori* reason why it should not affect another form of organism activity, behaviour. This belief is old and universal, for instance the Vedic culture of about 1500 BC believed onions encouraged sleep, legumes reduced aggression, and sesame seed improved memory (J. Henry, pers. comm., 1987).

NDCP—L

Behaviour causation. Behaviour causation is (*1*) multiple, (*2*) heterogeneous, and (*3*) tends to produce its effects 'catastrophically' (that is, by sudden change). In other words, (*1*) the appearance of any one behaviour is due to the action of multiple causes (sometimes separated into genetic, ontogenetic, predisposing and precipitating). (*2*) Between any two individuals (*a*) the same behaviour can be the result of different sets of causes and (*b*) different behaviours can have causes in common. (*3*) Whilst behaviours vary in intensity, all have thresholds for their appearance and so require a critical strength of causal factors to be elicited.

So with food: (*1*) diet is always only one of the many causal factors that produce a behaviour – to say that 'additives cause hyperactivity' might be a good public relations statement, but it is not scientifically coherent. (*2*) (*a*) The effect of diet is stronger in some individuals – additives have a significant effect in *some* children, and (*b*) the behaviours affected may be different (for example, overactivity or lethargy). (*3*) Eating a certain food may be followed by difficult behaviour one day but not another, simply because other causal factors are not present for the threshold to be reached (either within the nervous system, or outside it).

Psychosocial versus physiological causation. To state the obvious, which nevertheless seems to be forgotten by some critics, psychological problems do not imply psychological causes, in particular, problems in social behaviour do not imply an exclusively or even significantly psychosocial aetiology (one need not look further than the effects of epilepsy). May (1984) seems to forget this point when he criticizes Randolph, a pioneer of this field. May lists 'the many symptoms of reactions to foods according to Randolph, the prime Clinical Ecologist'. These are:

General – fatigue unrelieved by rest, weakness, sleep disturbance, excessive sweating, urinary frequency.
Respiratory – rapid breathing, excessive coughing and clearing throat.
Cardiovascular – precardial pain, tachycardia, palpitations.
Neurologic – poor concentration, parasthesias, dizziness, syncope, headache, blurred vision.
Behaviour – anxious, irritable, 'nervous' apprehensive, emotionally unstable.
Gastrointestinal – nausea, vomiting, diarrhoea, bloating, abdominal pain, dry mouth.
Muscular – Myalgic, nuchal spasm, muscle cramps.

Referring to Marks, May points out that all these are symptoms of *neuroses*, and strongly implies that therefore the involvement of food is to be viewed with extreme scepticism. This is an error. The central assertion is precisely that behaviour, amongst other functions, *can* be influenced by diet, and this is not disproved simply by noting that the symptoms are classified under the neuroses. Koranyi (1979) reports the high rate of undiagnosed physical problems in a psychiatric clinic population. May (*op. cit.*) reports that 'the findings of *scientific* studies (unreferenced), particularly with the exclusion of psychological influences, have revealed the manifestations of *true* immunologic sensitivity to food' [italics are mine]. These are '*Signs*: vomiting, diarrhoea, fatty stools, oedema, rash, hives, eczema; *Symptoms*: abdominal pain, borborygmi, dyspnoea, itchiness of skin, palpitation'. It cannot be determined from May's paper to what extent the lack of significant behavioural findings in the 'scientific' studies, is due to poor methodology and insensitive behavioural measurement discussed here (see also Hutt and Hutt, 1970a).

To anticipate, Randolph's list illustrates the mix of behavioural/psychological *and* physical complaints that typify an individual in whom diet plays a significant part in the causation of their problem.

Natural versus artificial. Finally there is the question of 'natural vs artificial'. The assertion of such organizations as the Hyperactive Children's Support Group is that *artificial* additives, amongst other things, are strongly implicated in the causation of hyperactivity. Again, artificial additives are excluded from the Feingold diet (for example, Feingold, 1975). Many food manufacturers now emphasize that their products are free of 'artificial additives' (which is probably no bad thing). It is important to remember, however, that 'artificial additives' are chemicals like any other food, and there are many 'natural' substances which are deadly. The criteria for artificiality are never made explicit, but they seem to be a mixture of 'new', 'commercial', or 'made from non plant or non animal sources'. (What about salt?)

There is a more interesting criterion that could be used, the evolutionary one. It need not be argued here that the human species is adapted to a very different lifestyle from that which obtains in western industrial societies, namely the hunter-gatherer lifestyle, which we started to leave less than 5000 years ago. Since genetic evolution is much slower than cultural evolution, it is a reasonable assumption that we remain physiologically more adapted to the hunter-gatherer way of life and to that diet, than to our own. In only the last 70 years (no time for any genetic evolution), great changes have occurred and include a great increase in the amount of refined and convenience foods, the consumption of additives, and of fat, dairy products, and sugar. [The rise in the consumption of 'junk' food led the American Public Health Association in 1979 to characterize the diet of adolescents (major consumers of junk food) as 'overconsumption malnutrition' (Schauss, 1985).] The reasons for these changes are interesting from an evolutionary point of view. Animal protein and fat, and sweet foods were an important part of the diet of the hunter-gatherer, but they were difficult to get. Therefore, there would have been selection for those individuals who were willing to work hard to get them. Nowadays, we are left with the genetic programming that makes these foods rewarding to consume, but they are easily available. Thus they can be overconsumed. On this basis, the criterion for 'artificiality' becomes whether or not a food was in the diet of our hunter-gatherer ancestors and, importantly, in that diet in the same proportion or amount. That is a purely empirical question. Amongst 'new' foods would not just be 'additives' but also, for instance, grains, dairy products, and refined foods such as refined sugar, now staple foods in Western societies. But none of these figured largely in the hunter-gatherer diet.

Interestingly Dohan and Grasberger (1973) found that schizophrenics on a milk- and cereal-free diet were released from hospital twice as fast as those given the regular hospital diet. Dohan *et al.* (1984) also compared two New Guinea populations for their rates of schizophrenia. Both consumed little or no milk, but one also consumed no grain, and they found the prevalence of schizophrenia reduced in this population. (These studies do not imply the strong hypothesis that grain is implicated in the aetiology of all schizophrenias.) Wheat and dairy products as well as some additives occur in most lists of the most common foodstuffs causing intolerance. Rippere (1983) surveyed a heterogeneous group of 85 allergy sufferers and found wheat and wheat products (61 per cent), cows' milk (40 per cent), and food additives and contaminants (38 per cent) topped her list. This sample was gathered by advertisement and many were connected with allergy organizations, so they were probably more knowledgeable than the general population and unrepresentative of it. Nevertheless, the prevalence of wheat and dairy products and some additives, especially tartrazine and benzoic acid and related compounds, appears in numerous studies of allergens (see Brostoff and Challacombe, 1987).

This finding should not only be seen in evolutionary terms, since it is to be expected that staple foods, those which are consumed in greatest quantities and from an early age, would be precisely those to which sensitivity would develop. There are three main reasons for this. First, sheer quantity of a foodstuff increases the chance of sensitivity developing; second, sensitivity is more likely to develop in the young (due partly to greater permeability of the gut membrane); and third, these foods are more likely to be present in the diet at times of increased vulnerability to developing a sensitivity (for example, during a viral infection), simply because they are a frequent component of the diet.

EMPIRICAL STUDIES

Next, I shall consider a few findings from two major areas:

(*1*) food intolerance, including food allergy, in children,

(*2*) the effects of sugar/refined carbohydrates.

These contain some clear findings of relevance to behavioural studies, and require less detailed knowledge of nutrition and human physiology. By contrast, more detailed nutritional and physiological knowledge is required to evaluate the effects of megavitamin diets or trace elements and use them in clinical practice. These will not be discussed in this paper, but reviews include Bryce-Smith (1986) and Schauss (1985). Nor shall I discuss the effects of behaviour on diet, as in anorexia nervosa, bulimia nervosa, food aversion, or food fads (see Royal College of Physicians and the British Nutrition Foundation report, 1984). These problems are within mainstream clinical psychology and are not caught up in the nutrition-behaviour controversy [although the consumption of large amounts of a certain food, is sometimes seen as a physiologically-based addiction to that food, and as evidence of an underlying intolerance of it (Randolph, 1956)].

Food intolerance

Food intolerance is defined by the Joint Report of the Royal College of Physicians and the British Nutrition Foundation (RCP-BNF, 1984) as 'a reproducible, unpleasant (i.e. adverse) reaction to a specific food or food ingredient and is not psychologically based. This occurs even when the affected person cannot identify the type of food which has been given'. This is distinguished from food aversion which 'comprises both psychological avoidance – when the subject avoids food for psychological reasons – and psychological intolerance, which is an unpleasant bodily reaction caused by the emotions associated with the food, rather than the food itself and which does not occur when the food is given in an unrecognizable form'. Food allergy is 'a form of food intolerance in which there is evidence of an abnormal immunological reaction to the food' (*op. cit.*).

The report lists mechanisms of adverse food reaction other than allergy or aversion and these include:

(*a*) a lack of particular enzymes (for example, lactase deficiency)

(*b*) pharmacological effects (for example, caffeine)

(*c*) a histamine releasing effect (for example, to shellfish or strawberries)

(*d*) an irritant effect on the mucous membranes of the mouth or bowel

(*e*) an indirect effect caused by the effects of fermentation of unabsorbed food residues in the lower bowel.

It is unfortunate that the popular use of the term allergy has greatly widened so that it is often synonymous with the term intolerance or even intolerance and aversion. Medical irritation at this imprecision has fuelled the polarization between 'conservatives' and 'cranks'.

The effects of food intolerance on behaviour can be directly on the nervous system or indirectly via the (usually) unpleasant symptoms the allergy produces. It is clear that both can occur (Pearson and Rix, 1987).

'Hyperactive' behaviour. The area I shall discuss is the effects of food on behaviour problems, especially 'hyperactivity', in children. The behaviour of children with hyperactivity/'hyperkinetic syndrome'/'attention deficit syndrome', is characterized by very short attention span, impulsivity, and overactivity. In such children aggressive and antisocial behaviour and learning problems often develop, but, it seems, as a secondary reaction (Weiss *et al.*, 1971; Satterfield *et al.*, 1982). However it is well known that children classified as hyperactive in the USA tend to be classified as having behaviour problems in the UK where the term 'hyperkinetic syndrome' is reserved for a small proportion of these children.

A major contribution the behaviour scientist can make to this area is to describe and analyse in detail the behaviour in question, in order that nutrition–behaviour studies need not suffer the poor understanding of behaviour that is not infrequently found. I shall adopt an approach strongly influenced by ethology.

These children's behaviour may be described as *motivational conflict behaviour*. Motivational conflict is well understood in ethology but hardly used in psychology or psychiatry. The motivations in question here are fear/frustration and whatever other motivation(s) are competing with it. [There are good grounds for regarding fear and frustration as belonging to the same motivational system (Gray, 1971).] When fear/frustration motivation is strong (that is, when the child is easily frustrated), compared to the other motivation(s) that are active, a state of motivational conflict exists where a number of behaviours can appear, these include:

(*i*)   the child is more likely to switch from the ongoing activity (he or she is said to switch attention, be distractible)

(*ii*)   the child can continue with the activity but slowly and/or showing avoidance behaviour simultaneously or alternately (he or she is said to dither, not have his or her mind on the job, be over tentative, timid etc.)

(*iii*)   the child can start responding to only partial (incomplete) cues, and respond with great intensity (he or she is said to be impulsive, careless and to rush or be overactive)

(*iv*)   the child may perform displacement activities – out of context activities, functionally the same as stereotypies (Hutt and Hutt, 1970b) (he or she is said to fidget, fumble, fiddle, scratch, and even show some more unusual, repetitive, simple behaviour). The specific goals of these activities are not important, all that matters is that the child does them successfully and so gets the feedback expected, whatever it is. They have a homeostatic function by providing successful feedback when the child is thwarted, reward when he or she is frustrated, and perhaps reducing anxiety/arousal at times of high anxiety/overarousal (Hutt and Hutt, 1970b; Richer, 1979)

(*v*) the child may show re-directed aggression.

(*vi*) the child may show regressive behaviour.

All children show all these behaviours on some occasions. Children differ in the situations where they show them and the frequency with which they are shown. This description embraces the fact that the dividing line between children with and without behaviour problems, or with and without hyperactivity, is not clear. The distinction does not depend on the child's behaviour alone but includes environmental factors and parents' or teachers' perceptions and ability to cope. All this throws doubt on the usefulness of fixed categorization of children, as opposed to their behaviour.

Children are described as hyperactive when they show (*i*) and (*iii*), when, in other words, they switch activities frequently and perform them quickly, intensely and to partial cues (impulsively and carelessly). These children fidget and fiddle, that is, they perform displacement activities frequently (*iv*). They also show the dithering and distracted behaviour which alternating or simultaneous conflict behaviour suggests to people (*ii*). What underlies all these 'hyperactive' behaviours is a low frustration tolerance (high fear/frustration motivation) and the motivational conflict which ensues.

Having analysed the behaviour this far, it is necessary to ask what causal factors affect it. It is clear that frustration tolerance depends on immediate environmental circumstances or the nature of the activity performed much more in some children than in others. The distinction between specific and pervasive hyperactivity (Schachar *et al.*, 1981) is similar. Where a child shows good frustration tolerance in some situations, diet is unlikely to be worth investigating. Where hyperactivity is less dependent on current situations and activities (it is always dependent to some extent), diet becomes one of the factors to be considered when investigating the causes of the child's low frustration tolerance – his or her hyperactivity.

Feingold diet. Feingold (1973) suggested that salicylates and artificial food colouring and flavourings were associated with hyperactivity, and that a diet free of them reduced it. His studies have been strongly criticized on methodological grounds (lack of objective behavioural measures, of control groups, of double blind procedures, etc). Subsequently, more careful controlled studies were carried out (Conners *et al.*, 1976; Williams *et al.*, 1978; Harley *et al.*, 1978; Swanson and Kinsbourne, 1980; Weiss *et al.*, 1980; Thorley, 1984). Results were mixed, and often within a single study an effect of the diet was shown on one measure but not on another. However, even these studies contained many flaws which have been summarized by Egger (1987):

– the effect of the control diet was not studied before it was used,
– washout periods were not inserted between test periods so there may have been carry over effects,
– in three studies the placebo substance was disguised in chocolate or sugar containing substances even though these probably have an adverse effect on behaviour,
– in two studies, challenges lasted only one or two days so symptoms may not have had a chance to develop. (A 'challenge' is when the person is given a substance, whose effect is being tested, after a period of not being exposed to it.)

Despite these criticisms the broad conclusion to be drawn from these studies is that the Feingold diet helped a minority of hyperactive children, but that many claims for it were exaggerated.

Food allergy hypothesis. Distinct from the very specific Feingold hypothesis is the *food allergy hypothesis*. The suspicion that food allergy may be implicated in some hyperactivity is an old one (Hoobler, 1916; Cooke, 1922). A recent major study (Egger *et al.*, 1985) has provided it with strong support.

Egger and his colleagues studied 76 children (60 boys, 16 girls, mean age: 7.3 years, range 2–15 years; 37 with adverse social factors in the family) who were 'socially handicapped by their behaviour', overactivity and inattention being prominent features. Sixty-six had associated symptoms such as headaches, abdominal pains, chronic rhinitis, aches in limbs, skin rashes (eczema, etc.), mouth ulcers, unusual thirst and seizures. The authors recognize that the sample may be unrepresentative (and a further study is under way in London to investigate this) although Egger (1987) argues that some of these associated symptoms were often only uncovered by careful questioning and so their prevalence in the general population may be higher than currently thought.

The study was in three main stages:

(*1*) A child was put on the oligoantigenic diet ('few foods' diet) which contained a dozen or so foods very unlikely to be allergenic. If the child failed to respond to the diet in four weeks, an alternative oligoantigenic diet was offered.
(*2*) The 82 per cent of children who responded to the diet were introduced sequentially to foods previously excluded by the diet, one new food per week. If the child responded to the food it was withdrawn, if not, it was included in the future diet. Fourteen did not respond to any of the foods.
(*3*) Foods identified in phase *2* were further tested in a double blind cross over trial.

This study clearly showed that food was adversely affecting the behaviour of a high proportion (82 per cent) of this group of children. The range of foods producing an effect was large, suggesting an allergic mechanism. Amongst the foods most frequently producing an effect were:

Colorant (tartrazine) and preservatives	27/34 (79%) reacted
Soya (given only to those who reacted to cow's milk)	11/15 (73%) reacted
Cows' milk	35/55 (64%) reacted
Chocolate	20/34 (59%) reacted
Grapes	9/18 (50%) reacted
Wheat	28/52 (49%) reacted
Oranges	22/49 (45%) reacted

Whilst the colorant and preservatives were top of the list, as the Feingold hypothesis would predict, no child reacted to them alone. Moreover foods containing salicylates were very low in the list. This is consistent with the largely negative findings of studies of the Feingold diet. Many children also experienced remission of their associated symptoms. Fewer children from families with adverse psychosocial backgrounds benefited from the diet (71 per cent vs 90 per cent). However more than half did, so such adverse conditions should not exclude children from dietary investigation. Egger (1987) emphasizes the disruption to family life and the expense of rigorous oligoantigenic diets with challenges. They should certainly not be routine for all hyperactive children.

Selection criteria. The criteria for selecting children for whom diet may play a role in their problems and who might therefore be helped by dietary intervention, are not yet completely clear but probably will include the following:

– Pervasive low frustration tolerance, leading to poor concentration/overactivity or lethargy (children are lacking in initiative and staying power, and are often pasty-faced). Overactivity and lethargy may alternate (cf., tension–fatigue syndrome).
– Parental handling, family relationships and the child's psychosocial history seem insufficient to account for the severity of the problem, but remember that adverse psychosocial history does not preclude dietary involvement as Egger *et al.* (1985) found.
– Other allergies or intolerances in the child or family,
– (Possibly) excessive consumption of, even craving for, certain foods,
– (Possibly) the existence of other physical features such as red ears or cheeks for no obvious reason, frequently pasty-faced, glittery-eyed.
– (Possibly) the absence of other medical conditions which might account for the child's behaviour. Pearson and Rix (1987) stress the importance of excluding 'organic brain syndromes'. But remember that Egger *et al.* (1985)

found that both hyperactivity *and epilepsy* remitted in many children after dietary treatment.

Because of the tendency to over- or under-diagnose food involvement in children's behaviour and learning problems, Thomas and I are developing a screening questionnaire, initially for teachers, which, we hope, will pick out those children most likely to have dietary (or inhalant or contactant) involvement. From a literature survey Thomas developed a list of symptoms often reported in children with food intolerance/allergy. Many could be seen in children whose problems have no dietary involvement. Our task is to see if a particular combination(s) indicates that dietary investigation would be valuable.

Clinical investigation and treatment. When a psychologist is treating a child for overactivity, behaviour or learning problems, and suspects that diet is worth investigating, he or she should do this in collaboration with dietetic and medical colleagues.

If an allergic response, in particular involving diet, is suspected to be influencing behaviour, then there are no valid biochemical tests for discovering which foods are being reacted to. Nor does the nature of the behaviour always give much clue, although some psychological reactions have been linked to certain foods. As long ago as 1621 Robert Burton, in *The Anatomy of Melancholy*, blamed milk and milk products for increasing melancholy; and dairy products are still often linked with lethargy and depressed mood. There is little alternative in the end to food avoidance and challenge, although the disruption of the full oligoantigenic diet can sometimes be avoided.

A first step can be a simple food-behaviour diary, in which parents record their child's behaviour daily and record everything ingested (including snacks, toothpaste, etc.). The purpose of this is to see if there are any obvious connections between taking in certain food or drink and behaviour. Frequently this reveals nothing for three main reasons:

(*1*) The time between ingestion and reaction is very variable, from a few minutes (in Type I allergic reactions) to well over a day. In addition there are often build up effects, and carry over effects, that is, it is necessary to eat a food several times in a short period for an effect to show, and the effect can last days after the child has stopped eating a food.

(*2*) The offending substances may be fairly constant in the child's diet and environment so changes would not be evident; their effect is masked. Staple foods, dairy and wheat products, citrus fruits and eggs, as well as chocolate and some of the additives are, in fact, among the most frequent allergens. Indeed children sometimes crave their allergenic foods in a classically addictive way (Randolph, 1956), and get the withdrawal reactions on deprivation.

(*3*) There may be no relationship between diet and behaviour. However, keeping a diary, and perhaps subsequently investigating a child's diet, might benefit the family's relationships and so the child's behaviour. Placebo effects can be genuinely beneficial. In such a case, although diet has no direct effect on behaviour via a physiological mechanism, the investigation of diet can be part of the psychological treatment of a child and the family, especially those who might be resistant to purely psychological approaches.

Another advantage of a diary is that it sometimes reveals to parents the poor quality and lack of variety of their child's diet which they then try and correct. Some then see improvements in their child's behaviour and general health. There is evidence that sub clinical deficiencies of nutrients impair behaviour (Schauss, 1985).

These are amongst the reasons why the discipline and length of the oligoantigenic diet is sometimes necessary. However there are further intermediate steps that can be taken before this. On the basis of an examination of the child's diet for imbalances, deficits and excesses, and of a knowledge of the foods most frequently reacted to, a modified diet can be suggested for the child by the dietitian which, for example, might exclude many colourings and flavourings, wheat and dairy products, eggs, citrus fruits and chocolate for a limited period, perhaps four weeks. Parents and, if appropriate, teachers should continue to record the child's behaviour and, if an improvement is observed, undertake controlled challenges. Ideally these would be double blind. However, this is usually extremely difficult to arrange in everyday clinical practice.

This procedure is sometimes sufficient to produce a satisfactory improvement. Part of the reason for this may derive from the cumulative effect of potential sensitivity-inducing nutrients, both in number and quantity, such that reducing the quantity of some and removing others altogether may be sufficient to take the child 'below threshold' (as well as reducing the risk of sensitivity developing to yet more substances). Other reasons may include the child being given a better quality diet, and the parents paying more positive and constructive attention to the child and his or her problems.

This phenomenon of the cumulative effect of sensitivity-inducing nutrients underlies the use of rotation diets in management. In a rotation diet an individual has foods from a certain class only once every four days with the intention of keeping the concentration of (potential) sensitivity-inducing nutrients below threshold. This procedure can also be diagnostically useful since the masking effects of other foods may be reduced (Radcliffe, 1987).

Other diagnostic tests, such as applied kinesiology (muscle strength testing in the presence of suspected substances), or pulse testing, are outside the scope of this paper.

Challenging with suspected substances must be done with care due to the rare but serious danger of the child entering anaphylactic shock. So challenges usually start with small quantities, followed by steadily increasing amounts.

If certain foods are found to affect behaviour such that they should be avoided, it is essential that the dietitian scrutinizes the child's diet for its nutritional adequacy. Reintroduction of small quantities is sometimes tried after about six months. Other methods can be used to desensitize the child but these will not be discussed here.

Some parents report dramatic and fast improvement in their child. However, in many cases, whilst attention span lengthens, behaviour problems maintain themselves by ordinary psychological mechanisms. In particular, the child's habitual behaviour and lack of skills continue to elicit adverse reactions from parents, other adults and peers; these attitudes to the child take time to change. Food is only one of many causal factors which may promote a child's difficult behaviour, and it should not distract attention from any maladaptive interactions that still exist in the family.

Contrary to the view of Gray (1986), 'blaming' food for the child's condition can often be therapeutic for a child and the family. It reduces hostility in family relationships and increases the chance of cycles of interaction developing which increase the child's security and self confidence and hence his or her frustration tolerance. Gray (*op. cit.*) argues that: 'Telling children that their diet is responsible for misbehaviour relieves them of responsibility for their actions, does not promote self-control, and may have far-reaching implications in terms of moral development'. Such a view implies that treating an individual on the basis of an understanding of the causes of behaviour necessarily means that responsibility, moral agency and scope for self control are removed. This is not so. It is perfectly possible to deal with people as both causally-influenced mechanisms and conscious, moral agents (see, for example, Richer, 1975). The psychological treatment programmes that accompany dietary investigation and treatment should ensure just that.

A discussion of the aetiology of food allergies is outside the scope of this paper but I shall mention two factors which have behavioural components. First, breast feeding and the avoidance of highly sensitizing foods such as cows' milk, both decrease the chance that sensitivities will develop (Soothill, 1987). Second, and more speculatively, the administration of antibiotics for viral infections tends to reduce many types of intestinal flora but not candida, which can then greatly increase its prevalence, sometimes resulting in chronic candidiasis sensitivity. This, in turn, it is argued, increases the chance of allergies developing, and has other consequences such as the child craving food rich in carbohydrates or yeast, and being hyperactive and irritable (Kroker, 1987).

As well as an allergenic diet having a direct effect on the central nervous system and behaviour, there are also indirect effects via the physical symptomatology of the allergy, its immediate discomfort and stress, the secondary medical consequences (for example, cerebral hypoxia in asthma), and the disruption and restriction it places on daily life (Pearson and Rix, 1987).

THE EFFECTS OF REFINED CARBOHYDRATES/SUGAR ON BEHAVIOUR

The consumption of simple sugar has increased more than 30-fold in the last 150 years in developed countries. The phylogenetic causes of the strong motivation to consume sweet foods have already been discussed. What enables it to be satisfied so frequently is the ready availability of sugar in large quantities; it has been estimated that to get through the average American's daily intake of sugar, someone would have to eat their way through hundreds of feet of sugar cane! (Schauss, pers. comm).

A major claim has been that reducing the amount of refined sugar, carbohydrates and additives in the diets of delinquents in institutions, and replacing these with complex carbohydrates such as fruit and vegetables, reduces violence and antisocial behaviour by between 21 per cent in one institution and 54 per cent in another (Schoenthaler, 1983). Ten institutions were involved in this study. A later study (Schoenthaler *et al.*, 1986) reported the effect of a diet low in sucrose and food additives on pupils in 803 New York city schools. There was a 15.7 per cent increase in the mean academic percentile rankings above the rest of the nation's schools, where before the dietary change there had been only a 1 per cent deviation.

Several mechanisms are thought to be involved, but a main one involves reactive hypoglycaemia. The symptoms of hypoglycaemia are being nervous, irritable, dizzy, forgetful, tired, clammy and/or sleepy. Those who have a high rate of these symptoms often have a high consumption of sugar and refined carbohydrates, leading to increased insulin release and rebound low blood sugar levels. Other mechanisms are thought to involve nutritional deficiency through the consumption of 'empty calorie' (junk) food (Schauss, 1985) made acceptable by additives which themselves may have a detrimental effect on brain metabolism (Schauss, *op. cit.*).

These results have been subject to some, not always coherent or fair, criticism (for example, Gray, 1986), generally claiming that other non nutritional explanations are possible. However, whatever the exact mechanism, the repeated findings of improvement hold out the promise of an inexpensive way of improving behaviour in penal institutions. In addition, whilst these studies do not claim to show that excess sugar-refined carbohydrates/additives in the diet of the general population are a significant cause of delinquency, they point to exciting areas for future research. Schauss and Simonsen (1979a) and Schauss *et al.* (1979b) showed that delinquents consumed more (but not statistically significantly more) refined sugar than non-delinquents.

Fishbein's (1981) study of adult male prisoners is interesting here. Using food frequency and symptomatology questionnaires, he divided the prisoners into two groups: 'hypoglycaemic' and 'non-hypoglycaemic'. He gave one half of each group a diet high, and the other half a diet low, in refined carbohydrates. Only the half of the 'hypoglycaemic' group given the diet low in refined carbohydrates showed any significant positive behavioural change, the other three groups showed no change. This study is interesting methodologically in that it attempts to separate out the susceptible individuals, and then show a differential effect, thus acknowledging the heterogeneity of behaviour causation – an essential feature for research in this area.

CONCLUSIONS

Diet does affect behaviour both by direct effects on the central nervous system and by indirect effects. The understanding of a field of such obvious complexity is not helped by the polarization of views that exists. There is a need for much more sympathetic and open minded but rigorous work like that of Egger *et al.*

Investigating and changing the diets of individuals with problems affecting their behaviour, needs to be combined with investigation and management of the psychological factors also always present.

It is instructive that large sections of the public and business world are taking action ahead of the scientific evidence, and it is unconvincing to dismiss the concern for a healthier diet as simply a passing fad with no foundation. The promise held out by greater understanding of the effects of diet on behaviour, and on health generally, is of an inexpensive contribution to the management of at least some of the problems which are now draining the resources of the health, education, social, law enforcement, penal and other services.

REFERENCES

BROSTOFF, J. and CHALLACOMBE, S.J. (eds) (1987). *Food Allergy and Intolerance*. Eastbourne: Baillière Tindall.

BRYCE–SMITH, D. (1986). Environmental chemical influences on behaviour personality and mentation. *International Journal of Biosocial Science, 8*, 115–150.

CONNERS, C.K., GOYETTE, C.H., SOUTHWICK, D.A., LEES, J.M. and ANDRULONIS, P.H. (1976). Food additives and hyperkinesis: a controlled double-blind experiment. *Pediatrics, 58*, 154–166.

COOKE, R.A.(1922). Studies in specific hypersensitiveness. On the phenomenon of hyposensitisation (the clinically lessened sensitivities of allergy). *Journal of Immunology, 7*, 219.

DOHAN, F.C. and GRASBERGER, F.J. (1973). Relapsed schizophrenics: earlier discharge from hospital after cereal-free, milk-free diet. *American Journal of Psychiatry, 130*, 685–688.

DOHAN, F.C., HARPER, E.H. and CLARK, M.H., RODRIGUE, R.B. and ZIGAS, V., (1984). Is schizophrenia rare if grain is rare? *Biological Psychiatry, 19*, 385–399.

EGGER, J., CARTER, C.M., GRAHAM, P.J., GUMLEY, D. and SOOTHILL, J.F. (1985). Controlled trial of oligoantigenic diet treatment in the hyperkinetic syndrome. *Lancet, vol. 1*, 540–545.

EGGER, J. (1987). The hyperkinetic syndrome. In J. Brostoff and S.J. Challacombe (eds) *Food Allergy and Intolerance*. Eastbourne: Ballière Tindall.

FEINGOLD, B.P. (1973). *Introduction to Clinical Allergy*. Springfield, Illinois: Charles C. Thomas.

FEINGOLD, B.P. (1975). Hyperkinesis and learning difficulties linked to artificial food flavours and colors. *American Journal of Nursing, 75*, 797–803.

FISHBEIN, D. (1981). Refined carbohydrate consumption and maladaptive behaviours: an experiment. *International Journal of Biosocial Research, 2*, 21–24.

GRAY, G.E. (1986). Diet, crime and delinquency: a critique. *Nutrition Reviews*, Supplement, May, 89–94.

GRAY, J.A. (1971). *The Psychology of Fear and Stress*. London: Weidenfeld and Nicolson.

HARLEY, J.P., RAY, R.S., TOMASI, L., EICHMAN, P.L., MATTHEWS, C.G., CHUN, R., CLEELAND, C.S. and TRAISMAN, E. (1978). Hyperkinesis and food additives: testing the Feingold hypothesis. *Pediatrics, 61*, 818–828.

HOOBLER, B.R. (1916). Some early symptoms suggesting protein sensitization in early infancy. *American Journal of Diseases in Childhood, 12*, 129.

HUTT, C. and HUTT, S.J. (1970a). An ethological viewpoint. In C. Hutt and S.J. Hutt (eds) *Behaviour Studies in Psychiatry*. Oxford: Pergamon.

HUTT, C. and HUTT, S.J. (1970b). Stereotypes and their relation to arousal. A study of autistic children. In C. Hutt and S.J. Hutt (eds) *Behaviour Studies in Psychiatry*. Oxford, Pergamon.

KORANYI, E.K. (1979). Morbidity and rate of undiagnosed physical illness in a psychiatric population. *Archives of General Psychiatry, 36*, 414.

KROKER, G.F. (1987). Chronic candidiasis and allergy. In J. Brostoff and S.J. Challacombe (eds) *Food Allergy and Intolerance*. Eastbourne: Ballière Tindall.

MAY, C.D. (1984). Food sensitivity: facts and fancies. *Nutrition Reviews, 42*, 65–71.

PEARSON, D.J. and RIX, K.J.B. (1987). Psychological effects of food allergy. In J. Brostoff and S.J. Challacombe (eds) *Food Allergy and Intolerance*. Eastbourne: Ballière Tindall.

RADCLIFFE, M.J. (1987). Diagnostic use of dietary regimes. In J. Brostoff and S.J. Challacombe (eds) *Food Allergy and Intolerance*. Eastbourne: Ballière Tindall.

RANDOLPH, T.G. (1956). The descriptive features of food addiction. Addictive eating and drinking. *Quarterly Journal of Studies on Alcohol, 17*, 198–224.

ROYAL COLLEGE OF PHYSICIANS AND BRITISH NUTRITION FOUNDATION REPORT (1984). Food intolerance and food aversion. *Journal of the Royal College of Physicians of London, 18*, 83–123.

RICHER, J.M. (1975). Two types of agreement – two types of psychology. *Bulletin of the British Psychological Society, 28*, 342–345.

RICHER, J.M. (1979). Human ethology and mental handicap. In F.E. James and R.P. Snaith (eds) *Psychiatric illness and mental handicap*. London: Gaskell.

RIPPERE, V. (1983). *The Allergy Problem: why people suffer and what should be done*. Wellingborough: Thorsons.

SATTERFIELD, J.H., HOPPE, C.M., and SCHELL, A.M. (1982). A prospective study of delinquency in 110 adolescent boys with attention deficit disorder and 88 normal adolescent boys. *American Journal of Psychiatry, 139*, 795–798.

SCHACHAR, R., RUTTER, M. and SMITH, A. (1981). The characteristics of situationally and pervasively hyperactive children: implications for syndrome definition. *Journal of Child Psychology and Psychiatry, 22*, 375–392.

SCHAUSS, A.G. (1985). Research links nutrition to behaviour disorders. *School Safety, 3*, 20–28.

SCHAUSS, A.G. and SIMONSEN, C.E. (1979a). A critical analysis of the diet of chronic juvenile offenders: Part I. *Journal of Orthomolecular Psychiatry, 8*, 149–157.

SCHAUSS, A.G., BLAND, J. and SIMONSEN, C.E. (1979b). A critical analysis of the diet of chronic juvenile offenders: Part II. *Journal of Orthomolecular Psychiatry, 8*, 222–226.

SCHOENTHALER, S.J. (1983). Diet and delinquency: a multi-state replication. *International Journal of Biosocial Research, 5*, 70–117.

SCHOENTHALER, S.J., DORAZ, W.E., and WAKEFIELD, J.A. (1986). The impact of low food additive and sucrose diet on academic performance in 803 New York public schools. *International Journal of Biosocial Research, 8*, 138–148.

SOOTHILL, J.F. (1987). Prevention of food allergy. In J. Brostoff and S.J. Challacombe (eds) *Food Allergy and Intolerance*. Eastbourne: Ballière Tindall.

SWANSON, J.M. and KINSBOURNE, M. (1980). Food dyes impair performance of hyperactive children on a laboratory learning test. *Science, 207*, 1485–1487.

THORLEY, G. (1984). Pilot study to assess behavioural and cognitive effects of artificial food colours in a group of retarded children. *Developmental Medicine and Child Neurology, 26*, 56–61.

WEISS, G., MINDE, K., WERRY, J.S., DOUGLAS, V. and NEMETH, E., (1971). Studies on the hyperactive child. VIII. 5 year follow-up *Archives of General Psychiatry, 24*, 409–414.

WEISS, G., WILLIAMS, J.H., MARGEN, S., ABRAMS, B., CAAN, B., CITRON, L.J., COX, C., McKIBBEN, J., OGAR, D., and SCHULTZ, S. (1980). Behavioral response to artificial food colors. *Science, 207*, 1487–1489.

WILLIAMS, J.J., CRAM, D.M., TAUSIG, F.T. and WEBSTER, E. (1978). Relative effects of drugs and diet on hyperactive behaviour: an experimental study. *Pediatrics, 61*, 811–817.

PERSONAL AND SOCIAL REHABILITATION AFTER SEVERE HEAD INJURY

Andrew Tyerman and Michael Humphrey

Severe head injury is a devastating experience for the individual, an acutely stressful life event for the family, and a major health problem for society. The impact is all the more disturbing due to limited public awareness of the effects of head injury. To learn that your loved one, whose life may be in danger, has suffered brain damage is acutely distressing for the family, and later profoundly disturbing for the patient.

It was estimated from the *Hospital In-patient Enquiry* that 142 000 head injured people were admitted in England and Wales in 1972, of whom two-thirds were male and over half aged under 20 (Field, 1976). The 5175 deaths represented nearly 1 per cent of all deaths. More recently Jennett and MacMillan (1981) estimated an annual attendance rate of 1778 per 100 000, and admission rates of 313 per 100 000 in Scotland and 270 per 100 000 in England and Wales.

Whilst recovery may continue over many years the more severely injured will be faced with permanent disability, which threatens the resumption of family, work and social lives. Head injury is especially tragic for the family and costly for society as it tends to affect teenagers and young adults with a further life expectancy of over 50 years. It is essential that these young people attain their maximum rehabilitation potential and whenever possible return to a productive and satisfying life.

The needs of head-injured people vary markedly with the severity of injury and associated disability. This chapter considers the severely head-injured adult (that is, coma >6 hours and/or post-traumatic amnesia (PTA) >24 hours), but will focus mainly on those with very severe injuries (PTA >7 days), for whom rehabilitation services are essential. The review draws upon Tyerman's (1987) study of 60 very severely head-injured patients (PTA > 7 days, median 10 weeks), admitted to two specialist neurological rehabilitation centres in Britain – the Wolfson Medical Rehabilitation Centre (Wimbledon) and the Joint Services Medical Rehabilitation Unit (RAF Chessington).

NDCP—M

On the basis of a long-term follow-up of 469 very severely injured patients (PTA > 7 days) from the Radcliffe Infirmary, Oxford, Roberts (1979) estimated that there will be an additional 210 totally disabled and 1500 severely or profoundly disabled persons after head injury every year in England and Wales. Numbers of head-injured people in the community are accumulating with a recent estimate that one family in every 300 has a member with persisting disability after head injury (Lancet, 1983). This involves a wide range of physical, cognitive and personality changes which, in combination, often prevent successful resettlement.

Physical disability is mainly neurological (see Roberts, 1979), but may include numerous orthopaedic and other medical complications (see Zalisky *et al.*, 1985). Of 60 very severely head-injured patients admitted to rehabilitation at an average of 7.8 months post-injury, Tyerman (1987) found that all except two had some physical disability, of whom 17 were totally dependent. Amongst 50 extremely severe cases (PTA >1 month) Thomsen (1974; 1984) found that 70 per cent had some physical disability and 20 per cent were severely disabled at 12–70 months, with no significant improvement at 10–15 years follow-up.

Cognitive impairment is a central feature of disability after head injury (see Newcombe, 1982; Brooks, 1984; Levin, 1985; for recent reviews). Tyerman (1987) found that all except one of his 60 patients had some intellectual impairment, of whom eight displayed specific language problems and seven marked visuo-spatial deficits, with all patients impaired in their memory and learning skills. In her long-term follow-up Thomsen (1984) reported that 80 per cent of her extremely severe group still exhibited memory problems at long-term follow-up. However, it is the accompanying personality and social changes which are the primary focus of the chapter.

PERSONALITY CHANGE

Personality change after head injury embraces a wide range of emotional and behavioural sequelae. Prigatano (1987) identified four classes of disturbance:

anxiety and catastrophic reaction
denial of illness or anosognosia
paranoia and psychomotor agitation
depression, social withdrawal and amotivational states.

These represent a combination of primary neurological damage and secondary psychological reactions. Ford (1976) contrasts primary changes, such as lack of insight, egocentricity, hyperactivity, impulsiveness and loss of emotional control, with secondary changes such as reduced self-esteem, loss of self-assurance and confusion arising from repeated failure and frustration. These secondary reactions include the broad spectrum of responses seen in other injured, sick or stressed people but with additional constellations of symptoms specific to brain injuries (Bond, 1984).

Muir and Haffey (1984) suggest that head-injured patients suffer a 'partial death' with a characteristic pattern of grieving which they have termed 'mobile mourning'. Common reactions include:

the search for certainty of recovery
fluctuations between euphoria and despair
exacerbated feelings of rage
breakdowns in links in the patient's 'personal system'
and 'learned helplessness'.

Such changes in personality have been investigated primarily through clinical ratings and relatives' perceptions.

Levin and Grossman (1978), for example, completed the Brief Psychiatric Rating Scale with 70 patients in a neuroscience unit: mild cases (conscious on admission) exhibited only somatic concern and anxiety; severe patients (unconscious >24 hours) exhibited more emotional withdrawal, conceptual disorganization, motor retardation, unusual thought content, blunted affect, excitement and disorientation. Agitation, aggression and sexually-explicit behaviour was also noted in a third. In a one year follow-up of 27 severe patients, ten reported depression, five anxiety and eight aggression, with four exhibiting severe disturbance (Levin *et al.*, 1979). Marked conceptual disorganization, lack of insight, decreased initiative and poor planning have also been reported on a modified Neurobehavioral Rating Scale (Levin *et al.*, 1987).

In his very severe group, Tyerman (1987) found that 85 per cent presented with problems in social behaviour on admission to rehabilitation, although few problems were regarded as severe. Marked changes in self-concept and high levels of distress were also found amongst 25 patients during rehabilitation (Tyerman and Humphrey, 1984). Poor social skills, high social anxiety and low self-esteem were still evident amongst 11 very severely injured patients (unconscious >1 week) at an average of 5.4 years post-injury (Newton and Johnson, 1985). Whilst appearing low, the reported suicide rate of 0.6 per cent was estimated to be three times the expected level amongst 291 very severely injured patients (PTA >1 week) at ten year follow-up (Roberts, 1979).

Other researchers have focused on the perceptions of relatives. Lezak (1978) identified five categories of personality change likely to create adjustment problems for the family:

an impaired capacity for social perceptiveness
reduced control and self-regulation; stimulus-bound behaviour

specific emotional reactions (such as apathy, silliness, irritability, altered sexual drive)
and an inability to profit from experience.

In a study of 50 severely head-injured young adults (PTA > 24 hours), Oddy and Humphrey (1980) found that 43 per cent of relatives reported adverse changes in personality at 6 months and 57 per cent at 12 months. The nature of relatives' perceptions of personality change was explored by Brooks and McKinlay (1983) on a semantic differential scale at 3, 6 and 12 months post-injury. The pattern of ratings of 'current' versus 'retrospective' personality was found to be established at 3 months, when reduced self-reliance and sensitivity and increased irritability were already striking. In a study of relatives' perceptions of 55 severely head-injured patients (PTA > 2 days) McKinlay *et al.*, (1981) found that, whilst 60 per cent reported personality change at 12 months, disturbed/inappropriate behaviour was much less common (20 per cent). However, the percentage reporting personality change rose to 74 per cent at 5 years with a marked rise in disturbed behaviour – 54 per cent now making threats or gestures of violence and 20 per cent displaying physical violence (Brooks *et al.*, 1986). Such changes have a marked impact upon social and family adjustment.

SOCIAL AND FAMILY CONSEQUENCES

In a 1–14 year follow-up of 150 patients (coma >6 hours), Jennett *et al.* (1981) reported 40 per cent to have made a good recovery (able to resume normal occupational and social activities), 40 per cent to have moderate disability (independent but disabled) and 20 per cent severe disability (dependent upon others for activities of daily living). Some degree of disability was evident in 97 per cent of cases.

The most commonly reported social outcome concerns return to work. In a review of 12 studies, Humphrey and Oddy (1980) found that occupational resettlement ranged from 50 per cent – 99 per cent. In their own study of 50 severely injured patients (PTA >24 hours) Oddy and Humphrey (1980) report a resettlement rate of 82 per cent at 2 years. However, in a 2–5 year follow-up of 58 more severe patients (unconscious >24 hours), Hpay (1971) found that, whilst 83 per cent had returned to work, 28 per cent were in a reduced capacity. In her 30-month follow-up of 50 extremely severely injured patients (PTA >1 month) Thomsen (1974) found that only 8 per cent had returned to previous work, 4 per cent to irregular work, 4 per cent to easier work, 4 per cent back to school and 8 per cent to sheltered work. Of the 40 reviewed at 10–15 years only five were in open employment and seven in sheltered employment (Thomsen, 1984).

However, it was the loss of social contacts rather than the lack of employment that was reported to be the most disabling handicap for patients and families. Of the 58 patients followed up by Hpay (1971), two-thirds had achieved a satisfactory adaptation to their previous social life, 20 per cent had been unable to re-adapt and 14 per cent were 'complete social outcasts'. In a detailed study, Oddy *et al.* (1978a) found that 38 per cent of severely head-injured patients reported impaired leisure activities at 6 months and the group enjoyed fewer social outings than orthopaedic controls at two years (Oddy and Humphrey, 1980). A marked lack of social activities at two years was reported by relatives of 44 very severe patients (PTA >7 days) from the Wolfson Medical Rehabilitation Centre: they reported fewer interests and hobbies, fewer friends, less social and sexual activity and a more lonely life than less severely injured patients (Weddell *et al.*, 1980). A dearth of activities was also evident at a 7 year follow-up – half had very limited contact with friends and 60 per cent had no boy or girlfriend (Oddy *et al.*, 1985).

Many studies have stressed the impact on the family. A six-stage model was proposed by Lezak (1982):

1 preoccupation with helping
2 anxious bewilderment at changes in the patient
3 anxious guilt-ridden depression characterized by feelings of helplessness and despair
4 realization that the patient has changed, that they are not responsible for the consequences, and that the patient is not going to change very much
5 active mourning
6 and, finally, re-organization and adaptation.

All caretakers of dependent patients may feel very isolated and trapped. Lezak (1978) highlighted the special problems of the spouse of the head-injured person – the 'single spouse', who is in 'social limbo' without a partner to share in an active social and sexual life, yet not free to seek one.

Panting and Merry (1972) reported great strain upon wives and mothers of 30 severely injured patients (27 unconscious > 24 hours) with 61 per cent requiring tranquillizers and sleeping tablets. Oddy *et al.* (1978b) found that 39 per cent of relatives seen within a month of injury were depressed on a self-report scale with a fall at 6 months but no further fall at 12 months. Similarly, McKinlay *et al.* (1981) found that the subjective burden upon relatives of 55 severely injured patients (PTA > 2 days), which was related to patients' cognitive and behavioural changes but not to physical disability or language impairment, did not diminish from 3 to 12 months. In a five-year follow-up of this group, Brooks *et al.* (1986) found a marked deterioration with twice as many relatives in the 'high burden' category (53 per cent) as at one year (24 per cent). In a related study of 42 severe patients (PTA > 2 days) Livingston *et al.* (1985a) found that 45 per cent of relatives reported a clinical degree of anxiety on the Leeds scales and 57 per cent on the General Health Questionnaire at three months. Problems were emerging in marital and close relationships but not yet in social, leisure and work activities. Significant psychiatric difficulties persisted during the first year with twice the level of dysfunction as in the general population and problems now beginning to emerge in social functioning (Livingston *et al.*, 1985b). However, it was noted that most of the group had not completed any formal rehabilitation programmes.

REHABILITATION AND OUTCOME

The Mair Report (1972) defined rehabilitation as the restoration of the person to the fullest physical, psychological and social condition. Some authors use the term as synonymous with treatment, but rehabilitation involves resettlement and re-adjustment – 'the training of the disabled to live the best life he can, not within the limits of his disability, but to the maximum of his ability' (Rusk *et al.*, 1969). This is not just a matter of meeting physical needs but emotional, social, educational and vocational needs, especially in a young adult group.

Reviewing services in the USA, Ranseen (1985) noted that most head injury rehabilitation teams include:

a physiatrist specializing in medical management
a physical therapist remediating physical impairments
an occupational therapist helping with basic self-care and community skills
a speech therapist evaluating swallowing mechanisms and providing therapy for language and communication disorders
nursing staff implementing medical and therapeutic programmes
a neuropsychologist assessing cognitive function and facilitating management of behavioural problems
and a social worker providing support and ongoing communication with families, helping families manage economic issues, and assisting in referral to after-care services.

A recent review of rehabilitation services in Britain highlighted the lack of clinical psychologists working with cognitive, behavioural and emotional problems after head injury (Gloag, 1985a and 1985b).

In contrast with the research on outcome there have been few evaluative studies of rehabilitation. In a study of progress in rehabilitation. Panikoff (1983) reported upon 80 severely head-injured patients (coma >6 hours, mean 31.6 days) at the Santa Clara Valley Medical Center in California. The percentage of 'functionally-independent' rose substantially during the first year with further gains at two years. Encouraging progress was also reported by Gjone *et al.* (1972) for 94 severe patients three months after admission to the Sunnaas Rehabilitation Centre, Oslo, with half able to resume their previous activities. In a 8–14 year follow-up of 30 very severe cases (PTA >7 days) 15 remained entirely independent, 7 partly dependent and 8 entirely helpless (Lundholm *et al.*, 1975).

In Britain, Gilchrist and Wilkinson (1979) followed up 72 very severe patients (unconscious >24 hours, median 4 weeks) from the Eastern Hospital, London, at 9 months – 11 years post-injury: 39 per cent were working, 38 per cent were at home, 18 per cent were in hospital (four in psychiatric hospitals) and 6 per cent had died (including two suicides). Similarly, amongst 44 very severely injured patients (PTA >7 days) from the Wolfson Medical Rehabilitation Centre, 11 per cent had returned to former jobs and a further 25 per cent were working full-time at a reduced level; but nearly half were receiving further care or at home inactive (Weddell *et al.*, 1980). At seven years, a few more had progressed from a reduced to a previous position and all of those employed at two years were still in work; but none without jobs had since found employment (Oddy *et al.*, 1985).

The outcome for the 60 very severe patients from the Wolfson Medical Rehabilitation Centre and Joint Services Medical Rehabilitation Unit was equally disappointing. After an average of four months' treatment, there had been impressive progress in functional independence but less change in social behaviour and no significant reduction in distress. At eight months' follow-up, on average 20 months post-injury, only three patients had returned to previous work or study and six to a reduced position, with over half at home inactive. Most complained of very limited leisure, social and sexual lives. Of ten married at the time of injury, seven marriages were intact but only two reported normal sexual relations. The lack of a partner for all but four others was a major source of frustration with only one new sexual relationship established (Tyerman, 1987).

At first sight such studies highlight the long-term social consequences of more severe head injuries. However, rehabilitation has in the past concentrated upon physical and functional independence rather than psychological and social skills. In a follow-up of 169 patients from the Loewenstein Rehabilitation Hospital in Israel, Najenson *et al.* (1974) found that many were not fulfilling their occupational potential. Accordingly, a year's vocational rehabilitation programme was designed to assist work and social re-integration through psychotherapy, cognitive and vocational training and prosthetic devices. Considerable gains were claimed for 13 patients within the therapeutic milieu but less success in improving behaviour outside the sheltered workshop environment (Rosenbaum *et al.*, 1978).

In response to research demonstrating the importance of cognitive and behavioural changes (for example, Najenson *et al.*, 1980), there is an increasing use of psychological methods in rehabilitation after head injury, especially in the USA. Ben-Yishay and Diller (1983), for example, describe a neuropsychological approach to cognitive retraining and Muir *et al.* (1983) report a behavioural approach to treatment at the Casa Colina Hospital for Rehabilitation Medicine in California. Whilst Powell (1981) stressed the benefits of combining neuropsychology with behaviour therapy in working with brain-damaged patients, Miller (1984; 1985) concluded that such approaches are still in the early stages of development and are as yet unproven.

In Britain, Lincoln (1981) pioneered the use of behaviour modification in general patient management and for specific problem behaviour at Rivermead Rehabilitation Centre, Oxford. Wilson (1987) subsequently developed an approach integrating neuropsychological and behavioural methods at the same centre, especially with memory problems. Wood (1984) described the token economy regime at the Kemsley Unit, St Andrews Hospital, Northampton, in the management of brain-damaged patients with severely disturbed behaviour. Jones (1985) ran an 'adjustment group' at the Joint Services Medical Rehabilitation Unit, in which patients were encouraged to consider how they projected themselves to others and how this, in turn, affected the way in which they were treated. Johnson and Newton (1987) report a weekly social skills group using role-play, videotaped feedback and discussion.

One of the most comprehensive approaches yet devised is an intensive six month 'Neuropsychological Rehabilitation Program' in Oklahoma (see Prigatano, 1986). Major themes include increased awareness, acceptance and understanding, cognitive retraining, development of compensatory skills and vocational counselling. Prigatano *et al.* (1984) report that 18 patients, admitted at an average of 22 months after severe head injury (coma >24 hours), showed greater improvement than a matched group of 17 untreated head-injured controls – improving in speed of information processing and becoming more reliable and less confused, helpless, withdrawn, hyperactive, anxious and depressed. Whilst nine patients were gainfully employed at follow-up compared with only six controls, this was still less than expected. It was concluded that improvement in neuropsychological status and personality is necessary but not sufficient to ensure a productive lifestyle for head-injured people. The programme was subsequently being revised to include 'job placement and maintenance skills'.

Such developments represent a major advance in the management and retraining of cognitive and behavioural skills, at least within the specialist centre. However, the early results from Israel and Oklahoma suggest problems in maintaining gains on return to the community. Indeed it is unlikely that such programmes alone will resolve the problems of resettlement, the social isolation of head-injured patients and the strain upon relatives, as described above. New initiatives will be required to promote long-term personal and social adjustment.

PERSONAL AND SOCIAL REHABILITATION

Psychological and social adjustment after head injury has, to date, been studied primarily through the perceptions of relatives and has tended to highlight the effects upon the family rather than the person. Van Zomeran and van den Burg (1985) argue that the patients are comparative experts in head injury and we cannot complete our understanding without investigating their subjective complaints. Patients' perceptions are of course influenced by their cognitive status, especially lack of insight, but that must not deter us from efforts to explore their experiences and develop appropriate interventions.

Subjective impairment, expectations of recovery, self-concept and emotional distress were studied by Tyerman (1987) amongst his 60 very severely head-injured patients. On admission to rehabilitation the group were inclined to underestimate their functional restrictions in mobility, self-care and performance skills, with a marked lack of insight into their cognitive impairment. They had very high expectations of recovery, with few doubting their return to independence and most expecting to regain their previous level of function. Marked changes in self-concept were also evident with patients rating their current selves lower than their past selves on 17 of 20 constructs on a Head Injury Semantic Differential Scale: seeing themselves as markedly more bored, unhappy, helpless, worried, dissatisfied, unattractive, forgetful, irritable, clumsy, dependent and inactive than prior to their injury.

On self-report scales 40 per cent were clinically anxious or depressed, but patients confidently expected to return to their former selves within a year. On discharge, after an average of four months, patients continued to underestimate their problems, lacking insight into their cognitive and personality changes and maintaining unrealistic expectations of recovery. There was only a slight increase in current self-concept as the higher ratings of patients with more accurate self-appraisal on admission were offset by lower self-ratings from those who had developed greater insight at discharge. The group continued to identify with their pre-morbid selves and few, as yet, appreciated the need for reappraisal of themselves and their lives.

At follow-up, eight months after discharge and 20 months post-injury, there was little overall change in current self-concept – whilst 26 subjects were more positive than on discharge, 27 were more negative. There remained a very marked discrepancy between ratings of present and past self but the future was now viewed less positively – midway between the present and the past. Less optimistic expectations of further recovery were now expressed amidst a growing realization of the extent and implications of residual impairment, with more patients beginning to appreciate that they would not regain their former skills and life style. A major concern is that such patients were reaching this painful realization at a stage when few were receiving any professional advice or support. In fact, more of the group were now clinically anxious or depressed on self-report scales than on admission or discharge.

This group of very severely injured patients made substantial gains in their functional independence during rehabilitation but with less change in self-perceptions, unrealistic expectations and levels of distress. However, in contrast with the intensive skills training, there was a marked lack of therapy for the emotional trauma of head injury. Acutely distressed patients were seen by a clinical psychologist or occasionally by a psychiatrist, but at neither unit was there provision for routine counselling of patients or their relatives.

Personal rehabilitation

A primary need is to provide regular information and explanation at a level compatible with the patient's cognitive and emotional status. Formal assessments provide a useful framework within which to explain the nature and effects of neuropsychological impairment. This may range from a broad outline of major problem areas to detailed explanation and feedback of test results and implications. It may help the patient's acceptance and understanding of particular problems to provide external illustrations, for example, in demonstrating problems of gait through the use of a mirror, in tape-recording dysarthric speech, in videotaping poor social skills. Whilst a minority of patients may require a behaviour modification programme, many behavioural difficulties can be productively addressed within the context of an ongoing counselling relationship.

Whilst initially serving a protective and motivating function, continued reliance on unrealistic expectations may impede progress in rehabilitation and re-adjustment. It is clear from the research presented that it cannot be assumed that patients will independently modify their expectations or recovery without skilled help. Systematic appraisal of subjective impairment and expectations will assist the clinician to judge at what stage, if any, to confront unrealistic expectations in order to seek a compromise between unreasonable optimism and despair. Prigatano (1986) suggests that the therapist should instil a sense of hope in both the patient and the family, which should be realistic, not 'blind, stupid or naive'. It will help to focus upon patients' immediate needs and a series of short-term attainable goals, such as independent dressing or memory for the daily treatment programme, rather than the uncertain long-term future.

The rehabilitation programme should, of course, be discussed with the patient and specific treatment goals negotiated to take due account of the patient's own priorities wherever possible. It is helpful to provide the patient with a record of areas of difficulty, the treatment programme and specific goals to compensate for their memory impairment. The charting of progress is crucial for those with severe memory problems whose sense of progress may be hampered by the lack of an internal baseline with which to compare their current performance. Regular re-assessments are important not just in monitoring progress and reviewing treatment goals but in moving patients and families forward in understanding the residual difficulties and in planning appropriately for the future. Clinical psychologists can thus fulfil a vital role in the overall rehabilitation process.

In the USA psychologists have assumed a dominant role in the organization and delivery of care for the head-injured patient. For example, in the Neuropsychological Rehabilitation Program in Oklahoma three neuropsychologists and a research psychologist work with just six to eight patients (Prigatano *et al.*, 1984). Whilst psychologists in Britain are not able to implement such labour-intensive programmes there is scope for a more psychological approach to head injury rehabilitation within existing constraints.

The Wolfson Cognitive and Communication Programme (Tyerman *et al.*, 1987) is a joint initiative to coordinate and evaluate a set course of rehabilitation for brain-damaged patients with primary psychological disability through individual and group sessions of occupational, physical, speech and psychological therapy, with medical, nursing and social work support. The planned role of the clinical psychologists in the programme involves routine neuropsychological assessment and consultations with patients and their relatives, individual rehabilitation counselling along the lines indicated above, cognitive retraining and behavioural management for selected patients, plus three weekly groups: educational groups to explain neuropsychological impairment; goal-oriented groups to set and monitor weekly functional or behavioural goals; and resettlement groups to discuss patients' problems and prospects in preparation for discharge.

Routine follow-up is vital as it is only on return home that patients are confronted by the full extent of their restrictions and come to realize that they cannot fulfil their former aspirations. Most require reassessment and advice on progress, further therapy and occupational prospects. Some are devastated by the loss of personal skills and change in social circumstances. Burr (1981) observed that head-injured people may be grappling with an altered perception of their own worth, their new found social stigma as a handicapped person, their dependence upon others, and their lessened freedom of choice of action. He concluded that they need supportive counselling to move from denial to acceptance, from a sense of loss to an appreciation of potential, from dwelling on the past to looking to the future, and from seeing themselves as sick to seeing themselves as different.

Amid the confusion of the present and the uncertainty of the future, patients often cling to the apparent security of the past. A more explicitly psychotherapeutic approach may now be required to help them to adjust to long-term disability. In this respect the therapist may have to assume the role of a 'surrogate information-processer' (Wexler, 1974) to compensate for the cognitive limitations of the head-injured person. Self-exploration techniques (such as self descriptions and semantic differentials) and personal construct therapy have provided a useful framework within which to assist head-injured people to let go of the past and to move forward to explore and appraise their new selves. In this way, they may be helped to plan more appropriately for the future. This process is illustrated in the following summary of a case which will be reported more fully elsewhere (Tyerman, A. in preparation).

A 26-year-old graduate was working as a sales executive when he suffered a head injury in a road traffic accident. He was unconscious for 18 days with a PTA of five to six weeks. On admission at three months post-injury he presented with mild weakness and uncoordination, double vision, poor memory and mild personality change. Formal testing revealed marked intellectual impairment (WAIS Verbal IQ 113, Performance IQ 88), reduced speed of information processing, and impaired memory and learning skills. He lacked insight into his cognitive and personality changes and had to be persuaded that he was not ready to return to work without first undertaking a programme of cognitive retraining exercises.

A reassessment four months later revealed encouraging progress in cognitive skills, and a gradual return to work in a reduced capacity was recommended. A further follow-up was prompted by the patient six months later, 14 months post-injury. His longstanding relationship with his girlfriend, with whom he shared a flat, had ended. He attributed this to his changed personality, having become impulsive, aggressive and unsettled. He was confused and distressed, feeling that he had lost control of himself and his life. He was seen fortnightly for four months to discuss the nature of his impairment and its effects on his work and relationships. He felt very guilty about his behaviour towards his ex-girlfriend. It was vital to help him to view this in the context of his head injury so that he could deal with his guilt over how he had 'mistreated' her. Whilst he was coping with work, albeit in a less demanding job, he decided to resurrect a dormant ambition to be a journalist, for which he enrolled in a postgraduate diploma course. A further assessment confirmed that his cognitive skills had continued to improve, but he agreed to prepare in advance by working on shorthand and typing skills.

In spite of successfully completing his diploma and launching himself in his new career he clung to his past self. He was in his own words 'trapped in a melancholic longing for the way things were'. He sought constantly to prove that he was back to his former self and even applied to join Mensa as proof of his intellectual recovery. He drove himself very hard in his work to the detriment of his social life and tended to avoid close personal relationships, making instant and frequently dismissive judgements about people he met. Only after regular psychotherapy could he begin to let go of the past and move forward to experience new relationships. This took the form of exploration of the nature of the change in his self-concept, using semantic differentials and self descriptions, and exercises in fixed role therapy (see Bannister, 1974). At the last contact, some four years post-injury, he was finally settled in a relationship with a new girlfriend.

Social and family adjustment

Whilst there are grounds for optimism that a range of cognitive and behavioural therapies will prove of some value in promoting long-term adjustment, the benefits of such intervention will be limited by the catastrophic nature of severe head injury. A major constraint is where the individual has no daily occupation, as was the case for over half of the Wolfson–Chessington series. Of 13 patients regarded as employable in a restricted capacity or under sheltered circumstances, ten were assessed at an employment rehabilitation centre, but in only one case did this lead on to any training or work. Employment rehabilitation services are clearly not attuned to the needs of the more severely head-injured. Whilst generally unable to work to the level normally expected in competitive employment, many can still make a valuable contribution if provided with an appropriate opportunity.

For those capable of work, direct liaison with employers to explain residual difficulties and the need for a graded return to restricted duties, will often give head-injured people the breathing space they require. The reassurance that gradual progress can be expected and that a review is planned or can be arranged may provide a valuable safety net. For those incapable of work, there is an urgent need for suitable sheltered work opportunities, following the example of the Birmingham Head Injuries Rehabilitation Unit (London, 1973), both as a step towards re-employment and as a permanent placement for the severely disabled.

The lack of leisure and social pursuits at follow-up is also disturbing, especially for those with no daily occupation and limited opportunities to make new friends. Many remain totally dependent upon the family for leisure and social activities. There is a need for a much greater emphasis on leisure pursuits in rehabilitation. The response of RAF Chessington was to introduce leisure options one afternoon per week as an integral part of the rehabilitation programme, ranging from photography to carriage driving (see Tyerman R, 1984). However, it is vital that such initiatives are maintained and developed on return to the community. In this respect the growing network of over 70 branches of the self-help group Headway (National Head Injuries Association) fulfils an important role. Headway House set up by the Cotswold branch as a local 'activity/therapy' centre (Fitzsimmons, 1984) offers a promising model for meeting these leisure and social needs, as well as providing continuous support and advice.

Recent research has highlighted the impact upon the family. Tyerman (1987) found a range of family problems, marked disruption to family life and great distress amongst relatives at follow-up (60 per cent anxious or depressed on self-report scales). Whilst Headway groups provide valuable support, more professional help is needed. This should include family education and counselling and family therapy in selected cases, as well as support groups (see Rosenthal, 1984). Lezak (1978) has provided some practical advice on the counselling of relatives.

Throughout rehabilitation, relatives need information and support. They frequently require advice about the management of cognitive and/or behavioural problems and may assume the role of co-therapist in home-based retraining programmes. Ultimately, relatives must attempt to re-establish their relationship as a parent, spouse or (less often) as a child. Parents may find it easy to revert to the role of carer but harder to allow more independence in line with recovery. Spouses may find the role of carer/therapist irreconcilable with that of sexual partner and may find the altered personality and behaviour of the injured patient no longer attractive or compatible with their own. Spouses with children may find themselves torn between the needs of their injured partner and the needs of their children. The children may themselves need help in coping with the strange and unpredictable behaviour of their head-injured parent. Clinical experience with selected cases suggests that marital, family and sexual therapy can often assist families to cope with the complex problems that arise.

CONCLUSIONS

Research on outcome after severe head injury has consistently highlighted the importance of psychological changes for both social and family readjustment. A number of rehabilitation programmes have recently been devised to address the psychological needs of head-injured patients. These have tended to focus on cognition and behaviour rather than changes in personality and self-concept. We must take due account of the perceptions, aims and expectations of severely head-injured people themselves if we are to aid their long-term adjustment.

Within their cognitive limitations head-injured people should be encouraged to 'co-manage' their own rehabilitation (Wright, 1983). This can be facilitated by general education about head injury, explanation and demonstration of specific problem areas, discussion of treatment goals, joint monitoring of progress, guided planning for the future and longer-term psychotherapy. There is a parallel need for educational, advisory and supportive counselling for relatives. Formal assessments can be timed to assist the process of re-adjustment for patients and relatives through detailed feedback and discussion. Above all, the patient and family must not be allowed to drift in limbo after discharge from intensive rehabilitation back into the community. Home-based retraining programmes attuned to the individual's interests and circumstances will need to be continued in combination with available local resources.

There is an acute need for more suitable sheltered work opportunities, as well as progressive day care facilities for the more severely disabled. The expanding network of Headway groups warrants additional resources and support in its efforts to compensate for the shortcomings of health and social services. Legislation to overcome the economic and social deprivation suffered by head-injured patients and their families should also be considered. These problems are magnified by the lack of a co-ordinated policy for rehabilitation after head injury and poor continuity between specialist and local services. Whilst more severely head-injured patients require specialized rehabilitation, all groups require a range of local services including clinical psychology. The Royal College of Physicians (1986) has recommended the provision of a head injury recovery service in each district and a clinical psychologist to supervize the long-term care of those with severe cognitive problems.

In Britain, clinical psychologists have tended to be preoccupied with problems of cognition and behaviour rather than the broader aspects of personality change. However, the research on outcome of head injury is unequivocal in identifying personality change as an area of primary concern. Clinical psychologists in the USA, and to an increasing extent in Britain, are becoming involved in the process and evaluation of rehabilitation after severe head injury. Alongside cognitive rehabilitation, behavioural management and social skills training, there is a need for a more psychotherapeutic approach to aid long-term personal and social adjustment.

REFERENCES

BANNISTER, D. (1974). Personal construct theory and psychotherapy. In D. Bannister (ed.). *Issues and Approaches in Psychotherapy*. New York: Wiley.

BEN-YISHAY, Y. and DILLER, L. (1983). Cognitive remediation. In M. Rosenthal, E.R. Griffith,, M.R. Bond and J.D. Miller (eds). *Rehabilitation of the Head Injured Adult*. Philadelphia: F.A. Davis.

BOND, M.R. (1984). The psychiatry of closed head injury. In N. Brooks (ed.). *Closed Head Injury: Psychological, Social and Family Consequences*. Oxford: Oxford University Press.

BROOKS, N. (1984) Cognitive deficits after head injury. In N. Brooks (ed.). *Closed Head Injury: Psychological, Social and Family Consequences*. Oxford: Oxford University Press.

BROOKS, N., CAMPSIE, L., SYMINGTON, C., BEATTIE, A. and McKINLAY, W. (1986). The five year outcome of severe blunt head injury: a relative's view. *Journal of Neurology, Neurosurgery & Psychiatry, 49*, 764–770.

BROOKS, N. and McKINLAY, W. (1983). Personality and behavioural change after severe blunt head injury: a relatives' view. *Journal of Neurology, Neurosurgery and Psychiatry, 46*, 336–344.

BURR, M. (1981). The rehabilitation and long-term management of the adult patient with head injury. *Australian Family Practitioner, 10*, 14–16.

FIELD, J.H. (1976). *Epidemiology of Head Injuries in England and Wales with Particular Reference to Rehabilitation*. London: HMSO.

FITZSIMMONS, R. (1984). *Report of first year of work August 1983–84*. Unpublished report available from Headway, Headway House, Headway Cotswold.

FORD. B. (1976) Head injuries – what happens to survivors. *Medical Journal of Australia, 1*, 603–605.

GILCHRIST, E. and WILKINSON, M. (1979). Some factors determining prognosis in young people with severe head injuries. *Archives of Neurology, 36*, 355–359.

GJONE, R., KRISTIANSEN, K. and SPONHEIM, N. (1972). Rehabilitation in severe head injuries. *Scandinavian Journal of Rehabilitation Medicine, 4*, 2–4.

GLOAG, D. (1985a). Rehabilitation after head injury. 1. Cognitive problems. *British Medical Journal, 290*, 834–837.

GLOAG, D. (1985b). Rehabilitation after head injury. 2. Behaviour and emotional problems, long-term needs, and the requirement for services. *British Medical Journal, 290*, 913–916.

HPAY, H. (1971). Psycho-social effects of severe head injury. In *Head Injuries: Proceedings of an International Symposium*. Edinburgh: Churchill Livingstone.

HUMPHREY, M.and ODDY, M. (1980). Return to work after head injury: a review of post-war studies. *Injury, 12*, 107–114.

JENNETT, B. and MACMILLAN, R. (1981). The epidemiology of head injury. *British Medical Journal, 1*, 101–104.

JENNETT, B., SNOEK, J., BOND, M.R. and BROOKS, N. (1981). Disability after severe head injury: observations on the use of the Glasgow Outcome Scale. *Journal of Neurology, Neurosurgery and Psychiatry, 44*, 285–293.

JOHNSON, D.A. AND NEWTON, A. (1987). Social adjustment and interaction after severe head injury. II. Rationale and basis for intervention. *British Journal of Clinical Psychology, 26*, 289–298.

JONES, S. (1985). The organization of a head injury rehabilitation unit. Pamphlet No. 20. Nottingham: Headway, The National Head Injuries Association.

LANCET (1983). Caring for the disabled after head injury. *The Lancet, II*, 948–949.

LEVIN, H.S. (1985). Outcome after head injury: Part II. Neurobehavioral recovery. In D.P. Becker, and T.T. Polvishock (eds) *Central Nervous System Trauma Status Report 1985*. USA: National Institute of Health.

LEVIN, H.S. and GROSSMAN, R.G. (1978). Behavioral sequelae of closed head injury. *Archives of Neurology, 35*, 720–727.

LEVIN, H.S., GROSSMAN, R.G., ROSE, J.E. and TEASDALE, M.B. (1979). Long-term neuropsychological outcome of closed head injury. *Journal of Neurosurgery, 50*, 412–422.

LEVIN, H.S., HIGH, W.M., GOETHE, K.E., SISSON, R.A., OVERALL, J.E., RHOADES, H.M., EISENBERG, H.M., KALISKY, Z.V.I. and GARY, H.E. (1987). The neurobehavioral rating scale: assessment of the behavioral sequelae of head injury by the clinician. *Journal of Neurology, Neurosurgery and Psychiatry, 50*, 183–193.

LEZAK, M.D. (1978). Living with the characterologically altered brain-injured patient. *Journal of Clinical Psychiatry, 39*, 592–598.

LEZAK, M.D. (1982). Coping with head injury in the family. In G. Broe and R. Tate (eds). Proceedings of the Fifth Annual Brain Impairment Conference. University of Sydney: Postgraduate Committee in Medicine.

LINCOLN, N. (1981). Clinical psychology. In C.D. Evans, *Rehabilitation after Severe Head Injury*. Edinburgh: Churchill Livingstone.

LIVINGSTON, M.G., BROOKS, D.N. and BOND, M.R. (1985a). Three months after severe head injury: psychiatric and social impact on relatives. *Journal of Neurology, Neurosurgery and Psychiatry, 48*, 870–875.

LIVINGSTON, M.G., BROOKS, D.N. and BOND, M.R. (1985b). Patient outcome in the year following severe head injury and relatives' psychiatric and social functioning. *Journal of Neurology, Neurosurgery and Psychiatry, 48*, 876–881.

LONDON, P.S. (1973). Workshop for disabled survivors of severe head injury. *British Medical Journal, III*, 393–396.

LUNDHOLM, J., JEPSON, B.N. and THORNVAAL, G. (1975). The late neurological, psychological and social aspects of severe traumatic coma. *Scandinavian Journal of Rehabilitation Medicine, 7*, 97–100.

McKINLAY, W.W., BROOKS, D.N., BOND, M.R., MARTINAGE, D.P. and MARSHALL, M.M. (1981). The short-term outcome of severe blunt head injury as reported by relatives of the head injured persons. *Journal of Neurology, Neurosurgery and Psychiatry, 44*, 527–533.

MAIR REPORT (1972). *Medical Rehabilitation: The Pattern for the Future*. Report of a sub-committee of the Standing Medical Advisory Committee of Scottish Home and Health Department, Edinburgh: HMSO.

MILLER, E. (1984). *Recovery and Management of Neuropsychological Impairments*. Chichester: Wiley.

MILLER, E. (1985). Cognitive retraining of neurological patients. In F.N. Watts, (ed.). *New Developments In Clinical Psychology*. Leicester: The British Psychological Society.

MUIR, C.A. and HAFFEY, W. (1984). Psychological and neuropsychological interventions in the mobile mourning process. In B.A. Edelstein and E.T. Couture (eds.). *Behavioral Assessment and Rehabilitation of the Traumatically Brain Damaged*. New York: Plenum.

MUIR, C.A., HAFFEY, W., OTT, K.J., KARAICA, D., MUIR, J. and SUTKO, M. (1983). The treatment of behavioral deficits. In M. Rosenthal, E.R. Griffith, M.R. Bond and J.D. Miller (eds). *Rehabilitation of the Head Injured Adult*. Philadelphia: F.A. Davis.

NAJENSON, T., GROSWASSER, Z., MENDELSON, L. and HACKETT, P. (1980). Rehabilitation outcome of brain damaged patients after severe head injury. *International Rehabilitation Medicine, 2*, 17–22.

NAJENSON, T., MENDELSON, L., SCHECHTER, I., DAVIV, C., MINTZ, N. and GROSWASSER, Z. (1974). Rehabilitation after severe head injury. *Scandinavian Journal of Rehabilitation Medicine, 6*, 5–14.

NEWCOMBE, F. (1982). The psychological consequences of closed head injury: assessment and rehabilitation. *Injury, 14*, 111–136.

NEWTON, A. and JOHNSON, D.A. (1985). Social adjustment and interaction after severe head injury. *British Journal of Clinical Psychology, 24*, 225–234.

ODDY, M., COUGHLAN, A., TYERMAN, A. and JENKINS, D. (1985). Social adjustment after closed head injury: a further follow-up seven years after injury. *Journal of Neurology, Neurosurgery and Psychiatry, 48*, 564–568.

ODDY, M. and HUMPHREY, M. (1980). Social recovery during the year following severe head injury. *Journal of Neurology, Neurosurgery and Psychiatry, 43*, 798–802.

ODDY, M., HUMPHREY, M. and UTTLEY, D. (1978a). Subjective impairment and social recovery after closed head injury. *Journal of Neurology, Neurosurgery and Psychiatry, 41*, 611–616.

ODDY, M., HUMPHREY, M. and UTTLEY, D. (1978b). Stresses upon the relatives of head injured patients. *British Journal of Psychiatry, 133*, 507–513.

PANIKOFF, L.B. (1983). Recovery trends of functional skills in the head injured adult. *American Journal of Occupational Therapy, 37*, 735–743.

PANTING, A. and MERRY, P.H. (1972). The long-term rehabilitation of severe head injuries with particular reference to the need for social and medical support for the patient's family. *Rehabilitation, 38*, 33–37.

POWELL, G.E. (1981). *Brain Function Therapy*. Aldershot: Gower.

PRIGATANO, G.P. (1986). Psychotherapy after brain injury. In G.P. Prigatano, (ed.) *Neuropsychological Rehabilitation after Brain Injury*. Baltimore: Johns Hopkins University Press.

PRIGATANO, G.P. (1987). Personality and psychosocial consequences after brain injury. In M.J. Meier, A.L. Benton and L. Diller (eds) *Neuropsychological Rehabilitation*. Edinburgh: Churchill Livingstone.

PRIGATANO, G.P., FORDYCE, D.J., ZEINER, H.K., ROUECHE, J.R., PEPPING, M. and WOODS, B.C. (1984). Neuropsychological rehabilitation after closed head injury in young adults. *Journal of Neurology, Neurosurgery and Psychiatry, 47*, 505–513.

RANSEEN, J.D. (1985). Comprehensive rehabilitation of head injured adults. *Maryland Medical Journal, 34*, 1176–1182.

ROBERTS, A.H. (1979). *Severe accidental head injury. An assessment of long-term prognosis*. London: Macmillan.

ROSENBAUM, M., LIPSITZ, N., ABRAHAM, J. and NAJENSON, T. (1978). A description of an intensive project for the rehabilitation of severely brain injured soldiers. *Scandinavian Journal of Rehabilitation Medicine, 10*, 1–6.

ROSENTHAL, M. (1984). Strategies for intervention with families of brain-injured patients. In B.A. Edelstein and E.T. Couture (eds). *Behavioral Assessment and Rehabilitation of the Traumatically Brain Damaged*. New York: Plenum.

ROYAL COLLEGE OF PHYSICIANS (1986). *Physical Disability in 1986 and beyond*. London: Royal College of Physicians.

RUSK, H.A., BLOCK., J.M. and LOWMAN, E.W. (1969). Rehabilitation of the brain-injured patient: A report of 157 cases with long-term follow-up of 118. In A.E. Walker, W.F. Caveness and M. Critchley (eds). *The Late Effects of Head Injury*. Springfield, Illinois: Charles C. Thomas.

THOMSEN, I.V (1974). The patient with severe head injury and his family: a follow-up of 50 patients. *Scandinavian Journal of Rehabilitation Medicine, 6*, 180–183.

THOMSEN, I.V. (1984). Late outcome of very severe blunt head trauma: a 10–15 year second follow-up. *Journal of Neurology, Neurosurgery & Psychiatry, 47*, 260–268.

TYERMAN, A. (1987). Self-concept and psychological change in the rehabilitation of the severely head injured person. Unpublished PhD Thesis, University of London.

TYERMAN, A. and HUMPHREY, M. (1984). Changes in self-concept following severe head injury. *International Journal of Rehabilitation Research, 7*, 11–23.

TYERMAN, A., ROWLAND, D., WILLIAMS, J., CRANCH, M., BENDALL, J., SIMONSON, P. and JENKINS, D. (1987) Proposal to coordinate and evaluate the Wolfson Cognitive and Communication Programme. Unpublished manuscript available from the author.

TYERMAN, R. (1984). Promoting leisure pursuits in the rehabilitation of the severely head injured. *Therapy Weekly, 10*, 5.

VAN ZOMERAN, A.H. and VAN DEN BERG, W. (1985). Residual complaints of patients two years after severe head injury. *Journal of Neurology, Neurosurgery and Psychiatry, 48*, 21–28.

WEDDELL, R., ODDY, M. and JENKINS, D. (1980). Social adjustment after rehabilitation: a two year follow-up of patients with severe head injury. *Psychological Medicine, 10*, 257–263.

WEXLER, D.A. (1974). A cognitive theory of experiencing, self-actualising and therapeutic process. In D.A. Wexler and L.N. Rice (eds) *Innovations in Client-centred Therapy*. New York: Wiley.

WILSON, B. (1987). Neuropsychological rehabilitation in Britain. In M.J. Meier,

A.L. Benton and L. Diller (eds). *Neuropsychological Rehabilitation*. Edinburgh: Churchill Livingstone.

WOOD, R.L. (1984). Behaviour disorders following severe brain injury: their presentation and psychological management. In N. Brooks (ed.). *Closed Head Injury. Psychological, Social and Family Consequences*. Oxford: Oxford University Press.

WRIGHT, B.A. (1983). *Physical disability – a psychosocial approach* (2nd ed.). New York: Harper & Row.

ZALISKY, Z., MORRISON, D.P., MEYERS, C.A. and VON LAUFEN, A. (1985). Medical problems encountered during rehabilitation of patients with head injury. *Archives of Physical Medicine and Rehabilitation 66*, 25–29.

EYEWITNESS TESTIMONY: SOME IMPLICATIONS FOR CLINICAL INTERVIEWING AND FORENSIC PSYCHOLOGY PRACTICE

Robert Sharrock

Early psychologists were quick to realize the applications of psychological research to legal problems, particularly those relating to testimony (Binet, 1900; Munsterburg, 1908). Nevertheless, recent years have seen an enormous growth in research in eyewitness testimony such that Wells and Loftus (1984) estimate that 85 per cent of papers in the area have been published since 1978. In part, this reflects a healthy trend towards applied rather than purely theoretical research, but it is also likely that the rigours of courtroom scrutiny and the apparent limitations of existing knowledge have provided an additional impetus to research. It is the purpose of this chapter to describe some recent developments in this area and to discuss their implications for clinical interviewing, in addition to the emerging speciality of forensic psychology (Haward, 1981).

Interviewing witnesses is in some respects analogous to performing a functional analysis (Wilson and O'Leary, 1980) of a patient's problems: in both, the aim is for a clear factual account of a set of events of interest. The implication is that the same factors that threaten the accuracy of eyewitness accounts, for example, observers' expectations, heightened arousal, and the style of questioning used to elicit information will also affect the reliability of *patients'* accounts, and should therefore be of interest to the clinician. (A complete account of the scientific basis of clinical interviewing is beyond the scope of this chapter. For further reading see Marzillier, 1976, and Shapiro, 1979.)

A sequential framework for memory is presented consisting of three stages: registration, retention and recall. At each stage, the factors that affect accuracy of recall are examined and some implications for clinical interviewing considered. Based on theoretical accounts of memory, some methods for enhancing memory are discussed which the clinician may well find of use. Finally, recent research in individual differences in eyewitness recall, particularly in suggestibility in interview, is considered; this should be of interest to the increasing numbers of psychologists, mainly clinically trained, who are asked to provide expert evidence to the courts (Gudjons-son, 1985a).

REGISTRATION

Salience and attention

A necessary condition of recall is that an event is initially perceived, which is, in turn, a function of the salience of a set of stimuli present in a situation and the expectations of the perceiver. At the level of perception, the conditions of encoding may be far from ideal in terms of lighting, movement and position. However, contemporary accounts of perception place great emphasis on the role of expectancies in the perception of stimuli (Neisser, 1967). For example, in one classic study (Allport and Postman, 1947) it was shown how subjects, when presented with a picture of a white person holding a knife alongside a black person, tended to report that the knife was held by the black person: prejudice may be a more appropriate word here than expectation.

Analogously, patients may fail to notice ambiguous but potentially relevant information, and instead perceive and subsequently report information that is consistent with their own understanding. In drawing from the social judgement literature (Nisbett and Ross, 1980), Watts (1983) argues that where there is no 'causal schema' to imply the relevance of a factor, it is less likely to be identified and reported. This suggests that a knowledge of the patient's understanding of a problem will provide a basis from which the validity of their account may be evaluated.

A further limitation is imposed simply by the limited capacity of attention (Miller, 1956). A patient cannot be expected to perceive consciously all the relevant cues and behaviour during a complex series of interactions, just as a witness cannot apprehend more than even a fraction of the details of a criminal scene. As Herbert (1981, page 21) points out, if the relevant behaviour consists of overlearned responses, a client may be quite unaware of his or her actions, in which case part of the aim of assessment will be to train the client to discriminate relevant from irrelevant events.

Stimuli that impose a degree of threat, or which are of particular concern to an individual, are likely to recruit preferential attention. In viewing criminal acts, Loftus (1979) has shown how attention may be drawn towards a weapon at the scene of a criminal act at the expense of face recognition, on which subsequent conviction may depend. Similarly in phobics, there is good evidence that attention is biased towards threat-related cues (MacLeod *et al.*, 1986; Watts *et al.*, 1986). The cost is that other potentially-relevant stimuli may well be overlooked by a patient, a possibility that should be borne in mind by clinicians. This may be most apparent where attention is inwardly directed towards somatic symptoms or negative thoughts, when attention to environmental events will necessarily be impaired. An obsessional ruminator, for example, may be unaware of some environmental triggers to their unwanted thoughts.

The influence of arousal

Although much criticized (for example, Andrew, 1974), the principles embodied within the Yerkes-Dodson Law (1908) continue to influence eyewitness research. It will be recalled that the Law posits an inverted U-shaped relationship between arousal and task performance, so that performance rises with increasing arousal until some optimum is reached after which performance declines. (Task difficulty provides an additional complication which is beyond the scope of this chapter; see Deffenbacher, 1983.) As predicted, increases in levels of arousal to relatively high levels, produced for example by exposure to filmed violent incidents (Clifford and Scott, 1978), produces a decrease in recall which is usually attributed to the narrowing of attention to those central stimuli which the perceiver regards as important (Easterbrook, 1959; Baddeley, 1972).

Clinically, it is notable that relevant events are often experienced by patients in highly-aroused states, which presumably serves only to reduce further the reliability of their reports during interview. Interestingly, the apparently reduced memory of murderers for the homicidal act has, in some cases, similarly been attributed to narrowed attention in a state of arousal (O'Connell, 1960) though motivational factors or the tendency to repress painful memories may also be relevant, in addition to the effects of alcohol (Taylor and Kopelman, 1984).

FACTORS OF RETENTION

The reliability of eyewitness recall (though not necessarily recognition), tends to decline as time elapses from a witnessed event (Loftus, 1979). The rate of decline varies with the nature of the material; memory for human faces, for example, may be relatively long lasting (Deffenbacher *et al.*, 1981). Similarly, as an event of clinical interest becomes more distant in time, it is to be expected that accuracy of report diminishes.

Bartlett's (1932) conception of memory helps to account for the reduced reliability of testimony with time, although its undoubted influence is not always acknowledged in recent research on eyewitness testimony. In asking subjects to recall meaningful passages of prose he noted how, with the passage of time, accounts became simplified and more consistent with the subject's prior attitudes and expectations. Details may be omitted and others heightened in importance so as to serve as anchor points for subsequent retrieval. Sometimes extraneous information may be added to rationalize the subject's recollection. In speaking of 'effort after meaning', Bartlett was emphasizing the constructive and active nature of memory, in contrast perhaps to some lay people's conception of memory as a video-recorder which can be replayed with total accuracy (Buckhout, 1974).

Misleading information

On the basis of Bartlett's theorizing, it is perhaps unsurprising that there is now good evidence that recollection can be altered by exposure to misleading or contradictory information following registration. Loftus (1979) has developed an interesting paradigm to investigate these fallibilities. Typically, subjects are shown a sequence of slides that depict an event. Then follows post event information that in some way contradicts the original information. Finally, a memory test is given which usually shows a decrease in recall.

It is important to take note of the variety of ways in which, in real life, misleading information may be encountered. A witness may alter his or her account on the basis of a newspaper report. A patient's report may be altered in the light of different accounts from other family members, or indeed other therapists – a factor that clinicians should not overlook. More importantly, misleading information may be present in the form of questions. For example, in one study subjects were asked: 'How fast was the white sports car going when it passed the barn?' Those exposed to this misleading question were six times more likely to report subsequently the presence of a barn which was absent from the originally-presented episode (Loftus, 1975).

Although the explanation of these results lies with the nature of forgetting itself, which is at present far from properly understood, it is of more than theoretical interest. Loftus and Loftus (1980) have argued that memories undergo irreversible transformations as related post event information is assimilated into an existing memory. The implication is that accurate recall becomes irretrievably impaired.

On the other hand, and more optimistically perhaps, Morton *et al.* (1983) have proposed a 'Headed Records Theory' of memory in which a hypothetical record is formed with every new relevant episode. A 'Heading' is attached to every one, through which a record may be accessed, and consists of a mixture of content and context, including representations of environmental cues and internal states such as mood or drug states. Misleading information is assumed to form a new record which, if accessed during subsequent tests, produces faulty recall. However, if testing provides the cues which allow access of the original record, recall should not be affected (see, for example, Bekerian and Bowers, 1983). The implication, to be considered below, is that providing witnesses, or indeed patients, with suitable cues may well enhance the quality of recall.

It has further been shown that misleading information produced more effect when it was embedded in syntactically-complex sentences, which Loftus (1981) attributed to a reduction in subject awareness that the material was misleading. On the basis of this and other research, Schooler and Loftus (1986) have proposed that recollections change only if the subject does not immediately detect discrepancies between the memory of the original event and the post event information. One is reminded here of Muscio's (1915, page 379) piercing observation, that a suggestion is only effective when it is not too obvious. The implication is that when the memory of a set of events of clinical interest is not wholly discriminable, then a patient's report may be particularly influenced by cues or expectations within a question. Further, suggestion may be maximally potent when there are only subtle differences between an interviewer's and interviewee's account, so that discrepancies between the two are not detected (Tousignant *et al.*, 1986).

CONDITIONS OF RECALL

Question forms

As early as 1900, Binet, in his book *La suggestibilité*, argued that whenever a question was posed, memory was 'forced' to the extent that the question implied or suggested a particular range of answers. Later writers developed simple taxonomies for question forms so that their degree of 'force' or suggestibility could be more precisely assessed. Lipmann (1911), for example, resolved questions into seven types, including:

the simple YES/NO: 'Was the man's shirt red?'

the 'determinant': 'What colour was the man's shirt?'

and the 'incomplete disjunctive' in which an incomplete range of alternatives are presented in the question, implying the veracity of one of them: for example, 'Was the man's shirt red or green?', as opposed to the 'complete disjunctive' in which the alternatives are a full set of the possibilities: 'Was the man awake or asleep?'

Muscio (1915) made a further distinction between what he called objective and subjective questions, examples being: 'Was there a blue car', or, 'Did you see a blue car' respectively; and found that the former elicited more cautious replies in the form of a greater proportion of 'don't know' replies. In his experiments, prophetic of much more recent research on eyewitness testimony, university students were shown filmed events and the effect of types of questions on the quality of recall was then studied. Among his findings – presented in admirable detail – were the marked suggestiveness of incomplete disjunctions, and the relative unreliability of questions containing either a negative or a definite article; the question: 'You *didn't* see *the* blue car then?' would be a good example of an intrinsically unreliable question, containing as it does a clear 'expectation' of a response. (See Richardson *et al.*, 1965, Ch. 7.)

Some recent research would appear simply to replicate earlier findings. Thus, Loftus and Zanni (1975) reiterate that use of the definite article produces a greater tendency towards affirmative replies. (For example: 'Did you see a black car?', which only minimally assumes the existence of a car versus: 'Did you see *the* black car?') The clear implication is that clinicians should always consider the effect of the type of question on recall.

This is nowhere more important than when interviewing children or the handicapped. Children have been found particularly suggestible to leading questions, confirming Stern's (1910, page 272) observation that 'the power of the suggestive question showed itself to be dependent in large measure on age'. In one study, when asked leading questions about objects not present in a film, children were highly likely to say yes (Dale *et al.*, 1978). The importance of age as such was shown by Cohen and Harnick (1980) who found that 9-year-olds agreed with false suggestions significantly more than 12-year-olds or college students. Interestingly, the two eldest groups did not differ, raising the possibility that in some situations 12-year-olds may be as resistant to leading questions as adults. Finally, Marin *et al.* (1979) showed how, in children, leading questions containing misleading information presented after a film affected not only immediate recall but recall to non-leading questions some 14 days later. This study illustrates the point that not only does the form of a question alter the quality of replies, but also that questions *supply* information as well as elicit it, and can thereby detrimentally affect subsequent retrieval.

It is important in children to distinguish biases in recall due to the style of questioning from cognitive limitations of memory due to the child's stage of development. Children aged under five lack verbal and imagery-based strategies for encoding memories, and have fewer experiences with which an event may be associated, although these skills develop rapidly to the age of ten (Brown *et al.*, 1983). However, memory for events within the child's experience is good (Lindberg, 1980), even for emotionally-charged material such as memories of being molested (Marin *et al.*, 1979). Thus, children are often competent witnesses in court, although the traumatizing effect of giving evidence should be minimized wherever possible (Yates, 1987).

Open-ended and specific questions

The evidence shows that specific questions provide cues that facilitate and make more complete recall, though at the potential cost of increasing errors, depending on the precise form and difficulty of the question. Marquis *et al.* (1972), for example, examined the relevance of this factor in the quality of recall of subjects presented with filmed incidents. They showed clearly that free report ('tell me everything you remember about the film') produced the most accurate but least complete reports. With difficult items, the use of specific questions and, to a lesser extent, of narrowing questions (for example 'tell me everything about the person you saw'), produced more complete replies at the expense of increased errors.

Similar results have been obtained with children. Dent and Stephenson (1979) presented 10- to 11-year-olds with filmed events. Three groups received different question techniques over two occasions; all later received specific questions, which enabled a demonstration of the minimal cost of first getting free replies to responding later to specific questions. The results confirmed that specific questions did increase the number of correct replies, but they also increased the number of errors, particularly with respect to descriptions of people. Free reports, in contrast, showed few errors. Unfortunately, it is not possible to assess from Dent and Stephenson's study the cost to later free report of initial specific questioning, although this circumstance resembles legal proceedings when appearance in court may be preceded by several instances of specific questioning.

The findings that information contained within a question may bias subsequent recall, or that specific questions may elicit information of which the interviewee is less than certain, have been taken to imply that specific questions should follow open-ended questions where the interviewer wants optimally accurate information (Hilgard and Loftus, 1979). Clinically, this is probably a sound generalization. As Nay (1979, page 96) points out, free report provides an account of a problem as the patient perceives it. In addition, information about the relative salience of problems might be gathered that might be overlooked if specific questions are relied on prematurely.

Nevertheless, there are occasions when leading questions are acceptable in interview. Richardson *et al.* (1965) notes the value of introducing an embarrassing area of discourse by using a leading question. Further, it is likely that the style of questioning provides the patient with expectancies about the nature and competencies of the therapist which may be an important component in treatment outcome (Wilson, 1980). To this extent, the occasional leading question, where an interviewee is reasonably confident of a response, may not necessarily be undesirable.

With more specific questions, because they carry increased risk of inaccuracies, there is a need to validate tentative findings and preliminary hypotheses against direct observations or reports of reliable informants. This is particularly true for children and the mentally handicapped, whose frequent inability or unwillingness to talk fluently may force the interviewer to use a strategy of specific or closed questions.

Early research found that people of poor education have a tendency to acquiesce, or answer yes to yes/no alternative questions (Cronbach, 1946;

Campbell *et al.*, 1960). This has recently been confirmed by Siegelman *et al.* (1981) in mentally handicapped people who were presented with opposite questions asking the same thing ('Were you happy?' versus 'Were you sad?'). However, it is not clear whether, in such people, acquiescence is a general response set, perhaps previously reinforced by social attention, or occurs particularly when questions are not fully comprehended. The implication is that yes/no questions should be avoided with children and the handicapped, and replaced by either/or questions. Further, the possibility that a question has not been properly understood should always be considered.

In addition to inherent problems of memory, there are of course clinical and motivational factors that may affect recall accuracy. A patient or a suspect may have a vested interest in not revealing the truth. Getzels (1954) noted the distortions that can occur in material that is injurious to a respondent's self-esteem. In cases of so-called functional or hysterical amnesia (for example, Nemiah, 1969) memory for traumatic events might be lost or repressed altogether, perhaps to preserve the self from distressing recollections. Recent research on mood and memory (Teasdale and Fogarty, 1979; Bower, 1981) shows how the recall of mood incongruent material may be impaired relative to congruent material.

FACILITATING ACCURATE RECALL

When memories are less than certain, Merton *et al.* (1956) suggested that frequent 'probes' and an encouragement of discussion may 'establish a network of associations' which would facilitate recall. Similarly, it was argued above that the 'headed records theory' of eyewitness memory suggests that recall may be made more accurate if cueing conditions are arranged which provide access to a memory of an original event rather than to representations of related but possibly misleading events.

This provides a basis for common memory enhancing strategies, for example, a witness being taken to the scene of a crime; but it also points towards the potential of assessing patients in as natural an environment as possible in order that the number of relevant cues or antecedents to dysfunctional behaviour may be maximized. A number of other strategies for assisting retrieval have been incorporated into a 'cognitive interview' by Geiselman *et al.* (1986). These include:

1. Mentally rehearsing the situational and personal cues at the time of the episode: the provision of cues related to appearance, speech, names and numbers.
2. The encouragement to report everything, not just what is regarded by the subject as being of importance.

3. The recounting of events in a variety of different orders.
4. The reporting of events from a variety of different perspectives.

A number of experienced police officers were trained briefly to use such methods and compared with other officers briefed to use a combination of open and closed questions; both interviewed subjects who had been exposed to a filmed criminal incident. Analysis of transcribed interviews showed a significant increase in the number of correct items of information elicited in the experimental group. Importantly, this was not accompanied by an increase in the number of errors, which might have resulted from subjects lowering their criterion for responding to uncertain memories. Neither was the effect due to an increased overall duration of questions, which were comparable in the two groups. Rather, the control group used significantly more questions, presumably of lesser quality.

Although these results are in need of replication in other contexts, they may well be of use in clinical practice to assist in the detective work of teasing out the functional determinants of problem behaviour. As was noted above, subjects' recall may well be limited by constraints on memory in addition to perceptions of what the patient, rather than the therapist, sees as relevant (Watts, 1983).

The use of hypnosis to assist recall has been advocated most convincingly in those cases in which a theoretical rationale can be advanced, for example, that following trauma certain memories may be repressed (Doreus, 1960). However, although hypnosis in itself may have therapeutic benefits, there is reason to doubt its usefulness in uncovering factual material, particularly in legal contexts. In a useful discussion, Orne (1979) warns us that a state of hypnotism is often accompanied by increasing tendencies to fulfil interviewers' expectations, to confabulate and to report uncertain memories with false confidence. He also argues convincingly that when used to assist the police in interviewing suspects, the accused's motivation to feign a state of being hypnotized must also be considered. Further, Zelig and Beidleman (1981) showed that hypnosis increased the tendency to agree with leading questions, but failed to enhance recall in response to non-leading questions; hence the need to exercise great care in the selection of questions in states of hypnotism.

Nevertheless, there may be *elements* of hypnosis that can be used to facilitate accurate recall. It is interesting in this regard that Geiselman *et al.* (1985) found no significant difference in the efficacy of their 'cognitive interview' and a hypnotic procedure, which were both superior to a standard interview. They raised the possibility that there is a factor of 'guided memory' common to both, although there is a need to define operationally the nature of these various memory enhancing techniques so that the efficacy of constituent components can be evaluated (Gudjonsson, 1985b)

The relationship between accuracy and confidence

One of the more counter-intuitive findings to emerge from this area of research has been the often low (but variable) correlations between eyewitness confidence in memory reports and accuracy (Wells and Murray, 1984). For example, Brown *et al.* (1977) presented people with pictures and later measured identification accuracy and confidence for each. They found that the mean confidence ratings when subjects were correct hardly differed from when they were incorrect. In other words, eyewitness confidence may in some circumstances be a relatively stable characteristic, and a poor indicator of accuracy, in spite of the widely-held lay belief that accuracy and confidence are closely related (Brigham and Wolfskiel, 1982).

On the basis of Bem's (1972) neo-behavioural approach to cognitive phenomena, Leippe (1980) suggested that people's stated confidence is derived from their perceptions of their own behaviour of making an identification. To paraphrase: 'I really must be sure that was the person because I chose him/her knowing I would be cross examined'. Further, it may be argued that whilst making an identification, subjects are less aware of their task-related thoughts than they are of the environmental stimuli to which they are attending, namely the faces in a line-up parade. Thus, when subjects were presented with videotaped feedback of making an identification, their confidence estimates became more realistic, arguably because they had access to their own behaviour or to cues to the accompanying cognitive events which they could then use to infer their certainty of the decision they had made (Kassin, 1985).

Kassin went on to advocate the video-recording of suspect identifications so that witnesses, as well as the court, could scrutinize their selection and assess more accurately their confidence. It might be noted that audiotaping of police interviews, as for example considered by the Royal Commission on Criminal Procedure (1980), might similarly assist eyewitnesses to assess their evidential confidence. However, the clinical implication is that replaying patients' videotaped recordings of relevant situations, for example, role plays of social encounters, may provide cues to behaviours and cognitive processes of which the patient is not fully aware at recall.

INDIVIDUAL DIFFERENCES

In contrast to the experimental approach to eyewitness testimony, characterized by, for example, the work of Loftus, the complementary individual differences approach attempts to address why individuals might respond differently to similar questions in similar conditions. For example, one interesting prediction from the Yerkes–Dodson law relates to the increased effect of stress during registration in individuals high in trait or state anxiety, at least for moderately stressful events.

Deffenbacher (1983) cites several studies in support of this, though variability in how accuracy was measured reduces the confidence that can be placed in his conclusions. For example, in one study (Zanni and Offermann, 1978) inaccuracy was measured by the endorsing of the presence of events not actually presented in a previously-viewed filmed sequence. Errors thus measured correlated in excess of 0.4 with 'Neuroticism' measured on the Eysenck Personality Inventory (1964), although this may reflect the response bias of those high on 'N' to 'yield' to leading questions (Gudjonsson, 1983) rather than impaired registration or memory.

Interrogative suggestibility

More recently Gudjonsson (1984a) has devised a direct measure of the construct of 'suggestibility' within interview, meaning the extent to which misleading information may be assimilated into memory and affect testimony. In brief, the individual is presented with a short story resembling the Wechsler Logical Memory scale. A measure of immediate free recall is elicited, and delayed recall is measured some 50 minutes later. A number of specific and leading questions are then given, producing one measure of suggestibility ('yield'). Next follows a most interesting and imaginative procedure which reflects Gudjonsson's attempt to make his test as analogous as possible to the police interview. Critical feedback is given by saying: 'You have made a number of errors. It is therefore necessary to go through the questions once more, and this time try to be more accurate'. The extent by which answers are then changed produces a second measure, called 'shift' that purports to measure sensitivity to interpersonal pressure. Principal components analysis showed this to be independent of 'yield'.

An impressive array of data has been gathered using this scale. In normal adults, for example, IQ correlates negatively and significantly with both measures of shift and yield. When these were added to produce a total suggestibility score (although the rationale for doing so is unclear given that they are thought to be independent) the correlation with 45 subjects was an impressive −0.55 (Gudjonsson, 1983). In a study of police interviewing of the mentally handicapped, Tully and Cahil (1984) found a similarly impressive correlation between IQ and total suggestibility of −0.69.

An even closer relationship has been demonstrated between memory on the free report part of the test and subsequent suggestibility (Gudjonsson, 1987), although part of this may be mediated by IQ since memory and intelligence are themselves related (Powell, 1979).

In a recent theoretical formulation (Gudjonsson and Clark, 1986), ambitious in its attempt to incorporate a range of relevant variables, suggestibility and its antithesis of resistance are regarded as methods of coping (Moos and Billings, 1982) with the stresses of the interview situation. The employment of these is determined by uncertainty, interpersonal trust and expectations.

Thus, when asked a question to which the answer is uncertain, some will give a suggestible reply on the basis of misleading cues in the question, although in Gudjonsson's own research uncertainty and suggestibility are only weakly related (Gudjonsson, 1983). Similarly, poor self-esteem may increase uncertainty, consistent with Singh and Gudjonsson (1984) who found that, in an adult sample, 'yield' correlated with poor self-esteem. On the other hand, there will be those who, on the basis of experience, develop resistant strategies. This helps to explain the finding in young offenders that suggestibility correlates negatively with the number of convictions, since they may be expected to have acquired resistant coping mechanisms over the course of successive interviews (Gudjonsson and Singh, 1984).

In spite of the considerable face validity of this measure, care is needed in generalizing from the test score to suggestibility in other interrogative situations. In particular, the negative feedback produced by the tester cannot be expected to reflect social pressures within some more formal police interviews. It will also be apparent that the scale makes use of verbal memory of an abstract story, while memory for visual events, though involving verbal coding, may be of greater relevance to the interrogation context.

APPLICATIONS TO FORENSIC CLINICAL PRACTICE

Taken as a whole, recent research on eye witness testimony highlights the vagaries of human memory, although as Loftus (1984) points out, mistaken identifications are the greatest single cause of wrong convictions. In American courts, for some time, experimental psychologists have been presenting expert evidence, explaining to juries the various factors involved in memory in the hope (as yet unproven except in simulated trials (for example, Loftus, 1980), that a more reliable assessment of the evidence can then be made.

On the other hand there are those psychologists (for example, Egeth and McCloskey, 1984) who do not regard current findings as sufficiently reliable to place them under courtroom scrutiny. They argue that lay people possess a sufficient understanding of basic memory and perception to which 'expert' evidence adds very little, although the poor relationship (against intuition) between accuracy and confidence noted above would appear to be one notable exception (Deffenbacher and Loftus, 1982). Further, it is argued, the burden of proof in criminal trials of 'beyond reasonable doubt' necessitates that eyewitness evidence is weighed up with suitable caution. These issues are far from resolved, although Egeth and McCloskey have probably overstated the case. Presumably jurors themselves are capable of evaluating the relevance and usefulness of expert evidence in a particular case.

In British courts, an expert's opinion is admissible if it provides the court with scientific information 'outside the experience of knowledge of a judge or jury' (Mitchell and Richardson, 1985). By precedent, matters of eyewitness testimony are assumed to lie within the province of the jury, so that expert evidence of a general educational kind is not admissible. Neverthe-less, psychological evidence relating to the reliability of witness evidence based on clinical assessment has been admitted. Gudjonsson and Gunn (1982), for example, showed how the reliability of the evidence of a mentally handicapped person might have been impaired by virtue of very poor intelligence and extreme suggestibility measured by individually centred tests. In addition, Gudjonsson and Haward (1983) show how interview statements may be analysed for their degree of complexity, and the likeli-hood that they were understood by an accused.

Gudjonsson (1986) has considered the contribution psychologists can and have made in the British courts and finds that recent scepticism (Hill and Griffiths, 1982) about the admissibility of, and demand for, psychological evidence is largely misplaced. For an account of the breadth of matters on which psychologists are well equipped to provide evidence, the interested reader is referred to Haward (1981).

False confessions, suggestibility and compliance

Psychologists might also be asked to assess 'suggestibility' of suspects who make confessions or admissions which they then retract. It is important here to distinguish between suggestibility as defined above when, due to uncer-tainty, memory is transformed by misleading post event information, from those occasions, when, although quite sure of a factual reply, a suspect produces a response in line with the interviewer's leading questions or pressure. Gudjonsson and Clark (1986) refer to this as compliance, whose relationship with interrogative suggestibility is at present unclear.

Criminal suspects may undergo lengthy police interviews in which a variety of interview strategies may be employed to encourage a confession (Irving and Hilgendorf, 1980). Precisely why some suspects manage to hold out against repeated police questions while others make admissions which may be subsequently retracted is largely unknown, although a resistant coping mechanism, possibly reflecting prior experience of similar interview situations, and an understanding of an individual's appraisal of the associ-ated costs and benefits of confessing or not at the time of the police interview are probably evident.

One finding by Gudjonsson (1984b) implicates the relevance of his measure of suggestibility, since those who made confessions which were later retracted scored as significantly more suggestible than those who consistently denied any involvement. However, these groups also differed in intelligence which accounts for most of the difference in their suggestibility. Self-esteem is another factor that may differentiate 'deniers' from 'false confessors', although research data on this is lacking. Finally, it is important to appreciate that research into compliance is likely to encounter a stiff test:

the courtroom verdict. Whether a confession is false or otherwise is for the jury to determine. The psychologist can only help the court to arrive at a decision.

Until these issues are resolved, when asked to assess compliance, the practising psychologist is best advised to rely on better established measures such as intelligence and literacy skills (since accused people are expected to read through and sign statements of their interview), in addition to relevant previous behaviours. Intelligence is particularly important since under the *Police and Criminal Evidence Act* (1984) and appended *Codes of Practice*, special precautions, notably the presence of a significant adult, are required when police officers interview mentally handicapped witnesses.

CONCLUSION

The aim of this chapter is to consider some of the recent research in eyewitness testimony and the implications raised for clinical interviewing and forensic psychology. Of course, care is needed in generalizing from the areas of research on interviewing witnesses in experimental settings and police interviewing to clinical practice, since the goals of participants will vary in each. Nevertheless, it is suggested that an appreciation of basic psychological processes of memory and attention provides a framework within which the reliability of patients' and witness' accounts may be evaluated, and even enhanced. Often the challenge for the clinician lies in applying theory and empirical generalizations to a particular case. This is nowhere more apparent than in legal applications of psychology, where expert evidence on an individual may be scrutinized by cross-examination in court. What is required, therefore, is an integrated account of the relationships between those environmental and intra-individual variables that bear upon the reliability of testimony. A start has been made, but there is a long way to go.

REFERENCES

ALLPORT, G. and POSTMAN, L. (1947). *The Psychology of Humour*. New York: Holt.
ANDREW, R.J. (1974). Arousal and the causation of behaviour. *Behaviour, 51*, 135–165.
BADDELEY, A.D. (1972). Selective attention and performance in dangerous environments. *British Journal of Psychiatry, 63*, 537–546.
BARTLETT, F.C. (1932) *Remembering*. Cambridge: Cambridge University Press.
BEKERIAN, D.A. and BOWERS, J.M. (1983). Eyewitness testimony: Were we misled? *Journal of Experimental Psychology: Learning, Memory and Cognition, 9*, 139–145.
BEM, D.J. (1972). Self-perception theory. In Berkowitz, L. (ed.), *Advances in Experimental Social Psychology, Vol.6*. New York: Academic Press.

BINET, A. (1900). *La Suggestibilité*. Paris: Schleicher Frères.

BOWER, G. (1981) Mood and memory. *American Psychologist*, *36*, 129–148.

BRIGHAM. J.C. and WOLFSKIEL, M.P. (1982). Opinions of attorneys and law enforcement personnel on the accuracy of eyewitness identification. *Law and Human Behaviour*, *7*, 337–349.

BROWN, A.L., BRANSFORD, J.D., and FERRARA, R.A. (1983). Learning, remembering and understanding. In Flavell, J.H. and Markman, E.M. (eds), *Handbook of Child Psychology*. New York: John Wiley & Sons.

BROWN, E.L., DEFFENBACHER, K.A. and STURGILL, W. (1977). Memory for faces and the circumstances of an encounter. *Journal of Applied Psychology*, *62*, 311–318.

BUCKHOUT, R. (1974). Eyewitness testimony. *Scientific American*, 231 [12], 23–31.

CAMPBELL, A., CONVERSE, P.E., MILLER, W.E. and STOKES, E.D. (1960). *The American Voter*. New York: John Wiley & Sons.

CLIFFORD, B.R. and SCOTT, J. (1978). Individual and situational factors in eyewitness testimony. *Journal of Applied Psychology*, *63*, 352–359.

COHEN, R.L. and HARNICK, M.A. (1980). The susceptibility of child witnesses to suggestion. *Law and Human Behaviour*, *4*, 201–210.

CRONBACH, L.J. (1946). Response sets and test validity. *Educational Psychology Measurement*, *6*, 475–494.

DALE, P.S., LOFTUS, E.F. and RATHBURN, L. (1978). The influence of the form of the question on the eyewitness testimony of preschool children. *Journal of Psycholinguistic Research*, *7*, 269–277.

DEFFENBACHER, K. (1983). The influence of arousal on reliability of testimony. In B.R. Clifford, and S. Lloyd-Bostock (eds), *Evaluating Witness Evidence*. Chichester: Wiley.

DEFFENBACHER, K. and LOFTUS, E.F. (1982). Do jurors show a common understanding concerning eyewitness behaviour? *Law and Human Behavior*, *6*, 15–30.

DENT, H.R. and STEPHENSON, G.M. (1979). An experimental study of the effectiveness of different techniques of questioning child witnesses. *British Journal of Social and Clinical Psychology*, *18*, 41–51.

DOREUS, R.M. (1960). Recall under hypnosis of amnesic events. *International Journal of Clinical and Experimental Hypnosis*, *8*, 57–60.

EASTERBROOK. J.A., (1959). The effect of emotion on cue utilization and the organization of behaviour. *Psychological Review*, *66*, 183–201.

EGETH, H.E. and McCLOSKEY, M. (1984). Expert testimony about eyewitness behaviour: Is it safe and effective? In Wells, G.L. and Loftus, E.F. (eds), *Eyewitness Testimony: Psychological Perspectives*. New York: Cambridge University Press.

EYSENCK, H.J. and EYSENCK, S.B.G. (1964). *Manual for the Eysenck Personality Inventory*. London: University of London Press.

GEISELMAN, R.E., FISHER, R.P., MACKINNON, D.P. and HOLLAND, H.L. (1985). Eyewitness memory enhancement in the police interview: Cognitive retrieval mnemonics versus hypnosis. *Journal of Applied Psychology*, *70*, 401–412.

GEISELMAN. R.E., FISHER, R.P., MACKINNON, D.P. and HOLLAND, H.L. (1986). Enhancement of eyewitness memory with the cognitive interview. *American Journal of Psychology*, *99*, 385–401.

GETZELS, J.W. (1954). The question–answer process: a conceptualization and some derived hypotheses for empirical examination. *Public Opinion Quarterly*, *18*, 80–91.

GUDJONSSON, G.H. (1983). Suggestibility, intelligence, memory recall and personality: an experimental study. *British Journal of Psychiatry*, *142*, 35–37.

GUDJONSSON, G.H., (1984a). A new scale of interrogative suggestibility. *Personality and Individual Differences*, *3*, 303–314.

GUDJONNSON, G.H. (1984b). Interrogative suggestibility: comparison between 'false confession' and 'deniers' in criminal trials. *Medicine, Science and the Law*, *34*, 56–60.

GUDJONSSON, G.H. (1985a). Psychological evidence in court: Results from the BPS survey. *Bulletin of the British Psychological Society*, *38*, 327–330.

GUDJONSSON. G.H. (1985b). The use of hypnosis by the police in the investigation of crime: is guided imagery a safe substitute? *British Journal of Experimental and Clinical Hypnosis*, *3*, 37.

GUDJONSSON. G.H. (1986). Criminal court proceedings in England. The contribution of the psychologist as an expert witness. *Medicine and Law*, *5*, 395–404.

GUDJONSSON, G.H. (1987). The relationship between memory and suggestibility. *Social Behaviour*, *2*, 29–33.

GUDJONSSON, G.H. and CLARK, N.K. (1986). Suggestibility in police interrogation: A social psychological model. *Social Behaviour*, *Vol.1*, 83–104.

GUDJONSSON, G.H. and GUNN, J. (1982). The competence and reliability of a witness in a criminal court: a case report. *British Journal of Psychiatry*, *141*, 624–627.

GUDJONSSON, G.H. and HAWARD, L.R.C. (1983). Psychological analysis of confession statements. *Journal of the Forensic Science Society*, *23*, 113–120.

GUDJONSSON, G.H. and SINGH, K. (1984). Criminal convictions and its relationship with interrogative suggestibility. *Journal of Adolescence*, *7*, 29–34.

HAWARD. L.R.C. (1981). *Forensic Psychology*. London: Batsford.

HERBERT, M. (1981). *Behavioural Treatment of Problem Children: A Practice Manual*. London: Academic Press.

HILGARD, E.R. and LOFTUS, E.F. (1979). Effective interrogation of the eyewitness. *International Journal of Clinical and Experimental Hypnosis*, *27*, 342–357.

HILL, A.M. and GRIFFITHS, R.C. (1982). English law and the psychologist. In Shapland (ed.), *Issues in Criminological and Legal Psychology*. Leicester: The British Psychological Society.

IRVING, B. and HILGENDORF, L. (1980). *Police Interrogation: The Psychological Approach*. Research Study No. 1. London: HMSO.

KASSIN, S.M. (1985). Eyewitness identification: Retrospective self-awareness and the accuracy-confidence correlates. *Journal of Personality and Social Psychology*, *49*, 878–893.

LEIPPE, M.R. (1980). Effects of integrative memorial and cognitive processes on the correspondence of eyewitness accuracy and confidence. *Law and Human Behaviour*, *4*, 261–274.

LINDBERG, M. (1980). Is knowledge base development a necessary and sufficient condition for memory development? *Journal of Experimental Child Psychology*, *30*, 401–410.

LIPMANN, P. (1911). Pedagogical psychology of report. *Journal of Educational Psychology*, *2*, 253–261.

LOFTUS, E.F. (1975). Leading questions and the eyewitness report. *Cognitive Psychology*, *7*, 560–572.

LOFTUS, E.F. (1979). *Eyewitness Testimony*. Cambridge, Mass: Harvard University Press.

LOFTUS, E.F. (1980). Impact of expert psychological testimony on the unreliability of eyewitness identification. *Journal of Applied Psychology*, *65*, 9–15.

LOFTUS, E.F. (1981). Natural and unnatural cognition. *Cognition*, *10*, 193–196.

LOFTUS, E.F. (1984). Expert testimony on the eyewitness. In Wells G.L. and Loftus, E.F. (eds), *Eyewitness Testimony: Psychological Perspectives*. New York: Cambridge University Press.

LOFTUS, E.F. and LOFTUS, G.R. (1980). On the permanence of stored information in the human brain. *American Psychologist*, *35*, 409–420.

LOFTUS, E.F. and ZANNI, G. (1975). Eyewitness testimony: the influence of the wording of a question. *Bulletin of the Psychonomic Society*, *5*, 86–88.

MacLEOD, C., MATHEWS, A. and TATA, P. (1986). Attentional bias in emotional disorders. *Journal of Abnormal Psychology*, *95*, 15–20.

MARIN, B.V., HOLMES, D.L., GATH, M. and KOVAC, P. (1979). The potential of children as eyewitnesses: A comparison of children and adults on eyewitness tasks. *Law and Human Behaviour*, *3*, 295–306.

MARQUIS, K.H., MARSHALL, S. and OSKAMP, S. (1972). Testimony validity as a function of question form, atmosphere and item difficulty. *Journal of Applied Social Psychology*, *2*, 167–186.

MARZILLIER, J. (1976). Interviewing. In Eysenck, H.J. and Wilson. G.D. (eds) *A Textbook of Human Psychology*. London: M.T. Press.

MERTON, R.K., FISKE, M. and KENDALL, P.L. (1956). *The Focussed Interview*. Glencoe: Free Press.

MILLER, G.A. (1956). The magical number seven, plus or minus two. *Psychological Review*, *63*, 81–97.

MITCHELL, S. and RICHARDSON. P.D. (eds) (1985). *Archtold: Pleading; Evidence and Practice in Criminal Cases*. London: Sweet and Maxwell.

MOOS, R. and BILLINGS, A.G. (1982). Conceptualizing and measuring coping resources and processes. In Goldberger, L. & Berkowitz, S. (eds), *Handbook of Stress: Theoretical and Clinical Aspects*. New York: Free Press, pp. 212–230.

MORTON, J., HAMMERSLEY, R.H. and BEKERIAN, D.A (1983). Headed records: A model for memory and its failures. *Cognition*, *20*, 1–23.

MUNSTERBURG, H. (1908). *On the Witness Stand: Essays on psychology and crime*. New York: Clark Boardman.

MUSCIO, B. (1915). The influence of the form of a question. *British Journal of Psychology*, *8*, 351–386.

NAY. W.R. (1979). *Multimethod Clinical Asssessment*. New York: Gardner Press.

NEISSER, U. (1967). *Cognitive Psychology*. New York: Appleton-Century-Crofts.

NEMIAH, J.C. (1969). Hysterical amnesia. In G.A. Talland and N.C. Waugh (eds), *The Pathology of Memory*. pp. 107–113. New York: Academic Press.

NISBETT, R. and ROSS, L. (1980). *Human Inferences: Strategies and shortcomings of social judgment*. Englewood Cliffs, N.J: Prentice-Hall.

O'CONNELL, B.A. (1960). Amnesia and homicide. *British Journal of Delinquency*. *10*, 262–276.

ORNE, M.T. (1979), Use and misuse of hypnosis in Court. *International Journal of Clinical and Experimental Hypnosis*, *17*, 311–341.

POLICE AND CRIMINAL EVIDENCE ACT (1984). London: Her Majesty's Stationery Office.

POWELL, G.E. (1979). The relationship between intelligence and verbal and spatial memory. *Journal of Clinical Psychology*, *35*, 335–340.

RICHARDSON. S.A., DOHRENWEND, N.S. and KLEIN, D. (1965). *Interviewing: Its Forms and Functions*. New York: Basic Books.

ROYAL COMMISSION ON CRIMINAL PROCEDURE (1980). London: Her Majesty's Stationery Office.

SCHOOLER, J.W. and LOFTUS, E.F. (1986). Individual differences and experimentation: Complementary approaches to interrogative suggestibility. *Social Behaviour*, *1*, 105–112.

SHAPIRO, M.B. (1979). Assessment interviewing in clinical psychology. *British Journal of Social and Clinical Psychology. 18*, 211–216.

SIEGELMAN, C.U., BUDD, E.C., SPANHEL, C.C. and SCHOENROCK, C.J. (1981). When in doubt say yes: Acquiescence in interviews with mentally retarded persons. *Mental Retardation, 19*, 53–58.

SINGH, K.K. and GUDJONSSON, G.H. (1984). Interrogative suggestibility, delayed memory and self concept. *Personality and Individual Differences, 5*, 203–209.

STERN, L.W. (1910). Abstracts of lectures on the psychology of testimony on the study of individuality. *American Journal of Psychology, 21*, 270–282.

TAYLOR, P.J. and KOPELMAN, M.D. (1984). Amnesia for criminal offences. *Psychological Medicine, 24*, 581–590.

TEASDALE, J.D. and FOGARTY, S.J. (1979). Differential effects of induced mood on retrieval of pleasant and unpleasant events from episodic memory. *Journey of Abnormal Psychology, 88*, 248–257.

TOUSIGNANT, J.P., HALL, D. and LOFTUS, E.F. (1986). Discrepancy detection and vulnerability to misleading post-event information. *Memory and Cognition* (in press).

TULLY, B. and CAHILL, D. (1984). *Police Interviewing of the Mentally Handicapped: An Experimental Study*. London: The Police Foundation.

WATTS, F.N. (1983). Strategies of clinical listening. *British Journal of Medical Psychology, 56*, 113–124.

WATTS, F.N., McKENNA, F.P., SHARROCK, R. and TREZISE, L. (1986). Colour naming of phobia related words. *British Journal of Psychology, 79*, 97–108.

WELLS, G.L. and LOFTUS, E.F. (eds) (1984). *Eyewitness Testimony: Psychological Perspectives*. New York: Cambridge University Press.

WELLS, G.L. and MURRAY, D.M. (1984). Eyewitness confidence. In Wells, G.L. and Loftus, E.F. (eds), *Eyewitness Testimony: Psychological Perspectives*. New York: Cambridge University Press.

WILSON, G.T. (1980). Towards specifying the 'non-specific' facts in behavior therapy: A social learning study. In M.J. Mahoney (ed.), *Psychotherapy Issues: Current Trends and Future Directions*. New York: Plenum.

WILSON, G.T. and O'LEARY, K.D. (1980). *Principles of Behavior Therapy*. Englewood Cliff, NJ: Prentice-Hall.

YATES, A. (1987). Should young children testify in cases of sexual abuse? *American Journal of Psychiatry, 144*, 476–480.

YERKES, R.M. and DODSON, J.D. (1908). The relation of strength of stimulus to rapidity of habit formation. *Journal of Comparative Neurology and Psychology, 18*, 459–482.

ZANNI, G.R. and OFFERMANN, J.T. (1978). Eyewitness testimony: An exploration of question wording you recall as a function of neuroticism. *Perceptual and Motor Skills, 46*, 163–166.

ZELIG, M. and BEIDLEMAN, W.B. (1981). The investigative use of hypnosis: a word of caution. *International Journal of Clinical and Experimental Hypnosis, 19*, 401–412.

EVALUATING COMMUNITY-BASED SERVICES

Paul Clifford and Sheila Damon

The closure of large long-stay hospitals and their replacement by community services now forms the centrepiece of most local development plans in the UK for both mental health and mental handicap services. It is also widely accepted that evaluation should be an integral part of such services, yet there is often no clear view of what should be evaluated, how, why and for whose benefit. Failure to answer such questions too often leads to the narrowing of research horizons and the adoption of unimaginative and sterile methodolgies. Our intention in this chapter is to help would-be evaluators consider some of these issues. The aim is both to provide a brief guide to contemporary research in our respective fields and to identify areas where there is room for innovation.

THE CONCEPT OF COMMUNITY CARE

Historically, a major factor in the promotion of community care for all client groups has been both professional and popular horror at conditions in long-stay hospitals. In the UK, these have been amply documented in the accumulated evidence of official enquiries and devastating exposées in the media over the past 20 years (see Martin's (1984) excellent book *Hospitals in Trouble*). These reports are indicative of a general move towards stronger insistence on the rights of the individual and on the accountability of public services. The growing acceptance of the need for evaluation is itself a reflection of this trend.

The revelation of poor hospital conditions is in itself insufficient to justify closing them altogether. A less drastic response would be to try to turn bad institutions into good ones. This has been seen as an inadequate response for a number of reasons. One set of factors is economic; large hospitals, often with deteriorating fabric, are increasingly expensive to keep open as their populations decline. Also, the availability of state benefits makes living outside hospital a much more practical possibility than it once was (see Warner (1985) for a discussion of the importance of this in the experience of deinstitutionalization in the US). Another set of factors relate to changes within the specialties themselves. Advances in methods of treatment, such as the use of behavioural training methods in the field of mental handicap, have transformed professions' view of what is possible. In psychiatry, an additional factor has been the widespread introduction of long-acting phenothiazines for people with psychotic symptoms; and behavioural methods of rehabilitation have also played their part.

At the level of ideas the most influential factor in the move towards community care has been the growing acceptance, publicly and professionally, that institutional environments can have harmful effects. At its most extreme this saw psychopathology as caused by, if not actually located in, the external environment; and both mental illness and mental handicap services were criticized for over emphasizing the difficulties of individuals and neglecting the impoverished social environment in which they were condemned to spend their lives. There is still a frequently unquestioning revulsion towards anything which looks like the old, bad services and an attraction to anything that, if not good, at least bears as few traces of the old as possible.

One problem with the term 'community-based services' is the heterogeneity of actual provision to which it refers. Perhaps the only common variable is that of a negatively-defined, geographical location: one which is not a large, long-stay hospital. This can lead to the unwarranted inference that services lacking in certain characteristics associated with hospitals will necessarily be associated with other desirable characteristics, most notably a higher standard of care and greater respect for the individual.

The initial assumption was that location away from hospitals and relative smallness of scale together constituted the essence of community care, and thereby avoided the worst aspects of the institutionalized hospital setting. More recently, community care has been conceived of as a constellation of services and facilities, including work, leisure, social relationships, education, personal social services, and access to mainstream medical care.

An increased emphasis on the positive aspects of client groups, rather than illness or disability has combined with a greater awareness of the importance of environmental variables to make comprehensive community care appear a realistic possibility. Community-based services are presumed to provide a more human, less stigmatizing environment for clients and to promote their development as valued members of the community. They assist an individual's acquisition of personal and life skills and enable her or him to be happier and more fulfilled. Or do they? This has perhaps been the central question around which research into community-based services has revolved.

The demonstration project

Attempts to answer it have often involved evaluating a new, model service set up with the explicit goal of providing an alternative to traditional modes of care. This has meant that the dominant research framework for both 'learning disabilities' and 'mental illness' has been *evaluation in the context of the demonstration project*. Such projects usually have three aims:

1 establishing that the new approach is workable
2 evaluation of its success in fulfilling specific goals and
3 dissemination of both findings and methods in order to change professional attitudes to care and broader social policy.

Fulfilling these aims ideally requires firm evidence of a link between the novel features of the service and its impact on clients. Two types of data have to be collected:

a. Descriptions of care settings which look at services to see whether they do actually incorporate the environmental characteristics and care practices that are considered desirable.

b. Outcome measures of how clients have fared under the new service. This typically involves comparing the progress of clients in hospital and matched samples who have had the benefits of the new community-based service. However, it may also involve case studies which look in detail at the experience of people whose contact with services centres around community settings.

In practice most studies have included both elements to varying degrees although conclusive evidence of a *causal* link between the new service and outcome has been relatively rare.

We will now consider how efforts to evaluate community services have developed, first in services for people suffering from severe mental illness (MI), then in services for people with severe learning disabilities (LD). In the final section we will discuss some factors that should guide the decision whether or not to embark on an evaluation and consider some directions that imaginative evaluations might take.

SERVICES FOR THE LONG-TERM MENTALLY ILL

Examination of the relationship between characteristics of the treatment setting and patients' psychological and social functioning has a long history going back to such classic works as Stanton and Schwarz's (1954) study of the mental hospital and Menzies' (1970) paper on social systems as a defence against anxiety. The emergence of methods of psychiatric rehabilitation in the fifties and sixties also produced a stream of research on the value of social treatments (for example, Barton, 1957). However, the modern era of research was signalled by Wing and Brown (1970) in their classic study of three hospitals. They showed that patients' clinical state varied according to how much activity they were engaged in and how institutional were the staff practices characterizing the setting.

Comparisons of hospital and community services

As the move to community care has gathered momentum, the focus of research has switched from hospital to the new settings. The initial aim has been to show that outcome in a community setting is as good if not better than outcome in a hospital setting. This is an important goal, but notably more modest than that of Wing and Brown who were attempting to demonstrate the relationship between the characteristics of a setting and outcome rather than just showing that one setting had a better outcome than another. An excellent review of such studies in the USA is provided by Braun *et al.* (1981). They come to only a modest conclusion about the efficacy of alternatives to hospital treatment.

The 'hospital' versus 'community' methodology tends to involve a global comparison of two populations, one in receipt of the new service, the other using traditional hospital services. This model in effect treats 'hospital' and 'community' as homogeneous treatments, the underlying model being that of the controlled clinical trial. This ignores both the obvious variability of community settings and Wing and Brown's demonstration of the variability of quality of care in hospital. Such comparisons do not usually specify in depth the characteristics of either the hospital or the new setting, and tend to focus on clinical and social outcome rather than looking in depth at the effect on outcome of key variables in the new service. Consequently, the measures adopted have usually centred around clinical state and social functioning rather than the minutiae of care practices or environments.

In the UK 'hospital' versus 'community' studies often revolve around hospital closure programmes rather than any specific innovation in methods of care or treatment. Two major studies under way are those of the TAPS team at Friern (Leff *et al.*, 1985) and the evaluation of the closure of Cane Hill hospital (Clifford and Holloway, 1987). Methodologically, the former study focuses on a comparison of 'stayers' and 'leavers', that is, people who stay are compared with people who leave hospital. The latter study focuses more on an assessment of the new settings and an evaluation of their impact on the quality of life of patients of varying levels of disability.

In the USA, although there has also been an interest in 'following-up' deinstitutionalized patients (for example, Lehman, 1983), the most interesting work has involved innovations in service provision. The best known example is the work of Stein and Test (1978), which has been replicated in Australia (Hoult and Reynolds, 1984).

Stein and Test developed a conceptual model for the development of community-based treatment programmes, a model also used by Hoult. This states that the avoidance of hospital treatment requires the following six elements:

material resources, such as food, shelter, clothing and medical care;
coping skills to meet the demands of community life;
motivation to persevere and remain involved with life;
freedom from pathologically-dependent relationships (on family, institutions);
support and education of community members who are involved with patients;
and a supportive system that *assertively* helps the patient with the previous five requirements.

Both sets of researchers randomly assigned referrals to either a treatment programme based on this model or to a more conventional approach involving hospital admission. The model-based programme was associated with less time spent in hospital, greater satisfaction with the treatment with respect to both patients and relatives, clinically superior outcome, and lower cost. An attempt to replicate the Stein and Test approach in this country is currently underway at the Maudsley (Marks *et al.*, 1987). Such research suggests that a psychiatric service can function effectively with very few acute or long-stay beds. The chosen ingredients of the alternative package are also of interest, particularly the emphasis on work with families and community members and the tackling of pathologically-dependent relationships. However, it is little more than suggestive of causal mechanisms and is most directly applicable only to people who have not already shifted base from home to hospital.

One problem with the 'hospital' versus 'community' methodology is that it fails to assess the effect on one part of a service system of developments in other parts; what Bachrach (1982) calls 'impact evaluation' as opposed to 'program evaluation'. Well-known phenomena are ignored, for example, the drastic drop in quality of care in hospitals consequent upon the implementation of closure programmes, or the effect on other parts of the service of a shift of resources to one model project or client group. Having half an eye on what goes on in hospital is also not conducive to studying the complex internal workings of new settings; the complexity and specifity of both clients and services can get lost.

In-depth studies of community care

An alternative method is needed that focuses more closely on what actually goes on in the services being provided. This is an established tradition of research in both learning disabilities (LD) and mental illness (MI) but, in recent times, has been more prominent in the former perhaps because the professional supporters of community care for learning disabilities have tended to concentrate their recent energies on the creation of better *care settings*, perhaps in the hope that existing treatments might then stand some chance of being implemented. They also began to suspect that the care settings themselves might be having a non-specific but beneficial effect on their clients.

Wing and Brown's study compared settings by producing a checklist of institutional practices that did or did not occur in a particular setting. In the USA, Moos' (1974) so-called 'Ward Atmosphere Scales' – rather less interesting than their name suggests – followed a similar tack. However, checklists tend to have limited applicability because of their lack of conceptual structure. They enable only crude comparisons between settings and are not easily converted into a coherent representation of the setting's mode of functioning.

The study of care settings and practices was pushed a stage further by the studies of King *et al.* (1971). Their focus was on operationalizing what was meant by an 'institutional' environment. Although initially developed for application to LD settings this approach has also been adopted for MI. Lavender (1984) nicely describes much of the work on quality of care in mental illness. He concluded that 'the lack of empirical work in all aspects of practice demonstrates that it is still far from clear which are the best practices to adopt' (page 77). Lavender (1985) also developed a set of questionnaires for monitoring the quality of care on long-stay wards using some of Raynes and Tizard's concepts and an Appendix to the Nodder Report (1977). The Model Standards Questionnaires looked at the physical environment, staffing levels and composition, ward management practices, individual programmes and contacts with the community.

Criterion based evaluations

A variant of the idea of empirically examining what goes on in a setting and judging whether or not it is 'institutional' in character is the formulation of a set of general principles or criteria against which any actual service may be measure. This has long been accepted practice in LD but it is only now being widely accepted in MI, as is the notion of the need for a formal operational policy. The best known approach that derives its measures from a clear philosophical statement of principle is that of normalization which has had a considerable impact on the development of LD services and, in recent years, become increasingly influential (though also strongly resisted) in MI. The principle of normalization endorses 'the utilization of culturally valued means in order to establish and/or maintain personal behaviours, experiences, and characteristics that are culturally normative or valued' (Wolfensberger, 1972). The quality of a service is judged by its degree of conformity to the principle as operationalized in the measuring instruments such as PASS and more recently PASSING (Wolfensberger and Glenn, 1975). A feature of these assessment methods is that practically all settings score very poorly. Whether this is taken to reflect the abysmal quality of psychiatric services or the idiosyncratic construction of the scale depends on one's ideological standpoint.

A comparable, though looser approach than normalization is that adopted by the organization Good Practices in Mental Health. In numerous local studies, criteria are devised against which local services are measured to see whether they conform to the notion of 'good practice' (for example, Sayce, 1987).

Although more reminiscent of complex value judgements than conventional evaluations, the last two methods highlight some of the pros and cons of focusing on the care setting. Both involve a refreshing shift of emphasis on to the 'human' rather than the 'service' side of 'human services'. They also make clear the value base underlying the evaluation and yield clear prescriptions for change. Such approaches also stress the importance of the management and organization of services to the quality of service delivery, thus giving attention to aspects of care that are not usually classified as 'treatment' in the medical sense but which may, nevertheless, have a strong impact on someone's experience of a service. The main disadvantages are fourfold. First, there is sometimes little empirical justification for the principles adopted. Wolfensberger (1972) argues that this criticism is ill-founded since it could equally have been applied to traditional hospital services but wasn't, so why should it be wheeled out as a criticism of normalization? His criticism of traditional services is correct, but there seems little reason why past errors should be repeated.

Second, the links between principles and practice are far harder to specify when it comes down to the nitty gritty of clinical work than with variables such as size or proximity to local services. Lavender (1987) attempts to link care practices with effects on clients by studying the effect of nurses ceasing to wear uniform on a long-stay ward. Shepherd and Richardson (1979) and Garety and Morris (1984) are rare examples of studies that relate a non-hospital service's philosophy of care to the staff–patient interactions that take place within it. Without this link the actual work of services may come under only limited scrutiny. More may be learnt about what a service is not doing than what it is.

Third, it is risky, if not tendentious, to assume that the same principles are applicable to all human services irrespective of their client population. For example, Clifford (1986) criticizes the philosophy of normalization for ignoring the relevance of an understanding of mental illness to the design and evaluation of such services; similarly, Millar and Roberts (1986) argue that an acknowledgement of death should be central to the functioning of services for the elderly.

Finally, there is the problem that no matter how good a service may seem when compared with *a priori* criteria this is no guarantee of its efficacy. To be truly evaluative, research has to relate what happens in a service to what happens to its users whilst in contact with the service and outside. Exclusive concentration on the quality of care, or other aspects of the environment or setting, however rigorously defined, cannot achieve this.

Recent trends linking care practices and client outcome

Recent years have seen increasing recognition of the need for more sophisticated measuring technology to relate what goes on in care settings to the lives of the clients that pass through them. A comprehensive model of rehabilitation outcome 'has the advantage of encouraging researchers to consider, during the process of research design, the specific outcomes that will and will not be affected by an intervention' (Anthony and Farkas, 1982). It is increasingly clear that the evaluation of community-based services requires both a multi-dimensional assessment of how each individual is faring *and* an analysis of the environments in which they spend their lives. There are promising developments in both areas:

(i) Outcome measures. Acknowledgement that the aim of psychiatric services for the most disabled clients is not the treatment of mental illness but the maximization of quality of life has led to a broadening of the concept of outcome beyond purely clinical indices. This distinguishes recent research from early hospital versus community studies.

Outcome measures are developing on two fronts. First, recently-devised schedules, such as those used by Clifford and Holloway, are much more precise in their measurement of key variables in an individual's social and clinical functioning. Second, methods are being evolved to assess the overall quality of life (QOL) of severely disabled individuals using both objective and subjective measures. Much of the published work is American. Both Lehman (1982) and Baker and Intagliata (1982) have shown that such assessment can be done reliably. The interest in this country is only beginning to be reflected in the research literature (for example, Gibbons and Butler, 1987). Central problems are the relationship between subjective and objective measures of QOL and the relationship between QOL and other clinical and social variables.

(ii) Assessing care settings. Developments in the assessment of care settings may be summarized under the concept of 'quality assurance' (Lalonde, 1982). Quality assurance refers to the ongoing monitoring of a service and conventionally refers to the collection of hard information about turnover,

costs, etc., rather than qualitative aspects of care or outcome. However, measures have been developed that focus on these (for example, Bigelow *et al.*, 1982). An important element in American quality assurance programmes is the 'case management' system which requires the review of a number of cases per year to ensure that standards have been complied with (Intagliata and Baker, 1983). Some studies have looked at the environment using Moos and Otto's (1972) Community-Oriented Programs Environment Scale (for example, Segal *et al.*, 1979). In the UK the most influential work has been that of Tizard as described below. Clifford *et al.* (1988) are one of a number of groups working to extend this approach to the monitoring of community settings.

SERVICES FOR PEOPLE WITH LEARNING DISABILITIES (MENTAL HANDICAP)

It is helpful to consider the evaluation of community services for this client group within two broader contexts. One is that of changing practices and patterns of service provision. The other is the changing preoccupations of psychologists engaged in intervention research, directed at understanding and ameliorating the learning difficulty itself. Mittler (1979) looked in some detail at developments in both areas, and their inter-relationships. Clarke and Clarke (1986) give an extremely succinct review of psychologists' work during the past three decades which also covers both aspects. Malin *et al.* (1980) gave a comprehensive account and critique of the whole range of mental handicap services in Britain at that time, but from their perspective as service evaluators. Shearer (1986) adopts a 15 year retrospective in her readable description of the development of community services in this country, arguing that it is within this period that the shift in the emphasis to the community has accelerated most markedly. She reminds us that many services which are labelled as 'community' by their planners may be effectively institutional, although situated outside the large hospitals they were intended to replace. Importantly (page 6), she points out that the decline in the population of the hospitals owes little to the transfer of residents, and more to the moratorium on admissions and the death of residents. For the evaluator, this means that comparative studies become decreasingly appropriate, as the populations of the two service settings become increasingly disparate. Nowadays, the typical hospital resident is likely to be older, more severely mentally handicapped, and more likely to have additional handicaps and other problems, both medically and psychologically, than his or her community counterpart.

Service evaluation has had the role of both a stimulus to change and a response to it. The extent to which those roles have been successfully enacted is arguable. Evaluation research in this country owes a great debt to the work of the late Jack Tizard (Clarke and Tizard, 1983). One of his basic assumptions, and that of the Thomas Coram Research Unit, which he founded, as well as of the many workers in the field whom he inspired, was that evaluation research, especially within the demonstration project model, should, could, and did have a fundamental role to play in influencing social policy and practice (for example, Tizard, 1974).

Emerson (1985) strongly argues the opposite case. From a detailed review of (largely) North American work, but with some reference to the British literature, he concludes that evaluation research has not been closely integrated with social policy formulation, nor with service improvement. He points to a lack of clarity in many studies about what should be evaluated, suggesting that the major use of research has been 'symbolic; that is, the non-functional use of data to justify pre-determined positions' and that there are many weaknesses in the concepts and methods used.

Evaluative research with this client group clearly presents challenges which can be absorbing for the researcher, and the issue of the ultimate impact of the work itself can easily be neglected. This risk is inherent in both research-based studies and evaluation conducted as part of on-going service provision.

The demonstration project

Evaluation within the 'demonstration project' model was undoubtedly the dominant research framework in mental handicap services during the period when it was still necessary to put strong arguments for more widespread community service developments. In retrospect, perhaps the real impact of such projects was simply the demonstration that such services were possible. The heyday of such work was during the 1970s and early 1980s, and much of it was concentrated in a small group of research centres, notably the Health Care Evaluation Research Team in Winchester (Kushlick and colleagues), the Mental Handicap in Wales Applied Research Unit (Blunden and colleagues), the Hester Adrian Research Centre in Manchester (Mittler and colleagues), the Thomas Coram Research Unit in London (Tizard, Kiernan and others), the Evaluation Research Group in Sheffield and the Sheffield Development Project (see Malin *et al.*, 1980), and the Department of Mental Health at Bristol University (Russell and Ward).

Comparisons of hospital and community services

Comparative studies of hospital and community services became impracticable as the differences between the populations of the two kinds of services grew, and apparently less relevant, as the shift to community provision gained momentum on ideological grounds. However, two major sets of comparative work merit particular attention. Following on from the Brooklands Experiment (Tizard, 1964) which demonstrated the developmental benefits to mentally-handicapped children of a small-scale child-centred approach to care, King *et al.* (1971) reported a major comparative evaluation study of existing child care settings in the NHS and local authorities. Their methodological innovations are still useful today. They carefully operationalized a set of measures of management and care practices which enabled them to distinguish clearly between institutional and child-centred approaches, drawing on the seminal work of Goffman (1961). These were summarized as: rigidity, block treatment, de-personalization and social distance between staff and children. They developed and tested a set of hypotheses to account for the differences in practices between the two types of setting, which enabled them to highlight relationships between child care practices deriving from organizational differences, and the functioning of the children on a range of behavioural and developmental measures.

In collaboration with the then Wessex Regional Hospital Board, Kushlick and his colleagues carried out a large scale comparison of the traditional hospital settings and the newer community units. The basis of the experimental methodology used in this set of demonstration projects was the assignation of residents to one or other type of care on a purely geographical basis. The new units were set up with minutely detailed operational policies, based upon the growing body of relevant research. The research team used both existing measures and their own innovatory ones to measure how residents fared under the different regimes. Kushlick *et al*'s submission to the Jay Committee in 1976 provides a useful distillation of the work and thinking of his group. See also Kushlick, 1969 and 1974, although HCERU (Health Care Evaluation and Research Unit), published much of its work independently.

These and other studies contributed methodologically to the set of available techniques for evaluating care settings. Techniques for assessing client outcomes have continued to multiply, but their origins owe more to the work of the intervention or treatment researchers, and to practising clinicians, than to evaluators.

Criterion-based evaluations

Later in the 1970s there emerged a growing consensus about the nature of 'good' services for people with learning disabilities. Evaluation shifted from a role of hypothesis testing and heuristics to one of prescription and quality assurance. This consensus was based partly on the findings of the service evaluators, but also on the work of more individually-oriented researchers working on behavioural treatment approaches and the growing ideological fervour of the normalization movement. This movement, in turn, was given impetus by the application of a coherent and well-operationalized philosophy to service demonstrations, especially in Scandinavia and North America (for example, Nirje 1970; Wolfensberger 1972; Grunewald 1978). In this country the consensus was distilled into a checklist approach to evaluation which assumed that we knew what good services should be like. The King's Fund document *An Ordinary Life* (1980) distilled and adapted thinking and practice from American sources such as ENCOR (East Nebraska Community Office for Retardation) with innovative work here, and became the much-quoted foundation for many new services established in the later 1970s and early 1980s. However, the diverse nature of such services, despite their claims to share a common philosophical origin, owes much to vagaries of interpretation. More precise and detailed checklists and service guidelines, also widely used, can be found in, for example, MENCAP's STAMINA documents, and the publications of the (now disbanded) National Development Group (see National Development Group, 1980). The more covert operations of the National Development Groups are also best seen as an adaptation of the checklist approach.

There was an implicit assumption that evaluation itself was an effective tool for the organizational change and the maintenance of good practice. The flaws in this assumption are readily apparent. The development of a much more sophisticated checklist approach to service evaluation which acknowledges the importance of the nature of the process as well as of the content of the evaluation can be seen in PASS (Programme Analysis of Service Systems' Implementation of Normalisation Goals). Wolfensberger and Thomas (1983) describe PASS and PASSING as 'tools for the objective quantitative measurement of the quality of a wide range of human service programs, agencies, and even entire systems. PASS measures service quality in terms of the service's adherence to (*a*) the principle of normalization, (*b*) certain other service ideologies, and (*c*) certain other administrative desiderata, all believed to contribute to service quality'. (See also Wolfensberger and Glenn, 1975, Flynn and Nitsch 1980.)

And now?

It is apparent that there has not only been a dramatic shift in the location of services away from hospitals and towards the community, but also in the rationale underlying service development, and thus of service evaluation. At the time of the behavioural revolution in treatment approaches, the main concern was to develop effective remediation techniques for the functional handicaps ascribed to the underlying learning disability. Experience suggested that the observed handicaps of institutional residents were also partly ascribable to the settings themselves. What began partly as a search for settings in which empirically-validated treatments could be more effectively carried out became more a pressure to create a constellation of services which conformed to ideologically-sound criteria. Indeed, there may be a paradox in seeking too actively to remediate handicaps within a 'people first' normalization ethos, especially when the methods of remediation, at their most intensive, may involve the creation of patterns of activity strikingly different from those of valued, non-handicapped people

Nonetheless, the dominance of the ideological basis of service development and evaluation, which has resulted in the consensus in favour of community services for people with learning disabilities, may have led to an excessive preoccupation with settings themselves to the relative neglect, ironically, of the individuals who use those services. In what follows, we suggest some future directions for service evaluation, in terms of aims, methods, frameworks and approaches to analysis. But the work of earlier researchers in this field has left us with a rich seam of approaches which may still find new uses. Although we have left behind many earlier preoccupations, a re-reading of earlier work still helps us to tackle more effectively the conceptual and research tasks which lie ahead. The greatest danger at the moment seems to be a sense that we already know what ideal services should look like, and that repeated application of existing evaluation techniques will function as adequate tools of quality assurance and organizational change.

A final point, particularly for this client group, is that we are again at a stage where there is a need for more basic research into the nature of the disability, and effective methods of helping individuals with learning disabilities. However, this work needs to be integrated with service development and evaluation; it is not a distinct and separate activity.

GENERAL ISSUES

Like any other psychological intervention an evaluation needs to be carefully thought out in relation to its goals, content and position in the service system. The motive behind a request for evaluation should be carefully considered before an evaluation is undertaken. For example, service managers may be wanting something called an 'evaluation' in order to satisfy themselves or their superiors that staff in the new facilities are not lapsing into past errors. Although a legitimate wish, evaluation may not be the best way to address it. Alternatively, the request for the psychologist to design and carry out an evaluation may mean that the problem of thinking in any depth about the way services are functioning is being avoided by being allocated to a 'specialist'. At its worst, 'evaluation' can represent yet another failure to look directly at what really goes on. For this reason, the request, or the urge, to evaluate should be taken as a cue to stop and think – both about the local origins of the desire for evaluation and the most appropriate response to it.

The best response may not be to carry out a formal evaluation. Green and Atkisson (1984) distinguish *evaluation* of a service, which tends to be on a one-off basis, using external assessors and objective methods from the *monitoring* of services which may be on a more ongoing basis. Resources may be better used in introducing a 'softer' form of service monitoring which could involve regular feedback to both providers of the service and service managers. This could easily involve members of the service rather than external researchers. The criterion-based assessments discussed above are particularly suited to the latter task but have the potential for refinement for both purposes. Lavender's work, previously referred to, is an example of this.

A decision may be made to go ahead and evaluate. In this case, it is essential to define what is to be evaluated. Is it the extent to which the service conforms to a particular criterion, such as being 'community-oriented' or 'client-centred'? Or, is there a genuine interest in outcome as measured by the extent to which a person's life is better in that environment? There is often ambiguity over whether community services are supposed to be a good thing *per se* or because they enhance the life of the client. These views are not mutually exclusive but have different implications for the potential evaluator. Similarly, it is important to know where the geographical and psychological boundaries of the service are deemed to be. Users and professionals may not agree.

In planning an evaluation three basic questions are:

1. To what extent is the service philosophically or morally satisfactory? This will be particularly relevant to services which are set up within a framework of normalization/social role valorization but will be equally important for any service that is trying to conform to a defined philosophy of care.

2. What is the impact of the service on the individual consumer? It will be important to consider the views of the users as well as whether the service reduces or enhances their disability and/or its handicapping effects.

3. Does the service run as intended? If it has an operational policy, implicit or explicit, to what extent does the practice follow that policy?

Each of these must be broken down into operationalized components for which appropriate measures need to be devised. Although it is tempting to take things off the shelf, there is tremendous scope for the methodological innovator. Traditional psychological evaluation techniques, founded on the need to evaluate treatment outcomes with individuals, are often inadequate when it comes to measuring the development of a service and its interactions with clients and staff. The use of matched control groups is an example of a methodology of limited applicability to the complex, multivariate nature of ordinary life. It is also easy to fall into the trap of only measuring the measurables when confronted with the difficulty of capturing qualitative aspects of experience using quantitative measures. For example, it is far easier to assess quality of life in terms of satisfaction with material conditions than in relation to an understanding of someone's internal, psychological functioning even though the latter may be of equal or greater significance. Another major problem facing evaluation of services for both client groups is the development of better measures of care settings. Its urgency is indicated by a recent review of outcome in residential programmes in the USA which suggested that most of the variance in social integration of the chronically mentally ill was attributable to environmental rather than treatment factors (Cournos, 1987).

Anticipating the successful completion of an evaluation, there are a number of other general points that need to be remembered. First, even if a service is given high marks by its evaluators, it will always be difficult to determine which aspects of the service constitute the critical variables. It will be equally difficult to identify which components of a service, singly or in combination, account for unsatisfactory standards.

Second, there is a need for caution in generalizing from the evaluation of a specifically-funded programme carried out by a team of dedicated innovators to a model that will be valid in more humdrum circumstances. Demonstration projects are typically well-endowed with respect to both research and clinical skills and it is inevitable that replications elsewhere in the context of mainstream provision will have less resources and lack the excitement inherent in the pioneering spirit of the originals. This means that demonstration projects can at best hope to persuade rather than to prove. However, even this does not always happen, history suggests that evaluation, even with dissemination, is rarely sufficient to affect policy. The implications of this is that thought must be given at the outset of a research project into planning how feedback might be genuinely influential, especially if evaluation is to be a thinly disguised lobbying tool.

If the request to evaluate is, in effect, a request to initiate or consolidate organizational change, then the best response may well not be an evaluation but, rather, a more explicit venture into the realms of organizational development work, bearing in mind – to paraphrase Georgiades and Phillimore (1987) – that organizations, like dragons, may well eat hero evaluators for breakfast.

It is not possible to make sense of the growing acceptability of evaluation without bearing in mind that the drive to create community-based services derives substantially from the perceived failure of the large hospital. Thus, a major motivating force for evaluating new services can be a belief that something bad was done in the past that must not be repeated. This has perhaps contributed to an exaggerated emphasis on the general humaneness of services (to compensate for past inhumanities) as opposed to specific functions they are intended to serve. Two corollaries have been that there has been a relative neglect of research that looks at the nature of people's disabilities or that examines their interactions with, and influence on, the character of services. These are glaring gaps in recent research in both fields.

There has also been a lack of investigation of the process of change. The stress on the discontinuities between the old and the new services rather than the continuities has led to a failure to follow through ideas that emerged from research into the old services.

Finally, then, a plea for less evaluation and more innovative and imaginative research into the way services function. Evaluations, by their very nature, are inclined to assume that the desired outcome is known and so tend not to be open-ended or exploratory. They also tend to stress what has worked, not the problems; the latter may actually be of more practical and theoretical interest. There is thus a place for more descriptive studies of the process of service development – evaluative methodologies treat settings as if they are constant rather than undergoing processes of growth or decline. It should also be remembered that answers to many of the fundamental questions regarding how best to provide human services are far from being answered. Thus the psychologist who is asked to contribute to service evaluation and begins to feel daunted by the task, should not feel inadequate as a professional, but merely, to quote the jargon, 'challenged'.

REFERENCES

ANTHONY, W.A. and FARKAS, M. (1982). A client outcome planning model for assessing psychiatric rehabilitation interventions. *Schizophrenia Bulletin, vol.8, no.1*, pp. 13–38.

BACHRACH, L.L. (1982). Assessment of outcomes in community support systems: results, problems, and limitations. *Schizophrenia Bulletin, vol.8, no.1*, pp. 39–60.

BAKER, F. and INTAGLIATA, J. (1982). Quality of life in the evaluation of community support systems. *Evaluation and Program Planning, Vol.5*, pp. 69–79.

BARTON, R. (1959) *Institutional Neurosis*. John Wright: Bristol.

BIGELOW, A.D., BRODSKY, G., STEWART, L. and OLSON, M. (1982). *The concept and measurement of quality of life as a dependent variable in evaluation of mental health services*. In G.J. Stahler and W.R. Tash. *Innovative Approaches to Mental Health Evaluation*. London: Academic Press.

BRAUN, P., KOCHANSKY, G., SHAPIRO, R., GREENBERG, S., GUDEMAN, J. and SHORE, M. (1981). *Overview: Deinstitutionalization of Psychiatric Patients: A Critical Review of Outcome Studies*. American Journal of Psychiatry *138*, 6.

CAMPAIGN FOR PEOPLE WITH MENTAL HANDICAPS (1981). *The Principles of Normalisation: a foundation for effective services*. Cambridge: Cambridge Free Press. Pages 30–31.

CLARKE, A.D.B. and TIZARD, B. (eds) (1983). *Child Development and Social Policy: The Life and Work of Jack Tizard*. Leicester: The British Psychological Society.

CLARKE, A.M. and CLARKE, A.D.B. (1986). Thirty years of child psychology: a selective review. *Journal of Child Psychology and Psychiatry, 27*, 719–759.

CLIFFORD, P.I. (1986). Why I haven't joined the Normies: Some doubts about normalisation. *South East Thames Rehabilitation Interest Group Newsletter*.

CLIFFORD, P.I. and HOLLOWAY, F. (1987). .*Evaluating the Closure of Cane Hill Hospital: Protocol for a collaborative research programme with South East Thames Regional Health Authority*. London: National Unit for Psychiatric Research and Development.

CLIFFORD, P.I., LAVENDER A. and PILLING, S. (1988). *QUARTZ: A Method of Quality Assurance for Community Care Systems*. London: National Unit for Psychiatric Research and Development.

COURNOS, F. (1987). The impact of environmental factors on outcome of residential programs. *Hospital and Community Psychiatry, vol.38*, No.8, pp.848–851.

EMERSON, E.B. (1985). Evaluating the impact of deinstitutionalisation on the lives of mentally retarded people. *American Journal of Mental Deficiency, 90*, 3, 277–288.

FLYNN, R.J. and NITSCH, K.E. (eds) (1980). *Normalisation, Social Integration, and Community Services*. Baltimore: University Park Press.

GARETY, P. and MORRIS, B. (1984). A new unit for long-stay psychiatric patients: organisation, attitudes and quality of care. *Psychological Medicine 14*, 183–192.

GEORGIADES, N.J. and PHILLIMORE, L. (1987). The myth of the hero-innovator and alternative strategies for organisational change in C.C. Kiernan and F.D. Woodford (eds), *Behaviour Modification with the Severely Retarded*, Associated Scientific Publishers: Amsterdam.

GIBBONS, J.S. and BUTLER, J.P. (1987). Quality of life for 'new' long-stay psychiatric in patients: The effects of moving to a hostel. *British Journal of Psychiatry, 151*, 347–54.

GOFFMAN, E. (1961). *Asylums: Essays on Social Situation of Mental Patients and Other Inmates*. New York: Doubleday.

GREEN, R.S. and ATKISSON, C.C. (1984). Quality Assurance and Program Evaluation – Similarities and differences. *American Behavioural Scientist, vol.27*, no.5, 552–582.

GRUNEWALD, K. (ed) (1978). *The Mentally Handicapped: Towards Normal Living*. London: Hutchinson.

HER MAJESTY'S STATIONERY OFFICE. (1979). *Report of the Committee of Enquiry into Mental Handicap Nursing and Care*. (Chairman Peggy Jay.) Cmnd. 7468. London: HMSO.

HOULT, J. and REYNOLDS, I. (1984). Schizophrenia: a comparative trial of community orientated and hospital orientated psychiatric care. *Acta Psychiatrica Scandinavia 69*, 359–372.

INTAGLIATA J. and BAKER, F. (1983). Factors affecting the delivery of case management services to the chronically mentally ill. *Adm. Mental Health, 11*, pp.79–91.

KING, R., RAYNES, N. and TIZARD, J. (1971). *Patterns of Residential Care: sociological studies in institutions for handicapped children*. London: Routledge and Kegan Paul.

KING'S FUND (1980). *An ordinary life: comprehensive locally-based residential services for mentally handicapped people*. (Project paper no. 24.) London: King Edwards Hospital Fund.

KUSHLICK, A. (1969). Care of the mentally subnormal. *Lancet, 2*, 1196.

KUSHLICK, A. (1974).*The Mentally Handicapped in Positions, Movements and Directions in Health Services Research*. Oxford: Nuffield Provincial Hospitals Trust and Oxford University Press.

KUSHLICK, A. FELCE, D. PALMER, J. and SMITH, J. (1976). *Evidence to the Committee of Inquiry into Mental Handicap Nursing and Care from the Health Care Evaluation and Research Team*. Wessex Regional Health Authority.

LALONDE, B.I.D., (1982). Quality Assurance. From M.J. Austin and W.E. Hershey (eds). *Handbook on Mental Health Administration*. San Francisco: Jossey-Bass.

LAVENDER, A. (1984). *Evaluation in settings for the long term psychologically handicapped*. PhD Thesis submitted for examination, University of London. King's College Hospital Medical School.

LAVENDER, A (1985). Quality of care and staff practices in long term settings. In F.N. Watts (ed.) *New Developments in Clinical Psychology*. Leicester: The British Psychological Society/John Wiley.

LAVENDER, A. (1987). Improving the quality of care on psychiatric hospital rehabilitation wards: A controlled evaulation. *British Journal of Psychiatry, 150*, 476–81.

LEHMAN. A.F. (1983). The well-being of chronic mental patients – assessing their quality of life. *Archives of General Psychiatry, vol.40*, 369–1276.

LEHMAN, A.F. (1982). Chronical mental patients: the quality of life issue. *American Journal of Psychiatry 139*, 10, pp. 369–76.

LINDSLEY, O.R. (1964). *Direct measurement and prosthesis of retarded behaviour. Journal of Education, 147*, 62–81.

MALIN, N. RACE, D. and JONES, G. (1980). *Services for the Mentally Handicapped in Britain*. London: Croom Helm.

MARKS, I., CONNOLLY, J. and MUIJEN M. (1987). The Maudsley daily living program: a controlled cost effectiveness study of community based vs standard inpatient care of serious mental illness. *Bulletin of the British Journal of Psychiatry*, Nov 1987.

MARTIN, J.P. (1984). *Hospitals in Trouble*. Oxford: Basil Blackwell.

MENZIES, I.E.P. (1970). *The functioning of social systems as a defence against anxiety*. London: Tavistock Pamphlet no.3.

MILLAR, D. and ROBERTS, V. (1986). Elderly patients in 'continuing care': a consultation concerning the quality of life. *Group Analysis, vol. 19*, pp. 45–62.

MITTLER, P. (1979) *People Not Patients*. London: Methuen.

MOOS, R.H. (1974). *Evaluating Treatment Environments: A social ecological approach*. Chichester: John Wiley.

MOOS, R. and OTTO, J. (1972). The Community-Oriented Programs Environment Scales: a methodology for the facilitation and evaluation of social change. *Community Mental Health Journal, 8*, 28–37.

NATIONAL DEVELOPMENT GROUP (1980). *Improving the Quality of Life for Mentally Handicapped People – A checklist of standards*. London: Department of Health and Social Security.

NATIONAL SOCIETY FOR MENTALLY HANDICAPPED CHILDREN (1977). *Stamina: Minimum standards for ESN schools, ATCs and Residential Homes*. London: NSMHC (now MENCAP).

NIRJE, B. (1970). The normalisation principle: implications and comments. *British Journal of Mental Subnormality, 16*, 2.

O'BRIEN, J. and TYNE, A. (1981). *The principles of normalisation: a foundation for effective services*. London: Campaign for People with Mental Handicaps.

REPORT OF A WORKING GROUP (1977). (NODDER Report). *Organisational and Management Problems of Mental Illness Hospitals*. London: Department of Health and Social Security.

SAYCE, L. (1987). *Questionnaire for the Assessment of Good Practices in Mental Health*. London: National Unit for Psychiatric Research and Development.

SEGAL S.P., EVERETT-DILLE L. and MOYLES E.W. (1979). Congruent perceptions in the evaluation of community-care facilities. *Journal of Community Psychology*, 7, 60–68.

SHEARER, A (1986). *Building a Community with People with Mental Handicaps, their Families and Friends*. London: Campaign for People with Mental Handicaps, and King Edwards Hospital Fund for London. (Distribution by Oxford University Press.)

SHEPHERD, G. and RICHARDSON A. (1979). Organisation and interaction in psychiatric day centres. *Psychological Medicine, 9*, 573–579.

STANTON, A. and SCHWARZ, M. (1954) *The Mental Hospital. New York: Basic Books*.

STEIN, L.I. and TEST, M.A. (1978). *An Alternative to Mental Hospital Treatment*. New York. Plenum Press.

THOMAS, D. FIRTH, H. and RENDALL, A. (1978). *Encor – A way ahead*. London: Campaign for the Mentally Handicapped.

TIZARD, J. (1964). *Community Services for the Mentally Handicapped*. Oxford: Oxford University Press.

TIZARD, J. (1974). Services and the evaluation of services. In A.M. Clarke and A.D.B. Clarke (eds) *Mental deficiency: the changing outlook*. London: Methuen.

WARNER, R. (1985). *Recovery from Schizophrenia: Psychiatry and Political Economy*. London: Routledge and Kegan Paul.

WING, J.K. and BROWN, G.W. (1970). *Institutionalism and Schizophrenia: a comparative study of three mental hospitals, 1960–1968*. Cambridge: Cambridge University Press.

WOLFENSBERGER, W. (1972). *The Principle of Normalisation in Human Services*. Toronto: National Institute on Mental Retardation.

WOLFENSBERGER, W. and GLENN, L. (1975). *Program Analysis of Service Systems' Implementation of Normalisation Goals*. Toronto: National Institute on Mental Retardation.

WOLFENSBERGER, W. and THOMAS, S. (1983). *Program Analysis of Service Systems' Implementation of Normalisation Goals*. Toronto: National Institute on Mental Retardation.

ASSESSING COST-EFFECTIVENESS

Steen Mangen

Before widespread adoption, medical and psychological treatments are required to establish their safety, quality and, in the longer term, their efficacy. However, until comparatively recently, they have not routinely had to demonstrate their efficiency in resource utilization. Since the introduction of cash limit planning in the National Health Service (NHS) in 1976, the question of cost containment has been increasingly prominent in Britain and in the intervening decade progressive welfare state retrenchment has engendered considerable effort in examining means of achieving 'value for money' through more efficient use of existing resources. The growing importance of this issue is manifested in the deepening 'welfare state crisis' in attempts to replace expensive institutional-based services with less expensive informal and community-based provisions, and in accompanying privatization policies which include the transfer of costs away from the public purse to the private realm of the family.

In Britain some form of cost benefit study is now routinely applied in the assessment of major health care options where at least one of these involves a large capital scheme (Department of Health and Social Security, 1981). The aim of this review is to assess the contribution such studies can make to the resolution of the question of efficiency of resource allocation for psychosocial interventions. Before discussing studies with direct implications for health care systems such as the British National Health Service, the principles of a major research model – cost-effectiveness analysis (CEA) – are introduced with particular attention being paid to what economists mean by cost. The problems of undertaking CEA are highlighted in the context of the psychosocial intervention studies reviewed.

Investing in the psychiatric system

The manner in which most new psychosocial interventions enter the psychiatric system is typically incremental and *ad hoc*. This situation is exacerbated by the failure to undertake formal evaluations of their relative status in the competition for health and welfare resources which are, according to an economist's definition, always scarce since they could be put to alternative uses. It is for this reason that health service planners have become increasingly preoccupied with ways of obtaining the best possible health care outcomes for any given level of resource service input. This essentially involves comparative analysis: weighing up the merits and limitations arising from two or more alternatives modes of intervention. One research tool which assists in this assessment is the cost-benefit study which has the attraction of bringing together the costs and benefits accruing from treatments into one analytical framework, thus permitting us to consider relative efficiencies in terms of cost-benefit ratios. Ultimately, of course, such studies are no surrogate for sound decision making, since other social and economic objectives need to be taken into consideration. Cost-benefit analyses (CBA), then, inform but cannot replace the political input in the policy-making process.

A logical pre-requisite of cost-benefit analysis is that the efficacy of the psychosocial intervention under investigation has been established. Since these economic studies are expensive to mount it would be scientifically inept to launch them as a preliminary analysis, although studies can be designed in such a way as to make use of clinical material already available which is then supplemented by further investigations.

Critically, CBAs of psychological interventions should incorporate a wide variety of outcomes which go beyond immediately observable effects on the service under review, such as: impact on utilization rates of other health and social services; changes in socio-clinical performance and in economic status of the patient and the family; perhaps effects on the wider community. Particularly where interventions involve innovative approaches, we may wish to extend the analysis to evaluate effects on existing service delivery and on the professional territoriality of each mental health agent.

As well as immediate costs and benefits, then, we need to consider the impact on other services, whose utilization may be differentially influenced by the patient's consumption of the therapy under review. Potential costs and benefits to other parties, including those only indirectly involved should also be evaluated. In short, 'externality effects' must be taken into account.

COST-BENEFIT AND COST-EFFECTIVENESS STUDIES

Cost benefit analysis is a generic term referring to various kinds of economic evaluations deriving from an operations research approach. Strictly speaking, CBA should only be applied as a term describing a comprehensive evaluation of all effects of alternative courses of action (for example, different therapies) expressed through a common resource unit, usually money.

The aim of such an analysis is to determine which of two or more treatments produces the greatest benefits in terms of achieving the most of a set of therapeutic objectives (the monetary value of the positive outcomes accruing) at the least cost (monetary value of resources consumed), or the most benefits at a fixed cost. CBA can be used to compare two alternative treatment programmes to reach the same objective – for example, behavioural or interpretive psychotherapy; or it can be applied to compare the relative costs and benefits of completely separate programmes – to aid decision making about whether, for example, to expand services for drug dependents or psychogeriatric patients.

There are clearly enormous problems in attempting a full cost-benefit analysis. In addition to the problems of how to measure the effectiveness of therapies which may have differing objectives, there is the question of what outcome variables to include as costs and benefits and, most critically, how to attach monetary values to them. There have been numerous strategies for resolution: panel consensus judgements, use of average insurance claims for loss of life or limb, surveys of the general public on the monetary value to be attached to particular therapeutic gains, and so on. In studies of physical medicine there have been various attempts to employ health status indicators through which standardized assessment of the benefit of clinical improvements are set against the costs of achieving it, the concept of 'quality adjusted life years' (QALYs) currently being the outcome measure most favoured.

Many of those involved in the field would subscribe to the view that it is ultimately inappropriate to attempt to monetarize outcomes that cannot be easily rendered in terms of cash. To do so makes the assumption that utility is coterminous with monetary value, a philistine act that conforms to Lord Darlington's definition of a cynic: someone who knows the price of everything and the value of nothing. Consequently, economic evaluations of mental health care have adopted the more restrictive, though perhaps more credible conceptual model of cost-effectiveness analysis (CEA). In CBA there are different potential outcomes that are valued in monetary terms; in CEA the outcome is fixed and expressed in non-monetary terms; It is the monetary costs of achieving this outcome via different therapies that is being compared. CEA, then, is technically only appropriate in situations where there is one uncontentious objective which is capable of being measured by a single outcome variable, for example, the average duration of inpatient admissions. As with CBA, the aim is to discover which therapeutic programme achieves a fixed objective at least cost or, alternatively, more of the objective at a fixed cost.

The formal requirements of CEA are rarely ideal for evaluative research in a specialty like clinical psychology, for it is rare indeed for there to be one explicit and fixed objective. Instead, socio-clinical outcomes from alternative therapies appropriate for the same patient group are likely to vary. In order to overcome the problems of attempting to examine costs and benefits over different service settings, the favoured solution is to express most differential outcomes in some reasonably unambiguous physical unit, such as bed-days, or in socio-clinical change scores, whilst other outcomes (which can be fairly unproblematically translated into monetary values) are so rendered. Glass and Goldberg (1977) offer a variant of this solution in their model of CEA whereby non-monetary and monetary effects of two therapeutic programmes are compared. If one programme results in a net benefit on both sets of effects, it is clearly the obvious candidate for adoption. On the other hand, if one programme produces, say, greater net non-monetary benefits but at a higher financial cost, policy-makers are at least made aware of the additional costs that must be borne if they decide to choose the more effective option.

Whatever the precise model ultimately employed, CEA incorporates both objective and subjective evaluative criteria. Although this approach may assuage the sensitivities of most research teams, it does not solve the problem of selection of benefits and non-monetary costs to include in the analysis, or of how to measure them, or of how many of the varying and sometimes conflicting interests to incorporate in determining the criteria to be employed in measuring outcomes (for example, those of patients, families, professionals, administrators or the wider community). These issues have implications which go beyond the scope of this Chapter (for further discussion see Yates, 1980; Ball, 1979). Even at the technical level there are still considerable problems to overcome. One of the major difficulties lies in the lack of commensurability of outcome data. Can one, for example, equate a 'unit' of improvement in social performance with a 'unit' of symptom alleviation and, if not, what subjective criteria should be used to weight them? A similar kind of problem occurs in situations where the distribution of intangible costs and benefits differs between settings. Different kinds of benefit may accrue in each: for example, day hospitals may offer more autonomy but inpatient wards more shelter. Each of these may be valued clinical outcomes, given a particular patient sample; the problem is how to render them commensurate.

Measurement issues of this kind are crucial. Too heavy a reliance on the 'easy measurement track' – collecting 'hard' financial data whilst neglecting less tangible effects – seriously underestimates a range of costs which are important to considerations of equity. There is, for example, an urgent need to incorporate more sensitive data on consumer preferences, including those of patients' families. Among these are feelings of autonomy, self-esteem and general variables connected with quality of life. Moreover, although there have been several studies of family burden and family coping styles, the field requires substantial development both at the conceptual and empirical level, as some feminist work argues (Finch and Groves, 1980; Dalley, 1988).

Of course, the costs of extending data collection have to be considered in the light of the expected value of those data to the analysis. This can pose particular problems in costing evaluations in mental health care where clients are often in receipt of services from a variety of agencies, each of which may involve a small number of the sample. However, since there is ample evidence that, for psychiatric patients, the direct costs of formal therapy represent a relatively small proportion of the total costs borne by the health and social services, and by themselves and their families, a convincing case must be made in any CEA that an appropriately comprehensive set of outcome measures has been included, so that 'externality effects' – the indirect costs or benefits accruing – can be reliably assessed. In this way we may be able to estimate the margin between private and social costs and benefits.

THE CONCEPT OF COST

In economics, 'cost' is strictly not financial cost but resources cost. The costs arising from any therapy lie in the consumption of scarce resources that could have been put to alternative uses. The real costs, then, are 'opportunity costs': the opportunities foregone by using resources for one purpose instead of another. The ultimate cost is the benefits that would have been derived had the resources been put to their optimal use (Drummond, 1980). Financial costs, on the other hand, are largely determined by accounting conventions. Unfortunately, in undertaking cost-effectiveness studies in health care we have to rely on accounting costs simply because these are the only data routinely available from NHS finance officers and social services departments. To render the data more valid for analytical purposes, modifications to costings are made, as appropriate.

One needs to be cautious about interpreting the apparent benefits of resource savings in terms of opportunity cost because its derivation can often be a hazardous exercise. Some resource savings may be more apparent than real if the resources released for alternative use cannot easily be amalgamated. Savings of 'units' of nurses' time, for example, may not be exploitable if they consist of one or two minutes here and there during the day and distributed among a large number of staff. Furthermore, such time saved may be used in carrying out lower priority tasks such as treating mildly symptomatic patients who might otherwise have spontaneously remitted or received support from their social networks. The question of redeployment of resources is, of course, ultimately one for policy-makers and managers and, thus, they will need to incorporate a range of factors other than the narrowly economic in arriving at their decisions. Though these factors lie outside the immediate concern of this chapter, they include important and topical issues such as the compatibility of pursuing efficiency with the goal of equity, although on the matter of distributive justice economics is strictly neutral, since the object is to measure costs and benefits accruing to society as a whole.

Marginal cost

Economic evaluations are generally more concerned with the extra cost incurred in expansion than with the total costs of the whole service. This is because interest lies in a therapy's impact on rates of psychological disturbance, given that such disorders cannot be totally eradicated. The valid concept is therefore 'marginal cost': the change in total costs attributable to marginal expansions of a treatment programme. This approach permits the existence of any spare capacity to be taken into account, since it is often the case that, say, a ten per cent increase in therapeutic activity may not demand a corresponding increase of resource input. The validity of this assumption is, of course, a function of the existing organizational structures and administrative practices, as well as of the volume of the expansion being contemplated. Thus, considerations of economies of scale come into play, since costs can change at different levels of operations; some expansions could, say, require additional administrative support or new accommodation. Furthermore, there may well be situations where existing spare capacity cannot be realistically exploited under prevailing circumstances.

Unfortunately for CEA, marginal cost data are not routinely available. Their accurate measurement requires detailed costing studies involving close observational 'time and motion' techniques. Most investigators undertaking CEAs do not have sufficient research resources to entertain such approaches and, instead, employ 'average' or 'unit' revenue costs, making amendments for capital cost implications of any service expansion. This solution which varies according to the degree of appropriateness is typically justified on the grounds that, as the service expands, average costs will approximate long-term marginal costs. However, this can result in an overestimation of long-run marginal costs, since an assumption of no spare capacity is usually made: that is, to expand the service in the long run will require an equal expansion of all inputs.

These problems are exacerbated by the unsatisfactory nature of the available unit cost data which are sensitive to patient and service mix. The Department of Health and Social Security (DHSS) *Health Service Cost Returns* give only 'speciality costs' which for the purposes of CEA are highly aggregated. In CEA, costing data have to be made more specific by modifying each element according to the level of service consumption of each patient in the sample. Psychiatric patients in day care, for example, vary considerably both in their frequency of attendance and use of the range of facilities on offer. Official statistics, however, do not make these distinctions and, thus, are a poor indication, both of actual resource utilization and potential savings that might be made by replacing one mode of care with another. One of the most contentious examples of this problem is presented by 'community care'. This was long argued in terms of its relative cheapness. But it is now common knowledge that easily rehabilitated patients, who can quickly be discharged from high-dependency psychiatric settings, present too favourable an impression of cost flows over time when 'hard core' clients are included in deinstutionalization programmes. Although CEA provides more sensitive economic analysis, each study relates directly to a particular patient sample and, in order to assess the relevance of the results for general policy-making, account must be taken of the representativeness of that sample and of the service being studied.

Shadow pricing

There are also situations where the current costs of some interventions may not reflect their true costs, especially when expansion of a programme becomes an option. If, for example, there is evidence of a difficulty in attracting qualified staff, with the result that services are understaffed, one is not justified in assuming that current average staffing costs will be valid when service expansion takes place. In cases like this the appropriate measure is 'shadow pricing' reflecting the full establishment staffing costs rather than present staffing costs. Otherwise, the service will be misrepresented as being cheaper than it should, or will, be. This problem is particularly germane to discussions of the relative costs of health and social care provisions. In some settings 'high cost' NHS facilities are caring for a more dependent clientele than 'low cost' non-health care facilities. It is perfectly conceivable that expansion of the latter services, which have often been underfunded, artificially low cost establishments, could result in heavy strain and eventual breakdown of the operation as a consequence of even a small increase in clientele. Alternatively, it might be necessary to employ more high cost professionals and deploy other therapeutic inputs to cope with the change of morbidity of the clientele being admitted, thereby eroding the initial low cost attractiveness of the service.

Discount rates

In undertaking CEAs the choice of time period for the examination of the flow of costs and benefits is absolutely vital. Unfortunately, in many studies the time span is dictated solely by project funding and is insufficiently long to allow for an appropriate appraisal, despite the frequent observation that initially high cost therapies can prove cheaper in the long run. As cost-benefit ratios may not be uniform over time, temporal considerations are crucial: therapy A may be more cost-effective than therapy B initially, but over time the reverse may be true because, among other things, one service may be more prone to inflationary effects than the other.

Not knowing how to take account of the differential timings of net benefits is a major problem for CEAs of mental health care. The standard approach is to apply a 'discount rate', a procedure which converts the value of future costs and benefits to their present values. The discount rate is therefore a value placed on the time that elapses before net benefits accrue. Put simply, it is the rate at which we are prepared to exchange present costs and benefits for those accruing in the future.

Since policy-makers generally prefer benefits to accrue earlier rather than later, a high discount rate indicates that a low priority has been attached to investing extra resources in a programme because its net benefits have been assessed as accruing only in the long term. Where policy-makers are completely indifferent as to when benefits occur (and this is rare) the discount rate would be set at zero. Low rates indicate that high value is attached to future benefits. The current Treasury recommended discount rate is five per cent per annum, although the DHSS usually applies a range of rates between two and ten per cent for sensitivity analysis to test differential outcomes arising from health service investments.

THE ECONOMICS OF MENTAL HEALTH CARE: SOME UK STUDIES

This review is largely restricted to British studies having direct implications for the current and potential practice of clinical psychology. A major constraint in interpreting the results of a majority of foreign studies relates to the specificity of each mental health system: that is, the degree to which it is dependent on private institutions, office practice and insurance reimbursement or, like the British NHS, is a socialized system which is tax funded and largely free at the point of consumption. It is clear from international studies that countries differ significantly in terms of the cost of health resource inputs which, in part, is due to varying administrative costs of national systems and to the form of reimbursement for mental health staff, particularly psychiatrists. For those interested in the American system, Newman and Howard (1986) provide valuable insights into issues such as lengths of treatment, the location of therapy and the cost of resource investments, including the question of fees and profits. Some American studies have been included in this review in situations where the specificity of the care system is not a paramount problem, thus, to some extent reducing the danger of misinterpretation of the implications for British practice.

Interest in economic issues in mental health care among British clinical psychologists has increased both as a result of their greater involvement in planning and, following the 1978 Trethowan Report, the expansion of their clinical roles. The need to use these personnel efficiently is all the more urgent, since currently there are just over two thousand clinical psychologists in Great Britain and it is likely that their opportunity costs are high. This issue has been well aired in the professional journals where some clinicians, for example, have questioned whether, despite the popularity of primary care attachment, psychologists are largely engaged in treating the mildly to moderately-impaired client, to the neglect of patients who are more seriously disturbed and who could benefit from their interventions (Spector, 1984).

Roberts (1974) classifies economic studies of health care as being concerned with the resource implications of (a) alternative types of care, including alternative therapeutic agents; (b) alternative places of care; and (c) alternative times of care. However, at present, most British psychological studies are stronger on clinical than economic analysis and comparatively few could claim to be formal CEAs, including some of the studies reviewed here, though they generally argue that substantial resources savings are implied by their findings. The high cost of mounting cost-effectiveness investigations in terms of time and money, combined with the need to obtain the co-operation of a large number of professional and lay respondents who are typically required to provide detailed information on resource consumption over time, is likely to mean that they will remain a rare resource for mental health policy-making and planning.

In the constraints imposed by the real world, most cost-effectiveness studies of psycho-social interventions contain serious deficiencies. In a research climate dogged by problems of funding, many studies are too small-scale for the task they are attempting to undertake. By their nature psycho-social problems are complex, but samples are small and tend to be overdetermined because of the extensive range of potential socio-clinical and economic variables needing to be incorporated. Problems of data interpretation can often occur in situations where there are too few patients in each cell. For example, in prospective studies there can be problems of extrapolation when only a handful of subjects, distributed unevenly among experimental and control groups, are subsequently discovered to receive a large number of expensive services, which in turn account for a high proportion of total costs incurred for the whole sample.

There can also be problems in treating earnings of patients and their families as outcomes, since the therapeutic programme that releases higher wage-earners back to employment will, on this criterion, automatically seem more cost-effective. The small scale of studies is often compounded by the relative brevity of their study periods, which diminishes the feasibility of applying a discount rate (see Chapman, 1979; Drummond *et al.*, 1986).

CEA and planning

A general observation to emerge from economic studies of mental health care is that only a small proportion of total health and social services costs are due to the consumption of the treatments being investigated. Indirect costs are much higher. This has immediate policy implications, since we cannot expect significant savings in total budgets to be achieved by the implementation of the experimental service. Moreover, we often cannot identify the impact of specific therapeutic inputs on socio-clinical outcomes, with the result that it is difficult to mount sensitivity analyses in which the level of particular resource inputs is manipulated to ascertain whether they have any effect on the achievement of clinical goals. These sorts of constraints mean that the actual role of many CEAs in policy-making may be modest.

Nonetheless, even if the level of specificity is less than would be desired for optimal resource investment, overall indications offer a positive contribution to planning. It has been found, for example, that expensive treatments (in terms of resource input) are associated with a greater level of effectiveness and in the long run they lead to lower levels of resource consumption: that is, they are more efficient. This is true for intensive therapeutic programmes which require high patient–staff ratios (Chapman, 1979). Weisbrod and colleagues (1980), in the best known study of its kind, found that community care in the USA was slightly more expensive but was associated with superior quality of service and clinical outcomes than institution-based solutions. However, several caveats must be added. The discharge of less severely disabled patients in the initial phase may give rise to too favourable a projection of cost savings in the long run, although these may be enhanced by the potential for capital savings, once whole sections or entire hospitals can be closed. A community-based system of care involves significantly different utilization of resources than does a hospital-based system (Wilkinson and Pelosi, 1987). But, if the new services operate as supplements to, rather than replacements for, medium and long-stay inpatient accommodation, as to a certain extent seems likely, resource savings may be less than originally envisaged.

Although most psychotherapeutic interventions have yet fully to establish their efficacy, several studies have indicated that their introduction is associated with reductions in inpatient length-of-stay, with obvious economic savings (Jones *et al.*, 1980; Chapman, 1979) as well as the alleviation, not only of psychiatric but also of physical symptoms (McGrath and Lowson, 1986). Typically, this is as far as most 'economic' considerations of psychotherapy go. Included in this category are studies pointing towards the efficiency of group psychotherapy in comparison to individual therapy for specified patient groups, and short-term as opposed to long-term therapy. In most cases the psychotherapy under review utilizes behavioural or interpretative models. Where psychotherapies have been compared the indications are that clinical results obtained by the former are equal or superior to those of the latter and, moreover, require substantially fewer hours of therapy (Spector, 1984).

Costs and the Therapeutic Role

Some investigations support the economic argument for greater effort to be made by psychologists in disseminating the principles of a particular therapy to lay people thus promoting its benefits to a wider clientele than would be the case if the therapy was administered only by clinical psychologists (Medlik and Fursland, 1984). Similar cases have been put forward for self- and mutual-help through such interventions as bibliotherapy and support groups.

A teaching and consultative role has also been advanced for psychologists in their relations with other professionals, notably general practitioners and nurses. Research directly or indirectly supporting this policy has been published in recent years. Catalan and colleagues (1984), for example, examined the effects of general practitioners adopting a psychotherapeutic approach to patients with minor affective disorders. The sample were offered brief counselling sessions by their general practitioners or were given routine, largely prescription-led interventions. They found that at follow-up, seven months later, counselling was associated with a decline in the prescription rate with no associated increases in therapeutic time.

Several studies have evaluated the potential for replacing higher-cost with lower-cost therapeutic agents who undertake interventions akin to those of clinical psychologists. An early paper by Marks and his colleagues, reporting the results of an uncontrolled investigation of the efficacy of nurse behaviour therapists, indicated that there was a decrease in resource consumption after therapy had been initiated amounting to about one hundred pounds (sterling) a year (Marks *et al.*, 1975). The authors estimated that, provided between 40 and 60 patients completed their programme annually and clinical improvements lasted for at least two years, the benefits of the treatment would outweigh its costs. In a subsequent investigation the Marks team provide further support for the role of nurses in treating patients, most of whom suffered from phobic and obsessive compulsive disorders, in a relatively small controlled trial of nurse therapy, comparing this treatment mode with routine primary care. At follow-up, one year later, the experimental sample achieved clinically superior results and there was a modest (four per cent) decline in resource consumption compared with an almost one-fifth increase in resource use by those seeing the GP, the majority of these differences being attributable to absences from paid work. Few economic differences, however, were statistically significant and the authors caution against extrapolation of the results to other treatment settings (Ginsberg *et al.*, 1984).

Our own prospective controlled CEA compared community psychiatric nursing (CPN) and routine outpatient follow-up for a patient sample largely comprising long-term attenders suffering from mild and moderate neurotic illnesses (Mangen *et al.*, 1983). Patients were allocated to experimental or control groups and followed up for a period of 18 months. No significant differences in socio-clinical outcomes were found. Patient satisfaction with CPN follow-up was greater, and the experimental group also recorded a higher rate of discharge from specialist mental health care, though many continued to see their GPs. On a narrow consideration of the effects on the 'psychiatric' budget, community psychiatric nursing was the cheaper option. However, taking into consideration the costs of all health and social services there were no significant differences, and it was found that both groups were large recipients of a wide range of services and benefits.

Several points must be raised before the results of our study can be interpreted appropriately. The study period of 18 months was judged by us to be too short to apply a discount rate, although Drummond and colleagues (1986) in a review of our study felt that it might have been appropriate. More important is the fact that the period is too brief to evaluate either long-term socio-clinical or economic effects and was dictated by funding rather than scientific considerations. A follow-up study is in progress to assess these effects in the five years or so since the sample was last interviewed. Finally, it is important to note that the costs of psychiatric care accounted for less than one-fifth of the amount of total public expenditure on this sample. Experimentation with modes of follow-up care like these may therefore have modest impact on public budgets, although they may be defensible on other grounds and are relevant to the wider concerns of policy-makers.

Psychologists and primary care

Primary care attachments of clinical psychologists have also been the object of investigation. Koch's uncontrolled retrospective study of his own practice indicated that the volume of prescriptions was reduced by half and that attendance at GP surgeries also declined in comparison with previous behaviour and that this was maintained at follow-up (Koch, 1979). Earll and Kincey (1982), in the best documented controlled evaluation of primary care attachments, found a more complex outcome. The principal psychological treatment adopted was based on a behavioural self-control model. The study was located in one general practice and patients were randomly allocated to clinical psychologist or routine GP follow-up. Use of health service resources was monitored for the duration of the experimental treatment period. The findings indicate that there was no significant difference in self-rated mental state at follow-up; as this was not recorded immediately after the treatment programme had terminated, short-term clinical gains could not be assessed. Regarding the pattern and frequency of prescriptions, GP consultations, outpatients appointments and inpatient admissions, there was no significant difference in outcome at seven months between the experimental and control group, although initially there had been a lower rate of prescribing among the group being treated by the psychologist. The level of patient satisfaction with treatment provided by the clinical psychologist was higher throughout the study period. Overall, the economic implications of this study are that the psychologist was complementing rather than substituting the interventions of the general practitioner, so that substantial savings in resources for equal clinical outcomes could not be expected.

PROSPECTS FOR CEAs OF PSYCHOSOCIAL INTERVENTIONS

Several authors have argued that CEAs must be presented in a form that is relevant to the concerns of planners and clinical teams (Roberts, 1974; Drummond *et al.*, 1986). They stress the importance of good descriptions of service settings, treatment modes and a full listing of resource utilization. Furthermore, to assist the planning of mental health services some justification should be given for the selection of the alternative forms of treatment that are the object of the CEA. This is particularly relevant in cases where organizational, professional or political considerations may have been at play in preventing the inclusion of certain service modes or, indeed, a placebo group for comparison.

Many CEAs of mental health care provide ambigious or 'marginal' results which do not render sufficiently clear guidelines for planners. Moreover, economic advantages have often been demonstrated in studies which are derived from local, small-scale settings and, thus, there is a need for planners to assess if these outcomes could be replicated elsewhere, given that some of the economic variables may be subject to local variation (for example, property prices and, to some extent, salaries). The degree of specificity of the data we are able to collect for CEA is, to a large extent, a function of existing organizational practices and we are often in a position where we are comparing the relative efficiency of sub-optimally organized services. At present there are few controlled studies of different organizational systems for delivering the same treatment and progress in this field may be difficult, given the tight coordination that might be required of a large range of mental health agencies, some of which are in the voluntary or private profit-making sector.

Nevertheless, there are encouraging developments in the general field of CEAs of health care. Drummond and colleagues (1986), for example, report that some studies examine whether new programmes are operating at optimal efficiency in terms of size of the operation, intensity of use and so forth, sensitivity analyses being undertaken to ascertain whether operational changes could lead to greater efficiency.

Although I have outlined the advantages of CEA for assessing the efficient use of resources, efficiency can never be the sole criterion in evaluating psychiatric services. Mental health policy-makers and planners have to have regard to the distributional effects of their decisions and may well have to seek the best compromise between efficiency, effectiveness and equity. They cannot be narrowly preoccupied with resource utilization to the neglect of issues such as the kind of services that are popularly demanded, the quality of the treatments on offer and the kind of status they afford patients who receive them (Drummond, 1980). In addition, the views of the professions and administrators have to be taken into account because there are potential costs and benefits accruing to them from innovations in service provision. These concerns go beyond the focus of this paper but mention should be made of the supremely sensitive issue of professional territoriality. Furthermore, because of compartmentalization of health and social service bureaucracies, there may be little, if any, incentive for managers in one service sector to reform practices which could achieve savings that ultimately accrue elsewhere.

Cost-effectiveness analysis is a valuable research tool, despite its methodological limitations. However, it remains an adjunct to, not a replacement for, difficult resource decisions in a large organization like the National Health Service. Its greatest strength lies in encouraging us to focus on the implicit and explicit values that are attached to specific policy goals.

REFERENCES

BALL, M. (1979). Cost-benefit analysis: A critique. In F. Green and P. Nore (eds). *Issues in Political Economy: A Critical Approach*. Basingstoke: MacMillan.

CATALAN, J., GATH, D., EDMONDS, G. and ENNIS, J. (1984). The effects of non-prescribing of anxiolytics in general practice. *British Journal of Psychiatry, vol. 144*, 593–602.

CHAPMAN, J.R. (1979). Techniques of economic analysis in psychiatric practice. *British Journal of Medical Psychology. vol. 52*, 91–97.

DALLEY, G. (1988). *Ideology of Caring: Rethinking Community and Collectivism*. Basingstoke: Macmillan.

DEPARTMENT OF HEALTH AND SOCIAL SECURITY (1981). Health Services Management: Health Building Procedures. HN (81)30. London: Department of Health and Social Security.

DRUMMOND, M.F. (1980). *Principles of Economic Appraisal in Health Care*. Oxford: Oxford University Press.

DRUMMOND, M.F., LUDBROOK, A., LOWSON, K. and STEEL, A. (1986). *Studies in the Economic Appraisal of Health Care*. Oxford: Oxford University Press.

EARLL, L. and KINCEY, J. (1982). Clinical psychology in general practice: A controlled trial evaluation. *Journal of the Royal College of General Practitioners, vol. 32*, 32–37.

FINCH, J. and GROVES, D. (1980). Community care and the family: A case for equal opportunities. *Journal of Social Policy, vol. 9*, 487–511.

GINSBERG, G., MARKS, I. and WATERS, H. (1984). Cost-benefit analysis of a controlled trial of nurse therapy for neurosis in primary care. *Psychological Medicine, vol. 14*, 683–690.

GLASS, N. and GOLDBERG, D. (1977). Cost-benefit analysis and the evaluation of psychiatric services. *Psychological Medicine, vol 7.,* 701–707

GOLDBERG, D. and JONES, R. (1980) The costs and benefit of psychiatric care. In L. Robins, P. Clayton and J.K. Wing (eds). *The Social Consequences of Psychiatric Illness.* New York: Brunner & Mazel Press.

JONES, R., GOLDBERG, D. and HUGHES, B. (1980). A comparison of two different services treating schizophrenia: A cost-benefit approach. *Psychological Medicine, vol. 10,* 493–505.

KOCH, H. (1979) Evaluation of behaviour therapy interaction in general practice. *Journal of the Royal College of General Practitioners, vol. 29,* 337–340.

MANGEN, S.P., PAYKEL, E.S., GRIFFITH, J.H., BURCHELL, A. and MANCINI, P. (1983). Cost-effectiveness of community psychiatric nurse or outpatient psychiatrist care of neurotic patients. *Psychological Medicine, vol. 13,* 407–416.

MARKS, I.M., HODGSON, R. and RACHMAN, S. (1975). Treatment of chronic obsessive compulsive neurosis by in vivo exposure. *British Journal of Psychiatry, vol. 127,* 349–364.

McGRATH, G. and LOWSON, K. (1986). Assessing the benefits of psychotherapy: The economic approach. *British Journal of Psychiatry, vol. 150,* 65–71.

MEDLIK, L. and FURSLAND, A. (1984). Maximizing scarce resources: Autogenic relaxation classes at a health centre. *British Journal of Medical Psychology, vol. 57,* 181–185.

NEWMAN, F.L. and HOWARD, K.I. (1986). Therapeutic effort, treatment outcome and national health policy. *American Psychologist, vol. 41,* 181–187.

ROBERTS, J.A. (1974). Economic evaluation of health care: A survey. *British Journal of Preventive and Social Medicine, vol. 28,* 210–216.

SPECTOR, J. (1984). Clinical psychology and primary care: Some ongoing dilemmas. *Bulletin of The British Psychological Society, vol. 37,* 73–76.

TRETHOWAN, W. (1977). *The Role of the Clinical Psychologist in the Health Service.* London: Her Majesty's Stationery Office.

WEISBROD, B.A., TEST, M.A. and STEIN, L.A. (1980). Alternatives to mental hospital treatment II: Economic benefit-cost analysis. *Archives of General Psychiatry, vol. 37,* 400–405.

WILKINSON, G. and PELOSI, A.J. (1987). The economics of mental health services. *British Medical Journal, vol. 294,* 139–140.

YATES, B.T. (1980). The theory and practice of cost-utility, cost-effectiveness and cost-benefit analysis in behavioural medicine: Towards Delivering More Health Care for Less Money. In J.M. Ferguson and C. Barr Taylor (eds). *The Comprehensive Handbook of Behavioural Medicine, vol. 3.* New York: Spectrum.

CONSULTANCY IN NON NATIONAL HEALTH SERVICE SETTINGS

Barrie Brown

This chapter explores the potential uses of consultation by psychologists working outside National Health Service institutions. Although the focus of the chapter is on the nature and scope of consultation itself, placing current NHS clinical psychology practice into its historical context may prove to be a helpful preamble.

The case for locating psychological interventions of all kinds for people with mental illness – assessment, treatment, advice, consultancy and prevention – away from the NHS institutions is based on a widely-shared idea that, for a variety of reasons, the majority of those who experience mental ill health rarely make use of formal mental health systems. The case for consultation as a preferred mode of psychological intervention is based additionally on a second widely-shared idea, that the application of psychological principles to foster change in organizations or systems in the community, that in turn facilitate good mental health through prevention and early intervention, directly attacks the root causes of mental ill health.

These are not new ideas. The last two decades have witnessed several attempts at innovatory change in the location and mode of service delivery, for example, the move into primary care and social services organizations (Brown, 1985a). But neither innovation appears to have generated genuine innovation in practice methods, even if the practice has a new location outside the NHS.

It seems worthwhile, therefore, returning for a moment to examine critically the ideas underpinning the widespread view that psychologists should be working outside NHS institutions. Evidence in support of the first notion, that the bulk of the demand for psychological services does not pass through the hospital gates, can be found in the early study by Shepherd *et al.* (1966) of psychiatric illness in inner city general practice. This study showed a prevalence of psychiatric disturbance of upwards of ten per cent, a finding replicated in a later study by Goldberg and Blackwell (1970). Furthermore, the prevalence of mental ill health has been shown to vary widely in different socioeconomic and ethnic groups (Srole *et al.*, 1962). Further, mental health resources, including psychologists, offer the least in the way of quality and quantity of service to these very groups (Ryan, 1969).

It was evidence such as this that led The British Psychological Society to make a strong case for increasing the number of clinical psychologists in order to better meet the mental health needs of the community (British Psychological Society, 1973) almost a decade after similar conclusions were reached in the USA by the Joint Commission on Mental Illness and Health (1961).

Simply increasing the numbers of psychologists, however, was unlikely to achieve much benefit for the clients if the system of mental health care in which they worked was not itself accessible to the bulk of the people in the community who needed it. Even as the BPS report was published, evidence was emerging (Wing and Hailey, 1972) that referral to psychiatric services reflects neither the severity of the problems nor the efficacy or actual availability of the means to deal with it. Similar findings were reported on a national scale in the USA by the Joint Commission (1961).

Such data began to convince the profession that clinical psychology had a new challenge; as Sundbert *et al.*, (1983) put it, to develop methods which emphasized 'prevention, skill acquisition, early detection, the spread of effect through the use of non-professionals, volunteers and community networks' (page 269).

This challenge was only tackled in the USA after the early attempts to implement mental health programmes in the community had been exposed in a series of evaluations as failures (Roen, 1971; Biegel and Levenson, 1972; Golann and Eisdorfer, 1972; and Zax and Specter, 1974). Each of these studies showed that, if the central aim of the mental health service was to achieve greater impact on the welfare of the poorest and most disadvantaged groups in the community, particularly in inner cities, there had to be attempts to 'transcend professional territoriality, cross disciplinary barriers and overcome narrowly delineated latitudes of concern' (Roen 1971, page 777). Only then would clients other than the articulate, mobile and employed win access to the service.

In a more theoretical sense, the shift in emphasis in practice had to be from an exclusive concern with the nature of the individual and intrapsychic problems to a focus on the problems that individuals and groups face in coping with their social, physical, cultural, economic and even political environments.

This change in emphasis required new methods to be employed as well as reaching new groups of clients. Such a change was perhaps exemplified by the 'social action' movement of Roman and Schmais (1972). Their approach demanded that psychologists should not allow professional boundaries to impede the scope of their interventions – housing, transport, employment and literacy were each seen as essential ingredients of a comprehensive approach.

In spite of (or perhaps because of?) his radical approach, Roen has hardly influenced even the most committed proponents of community psychology on this side of the Atlantic, at least up to the early 1980s (Brown, 1985b). In the absence of any further significant data since 1985, that conclusion still holds.

Nevertheless, as opportunities now proliferate for clinical psychologists to change their practices to facilitate the transfer of the care of the chronically mentally ill and handicapped from large remote hospitals to local communities, the demand for them to engage with priority care groups, their carers, and pressure groups in the community, will increase. Innovation, breaking down professional barriers, and a commitment to prevention and education are likely to prove essential if clinical psychologists are to succeed in influencing the way health and local authorities and even central government go about funding and organizing the transfer of care to the community.

In these new tasks, traditional practice methods alone are unlikely to be of great value to clinical psychologists. New methods in new locations are required. In particular, there are reasons to think that consultancy will prove a useful mode of work.

PRINCIPLES OF CONSULTATION

An influential early proponent of consultation was Gerald Caplan, who described it as a collaborative process between professionals (Caplan, 1964). The purpose of consultation was to focus on work-related problems of the consultee rather than personal or psychological problems, thus differentiating consultation and psychological therapy. Since Caplan, a succession of writers have delineated three common principles which seem to underpin the nature of consultation (most recently, Parsons and Meyers, 1984). They are:

1. Non-hierarchal interchange.
Consultation involves two professionals – the consultant and consultee, both of whom have their own zone of expertise. Consultation takes place when one (the consultee) asks the other (the consultant) to provide advice, usually about how to solve a problem. The relationship remains non-hierarchal because the consultee maintains an active involvement in the ensuing process of developing new approaches to solving the problem. Maintaining the non-hierarchal relationship may prove difficult, since the consultee often assumes that the consultant is more skilful, knowledgeable or competent, and downgrades his or her own status accordingly – what Caplan describes as 'one-downmanship' (Caplan, 1970). One way to counteract this is for the

consultant to focus on the consultee's role in generating innovative plans to deal with the problem.

2. Primary focus on the consultee.
Throughout the process of consulting, the consultant should work towards the goal of helping the consultee to facilitate innovation and retain complete responsibility for implementing any consequential action.

3. Freedom to accept or reject.
Since the final responsibility for implementation is the consultee's, accepting or rejecting the consultant's recommendations arising out of the consultation process must be a mutually agreed option for the consultee. There must be no hint of indirect coercion, such as any suggestion by the consultant that harmful repercussions will result if his or her conclusions are rejected in any consequential action.

Much has been written about the process of consultation that indicates the difficulty of achieving these three principles in practice. The fact that the consultee asks the consultant to provide expertise to help solve a problem encourages the notion that the consultant is superior. The consultant, of course, is also highly motivated to win the consultee's acceptance of his or her advice and where consultancy processes are written down, the consultee knows that his or her rejection of advice will possibly become part of the public record if there are later serious consequences. For these practical reasons, violations of the three principles have been found to be common in at least one review of the general application of consultation practice (Parsons and Meyers, 1984). Consultants were found to determine the problem, select assessment techniques and propose intervention strategies much more frequently than consultees.

The focus evident in much of the work initiated by Caplan and developed by others such as Parsons and Meyers (1984) has been on the consultee's own performance. A second more recent development in the description and analysis of consultation has been on what Caplan (1970) referred to as 'programme-centred consultation'. That is, where the consultant helps the consultee with a technical problem such as how to introduce new technology or how to meet training needs in an organization. Whereas Caplan was primarily concerned with the *process* of consultation, this more contemporary approach has added the need for the consultant to possess real expertise in the *content* of the consultee's problem (for example, see Parsons and Meyers, 1984, or Gallessich, 1982).

EXAMPLES OF CONSULTATION

As an illustration of collaborative consultation, the following examples are drawn from the author's direct experience of working in a variety of extra-NHS contexts in recent years.

In one example, a group of parents of teenagers in South East Inner London banded together with the support of their local MP and his media friends to do something about their adolescents' heroin sniffing. The group consulted with the author in three meetings in the homes of group members about what statutory and non-statutory services were available to them and to seek advice on how to write and submit a proposal to the Department of Health and Social Security to fund a self help walk-in advice centre for young heroin users in their community. The author provided information, gave advice about writing a grant proposal and brought the group into contact with members of the local authority who were interested in drug abuse services. The Centre was funded by the Department of Health and Social Security and operated with staff who were themselves former addicts. The three principles of collaborative consultation are evident in this example. Unfortunately, a comprehensive evaluation of the evaluation process is not.

In a second example, an organization of families with a handicapped member in South West London asked the author to provide consultation to member families so as to enhance skilled parenting, encourage the development of pressure groups within the organization to press for better services from local health and education authorities and give practical advice on how to refer for help. Again, the three principles – non-hierarchal interchange, focus on the consultee's perspective, and the freedom of the consultee to accept or reject the consultant's advice – were to the fore, but funding to mount a systematic evaluation of the project was not available. The need for a consultant to have a technical knowledge of the consultee's problem was also evident.

A third example of carying out consultation in a non-NHS setting involved the author in advising on the evaluation of an 'Intermediate Treatment' project in a London Borough.

During 1983 and 1984 a voluntary organization involved in providing an alternative to custody for adolescent offenders established 'Wellhall', funded by the DHSS (LAC 83(3) initiative). This was intended to provide an intensive programme of education, social and life-skills training and a specific focus on changing the youths' attitudes to their own criminality.

The rationale and operational policy for the project has been described elsewhere (Rose *et al.*, 1984).

When the psychologist was asked to advise the project in 1985, it had already developed specific aims and objectives and detailed operational plans which it was implementing with considerable success. In a series of early meetings with the managers of the project it became clear that what was missing, they felt, was a means of evaluating the effectiveness of its methods and the extent to which aims and objectives were being achieved. Evaluation was important to them, because funding for Wellhall would revert to the local authority after the DHSS grant expired in 1986 and evidence of impact and worth would be essential.

There followed a fortnightly meeting between the consultant and the project staff at which a proposal for evaluating the project was drawn up. This proposal contained several elements. First of all, it was necessary to identify what was being offered to each young person in the programme. Wellhall worked with up to about eight young people at a time, and work with the group was broken down into specific activities such as interactive group teaching, group skills training, or group leisure activity. Some individual work was also undertaken, and this too was broken down into specific categories (for example, behavioural counselling or assessment interview). The categories were selected by the project staff and no new material for assessing or analysing activity was brought into the situation by the consultant. In fact, from the point of view of the project team, what was achieved at this early stage was simply a clarified reflection of what was already being undertaken. The consultant's role was limited to guiding the discussion such that useful questions about what Wellhall was doing were posed by the team themselves, and options selected.

The options eventually selected by the project team were as follows:

(*1*) The team should aim first to assess whether the personal objectives for each individual young person pinpointed during the assessment phase were actually being attacked in his or her programme.
(*2*) The second aim would be to build up a descriptive picture of the kinds of targets being commonly identified as the numbers of young persons passing through Wellhall increased.
(*3*) Finally, some reliable and valid measures of the youth's behaviour and attitudes would be required so as to link specific programmes with outcomes.

Having identified its aims, the project team then went on to design a series of progress evaluation scales – 5-point scales filled out by the young people on themselves. Scale items were drawn from a wide range of published ratings and measures used in evaluating mental health programmes and carefully matched against the aims of the evaluation. Typical scale items were 'showing concern', 'frequency of going to school', 'getting upset in arguments', 'getting into fights' and 'feeling worried or moody'.

The package of evaluation methods was then piloted by the team and refined. The entire consultation process had been completed within six months. The DHSS funding expired and responsibility for Wellhall was accepted by the local authority.

These three examples clearly illustrate the three principles of collaborative consultation described by Caplan (1964). They also highlight the combination of content with process objectives for the consultation.

BASIC RESEARCH

Although it is now more than 20 years since Caplan first began to develop both the conceptual framework and practical methodology of consultation, there has been little systematic study of the conceptual or practical issues in the psychological literatures. Instead, research has tended to focus on actual settings and client groups rather than concepts or methods, particularly in educational settings with adolescents, in child health and in community mental health. Much of the research has been descriptive, with little attention paid to the impact of the constituent components of consultation. With a few exceptions, the literature has at best posed the question: 'Does consultation work?' rather than asking, 'How does it work?'

Researchers have concentrated on asking questions about specific and non-specific behaviours associated with successful consultation.

(a). Specific consultant behaviours. A series of studies at the University of Cincinnati of effectiveness in consultation has demonstrated that consultants who are skilled in applying the three principles were much more effective in improving the ability of teachers to work with a problem child in the classroom (Curtis and Watson, 1980). In a second study, Curtis and Zins (1981) also found that teachers preferred to work with consultants who used collaborative techniques, and that their use resulted in generalization of more skilled teaching behaviour beyond the specific consultation case (Meyers, 1981). Each of these studies has employed an objective measure of teacher behaviour (the Consultant Observational Assessment Form), adapted from earlier research developing operational definitions of collaborative consultant behaviours (Curtis and Anderson, 1975).

(b). Non-specific consultant behaviours. Another theme in consultation research has been the exploration of non-specific consultant behaviours associated with success and failure of consultancy, again with teachers of difficult pupils. Fine *et al.* (1974) first observed that behavioural consultation with teachers was more likely to fail if the consultant was judged to be insensitive to implicit or unstated concerns of the teacher. In a second study. (Schowengerdt *et al.*, 1976) tested a number of predictors of teacher satisfaction with consultation and found that perception of the consultant's facilitative characteristics was most powerful. Similarly, Wilcox (1979) found that the consultee's attitude towards consultation in a mental health service context was predicted by high observed level of such consultant behaviours

as acknowledging feelings and facilitating the consultee's expression of feelings and different points of view.

Basic research such as this has led to the development of descriptive lists of consultant behaviours which enhance collaborative consultation (for example, Parsons and Meyers, 1984) and to methods of assessing effectiveness. The Parsons and Meyers (1984) list, for example,includes:

1. Facilitation – eliciting the consultee's observations, ideas and previous actions rather than taking over responsibility for analysing and solving the problem.
2. Equity – viewing the consultee as a colleague rather than the recipient of the consultant's ideas, expertise and information.
3. Empathy – communicating the consultee's perception of the problem accurately rather than imposing the consultant's own phenomenological world on the situation.
4. Ventilation – allowing free expression of feelings by the consultee.
5. Summarizing – periodically summarizing the main ideas of the consultee.
6. Strategy generation – the interaction leads to ideas about the action to cope with the problem.

The third example of consultation described above illustrates at least some of these operational criteria. Facilitation was prominent throughout the process, with both responsibility for the evaluation and the major contribution of ideas and actions coming from the Wellhall team itself. Equity in the professional relationship was emphasized throughout this process. The consultant, a clinical psychologist, brought prior knowledge of doing research and a thorough knowledge of delinquency to the consultation, but the team brought its own ideas about appropriate techniques, what they could achieve as social workers with the young people and what would probably work. And so on, through each of the operational definitions. It should be emphasized that both the consultant psychologist and the Wellhall team were aware of the principles of collaborative consultancy and attempted to adhere to them as closely as possible. Both understood that a combination of process and content consultancy was to be employed.

EVALUATION IN CONSULTATION

In spite of the growing interest in the consultation approach in the community as an alternative location and method for clinical psychologists, perusal of the literature reveals a virtual absence of systematic evaluations of the approach. Yet, curiously, the need to count the costs and benefits of practice by NHS psychologists has never been stronger than now, under the pressures of performance measurement, individual performance review and general management. It is essential, if psychologists are to succeed in redeploying their expertise out of NHS institutions to new tasks such as consultation that systematic evaluation of their interventions is carried out.

Perhaps the most useful concluding remarks that can be made in this brief review of the use of consultation in non-NHS settings, therefore, should highlight the need for the innovative clinical psychologist to build evaluation into his or her consultation practice and to suggest helpful practical ways this can be done.

The most important issue in evaluation is to avoid giving consideration to it only after the process and procedures of the consultation have been formulated and implemented. Evaluation cannot be successfully grafted on after the consultation has been completed, but should ideally be integrated into the entry, goal-setting and delivery systems of the consultation.

Evaluation of consultation takes two forms, process and outcome, reflecting exactly the dual emphasis on process and content aims. Both are essential to systematic comprehensive evaluation.

Process evaluation

Process evaluation seeks to assist both the consultant and consultee to take decisions about continuing or modifying the intervention. It can be achieved only by setting aside time in the consultative interchange. This can be achieved informally by asking consultees for their feelings about the plan of action and proposing adjustments to the plan in the light of the responses. Such informal process evaluation should be virtually continuous.

More formal process evaluation will also be necessary even though, in practice, many consultants may resist such activity because they believe it to be the zone of expertise of the researcher rather than the practitioner.

The use of formal data collection procedures is certainly time-consuming, but the extra time allocated to the data can be reduced to a minimum by setting out clear guidelines and using explicit and agreed assessment techniques. For example, the consultant may need to complete a checklist of actions taken at each stage of the consultation process.

Outcome evaluation

Both the consultant and consultee are necessarily interested in the outcome of the consultation. For both, the most exacting test is whether the aims and objectives of the consultation have been achieved. Secondary issues are to assess the extent to which the achievements can be attributed to the consultation; what aspects of the process enhanced the outcome and what inhibited it; was the intervention of greater or lesser value than alternative interventions; and what other unintended non-specific gains and losses has the consultation generated?

A model outcome evaluation of consultation, therefore, probably requires the consultant and consultee to agree on completion of each of the following steps:

(*a*) specify what outcomes are desired
(*b*) specify what measures are to be used to assess (*a*)
(*c*) identify necessary intervention inputs from the consultant and the consultee
(*d*) design the intervention so that (*c*) can be shown to link to (*a*) and (*b*)
(*e*) implement the intervention, carrying out process evaluation and altering (*a*) to (*d*) as necessary
(*f*) feedback analysis to consultee in the form of a report, verbal and/or written, to manager and all other staff involved in the intervention
(*g*) set new aims and objectives or discontinue.

Within each of these steps there are a wide variety of options for the consultant to engage in outcome evaluation. Many of these options have been described in a manual of evaluation for practitioners in the NHS (Brown and Barker, 1987).

CONSULTATION OUTSIDE THE NHS. WHERE NEXT?

This chapter has argued for the relevance of collaborative consultation as a cost-effective process which allows clinical psychologists to engage in applying psychological principles to changing systems, organizations and broader influences outside NHS hospitals. These extra-NHS locations, it is widely asserted, are the root cause of mental ill health. The use of collaborative consultation is likely to be most relevant in such settings as community health organizations, self help groups, non-NHS welfare and benefit services and many other locations in the community network as responsibility for the care of the long-term mentally ill and handicapped is transferred from large, remote institutions.

There is, however, much need for caution in embracing collaborative consultation. After all, there is, as yet, virtually no systematic evaluation of the approach. Yet, it could be argued that there has been no more advantageous time than the present to add a new battery of cost-effective techniques, if that is what collaborative consultation turns out to be in the cold light of evaluative research, to the traditional tasks of assessment and treatment of individuals and groups. The new tasks facing health and local authorities in caring for the chronically sick and disabled will demand a greatly expanded role for psychologists. The rising tide of the elderly, in particular, poses a great challenge to the profession. But, if clinical psychologists are to develop effective practice in the community, they will have to examine their own professional organizations and aspirations. The failures of the early mental health centre movement in the USA are clear: the failure to secure funding and professional commitment for evaluation or innovative practice is particularly relevant. Yet the same failures are already evident in this country in our failure to carry the best of academic and reseach endeavour into clinical psychology practice outside (some might say also inside) the NHS. This chapter argues the case for using collaborative consultation as an appropriate new approach and makes a plea for developing the approach within a systematic evaluative framwork.

REFERENCES

BIEGEL, A and LEVENSON, A (1972) *The Community Mental Health Center: Strategies and Programs*. New York: Basic Books.

BRITISH PSYCHOLOGICAL SOCIETY (1973). Report on the role of psychologists in the Health Services. *Bulletin of the British Psychological Society, 26*, 309–330.

BROWN, B. (1985a). Community Psychology: some alternative models of organization and practice. In J. Karas (ed.). *Current Issues in Clinical Psychology, Vol. 1*. London: Plenum Press.

BROWN, B. (1985b). Community psychology: A new location perhaps, but the same old methods, clients and aspirations. In A. Gale, J. Radford and M. Taylor (eds). *Psychology in the 1990s*, London: Association for the Teaching of Psychology.

BROWN, B. and BARKER, C. (1987). *The Evaluation Practice Pack*. London: Bloomsbury Health Authority.

CAPLAN, G. (1964). *Principles of Preventive Psychiatry*. New York: Basic Books.

CAPLAN, G. (1970). *The Theory and Practice of Mental Health Consultation*. New York: Basic Books.

CURTIS, M. and ANDERSON, T. (1975). *Consultant Observational Assessment Form*. Cincinnati: Department of Educational Leadership, University of Cincinnati.

CURTIS, M. and WATSON, K. (1980). Changes in consultee problem clarification skills following consultation. *Journal of School Psychology, 18*, 210–221.

CURTIS, M. and ZINS, J. (1981). Consultative effectiveness as perceived by experts in consultation and classroom teachers. In M. Curtis and J. Zins (eds). *The Theory and Practice of School Consultation*. Springfield, Illinois: Thomas.

FINE, N., NESBITT, J. and TAYLOR, M. (1974). Analysis of a failing attempt at behaviour modification. *Journal of Learning Disabilities, 7*, 12–17.

GALLESSICH, J. (1982). *The Profession and Practice of Consultation*. San Francisco: Jossey-Bass.

GOLANN, S. and EISDORFER, C. (1972). *Handbook of Community Mental Health*, New York: Appleton-Century-Crofts.

GOLDBERG, D.P. and BLACKWELL, B. (1970). Psychiatric Illness in General Practice. *British Medical Journal, 2*, 439–443.

JOINT COMMISSION ON MENTAL ILLNESS AND HEALTH (1961). *Action for Mental Health*, New York: Basic Books.

MEYERS, J. (1981). Mental Health Consultation. In T. Kratochwill (ed.). *Advances in School Psychology, vol. 1*, New Jersey: Erlbaum, Hillsdale.

PARSONS, R. and MEYERS, J. (1984). *Developing Consultation Skills*. San Francisco: Jossey-Bass.

ROEN, S.R. (1971). Evaluative Research and Mental Health. In A.E. Bergin and

S.L. Garfield (eds). *Handbook of Psychotherapy and Behavior Change*. New York: Wiley.

ROMAN, N. and SCHMAIS, A. (1972). Consumer participation and control: A conceptual overview. In H. Barton and L. Bellack (eds). *Progress in Community Mental Health, vol. 2*. New York: Grune and Stratton.

ROSE, J., JONES, D. and MURRAY-SMITH, D. (1984). The Wellhall Project Manual. London: Rainer Foundation.

RYAN, W. (1969). *Disorders in the City: Essays on the Design and Administration of Urban Mental Health Services*. Cleveland: Case Western Reserve.

SCHOWENGERDT, R., FINE, M. and POGGIO, J. (1976). An examination of some bases of teacher satisfaction with school psychological services. *Psychology for Schools, 13*, 269–275.

SHEPHERD, M., COOPER, B., BROWN, A. and KATTON, B. (1966). *Psychiatric Illness in General Practice*. Oxford: Oxford University Press.

SROLE, L., LANGER, T.S., MICHAEL, S.J., OPLER, M.R. and REMIE, T.A. (1962). *Mental Health in the Metropolis, vol. 1*. New York: McGraw Hill.

SUNDBERG, N.D., TAPLIN, J.R. and TYLER, L.E. (1983). *Introduction to Clinical Psychology*, Englewood Cliffs: Prentice-Hall.

WILCOX, R. (1979). Variables Affecting Group Mental Health Consultation for Teachers. Proceedings of the 85th Annual Meeting of the American Psychological Association, San Francisco.

WING, J.K. and HAILEY, A.M. (1972). *Evaluating Community Psychiatric Services*. Oxford: Oxford University Press.

ZAX, M. and SPECTER, G.A. (1974). *An Introduction to Community Psychology*. New York: Wiley.

SUBJECT INDEX